"Here, at last, is America revealed, warts, weirdness, wonders and wacki-ness. This book is honest, it's outspoken and it rips the lid off complacent interpretations and guidebook clichés. Devour it and discover a country you never knew before."
— David Yeadon, author of *Lost Worlds* and *The Back of Beyond*

"The *Travelers' Tales* series is altogether remarkable."
— Jan Morris, author of *Journeys*, *Locations*, and *Hong Kong*

"For the thoughtful traveler, these books are an invaluable resource. There's nothing like them on the market."
— Pico Iyer, author of *Video Night in Kathmandu*

"This is the stuff memories can be duplicated from."
— Karen Krebsbach, *Foreign Service Journal*

"I can't think of a better way to get comfortable with a destination than by delving into *Travelers' Tales*…before reading a guidebook, before seeing a travel agent. The series helps visitors refine their interests and readies them to communicate with the peoples they come in contact with…."
— Paul Glassman, Society of American Travel Writers

"*Travelers' Tales* is a valuable addition to any pre-departure reading list."
— Tony Wheeler, publisher, Lonely Planet Publications

"*Travelers' Tales* delivers something most guidebooks only promise: a real sense of what a country is all about…."
— Steve Silk, *Hartford Courant*

"*Travelers' Tales* is a useful and enlightening addition to the travel bookshelves…providing a real service for those who enjoy reading first-person accounts of a destination before seeing it for themselves."
— Bill Newlin, publisher, Moon Publications

"The *Travelers' Tales* series should become required reading for anyone visiting a foreign country who wants to truly step off the tourist track and experience another culture, another place, first hand."
— Nancy Paradis, *St. Petersburg Times*

TRAVELERS' TALES GUIDES

AMERICA

TRUE STORIES OF LIFE
ON THE ROAD

TRAVELERS' TALES GUIDES

AMERICA

TRUE STORIES OF LIFE
ON THE ROAD

Collected and Edited by
FRED SETTERBERG

Series Editors
JAMES O'REILLY AND LARRY HABEGGER

TRAVELERS' TALES, INC.
SAN FRANCISCO, CALIFORNIA

Travelers' Tales: America
Collected and Edited by Fred Setterberg

Cover design by Judy Anderson, Kathryn Heflin, and Susan Bailey
Cover photograph: Copyright © Bill Hatcher 1998/Adventure Photo and Film.
   A climber near the Mt. Rushmore monument in the Black Hills of South Dakota.
Illustrations by James Dowlen
Map by Keith Granger
Page layout by Patty Holden, using the fonts Bembo and Boulevard

Distributed by O'Reilly and Associates, Inc., 101 Morris Street, Sebastopol, CA 95472

Printing History
January 1999:   First Edition

ISBN: 1-885211-28-7

*Here is not merely
a nation but a teeming
nation of nations.*

—WALT WHITMAN,
Preface to *Leaves of Grass* (1855)

To Anne Fox,
Godmother of many books

Table of Contents

Part Two
SOME THINGS TO DO

Part Three
GOING YOUR OWN WAY

Part Four
IN THE SHADOWS

America: An Introduction

Travel made America.

Consider a mere 200 years ago. The North American continent—Atlantic to Pacific, tropical gulf to the ice fields of Hudson Bay—qualified as terra incognita. Coronado, Balboa, and de Soto had failed to slog across sufficient acreage of swamp, desert, river, and high plateau to piece together a serviceable map. Lewis and Clark still waited to penetrate the continent. The 500 Native American nations, the original residents, remained largely unaware of each others' presence—and would only gradually perceive that the trickle of interlopers from Europe, Africa, and Asia presaged an unpluggable fount of humanity whose excess would utterly transform the land mass now presumptuously named after a 15th century Italian navigator who never trod upon its shores.

"This new man, this American," as Hector St. Jean de Crevecoeur called the recent arrivals, knew almost nothing about their new country as a geographical entity, a real place.

America was ripe for crossing, and recrossing, and zigzagging without inhibition or boundary. And what is America today?

Any single characterization fails. Most of our nation's 280 million citizens now live in cities or suburbs; yet coast-to-coast air travel reveals the continental belly to be astonishingly empty. (We're not crowded Hong Kong or even the Netherlands.) We enjoy immense, historically unprecedented affluence. But the gap between our rich and poor is the widest of any industrial nation— and growing. (Our aspirations for socio-economic equity seem to waver between Sweden and Brazil.) Our population is still largely derived from European immigration. Nevertheless, the recent influx of newcomers from Asia and Latin America promises to reinvent our society once again, eventually forging something unexpected and unpredictable—and as usual, without the benefit of blueprints.

Two hundred years ago, parochial Europeans insisted that everything American—its mountains, rivers, plants, animals, and people—must necessarily be smaller, less energetic, more dissipated and duller than their Old World counterparts. Thomas Jefferson would buy none of that. He countered righteously, if erroneously, that the brave hearts then journeying westward might eventually stumble upon prehistoric mastodons—thus obliquely establishing the fact that America has frequently been off-kilter even in its own most basic self-concept.

Today the argument over grandeur is finished. Travelers now criss-cross America for what they'll never find at home: days worth of plains passing by, the Rockies and Sierras pitched to dizzying heights, two great oceans and three dissimilar coasts, the painted desert, the Mississippi River, the ancient redwoods. During summers at Zion National Park or Yellowstone or Yosemite, you'll almost certainly hear German spouting from the campsites. (Up in the Rosebud Reservation in South Dakota, you might even catch enterprising idolators of the earliest Americans exercising their skills in Lakota.) And need we compare New York to the old York?

For many of the most recent arrivals—particularly from South America, Central America, and Mexico (which, undeniably, is North America)—our country more accurately remains *El Norte* or *los Estados*. Yet traditional notions of "America"—expansive, promising, perilous, unique—retain their currency on a transnational basis.

Travels in America today reveal it to be a place where the lights of Caesar's Palace in Las Vegas beckon in lurid competition with the Statue of Liberty's torch of freedom; where whole families float boldly down the Colorado River to inspect the Grand Canyon on their summer vacation and then flit home via the airport hubs of Denver, Dallas, and Atlanta. Travelers in modern America confront the mid-day action in mid-town Manhattan and the scramble along L.A.'s freeways; they face the frantic, numbing, risky bustle of inner cities, edge cities, Levittowns plastered coast-to-coast.

Undeniably, we're a restless nation of movers; but we're squatters, too. We're a haven for immigrants where the previous generation too often bares its teeth at the latest newcomers. We're a magnet for tourists from older, more cultured, commensurately lovely lands whose existence we barely acknowledge.

Then how, finally, should we characterize this country that continues to engage, enrage, confound, and inspire the rest of the world—even as it ceaselessly draws visitors to its shores and sends the rest of us bouncing around its borders?

I think all we can say is that it's vast, copious, and contradictory. From Many, One.

"Always have a guide in the U.S.," writes Englishman Adam Nicolson in his essay in this book, "it's a much more foreign place than you think."

Good advice—as far as it goes. These fifty states and assorted possessions (how easily we forget our imperial grasp of Puerto Rico, the Virgin Islands, American Samoa, Guam) comprise one of the grandest, strangest, most influential societies ever to stake out borders on planet Earth. Yet even those of us who have always lived here may benefit from the eyes and insights of plucky travelers—be they peregrinating foreigner or uprooted resident. In truth, we need regularly to be reminded about the kind of daft and beguiling land we inhabit.

This book is that kind of reminder: tales of travelers who have walked, flown, driven, paddled, sailed, galloped, hitch-hiked, and otherwise traversed the breadth and depth of America—and lived to puzzle out the meaning of their journeys.

Despite the best efforts of Hollywood, Madison Avenue, Wall Street, and Wal-Mart, American variety perseveres. It even prevails—if you're determined enough to go looking for it. Sue Hubbell found American variety in a small Michigan town overrun with magicians. Calvin Trillin found it when he sat down in

New Orleans to devour a tasty plate of rodent. Marshall Krantz found it along Nevada's Alien Highway. And when Garrett Hongo and Anthony Walton returned to their respective family homes in Hawaii and Mississippi, they found that variety still pertained there, too. Indeed, most of the writers included in this volume have employed the cunning strategy of slipping off main-traveled roads to root around in some American patch that doesn't look, sound, smell, or feel like every other part. Others have walked straight into the darkened heart of the homogenizing corporate logo: Dave Barry does Disney World, while Mr. Nicolson strolls through a Connecticut shopping mall.

In every case, the writers have found something sufficiently ex-citing, beautiful, moving, disturbing, or funny to take the enormous trouble of writing well about their experience. Thus, they save us the considerable effort of physically following in their footsteps.

In the end, truly knowing America is probably too great a task for any one traveler. The United States of America, the USA, *El Norte*, the Capital of the 20th Century (and who can say about the 21st?) is simply too damn big. Too multitudinous and various. Too unexpectedly and exhilaratingly unusual.

Earlier this century, the English writer G.K. Chesterton pro-claimed that America was "a fairyland of happy lunatics and lovable monsters." I don't know if he ever caught a glimpse of the Grand Canyon, but it does sound like he had a terrific trip.

—Fred Setterberg

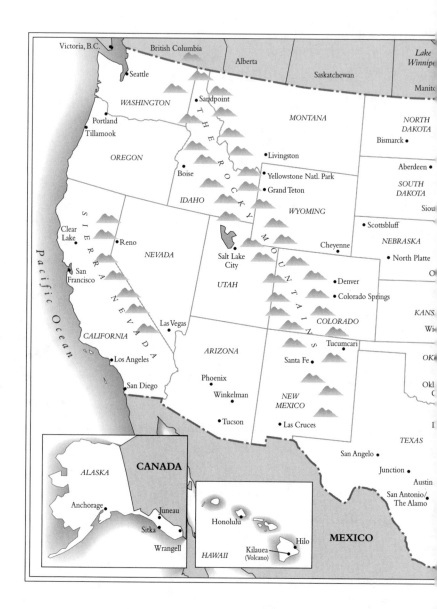

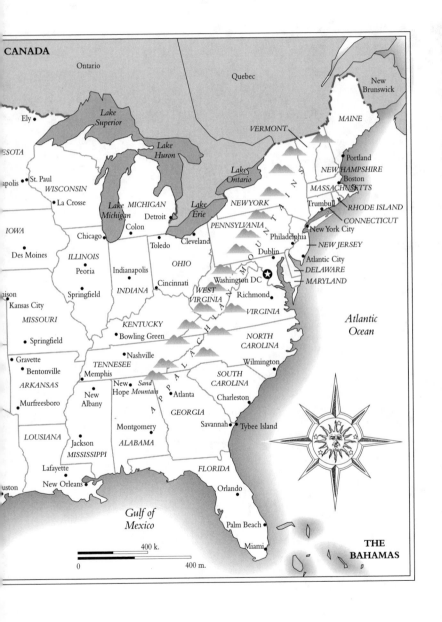

PART ONE

ESSENCE OF AMERICA

JERRY ELLIS

Walking the Trail of Tears

Along this route marched his Cherokee ancestors.

THE MAN WALKING DOWN THE ROAD REMINDS ME OF CHARLES
Manson. His hair is wild and curly and he wears no shirt. In his
right hand is a rock big enough to splatter a man's skull from here
to New York. His eyes are crazed, as if the whole world is chasing
him and he wants to say, No more, I'll kill every last one of you.
He walks my way.

I've been on the Trail for almost a week now and my confidence has grown. But I don't relish the thought of having to deal
with a maniac, especially one with a rock in his hand. How does
one greet another walker with murder in his eyes? *Hello, nice day
we're having* just doesn't fill the bill. I could act crazy and howl before we come within reach of each other. That might give me the
upper hand. It could, however, only serve to make him overreact
and jump me while introducing my head to his trusty rock.

He comes closer with each step and I now see that he has tat-
toos on both arms. I can't make out what they are, but on his chest
is a dragon breathing fire.

If he attacks me, I'm at a great disadvantage with a 50-pound
pack on my back. It could be in my favor if I knocked him to the
ground. I could then leap into the air and land atop him to squash

3

him like a TV wrestler. But this isn't TV Land. He might have his own thoughts about just lying there while I execute a Flying Pack.

I don't scare easily, but this is my first experience ever with a crazed man carrying a rock in my direction. Adrenaline shoots through my body and my mind goes weird. What if he's read about me in the newspaper and has fixated on me as some kind of enemy? Maybe he's a white supremacist and hates Indians with all his heart. He could want to knock me off with a rock as some sort of primal ritual.

From the prison camps they were started westward to Indian Territory. On the long winter trek, one of every four Cherokees died from cold, hunger, or disease. They called the march their "trail of tears."

◆

—Dee Brown, Bury My Heart at Wounded Knee: An Indian History of the American West

As he gets to within a few feet of me my instincts take over. I'm ready to slide the pack from me and use it as a shield if I have to. As we step closer toward each other all my senses are heightened. The crunch of his feet against the ground is piercing. The rock in his hand becomes twice as big and the dragon on his chest looks as mean as he does. His eyes are charged with such rage that they seem to bulge from the sockets. His mouth is open and his upper lip is twisted as if he fights for his next breath.

I'm a spring wound too tight. My arms and legs have more energy than they know what to do with. Come on, come on past me, you crazy son-of-a-bitch. Come on by. Come on, *come on.* And finally it's over with. He's behind me and the danger's gone. But *behind* me? I hurry to turn my head and make sure he hasn't lifted the rock. No, he continues on down the road like a man obsessed with purpose and destination.

I've met thousands of people in 41 years, but most of their faces have become lost in time. I'll *never* forget the caveman who just passed. Who was he and where was he going?

*

I've been using a map of the Trail of Tears, but I'm not sure which route to take—north or northeast—when I reach Gravette, Arkansas, in the Ozarks. I breeze into the newspaper office and ask the owner if he's up on local history enough to direct me down the Trail.

Not me, he says. You want to talk to Lewis Day. I'll phone him right now and see if he's in.

Lewis Day is in and I'm given directions to the funeral home he owns and operates. I can't say I'm overjoyed about getting a history lesson where a cold body is surrounded by flowers. I must've seen too many Dracula movies when I was a kid. I always have this slight suspicion that a corpse will rise up and grab me.

I take a right two blocks from the newspaper office and see the park with the World War II plane. Across the street from it is the funeral home, and there in the window, with his nose against the glass, is Lewis.

Come right on in, he says. Come right on in and make yourself at home.

I enter his office and the police scanner is on, complete with crackles and pops as a dispatcher gives directions to a car wreck. Why, you old devil you, waiting on a warm one to come in. He appears, however, to be anything but an opportunist: his tone and manners are nothing less than an old-fashioned gentleman. He's 72, and six feet tall with a full head of gray hair. It's easy to imagine him with a mint julep in his hand.

Oh yes, he says. I know the Trail of Tears in this area like the back of my hand. I've walked twenty-three miles of it myself over the years. Look out the window here. See there, where the ridge starts? That's where the old stagecoach road made the bend and the way the Indians came. My great-grandfather was a full-blooded Cherokee. He lived just down the road here and was a blacksmith for the stagecoach line. Come on outside. I have something to show you.

As we start out the door he cocks an ear to the police scanner. A man can't overlook business too long.

I follow him under a tree and onto the yard to the left of the funeral home. He stops at a rosebush, bursting alive with sixty or seventy red flowers. His eyes beam and his lips part with a smile that can stem only from a great gentle pride.

This bush has been in my family for over 150 years, he says. My Cherokee ancestors brought it from North Carolina in 1830. It's been transplanted four or five times. My parents cared for it while I was in college and in World War II. I'm afraid to move it anymore. Don't think it could take it. I sent a blossom to the National Rose Society. They had never seen one like it before.

It has a great will to live, I say.

I want you to have this, he says.

He reaches down to break a rose from the ancient bush. As he does so his hand trembles and I think of my friend Dan, back in Oklahoma City. He's one of the few men I know who could truly savor this rare moment as the old gentleman hands me the blossom, a trace of his soul.

I'll cherish it all the way back home, I say. I'll include it in the burial ritual I was telling you about.

Do whatever you like, he says. I'm glad you like it. Now, when you go down that hill there, in about, oh, a half mile, you'll come to a spring at the base of a house on your left. That's where the stage stopped. It's also where the Cherokee got water on their march.

We go back to his office. He gives me a detailed map of the Trail on to Missouri. I place the rose in my pack with the buckeye and the apple seeds. I like this old man a lot and shake his hand again just to touch him one more time.

As I go out the door the scanner's volume increases. Business just might be looking up.

I had hoped by now that the days would be cooling off with September winds. But they aren't. The thermometer climbs into the nineties everyday, and now that I'm in the Ozarks the hills are steeper, harder to climb. I've stopped a lot of my bellyaching about the pain in my feet though. I accept it and even look forward to it in a strange kind of way. I want to see if I can handle it and grow from it. It's as if raw determination from my teenage years is being reborn. My body, mind, and spirit are finding a new excitement with each other.

Trees and creeks and birds are no longer *out there*. I'm becoming one with them. In fact, I'm becoming dependent on the loud and jubilant cries of the blue jays. Three or four to a group, they often fly before me and sing as if to promise that all is safe. Some Cherokee believed that they were a sign of good times. When I camp in the evenings, I listen for their calls and pitch my tent under the biggest oak I can find near them. When the darkness quiets them, I depend upon the owl to assure me that I'm in the right spot.

My shirt is soaked with sweat by the time I reach a hilltop overlooking an old house at the next bend. I march to it and find the historic spring, only three or four feet from the road itself. I take off my hat and kneel to the water in the very spot where thousands of Cherokee also did the religious ritual of *going to water*. As if their spirits linger, the water ripples and goosebumps rush up my arms. If the Earth is our Mother, then water must be her heart. How often I have taken it for granted by simply turning a chrome or porcelain handle.

I stick my hands down into the spring and fill them. I raise the cool water to

---

Sometime during this first week of May 1877, Sitting Bull crossed the *chanku wakan*—the sacred road— into Canada.

"They told us this line was considered holy," remembered Robert Higheagle, a boy in the village. "They called that a holy trail. They believe things are different when you cross from one side to another. You are altogether different. On one side you are perfectly free to do as you please. On the other you are in danger."

◆

—Robert M. Utley, *The Lance and the Shield: The Life and Times of Sitting Bull* splash my face. I feel I am baptizing myself somehow. I'm washing away old skin, dropping some defenses. As simple—is it simple?—as it is, my life is taking on a new meaning. I have purpose like never before. I'm doing what I believe in, come men with roses or men with rocks. I'm almost in step with my drummer. There's an old Indian saying. *A man's soul can only travel as fast as his feet can carry him.* Perhaps between here and home I'll catch up with myself.

I splash my face again with the spring water, and recall how I loved to draw water from the well at my grandfather's house. Lowering the bucket into the earth and hearing the *splash* when it hit the underground lake seemed like magic. I couldn't wait to crank the windlass to bring the catch to the surface. It was both thrilling and sensual to pull the release trigger and watch the new waterfall rush into the drinking bucket. It was like climbing a tree or swinging on a vine across a creek. A bond was made with Nature, a secret friend who always offered a lift with its mystery. Over the years, living in New Orleans, Chicago, L.A., and San Francisco, I forgot that mystery and failed myself. Some days I could see nothing but work, cars, TV, and people. Nature was nothing more than an old toy. I had buried it without realizing it and didn't know what I longed for when I sometimes ached with loss. I had amputated a part of myself and the phantom lingered. When I would leave the cities and go back to the mountains of Alabama, I would find the power and peace of Nature again. I would swear that I would never again forget it and get caught up in the rat race back in the cities. I didn't lie on purpose.

I lower my hands into the spring again to wash my face and arms. It's cooling as it runs down the skin and I wish that the right woman was here to pour it over my neck and down my back. I would gladly return the favor.

I want to drink from the spring, but I'm afraid to. I can't be sure that it's free of pesticides and bacteria. I walk on.

Back home in Alabama, I've often been amused at how many country drivers wave at total strangers as if they're friends. I have returned their hand-hellos, but never initiated them. I never felt the need. Now, walking down the road, I begin to appreciate that most simple and primitive form of communication. I want to make contact and be part of strangers' lives if only for a fleeting moment. In return for my waves, I get polite waves, surprised waves, gawking waves, amused waves, flattered waves, loving waves, and there are those who refuse to wave but point as if the others in the car are on a tour of roadside attractions. Then there are the guys who nod but don't dare wave because *real men* can't appear too friendly. The truly cool ones simply lift one or two fingers from the steering wheel to let me know they can see me, but don't have time to think about me. Those who hold up their thumbs as if hitchhiking are, I suppose, frustrated artists combing the countryside for the perfect picture to paint.

A truck hauling chickens roars around the coming curve and I grab my hat to prevent it from being blown to the ground. The driver

In my experience, each country has a flavor all its own, a mystique unique to it and its people. This flavor, or "feel," is independent of topography, flora and fauna, temperature, climate, or even smells. It springs from the old nature spirits, gods, ghosts, witches, and demons, which are a vital part of most peoples' worlds. White Americans have very few spirits, so their country is by comparison apt to feel empty and barren based on this supersensory scale. The flavor of Hopi and Navajo country was almost palpable, and I began to catalog mentally the places I visited in terms of the feelings they evoked. I was discovering a new kind of geography.

◆

—Edward T. Hall, *West of the Thirties: Discoveries Among the Navajo and Hopi*

jerks his hand from the steering wheel and gives me the peace sign. I barely get my hand into the air as he zooms past, to leave a few feathers floating over me and the two horses in the nearby pasture. He isn't the first on the walk to offer the peace sign and I'm amazed each time it happens. I thought the symbol was dead and buried way back yonder in the early seventies. Why, the next thing you know some fool will want to talk about love and understanding.

As I approach Bentonville, Arkansas, the rolling hills stretch before me, covered with small oaks and pastures where horses and cattle graze, goldenrods waving in the breeze along barbed wire fences. A meadowlark sits on a fence post and opens its tiny beak to sing a welcoming song. A creek between two hills meanders into the shaded woods, where an old barn crumbles to the ground, pokeberry bushes hanging heavy with their clusters of purple fruit. A vine snakes around a hickory, and a new squirrel bed rides in the fork of two limbs, the leaves used for the building turning from green to yellow and brown. A hawk circles gently and gracefully overhead as if there's not a worry in the world.

As I get closer to Bentonville, little country houses are replaced with modern ones. I can't imagine where the money comes from, here in the Ozarks, till I remember that the world's richest man, Sam Walton—owner of Wal-Mart—lives here. Some of his offices and warehouses pad local pockets. Part of me wants to spit anytime I think of a chain store because each one looks just like another one, smothering individuality. But if I spit now, I'll be doing it against the wind. The hat I'm wearing, a gift, came from old Sam's store back in my hometown. I still haven't figured out why they had to chop off the magnificent ridge there to construct the building instead of working it into the natural contours of the land. To do such a thing is like taking off a woman's breast when it's in perfect health. I guess they X-rayed and discovered that the earth had a giant tumor or something.

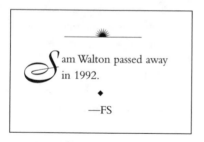

Sam Walton passed away in 1992.

◆

—FS

I'm down to my last drop of water and I swear that I'll never take it for granted again as long as I live. I stop at a house with a little office offering tickets to a cave in the backyard. Nobody's here and I bend over a glass case containing arrowheads and human bones found in the cave. When a ghostly shadow falls atop the case, I spin around to find a young man in the doorway.

You work here? I say.

Not usually, he says, but I do today. I'm home for a visit. Ready for it too. I just finished training for Special Forces. The last day we had to walk twenty-six miles with sixty-five pounds on our back. I *ran* the first eight miles. That was a week ago and the feeling hasn't returned to my big toe yet.

As I rolled up my dew-covered tent this morning I promised myself I'd get a motel tonight so I could take a shower. *That won't be necessary*, said my inner voice. *You'll be staying with a family tonight.* Now my head is often juggling thoughts, but when my inner voice speaks I take it as a premonition. Lewis Day was so kind that I just knew he would invite me to stay in his home tonight. Okay, I was wrong about that. But now here's Dough, a fellow walker. That inner voice must've been referring to him and his parents, who own the cave. That, or I was just plain old caught up in wishful thinking when I was half asleep this morning. We go outside and I fill my canteen with water from the garden hose.

In three more days, says Dough, I leave for language school. To study Spanish. Guess I'll be off to Colombia after that to fight in the drug war. Just hope we don't get ourselves into another Vietnam.

Maybe I need to trade my inner voice in on a newer model. Dough doesn't as much as hint that I should spend the night with his folks or even pitch my tent in the yard. I down another mouthful of water and return my canteen to the pack.

Don't forget to duck, I say.

What?

If you go to Colombia, I say.

Oh, yeah, he says. *That* duck.

I arrive in a small Arkansas town, to enter a gas station to use the phone to check on a motel for the night. The cheapest place in town turns out to be Ozark Hill.

Wait a minute, says the mechanic. I heard you on the phone. I got a wife and two kids, but if you don't mind them you can stay at my place tonight. I know what it's like to be on the road. I used to bum around a lot myself.

His name is Bob and he's in his late twenties. He's small and his hands are covered with enough dirt and grease to choke a man who has little will to live. I try to read his eyes to see if I want to accept his invitation. I'm uneasy.

That's a generous offer, I say. You sure your wife won't mind?

No, no, he says. I'm sure. I got another hour to work and she'll be by with the kids to pick us up.

> *N*o one really knows how many Indians died as a result of the European colonization of North America, because no one knows how many inhabited the continent before Columbus arrived. For many years, historians believed that in 1500 the native population might have numbered about one million in the area of the present-day United States. More recent estimates vary widely, from fewer than two million up to sixteen million.
>
> ◆
>
> —Fergus M. Bordewich,
> *Killing the White Man's Indian: Reinventing Native Americans at the End of the Twentieth Century*

He seems sincere, but I only met the guy five minutes ago. I'm anxious that he has something up his sleeve: A rock, like the man I met on the side of the road? His *voice*, I must hear his voice some more.

I don't want to put you out any, I say.

No, he says. I'm a good judge of character. You'd add something to our evening.

I don't like motels much anyway, I say, offering my hand.

He pulls out a cigarette and lights it. As he blows smoke he looks around us as if to make sure no one can hear us.

I should tell you something right now, he says. Before my wife gets here. It might change your mind.

What are you talking about? I say.

Well, he says. There's something me and my wife like to do at night. We don't let our kids see us, but...

Two miles after I passed the man with the rock this morning I saw a paperback book in the weeds alongside the Trail. The title read *Bent Love*. I picked it up and discovered a photograph of two men with a women. Let's just say she had more than her hands full and appeared to be the happiest person in the world, even if it was a bit painful. I salute the cliché *to each his own*, but if the mechanic is about to suggest a threesome tonight he's barking up the wrong leg.

There's not much I haven't seen, I say. Why don't you just spit it out?

He takes another draw from the cigarette, blows a cloud of smoke, and drops it to the ground. He crushes the cigarette with his foot.

Like I said, he says, we don't let our kids see us and we only do it at night. What I'm trying to say is that we like to smoke a little dope to unwind. Do you smoke or will it bother you when we do?

Welcome to America: down the road I met a soldier in the drug war and now I meet a rebel in the counterforces. No doubt about it, our streets aren't lined with gold, they're lined with dope.

I don't smoke, I say. What you and your wife do is your business.

You didn't strike me as somebody who'd play God, he says. Just thought I'd check it out before it was too late. A lot of people confuse grass with crack or smack. We don't do any hard drugs, but I have to have a little something at night to deal with this shit job. It's all I can do to make ends meet one week to the next. I got a dream to help keep me going though. Come back here and I'll show you.

And so another night was settled.

Jerry Ellis is a playwright and author, with a particular interest in Native American history. He has traveled the Pony Express Trail by foot, horseback, and covered wagon. This story was excerpted from his first book, Walking the Trail: One Man's Journey Along the Cherokee Trail of Tears.

✶

I like to think of the story I heard a Kiowa tell once. A famous writer, he was speaking to a huge crowd of non-Kiowa at a public ceremony on the Mainland. He said that when he was a child growing up on his grandfather's ranch near the reservation in Oklahoma, he'd come upon a box of huge animal bones under the rafters of the barn across from the house. He asked his grandmother what they were. "They are the bones of a great horse," his grandmother told him. "A horse of great strength that helped the Kiowa people." Legends grew around the horse. The horse led the way on a long pilgrimage to the source of all souls. And led the way back. It was a magical horse. These bones in the barn were his. The boy was to notice how large they all were, how huge the jaw, how massive the teeth and eye sockets. He went to the barn nearly every day, making the bones part of the circuit of his daily play.

One day, the boy went to the barn and the bones were gone. The boy felt sick inside. The bones had become part of his routine, a focus for his regimen of games and travel through what had become an *imaginative* world as well as an authentic landscape for his entire being. What happened? He asked his grandmother. She told him someone had stolen the bones. Why? No one knew for sure, but perhaps for greed, to exhibit in a traveling show, or, most strangely, for nothing at all. It could have been purposeful—to deprive the Kiowa of a glory, stealing the monument to a former time, an old way of life, an order of imagination. Who could know? The horse's bones had tied the child to the landscape and to stories of his Kiowa people. And it tied the people to the very grand story of their annual migrations up through the land corridor from Oklahoma to North Dakota, to the expanded universe of the entirety of the Great Plains itself. To heaven.

—Garrett Hongo, Volcano: A Memoir of Hawai'i

DUNCAN McLEAN

⋆ ⋆ ⋆

Nashville Cats

On the hunt for western swing,
a Scotsman tracks the legacy of
Bob Wills and his Texas Playboys.

THE GUITAR-SHAPED POOL IS CLOSED FOR REPAIRS. I GOGGLE MY hands and peer through the meshed-glass door. Corridor light shines off the water and shimmies up the far wall, flichtering across patches and tracks of raw concrete where the tiles have come unstuck. The air is saturated with chlorine. The vapour's so thick that my nostrils fizz and burn when I breathe in. That's good though: it burns out the last traces of my brown box-room's stink. (Sweat-soaked sheets, reconditioned air, stale fag-reek, businessman's beer belch.) There's a plop in the pool; another clump of little tiles scabbing off the ceiling into the deep end. The water ripples, the edges slosh, light-shards shiver up the walls.

I turn and walk away: down the corridor, across the murky, stained lobby, out into the hot Nashville night.

The day's been spent chasing ghosts around the Country Music Foundation. Their museum has Ira Louvin's mandolin, Little Jimmy Dickens' sequinned stage-suit, Hank Williams' scribbled lyrics. These are holy relics, it's true, but still only relics: husks, shells. Jimmy's suit stands there, the chest puffed out, the arms stiff, the whole get-up full of emptiness. It floats a few inches off the

15

ground as if modelled by some invisible hillbilly. Like I said: a husk. The body's long gone. The spirit too.

Downstairs in the chill vaults of the record library, the spirit feels closer. Listening to ancient crackly 78s through heavy, leather-upholstered headphones, there are times when I think I'm about to catch it. Through a hiss of static, over a frantic background of fiddle, sax, trombone, and tub-thumping two-four bass and drums, two vocalists—one singing swingingly, the other yelping joy-ously—urge their listeners to *Get With It:*

Rhythm here, rhythm there
Rhythm floating everywhere
Get with it, oh get with it
Red hot rhythm now

Some like to stomp, some like to hop
But give me the shimmy or the eagle rock
Get with it, oh get with it
Red hot rhythm now

This is Bob Wills and his Texas Playboys. This is their first recording session, in Dallas, September 1935, the one where the heat was so intense in the makeshift studio that big fans were angled to blow over barrels of ice in the direction of the sweat-lashed band.

This is the hottering chili-pot of New Orleans jazz, old coun-try fiddling, big-band swing, ragtime, blues, pop, mariachi and conjunto that dominated Texas, Oklahoma, Louisiana, and be-yond—all the way to San Francisco in the west, Memphis in the east—from the mid-Thirties till mid-Elvis. *This is western swing.*

It's square dances, reels, and schottisches, stomps, rags and waltzes. It's strings, brass and lap steel guitars, jive-talking, yodelling and scatting. It's the stuff I chanced across in a junk shop in Edinburgh five years ago—one scratchy LP's worth of it—the stuff that has been sending jolts of musical electricity through me ever since. It's the reason I'm three thousand miles from home, six hundred miles from anyone who knows anything more about me than the name on my credit card.

I am not from these parts. I've come a long way in search of real live western swing. I won't find real live Bob Wills, that's for sure: he's been dead twenty years. But his spirit lives on; I know it, I feel it. It lives on…somewhere. Not in the battered fiddle in the museum-case upstairs, not even in his three or four hundred vintage recordings down in the cool catalogued vaults. Nowhere in Nashville, probably; Bob always considered himself a jazz man, never thought he had anything in common with corny country music, always said that folk here didn't understand what he was *after*. (Cause he was always after something: he rarely, if ever, found what he was looking for—in life or music. It's this restless searching for new sounds and inflections and ways of twisting old tunes that makes his music so startling, so stimulating, so endlessly fresh and exciting.)

And now I am after something. I don't know exactly what it is, and I don't know exactly where I'm going to find it. But *somewhere* out there, further south and further west—out amongst the country dancehalls, the ranch to market roads, the old musicians hunched over tin-tack pianos and tenor banjos—somewhere in the wide, sun-struck wilds of Texas, that's where I'm going to track down the spirit of Bob Wills. That's where I'm going.

The first eating-place I come to is BK's Country Cafe. Posters in the window announce that this is their songwriters' night. Makes no difference to me; I haven't eaten all day. I walk in.

> *S*ooner or later, all vagabonds discover that something strange happens to them en route. They become aware of having wandered into a subtle network of coincidence and serendipity that eludes explanation. On tiptoes, magic enters.
>
> ◆
>
> —Ed Buryn, *Vagabonding in the USA: A Guide for Independent Travelers and Foreign Visitors*

BK's is a small, dark place with a serving hatch and bar at one end, a tiny stage at the other, unoccupied. It's easy to find a table; the place is less than half full. At scattered seats across the room, eight youngish men sit tuning and retuning and reretuning guitars. Some of the tuners are sitting with one or two or a whole gang of friends, partners, supporters. In fact, apart from me, everybody seems to be either tuner or supporter: at this amateur level, songwriting is apparently a participatory activity like angling, or knitting, not a spectator sport like baseball or Willie Nelson.

A waitress flits about, bringing long-necked beers, coffee and platters of barbecued meat to the tables; and somebody else, a big guy, goes from tuner to nervous tuner with a pen and clipboard, taking down names, giving out places in the running order. He gets to me before the waitress does.

You not brought your guitar?

Eh…no.

He grins, leans on the table to tick his clipboard. No problem, I'll fix you one.

No, listen…

You're not going *a capella* are you?

I splutter. Too right I'm not!

Fine, that's settled then. Now, three songs only, that's the limit. You got three?

Well…

Sure you have! Every one a hit, eh? He laughs. Right, you're on second. Good luck, buddy!

Thanks, I say, but…

Oh, what's your name?

Listen, we're at cross purposes. I didn't come here to sing.

You didn't?

No, I'm just trying to get something to eat.

To *eat*?

Yeah, can I do that? I mean, this is a cafe, isn't it?

Well…sure. He laughs again, looks around for the waitress and waves her over.

Yeah? she says. What is it, Grady?

This guy wants to eat, says Grady. *Just* to eat.

Well, not *just*, I put in. I'll listen as well. I look from Grady to the waitress and back again. I'll eat and listen and watch at the same time. Is that okay?

Sure, says the waitress.

Sure, says Grady. It's just unusual, that's all.

I shrug. I'm a spectator here, I say. I'm not joining in.

Well, if you change your mind, just let me know…

The waitress takes my order, and I sit back and sip on my beer. Grady is up on stage doing an MC routine, stuff about arriving in a cab and leaving in a Cadillac. Everybody laughs, then Grady introduces Billy Ray Pinkerton, all the way from Elgin, Alabama. A big BK's welcome for Billy Ray…

A tall lantern-jawed guy in a t-shirt and waistcoat climbs on the stage. He has a very expensive Ovation guitar, which he plugs in, tunes, strums, tunes, then strums again.

This one's called, "Since You Left I Feel Like Starting Colonic Irrigation, Cause I Miss My Pain In The Ass," he announces, and strikes a bold chord on the guitar. Actually, that's a joke, he says.

Somebody laughs loudly at a table down the front.

Thanks Myra. He nods, grins. But seriously, I'd like to start with this one…

And he launches into a song. It's so vague in its imagery, so twisted in its syntax, so abstract in its language, that even before the first verse is through I'm completely lost; I haven't the faintest idea what he's singing about. The chorus doesn't help much. It goes something like:

Expeditions of immorality in the modern world today
Explorations, navigations, trying to find the way
Seeking to locate the route that leads to what we're
looking for
You'll know it when you find it, my daddy said of
yore.

Each of the verses describes a different expedition in immorality. I think. Halfway through what must be about the eighteenth verse, the waitress brings my food, and with relief I turn my attention to pulled pork, onion rings and hot pepper sauce.

The food is fantastic. The songwriters are dire. Every single one of them. By the time I hear the fifth one introduce himself by saying, *I don't want to be just another cowboy singer, I want to be a cowboy singer pushing Jesus*, I'm ready to leap up there, batter him around the skull with his expensive guitar (they all have expensive guitars) and launch into the "Colonic Irrigation Song." I've had plenty of dull moments to work out my own version of it...

But I don't. Instead I sign for the waitress to bring me the bill, and drag some dollars out of my pocket. When she arrives, the saucer has a thick felt-tip marker on it as well as the little slip of till paper.

Thanks, I say. But I'm paying cash, I don't need a pen.

Hey, she says. The pen's for the wall. Would you sign it for us?

I look at her. Pardon?

Everybody that comes here on a songwriters' night has to sign the wall. In case they get famous, see.

But I haven't sung anything.

She shrugs. It don't matter. Go on! There's a space right there above the sauce bottle.

I look at the wall behind the table. She's right: there are scrawled names and good wishes, and posters and promo pics of nearly famous folk in black hats and big hair-dos all across the wall. But right above my chili sauce bottle there's a definite space.

I pick up the pen. Are you sure? I say.

Sure I'm sure. Hey, you might end up *anybody*. Then we can cut that piece of the wall out.

And burn it?

Sell it.

I pop the top off the pen. Right, I say. What am I going to write?

Anything you like. She takes the saucer with my dollars on it and heads off for the bar, sashaying between the tables, the guitar cases, the tapping and twitching toes.

I suck the end of the pen for a second, then reach out, hesitate, reach out again, and rest the tip of the pen on the wall. This is my chance to make my mark on Nashville, to give the country music establishment something to chew on. It doesn't matter a bean who I am. The person I want to bring to their attention is The King Of Western Swing. So I lean over and write, slowly and carefully:

BOB WILLS IS ALIVE AND WELL

AND LIVING IN

I stop. That's not right. What *is* it that folk write up? Oh aye. BIRD LIVES! ELVIS LIVES! That's it: not a bloody address book, HENDRIX IS ALIVE AND WELL AND LIVING IN anywhere, but a bold statement of faith, HENDRIX LIVES! But now I'm committed. I've started so I'll have to finish. Where could Bob be? IN THE HEARTS AND MINDS OF TEXANS EVERYWHERE...IN HILLBILLY JAZZ HEAVEN...IN LYLE LOVETT'S QUIFF...No no no, none of those would do. Out of the corner of my eye, I see the waitress coming back with my change. Up on stage another expensive-guitar-and-a-paisley-waistcoat hopeful is singing too many words with too few ideas behind them, too many notes with too little tune. I've got to get out of this place.

I read my sentence so far, then write the first word that comes to mind: SIN.

In the words of swing steel colossus Bob Dunn, at the end of his brief sojourn in Nashville in the late thirties, *I can't handle this shit. I'm going down to Cowtown.*

Duncan McLean was born in Aberdeenshire and now lives Orkney. His collection of stories, Bucket of Tongues, *won a Somerset Maugham Award in 1993. This was followed by two novels,* Blackden *and* Bunker Man. *He has also written for stage and television. This piece was excerpted from his book,* Lone Star Swing: On the Trail of Bob Wills and His Texas Playboys.

✳

Traditional jazz has never seemed risky enough to me. But as the band inside Preservation Hall continued to bang out one number after another, the piano, bass, drums, banjo, clarinet, and trumpet swelling into a sea of collective fakery with sufficient spirit and peculiarity to challenge all the conventional harmonies, I caught for an inspired instant how truly daring the music must have felt at its inception. Even now the friction of creation showed sparks—the painful *hilarity* of squeezing something unheard before from a motley collection of instruments only recently transported to these shores. The band rumbled on, and I realized there was nothing at all quaint about this music; it had always been full of risk, unstable, and liable to combust.

The bass player at Preservation Hall seemed determined to prove this point. He launched into a flutter of notes that were both too rapid and dissonant for New Orleans vintage jazz, playing more like Charles Mingus than Pops Foster. He scurried up the instrument's neck from the bridge to the scroll, shattering the tune. The other players grunted encouragement. Together they were demonstrating how music—culture—argues, blends, dissolves, mutates, advances. The odd bird who hears something different plucks his strings too quickly or queerly or flat out plunks the *wrong* note, but he does it over and over until it sounds right. He finds his own groove and fashions new music from the old.

And that's exactly what American music—American culture—has managed to do. As the bass player was now showing, our nation's truest anthem contains the funeral dirge of the New Orleans street band combined with the whorehouse piano and the last slave's work song and the bickering melodies of two hundred disparate points of origin, from Marseilles to Dakar, from Manaus to Guangzhou, now stretched out over the American plains like the hide of some mythical beast: the confluence of influences that nobody will ever be able to pick apart note-for-note. It has long been a sophisticated complaint to jeer that America has "no culture," but there couldn't be a sillier idea. We have more culture than one people will ever be able to digest. And that helps explain why the melting pot sometimes bubbles up—and when we least expect it, explodes.

—Fred Setterberg, *The Roads Taken: Travels Through America's Literary Landscapes*

TONY HORWITZ

* * *

Battle Acts

The Civil War lives—on weekends.

In 1965, a century after Appomattox, the Civil War began for me in a musty apartment in New Haven, Connecticut. My great-grandfather, leaning far over in his chair, held a magnifying glass to his spectacles and studied an enormous book spread open on the rug. Peering over his arm, I saw pen-and-ink soldiers hurtling up at me with bayonets. I was six, Poppa Isaac a hundred and one. Egg-bald, barely five feet tall, he lived so frugally that he cut cigarettes in half before smoking them. An elderly relative later told me that Poppa Isaac had bought the book of Civil War sketches soon after immigrating to America, in 1882.

Years later, I realized what was odd about this one vivid memory that I had of my great-grandfather Isaac Moses Perski. He had fled tsarist Russia as a teen-age draft dodger and arrived at Ellis Island without money or English or family. He had worked in a Lower East Side sweatshop and lived literally on peanuts. Why, I wondered, had this thrifty refugee chosen as one of his first purchases in America a book in a language he could barely understand, about a war in a land he barely knew, and why had he kept poring over that book until his death, at a hundred and two?

By the time Poppa Isaac died, my father had begun reading

aloud to me each night from a photographic history of the Civil War: page after page of sepia men leading sepia horses across corn-fields and creeks; jaunty volunteers, their faces framed by squished caps and fire-hazard beards; barefoot Confederates sprawled in trench mud, their eyes open and their limbs twisted like licorice. The fantastical creatures of Maurice Sendak held little magic com-pared to the man-boys of Mathew Brady who stared at me across the century that separated their life from mine.

Before long, I began to read aloud with my father, chanting the names of wondrous rivers like Shenandoah, Rappahannock, and Chickahominy, and wrapping my tongue around the risible names of Rebel generals such as Braxton Bragg, Jubal Early, John Sappington Marmaduke, William (Extra Billy) Smith, and Pierre Gustave Toutant Beauregard. I learned about palindromes from the surname of the Southern sea captain Raphael Semmes. And I began to match Brady's still-deaths with the stutter of farm roads and rocks that formed the photographer's backdrops: Mule Shoe, Bloody Lane, Devil's Den.

I also began painting the walls of our attic with a lurid narra-tive of the war: rebel soldiers at Antietam stretched from the stairs to the window. General Pickett and his men charged bravely into the eaves. The attic became my bedroom, and each morning I woke to the sound of my father bounding up the attic stairs, blow-ing a mock bugle call through his fingers and shouting, "General, the troops await your command!"

Twenty-five years later, early one winter morning, the Civil War reentered my life with the sound of gunfire outside my house in the foothills of the Blue Ridge Mountains. I looked out and saw men in gray uniforms firing muskets on the road. Then a woman popped up from behind a stone wall and yelled "Cut!" The firing stopped, and the Confederates collapsed in our yard. It turned out that our village had been chosen as the set for a TV documentary on Fredericksburg, an 1862 battle fought partly along Colonial-built streets that resembled ours. But the men weren't professional actors, and they were performing for little or no pay. "We do this sort of thing most weekends anyway," said a lean Rebel with gunpowder smudges on his face and the felicitous name of Troy Cool.

I'd often read in the local paper about "reënactors" who gathered by the thousands on spring and summer weekends to re-create Civil War battles using smoke bombs and reproduction muskets. This fast-growing hobby now had an estimated 40,000 adherents, whose rank had gone beyond mock soldiers to include nurses, surgeons, preachers, even embalmers. Cool and his comrades explained that they weren't average reënactors—a term that they spoke with obvious distaste. Rather, they thought of themselves as "hard cores"—purists who sought absolute fidelity to the 1860s: the era's homespun clothing, antique speech, sparse diet, and simple utensils. Strictly followed, this fundamentalism produced a time-travel high, or what hard cores called a "period rush."

"Look at these buttons," one soldier said, fingering his gray wool jacket. "I soaked them overnight in a saucer filled with urine." The chemicals oxidized the brass, giving it the patina of buttons from the 1860s. "My wife woke up this morning, sniffed the air, and said, 'Tim, you've been peeing on your buttons again.'"

In the field, the hard cores ate only foods that Civil War soldiers ate, such as hardtack and salt pork. And they limited their speech to mid-19th-century dialect and topics. "You don't talk about *Monday Night Football*," Tim explained. "You curse Abe Lincoln or say things like 'I wonder how Becky's getting on back at the farm.'"

The men paused to point out a hard core named Robert Lee Hodge who was ambling down the road toward us. Hodge looked as though he had stepped from a Civil War tintype: tall, rail-thin, with a long, pointed beard and a frayed and filthy uniform the color of butternut.

As he drew near, Troy Cool called out, "Rob, do the bloat!" Hodge clutched his stomach and crumpled to the ground. His belly swelled grotesquely, his hands curled, his cheeks puffed out, his mouth was contorted in a rictus of pain and astonishment. It was a flawless counterfeit of the bloated corpses photographed at Antietam and Gettysburg which I'd so often stared at as a child.

For Hodge, it was also a way of life. He told me that he acted in Civil War movies and frequently posed—dead or alive—for painters and photographers who reproduced Civil War subjects and techniques. "I go to the National Archives a lot to look at the Civil War photographs," he said. "You can see much more detail in the original pictures than you can in books." Hodge reached into his haversack and, to my surprise, handed me a business card. "You should come out with us sometime and see what a period rush feels like," he said. I glanced at the card. It was Confederate gray; the phone number ended in 1865.

When I called Rob Hodge, a few weeks later, he renewed his offer to take me out in the field. The Southern Guard, the unit Hodge belonged to, was about to hold a drill to keep its skills sharp during the long winter layoff. "It'll be forty-eight hours of hard-core marching," he said. "Wanna come?"

Hodge gave me the number for the Guardsman who would serve as the host of the event—a Virginia farmer named Robert Young. I called Young for directions and asked him what to bring. "You'll be issued a bedroll and other kit as needed," Young said. "Bring food, but nothing modern. Absolutely no plastic." I put on old-fashioned, one-piece long johns, a pair of faded button-fly jeans, muddy work boots, and a rough cotton shirt that a hippie girlfriend had given me twenty years before. I tossed a hunk of cheese and a few apples into a leather shoulder bag, along with a rusty canteen and a camping knife.

Two young Confederates stood guard at the entrance to the drill site, a four-hundred-acre farm in the bucolic horse country of the Virginia Piedmont. One was my host, Robert Young. He welcomed me with a curt nod and a full-body frisk for 20th-century contraband. The apples, he said, had to go, because they were flawless Granny Smiths—nothing like the mottled fruit of the 1860s. The knife and the canteen and the shoulder bag were also deemed too pristine, and so was my entire wardrobe. Even the union suit was wrong; long johns in the 1860s were two-piece, not one.

In exchange, Young tossed me scratchy wool trousers, a filthy shirt, hobnailed boots, a jacket tailored for a Confederate midget, and wool socks that smelled as though they hadn't been washed since Second Manassas. Then he reached for my tortoiseshell glasses. "The frames are modern," he explained, and he handed me a pair of wire-rimmed spectacles with tiny, weak lenses. Finally, he threw a thin blanket over my shoulders. "We'll probably be spooning tonight," he said.

Spooning? His manner didn't invite questions. Half blind, and hobbled by the ill-fitting brogans, I trailed him to a farm building behind the antebellum mansion that I'd seen from the road. We sat shivering inside, waiting for the others. Unsure about the ground rules for conversation, I asked my host, "How did you become a reënactor?"

He grimaced. I'd forgotten that the "r" world was distasteful to hard cores. "We're living historians," he said. "Or historical interpreters, if you like." The Southern Guard had formed the year before as a schismatic faction, he said, breaking away from a unit that had too many "farbs."

"Farb" was the worst insult in the hard-core vocabulary. It referred to reënactors who approached the past with a lack of verisimilitude. The word's etymology was obscure; Young guessed that "farb" was short for "far be it from authentic" or, possibly, an anagram of "barf." Violations serious enough to earn the slur included wearing a wristwatch, smoking cigarettes, smearing oneself with sunblock or insect repellent, or—worst of all—fake blood. "Farb" was a fungible word: it could become an adjective ("farby"), a verb ("Don't farb out on me"), an adverb ("farbily"), and a heretical school of thought ("farbism") or behavior ("farbiness"). The Southern Guard remained vigilant against even accidental farbiness; it had formed an "authenticity committee" to research subjects such as underwear buttons and 1860s dyes.

Rob Hodge arrived, and greeted his comrades with a pained grin. A few days before, he'd been dragged by a horse while playing Nathan Bedford Forrest in a cable-TV show about the

Rebel cavalryman. The accident had left Rob with three cracked ribs, a broken toe, and a hematoma on his tibia. "I wanted to go on a march down in Louisiana," Rob told us, "but the doctor said it would mess up my leg so bad that it might even have to be amputated."

"Super hard-core!" the others shouted in unison. As the room filled, with twenty or so men greeting each other with hugs and shouts, it became obvious that there would be little attempt to maintain period dialogue. Instead the gathering took on a peculiar cast—part frat party, part fashion show, and part Weight Watchers meeting.

"Yo, look at Joel!" someone shouted as a tall, wasp-waisted Guardsman arrived. Joel twirled at the center of the room, sliding out of his gray jacket like a catwalk model. Then, reaching into his hip-hugging trousers, he raised his cotton shirt.

"Check out those abs!"

"Mmm."

"Awesome jacket. What's the cut?"

"Type One, early to mid '62, with piping," Joel said. "Cotton-and-wool jean. Stitched it myself."

"Way cool!"

Rob Hodge turned to me and said, "We're all GQ fashion snobs when it comes to Civil War gear."

"CQ," Joel corrected. "Confederate Quarterly."

The two men embraced, and Rob said approvingly, "You've dropped some weight."

Joel smiled. "Fifteen pounds just in the last two months. I had a pizza yesterday but nothing at all today."

Losing weight was a hard-core obsession. Because Confederate soldiers were especially lean, it was every Guardsman's dream to drop a few pants sizes in order achieve the gaunt, hollow-eyed look of underfed Rebels. Joel, a construction worker, had lost eighty-five pounds in the past year. "The Civil War's over, but the Battle of the Bulge never ends," he said, offering Rob a Pritikin recipe for skinless breast of chicken. At the encampment, there was no food—local or otherwise—in sight. Instead, the men puffed at corncob pipes and took swigs from antique jugs filled with Miller Lite.

Near midnight, we hiked a few hundred yards to our bivouac spot, in a moonlit orchard. My breath clouded in the frigid air. The thin wool blanket I'd been issued seemed hopelessly inadequate, and I wondered aloud how we'd avoid waking up resembling one of Rob Hodge's impressions of the Confederate dead. "Spooning," Joel said. "Same as they did in the war."

The Guardsmen stacked their muskets and unfurled ground cloths. "Sardine time," Joel said, flopping to the ground and pulling his coat and blanket over his chest. One by one, the others lay down as well, packed close, as if on a slave ship. I shuffled to the end of the clump, lying a few feet from the nearest man.

"Spoon right!" someone shouted. Each man rolled onto his side and clutched the man beside him. I snuggled against my neighbor. A few bodies down, a man wedged between Joel and Rob began griping. "You guys are so skinny you don't give off any heat," he said. "You're just sucking it out of me!"

After fifteen minutes, someone shouted "Spoon left!" and the pack rolled over. Now my back was warm but my front was exposed to the chill air. I was in the "anchor" position, my neighbor explained—the coldest spot in a Civil War spoon.

Somewhere in the distance, a horse snorted. Then one of the soldiers let loose a titanic fart. "You farb!" his neighbor shouted. "Gas didn't come in until World War One!"

This prompted a volley of off-color jokes, most of them aimed at girlfriends and spouses.

"You married?" I said to my neighbor, a man about my own age.

"Uh-huh. Two kids." I asked how his family felt about his hobby, and he said, "If it wasn't this, it'd be golf or something." He propped himself up on one elbow and lit a cigar butt from an archaic box labelled "Friction Matches." "At least there's no room for jealousy with this hobby. You come home stinking of gunpowder and sweat and bad tobacco, so your wife knows you've just been out with the guys."

The chat died down. Someone got up to pee, walked into a tree branch, and cursed. One man kept waking himself and others with a hacking cough. And I realized that I should have taken off my wet boots before lying down; they'd become blocks of ice. My neighbor, Paul, was still half awake, and I asked him what he did when he wasn't freezing to death in the Virginia hills. "Finishing my Ph.D. thesis," he muttered. "On Soviet history."

I finally lulled myself to sleep with drowsy images of Stalingrad, and awoke to find my body molded tightly around Paul's, all awkwardness gone in the desperate search for warmth. He was doing the same to the man beside him. There must have been a "Spoon right!" in the night.

A moment later, someone banged on a pot and shouted reveille: "Wake the fuck up! It's late!" The sky was still gray. It was not yet six o'clock. No one showed any sign of making breakfast; instead, the Guardsmen formed tidy ranks, muskets perched on shoulders. As a first-timer, I was told to watch rather than take part. One of the men, acting as drill sergeant, began barking orders. "Company right wheel, march! Ranks thirteen inches apart!" The men wheeled and marched across the orchard, their cups

"*W*hen visitors come [to Appomattox] they expect to find a courthouse and nothing else," Ron Wilson told me. "They want to see where all those men who struggled for so long brought things to a conclusion. But then they find that they're in a village, walking old roads, smelling country smells, looking at cows in the fields, slowing down to a different pace. We've gotten them out of the automobile and back to an earlier time. We try to bring about a contemplative feeling: to get people to reflect on where this nation has been and what it has come from, to realize that after the Civil War it could never have gone back to the way it was before. It had been pushed forward."

◆

—William Zinsser, *American Places: A Writer's Pilgrimage to 15 of This Country's Most Visited and Cherished Sites* and canteens clanking like cowbells. In the early morning light, their muskets and bayonets cast long, spirelike shadows. "Right oblique, march! Forward, march!"

The mood was sober and martial—except for one hungover soldier, who fell out of line and clutched a tree, vomiting.

"Super hard-core!" his comrades yelled.

Rob Hodge called a month later to tell me that the first major event of the "campaign season" was coming up: the Battle of the Wilderness. Eight thousand reënactors were expected to attend, plus twice that number of spectators. "It'll be a total farbfest," Rob predicted. Hard cores, he said, were ambivalent about battle reënactments. After all, it wasn't easy to be truly authentic when the most decisive moment of any battle—the killing of one's enemy—couldn't be reproduced. Hard cores also felt that crowds of spectators interfered with an authentic experience of combat. But Rob planned to go anyway, to scout fresh talent for his unit.

The day before the reënactment, Rob dropped by to lend me some gear, which included a "trans-Mississippi shell jacket" and a smooth-sided 1858 canteen. "With this kit," he said, "people will think you're hard-core even if you act like a total farb." We made a plan to meet at the farm where reënactment was scheduled to take place.

*T*his country is a land mass that could be called anything, and for people to act like this is some kind of sacred territory is an insanity. It's just a bunch of people trying to live together, and if we're not going to be part of a dream of equality—a part of a dream of that which is the best of us, the idea that people help one another— if we're not going to do that, then this land mass doesn't any more deserve to be revered than anything else.

◆

—Nikki Giovanni, *Shimmy Shimmy Shimmy Like My Sister Kate: Looking at the Harlem Renaissance Through Poems*

The real Battle of the Wilderness was fought in jungly Virginia woods in May, 1864. Lee slammed into Grant's advancing Army, hoping that surprise and the tangled terrain would disorient his far more numerous foe. Units of both Armies got lost and the woods caught fire, cremating many of the wounded. Grant lost 17,000 men, twice as many as Lee. But the North could bear such losses better than the South, and Grant pressed on, waging the grisly war of attrition that led to Lee's surrender at Appomattox the next spring.

Today's Civil War "battles" were easier to navigate. After driving across the Rappahannock and Rapidan rivers, I spotted a roadside placard that read "Battle of Wilderness." A bit farther on a sign pointed to "C.S.A Parking Area." A woman sat behind a bridge table, chatting on a cellular phone. "Are you preregistered?" she asked me. I mumbled something about the Southern Guard. "Well, just fall in," she said, glancing at her watch. "Afternoon battle's about to begin."

Just beyond the parking lot and a row of portable toilets, several thousand Confederates mustered as drums rolled and flags unfurled. I scanned the long lines of gray but couldn't find any of the Southern Guard. A ragtag troop marched past, led by a lean, strikingly handsome figure. He wore wire-rimmed spectacles and a battered slouch hat, brown and curled, like a withered autumn leaf. He looked like a cross between Jeb Stuart and Jim Morrison.

I saluted him and said, "Sir, I've lost my unit. May I fall in with yours?"

"Certainly, private," he drawled. "I regret to say that one of our men fell in this morning's fight. You may take his place."

He pointed me to the rear rank, between two middle-aged men. The one to my left, who identified himself as Bishop, had graying hair and what looked like red finger paint smeared on his face. Bishop had been wounded in the morning clash. He pointed to his stained cheek. "Yankee bullet just bounced off me," he said. He reached into his pocket and pulled out a tube labelled "Fright Stuff: Fake Blood." "Got it at a gag shop," he said. "It's mostly corn syrup, with some dye and chemicals mixed in."

The soldier to my right, a huge, long-haired man named

O'Neill, told me that he'd fought as a Marine in Vietnam. When the Rebel Army halted, confused over where it was headed, O'Neill muttered, "Just like the military—a continual fucking screw-up."

I'd joined Company H of the 32nd Virginia, from the Tidewater area in the state's southeast. The handsome man in command was Captain Tommy Mullen, a carpenter. O'Neill worked as a receptionist in a museum. Bishop was a cop. Many of the others worked in the shipyards around Newport News. "We're a bunch of average Joes, pretty much like the Confederates of old," Bishop said.

"Bullshit!" O'Neill protested. "We're a bunch of fat slobs who couldn't hack it in the real Civil War for an hour."

We reached a line of trees. "Watch the poison ivy!" one man called out. As we were marching through a manure-laden pasture, someone yelled, "Watch the land mines! And the electric cable." O'Neill explained that a film crew was recording the battle. "My brother's on the other side, in the Sixty-ninth New York," he said. "He lives in New Jersey. I'm hoping to get filmed capturing him."

We stumbled through brambly woods until Captain Mullen ordered us to halt. Then he gave us a few stage directions. "The Yanks get hit big time, forty-five percent casualties," he said. "But those Rebs to the right of us are going to get overrun, so we've got to counterattack and chase the Yanks back." Artillery began pounding in the field just beyond the woods. Each time the cannon boomed, the ground shook and pine needles showered down around us. A foul gray smog seeped in among the trees. "Suck it in, boys," Captain Mullen said, resuming his Civil War persona. Troops to the right of us hoisted their guns and flags and rushed out of the woods, vanishing into the smoke and noise. There was a keening Rebel yell and the crackle of small-arms fire. I started to feel butterflies. Crouching in the woods, peering into the smoke, and listening to the percussion of guns and artillery, I sensed a little of what one of Mathew Brady's soldiers must have felt, with no idea who was winning the battle or even what his part in it should be.

"Prime muskets!" the captain barked. All around me, the men of the 32nd bit open paper cartridges and poured black powder down their rifle barrels. I was the only man without a gun. I asked the captain what part I might play in the combat. "If one of our men should fall, pick up his musket and fight on," he said. He added, "If no one goes down, run around awhile and then take a hit. We can always use casualties."

Back in line, I told Bishop about my orders. "Casualties are a problem," he said. "Nobody wants to drive three hours to get here, then go down in the first five minutes and spend the day lying on cow pies." O'Neill cut in with a safety tip about dying. "Check your ground before you go down," he said. "I've gotten bruises from falling on my canteen. Also, don't die on your back, unless you want sunburn." Shoulder to shoulder, we marched out of the woods and into the clouded field. We marched forward, then sideways, blinded by smoke. Somewhere a fife tootled "Dixie."

Captain Mullen took out binoculars and peered through the gloom. "Halt!" he shouted. Just ahead, we heard a murmur of voices and what sounded like triggers cocking. At the order "Form battle lines!" ten men knelt, rifles at the ready, with ten others standing right behind. Then the smoke cleared, revealing a crowd of spectators in lawn chairs, aiming cameras and videos at us. "There they are!" one of the spectators shouted, and a hundred shutters clicked.

"Company, left!" Mullen yelled, wheeling us sharply around and back into the smoke. Suddenly, fifty or so Yankees appeared just in front of us, as startled as we were. Upon Mullen's next command—"Fire at will!"—flames licked from the muskets and bits of white cartridge paper fluttered all around us. The blanks made a deafening roar. Like street mimes, the Yankees aped our motions precisely. Then both sides frantically loaded and fired again. "Pour it in, boys!" the captain shouted.

I put my fingers in my ears and crouched beside O'Neill. The Yankees were no more than twenty yards in front of us, firing round after round. I waited in vain for one of our men to go down.

"Damn Yanks can't shoot straight," O'Neill said, lips black with powder. Apparently, the Rebels couldn't aim, either. Despite the withering fire, only one Federal had gone down. "Yanks never take hits," O'Neill griped. "Fuckin' Kevlar army."

Then, obeying the battle's script, the Yankees suddenly turned and ran. Mullen drew his sabre. "Look, boys," he said, "they're turning tail! Drive 'em boys! Drive 'em!"

"No-account Yankees!"

"Candy asses!"

"Take no prisoners! Kill 'em all!"

We reached a field littered with blue figures. Several of the dead lay propped on their elbows, pointing Instamatics at the oncoming Rebs. "O.K., boys," the captain said after we'd poured imaginary lead at the enemy for fifteen minutes. "Time to take some hits."

Bishop reached into his pocket for the Fright Stuff. Smearing the bright-red goop on his temples, he asked me, "Want a squirt?" I shook my head, imagining what Rob Hodge would say if I returned his uniform with fake bloodstains. "Watch for land mines when you go down," Bishop reminded me.

The Yankees unleashed another volley. I clutched my belly, groaned loudly, and stumbled to the ground. O'Neill flopped on his side like a sick cow, bellowing, "I'm a goner! Oh, God, I'm a goner!" Then he spotted his brother from New Jersey, lying in the grass nearby. "Hey, Steve, they got you, too! Just like Civil War, brother against brother!"

A few minutes later, the battle ended with the playing of "Taps" and the order for us to "resurrect" and shake hands with enemy corpses. Combat wasn't scheduled to resume until the next day, so the soldiers and spectators scattered—to the portable toilets and to a huge tent encampment called "the sutlers' row." ("Sutler" was a Civil War term for merchants who provisioned the Armies.) North and South mingled peaceably here along dirt streets lined with shops selling uniforms, hoop skirts, and other period items. The atmosphere was self-consciously quaint—one store was labelled "The Carpetbagger" and another "War Profiteer Serving Both North and South." I wandered over to the "civilian camps." In a Rebel tent I came upon a Soldiers Aid Society, where women dressed as Southern belles sat knitting socks, sipping Confederate coffee (parched corn sweetened with dark molasses), and gossiping about their Northern counterparts. "Yankee women, of course, may not be of the highest moral order," one woman drawled.

In the nearby Union camp, I was handed a schedule of events that included a square dance, a women's tea, and an outdoor church service at which two reënactors were to be married. For all the military bravado, reënacting seemed a clean-cut family hobby, combining elements of a camping trip, a country fair, and a costume party. It was also becoming clear that the hobby attracted mostly conservative, middle-class people who were nostalgic for what they imagined was a simpler, slower, and more neighborly world, one that had distinct social roles. "It's an era lost that we're trying to recapture," a Union campwife named Judy Harris told me as she washed clothes in a tub. "Men were men, and women were women. It was less complicated." A soldier walked past, tipped his hat to Harris, and said "Evening, ma'am." She smiled and said to me, "See what I mean? No one's that polite in real life anymore." Harris, who said she worked as a data processor, added, "No one asks what you do for living. You could be a dentist or a ditch digger. See that general over there? He's probably pumping gas at Exxon during the week."

While women like Harris were welcome in civilian camp, the same wasn't always true on the battlefield. A female reënactor dressed as a male soldier had successfully sued the National Park Service following her expulsion from a 1989 battle. (She was caught coming out of the women's bathroom.) Ever since, a few women had dressed and fought as soldiers, despite grumbling from male reënactors. A different sort of cross-dressing—Southerners clad as Northerners, and vice versa—was encouraged. The reason became obvious as I toured the Union camp. Blue had outnumbered gray almost two to one at the real Battle of the Wilderness; the opposite was true here. In fact, a shortage of Yankees was endemic to reënactments—particularly to those staged below the Mason-Dixon Line. So it helped to carry two outfits, in case the other side needed you. Reënactors called this "galvanizing," which was the Civil War term for soldiers' switching sides during the conflict.

One reason for the preponderance of Rebels was the instinctive sympathy that Americans feel for the underdog. "When I play Northern, I feel like the Russians in Afghanistan," a Reb from New Jersey explained to me. "I'm the invader, the bully." The South also had the edge in terms of romance. Conformist ranks of blue couldn't compete with Jeb Stuart, Ashley Wilkes, and other doomed cavaliers of the Confederacy.

Wearing gray had little to do with politics; the awkward racial questions surrounding allegiance to the South didn't intrude. (Although the film *Glory* had inspired the creation of several units modelled on its black regiment, most reënactments remained virtually all-white affairs.) Many reënactors spoke of a desire to "educate the public," yet their concerns seemed essentially ahistorical: North and South, murderous foes for four years, were now blandly reconciled—interchangeable, even—in a spectacle that glorified the valor and the stoicism of both sides. "We're not here to debate slavery or states' rights," Ray Gill, a gray-clad Connecticut accountant, told me. "We're here to preserve the experience of the common soldier, North and South."

That night, a sudden downpour drove the soldiers into their tents, and I headed off in search of Rob Hodge. I finally found a few Southern Guardsmen, hunched at the rear of a sutler's lean-to, who told me that Hodge had become so disgusted with the luxury of even this modest shelter that he had decamped to a nearby field. I found him there the next morning, wringing out socks over a sodden fire. "I wanted to see what it's like to be soaked and cold on the night of battle," he said. "Now I know—it sucks."

I sat with him while he cooked salt pork in a half-canteen that served as his frying pan, poking the sowbelly with a bayonet. After half an hour, the pan had become a puddle of grease, with fatty chunks bobbing atop the scum. Rob skewered a piece and dangled it beneath my nose. "C'mon," he coaxed, "just think of it as blackened country ham." He took a chunk in his mouth and I did the same. We gasped, our eyes filling with tears. The meat didn't resemble meat at all; it tasted like a soggy cube of salt. "I bet this stuff killed more Rebs than Yankee bullets ever did," Rob groaned, dribbling the pan grease onto his trousers and dabbing a bit in his beard.

Back home, I pulled Poppa Isaac's book of Civil War sketches from the shelf. The title had rubbed off its spine and the pages discharged a puff of yellowed paper dust when I opened the massive cover. Turning the pages, I wondered again what had led my great-grandfather to buy this book soon after emigrating from Russia. The only clue I found was near the end of a Robert Penn Warren essay about the Civil war. "A high proportion of our population was not even in this country when the War was being fought," Warren wrote. "Not that this disqualifies the grandson from experiencing to the full the imaginative appeal of the Civil War. To experience this appeal may be, in fact, the very ritual of being American."

As a teen-age émigré with no family in America, Poppa Isaac must have felt profoundly adrift when he disembarked at Ellis Island, just seventeen years after Appomattox. Perhaps, having come from learned, rabbinical stock, he sensed that the complex saga of the Civil War was an American Talmud that would unlock the secrets of his adopted land and make him feel a part of it. Or perhaps, like young immigrants today who so quickly latch on to brand names and sports teams, he was drawn to the Civil War as a badge of citizenship. After all, as Warren wrote, "To be American is not... matter of blood; it is a matter of an idea—and history is the image of that idea."

Tony Horwitz is a senior writer for The Wall Street Journal *and winner of the 1995 Pulitzer Prize for national reporting. He is the author of* One for the Road *and* Baghdad Without a Map. *This story was excerpted from his recent book,* Confederates in the Attic.

★

Here at Vicksburg an organized, modern commercial society had struck the older feudal order a harsh blow. I had parked my car just north of the

West Virginia Memorial at the spot where, on May 19, 1863, William Tecumseh Sherman sent wave upon wave of Union soldiers against the rebel position at Stockade Redan, only to see each attack bloodily repulsed. A series of charges three days later also failed. The rebels had dug into the green hillsides, shaded by live oaks and maples, with extensive trenches and tunnels, and the courage and dedication of the Yankees who charged are beyond measure. Surveying the scene while considering the larger aspects of the war, I couldn't help wondering what had motivated those foot soldiers. For what did they think they were fighting?

Earlier I'd spent an hour at the Illinois Memorial, a white granite-and-marble rotunda nestled on another of the park's quiet hills. The dome of the memorial is modeled on the Pantheon in Italy, and cast in bronze inside are the names of the 36,325 soldiers from Illinois who participated in the Vicksburg campaign. Ulysses Grant was from Illinois, of course, as was Abraham Lincoln. My parents had viewed Illinois as the vehicle of their liberty—most blacks in Mississippi viewed the Illinoisans as liberators—and our family had risen from sharecroppers to suburbanites because of the opportunity and personal freedom afforded many blacks in that state. The names on the wall in bronze had had something to do with that rise. The domed roof of the rotunda is open to the sky, and on the day I was there, surrounded by all those names and my awareness of what they'd done—enduring a winter in the open, digging trenches and canals to try to divert the river, following the enemy into tunnels for hand-to-hand combat, running miles in the dark in close formation, fording the river twice, throwing siege upon siege at an almost unbreachable opponent—the sky was clear blue through the opening, everything was perfectly quiet and completely still, and in that moment it was a simple thing to feel respect and admiration and awe for all the possibilities of the human spirit.

—Anthony Walton, *Mississippi*

✦ ✦ ✦

Desert Dreams

An Englishman falls hard for
the American way.

I MET FRANKIE WHEN I WAS TWENTY-TWO, AND I COULD HARDLY believe my luck. She was a wild artist from New York City. A peroxide blonde who wore black miniskirts and silver space-age ankle-boots fit only for the Manhattan sidewalks. She sang for an underground rock band, was three years older than me, and taught me all kinds of things I had never imagined before. We met in London, exchanged one long kiss, and the day after she flew home she called me from across the ocean.

Our first telephone conversation, she in Manhattan, and I in my mother's house, in a quiet English Village: "I want to see you. Come over here." Her words came down the satellite line as a whisper.

"What?"

There was a pause. "I can't wait to see you." Another pause. "Come over here."

She was actually asking me to go to New York to see her. I couldn't believe it. Nor could I go, but a month later she came to England with her family to celebrate Labor Day. I caught the train up to London dressed in my brother's dinner jacket on a cold, rosy evening, the sky darkening slowly, the west showing pale through the bushes lining the tracks. The little train panted across Buckinghamshire towards Marylebone station, and by the time the brick walls of London were rolling past it was getting dark.

At eight o'clock I made my way to the Dorchester Hotel, where Frankie's wealthy stepfather had booked a sixteen-place table for all of his extended family. At midnight Frankie sat down on the edge of the queen-size bed in her room and unbuttoned her shirt. At twelve-thirty someone knocked at the door. Just then her ankles were positioned right under my chin, shackled by her leggings, and she was wailing softly into my ear. All of which, the position no less than its effect, was new to me.

We stopped and listened. The knock came again.

"Who is it?"

"It's me." It was her elder sister. Apparently she didn't know what to say next. "I wondered what happened to you." She hesitated. "You're doing it, aren't you? Oh well. I guess I'm going to bed."

You're doing it. A sister just saying it. *Oh well.* I didn't know people could talk like that. These people were truly uninhibited, quite unlike anyone I had ever known before. And it suddenly struck me that right then and there I was forging a link with them, driving an iron stake into their rock to tether myself to.

Two days after that Frankie called to tell me: "We better just grab the bull by the horns. No sense waiting around."

We flew to America the next day.

Coffee, whisky, sex, ketchup—even the same things tasted different in America. Sunsets looked different. They were brilliant and cold and spoke of big spaces and made you feel hollow, like a wind was blowing through you. I remembered one in particular. Frankie was in New York City and I was three hours away on Long Island, staying with a friend in a wooden cottage among the dunes. She had been staying out in the country while she completed a big canvas in the city.

"I miss you," her soft voice breathed down the line. "I miss all of you."

I knew what she was talking about. I could already feel the gentle weight of her breasts on my chest.

I went out for a walk, my legs shaking as I shuffled down the sand dunes. Inside the house they were heating sake on the wood stove, cooking broccoli and garlic chicken. Outside it was cold and dark and falling. The trees across the inlet were already black, and the sand was a pale glow, insubstantial. The black water carried the most fragile image of light, like gold leaf spread across the surface, or like a saucer of mercury trembling as someone carries it across a room. But up above, the sky was a defiant display of orange and crimson and lime. The colours had been applied in big strokes ignoring the laws of the spectrum, lying where they wished. Across them scrawled the fantastic graffiti of jets entering and leaving Kennedy Airport. Once a jet winked at me, a brilliant star at the front of a twin line, and vanished. Then I saw, through the black trees across the water, a blurry, pallid shape, a fleece hung in the trees. It startled me, even though I knew it was the moon.

I was jubilant. I went north to Portland, Maine, and found work on a trawler called the *Nordsee*. We were lucky and kept running into schools of monkfish, which were fetching high prices that season. After a month I had two thousand dollars, more money than I had ever had before. Frankie came up to join me and we moved inland. I got a job at a local airport in Vermont, and Frankie took a studio in a converted warehouse.

Every morning at seven-thirty I went out into the cold fall air, jumped into the airport Jeep and rattled down the hills to work. I didn't come back till night, when Frankie and I would watch videos and drink vodka and Michelob and make love, while outside our cabin the leaves turned yellow then gold then red, as the autumn fell on Vermont.

Sometimes I went to visit her in her studio. The big high hall had been partitioned into a number of work spaces. Pictures had been pinned up on the screens dividing them, and you could hear a continual soft babble of relaxed chatter and laughter as the artists worked away. Frankie used to work on the floor of her unit, with a wheeled lamp and pots of her various odd materials spread out around her, among rags, sponges, rulers and old pens. Instead of using paints, she was experimenting at the time with beeswax, old tea, tar and glue, and recently she had found a bag of school erasers by the roadside, which she had taken to carving up and using as printing stamps in her pictures.

One Saturday afternoon I found her laying out black and white monoprints on top of one another, ready for storing. A fat roll of duct tape sat beside her. Her ponytail was unusually bright just then, radiant gold in the chalky air of the hall. I bent down, lifted it, and kissed her neck. She let out a soft laugh, but didn't look at me. She was warm like she was in bed after sex. Her fingers were smudged with ink and she was arranging the sheets carefully by the edge, using only her fingertips. She set another picture down and I picked up her left hand. The grey-silver ink smears highlighted the grain of her fingers, made them look metal. I kissed the tips and let the hand go. She stayed as she was, not unhappy that I was there, but not wanting to break her attention either.

From a corner of the room came a high peal of laughter. Then a man walked in. He had fair hair cut very short, and blond stubble on his jaw, picked out by the curiously illuminating light in the hall. His face was somewhat rounded, but tanned and suave-looking. He was a little plump, but he carried it smoothly, and it suited him. There was a self-possession about him, an ease, that was immediately appealing.

He glanced at me, smiling faintly. It looked like the kind of smile he would always have on his face. Then he looked down at Frankie. "I've got it," he said. He was holding a small clay sculpture by his side. The subject of the piece was hidden in his hand.

"Hi, Joel." She didn't look up, but stayed hunched over, squatting, fingering her paintings. "Joel, this is Henry."

Joel stepped towards me and held out his hand. Something made me hesitate before taking it.

"How's it going?" he asked her.

"Fine."

The three of us were silent a moment, listening to the rustle of her stiff papers.

"You can put it down over there," she said.

She meant the little wooden cabinet by the door. He set the sculpture down. The clay made a quiet thud. It was a female nude reclining with one leg straight, the knee of the other raised, all done with rough knife-marks. It was a good piece. The proportions were right and it had a certain relaxed sophistication. I knew right away that it was Frankie. It surprised me. She hadn't told me she was modeling for anyone.

Joel glanced at her, then smiled at me steadily.

"So, Henry," he said, apparently at ease, "what do you do?"

"Right now I'm between boats," I said. I liked the expression. It hinted at a painful separation, though I had no intention of returning to fishing boats, and it sounded better than cleaning the toilets and pumping gas at an airport.

Joel glanced at my shoes—roughed-up deck shoes from K-Mart—and nodded. I asked what he did. He shrugged his shoulders. His blue-grey eyes rested easily on mine. "I'm an artist. I paint pictures and make things. Things I like."

A streak of sunlight found my left cheek from a high window. I stepped out of it. "Do you make a living like that?"

"You don't need money where I live."

"Where do you live?" My voice sounded higher than I wanted.

"New Mexico."

"How can you live without money?"

"Come to New Mexico and see. It's a cool place." He chuckled. "The coolest. The only place for an artist. Where else is there? Forget New York and LA. Forget Europe. Europe's all over. Santa Fe's the only real community right now. It's Paris in the '20s all over again. You know where I live? At the foot of the Blood of Christ Mountains. That's what they call them. The Sangre de Cristos. Every dawn and sunset they turn red, red as—" He shrugged. "As red as blood."

He arranged to meet up with Frankie later. I watched him as he walked towards the door, moving slowly and easily and somehow brightly, as if bathed perpetually in his own private sunbeam. I couldn't help feeling curiously privileged to have met him. This artist from New Mexico had breezed over to Vermont, made some sculptures, some things he liked, and soon would ride back to the south-west, to the land of the free.

It got me thinking about New Mexico. Frankie sometimes talked about the Four Corners region of the south-west, where she had gone hiking when she was eighteen. She showed me a photograph she had taken there of an adobe farmhouse. Its wicket fence and window frames and front door were all painted with the same peeling blue-green paint, a good colour against the adobe walls. I liked the photograph, and began to imagine living in such a house with Frankie. She would paint there and I would support us with some kind of simple labour, in a bar or on a farm. Not only that, but Frankie's eyes were the same colour as that green paint. They even had the same chipped and peeled look when you studied them closely.

I started dreaming about New Mexico. I had one particularly vivid dream in which I was a poet who lived in a large studio with white

I have been suspicious of the "poor, starving artist" (and the American idea of poverty) ever since my encounter with one. He was living in a spacious cabin in the woods, writing a book, naturally. A friend who knew him well thought I should meet him since I too was digging in the writing mine pit. He asked if we had brought any meat to cook for dinner, as he was too poor to afford any. We had not. But as we boiled lentils and baked potatoes, it turned out that the starving artist used a credit card to make long distance phone calls and had driven four hours to San Francisco just to buy a pair of very expensive hiking boots. Inwardly, I raged at his "poverty." I ate everything there was so there would be no leftovers for him. I'm sure he would be able to charge a meal at the boutique cafe in town. Soon after, I came across the American expression "trust-fund baby."

◆

—Rajendra S. Khadka,
The Hovering Hindu: An Education on Two Continents

floorboards. I was sitting on a cushion on the floor with a girlfriend facing me, a blue china teapot steaming between us. Outside
there was silent desert all around, and a high still sky, and I felt profound contentment, living a life that suited me. My girlfriend
could feel the calm in me too, and loved me for it.

I woke up from the dream and lay beside Frankie in the pre-
dawn dark on our mattress, sure that New Mexico was the place
for us. The Atlantic was a harsh ocean, and created lives to match
for its people. Britain, New England, Scandinavia were countries
where you needed Viking and Teuton genes, so the rain in your
eyes made you feel tough, not cold. I had lived in the north too
long, I suddenly realized. Further west, nearer the Pacific, in the
desert of the south-west, I would be able to lead a warm, quiet life,
something very different, something I wanted.

Once a month a priest used to fly into the airport. He was
known as the Flying Father and flew a Mooney, a fast, single-engine plane with a cut-back tail and retractable landing gear, the
most desirable of all small planes, making his way across America
on some obscure mission, stopping off here and there to lead certain congregations in their worship—in Iowa, Indiana, the
Dakotas, Illinois, as well as Vermont. His home town was
Carrizozo, New Mexico.

I liked him. He would come taxiing briskly to the pumps and
tell me to fill her up. "Always like to be ready for a quick getaway,"
he would explain with a chuckle. He had a lined suntanned face,
cropped silver hair and steely eyes, and looked as though he had
been toughened and cured by the New Mexican skies. He always
wore a black poloneck and exuded a bright, tough spirituality, as if
he came out of a pure, ascetic life in the south-western desert. I
asked him what it was like out there, and he told me, "You better
come and see for yourself some day."

Meanwhile Frankie was becoming withdrawn. We talked less
and less. Often she didn't get back from her studio till late, and
sometimes she spent the night there. Then one Saturday a gale
blew all night long. We woke up on Sunday morning to find our
cabin no longer standing in a forest, but in a desert of stark tree

trunks. It was as if the house were suddenly floodlit. The living room, which previously had seemed heavy and dark with its drapes, was suddenly bright, and grime marks had appeared on the door of the fridge overnight, while the kitchen sink looked whiter than ever before. What had been a lawn outside was a marsh of leaves.

We sat at the table with cups of coffee steaming brightly between our fingers. One of us was going to make pancakes, neither yet felt ready to do it. Things had been getting increasingly strained between us, and in the unforgiving clarity of that first morning of winter we both knew the time had come to do something about it.

But we had different ideas about what to do. Frankie got up from the table and climbed into the sleeping loft. I heard a tap running in the bathroom, then her clicking tread moving to the bed. From the knocks and creakings of the floor, and the rustlings, I could tell that she was going back and forth between the closet and the bed.

She came down the ladder with a suitcase, said she would call me in a couple of days, and left. I heard her truck start up and sit there idling for a while, as if she wasn't sure whether to move off, then the sound of the engine drew away. I sat watching the white steam from my coffee cup rise through the air of what had been our dark kitchen, and tried to lift the cup to my lips, but couldn't summon the will.

Then on a sudden impulse I ran outside, leapt into the Jeep and skidded off down the track. I guessed that she was probably heading back to New York, and once I hit the tarmac at the bottom of the hill I slammed my foot down and roared towards town, which she would have to pass through on her way south. She didn't have more than a couple of minutes' start on me. I overtook a Buick station wagon, then a purple Volkswagen Jetta, then settled into the long smooth stretch of easy bends that eventually delivered you to the white steeple of the Episcopalian church on the edge of town. I had just passed the church when I saw her truck up ahead.

She had parked at the roadside. I drew up alongside and looked in. It was empty. I drove on a little further and thought about what to do. She might have stopped to buy something, in which case I could find her when she came out of whichever shop it was. Or she might have decided to move into town, in one of the clapboard houses on the street, most likely the one she had parked outside, in which case perhaps I should go and knock on the door. But who would answer? What would I say to them? And I hadn't even begun to think about what I would actually say to Frankie. All I knew was that I didn't want it to end like this.

My deliberations were cut short when Frankie came out of the house followed by a man, the sculptor, Joel. He carried two kitbags slung over either shoulder, and held a wide shallow box in front. I saw her attempt to take the box. He shook his head. She went ahead and opened the back of the truck, where he deposited his belongings, while she climbed into the cab and leant across to unlock his door.

It was an overcast day, very cold. Winter had truly arrived now in New England. My breath came out in a cloud of steam and fogged up the windows, which I wiped clear with my elbow. Joel was wearing a dark-grey car coat and a pair of green slacks. I watched him rub his hands together and blow on them, then pull open his door. I wondered where they were going, then suddenly understood. A day like this, the first day of winter in Vermont— it was the perfect day to begin a long road trip. It was a day on which to leave for the desert. Joel, with his bronze face and short blond hair, didn't belong in a northern winter. He was migrating now, going back home to the sunny desert, and Frankie was going with him.

I was shocked. I sat still, not knowing what to do. The truck's headlights came on, and they drove right past me without noticing. The traffic light was green and they drove straight on through. A neat little tail of exhaust smoke fluttered in the cold air behind them, like a train of tin cans tied to a wedding car.

I didn't move. I felt like I had lost a layer of clothing, or a layer of skin. A long warm night was over and now I was waking to the cold light of day. I felt like I was standing under a new sky. Nothing seemed familiar.

I got out and wandered around town, acutely aware of all sights and sounds and sensations. Two icy grips had seized my wrists where the cuffs of my jacket ended. An aeroplane droned noisily by overhead, hidden in low clouds, sounding fat and slow like a bumblebee, and I realized I knew it was a Cessna 152. I had subconsciously learnt the different plane noises at the airport. The cars, the houses, the trees, all seemed to have had a film shaved off them by the cold. Then I heard a bell clanging nearby, and dumbly turned down a side street towards the sound.

It was coming from a modern church called the Reformed Catholic Assembly. The doors were wide open and I walked straight into the brightly lit interior, where a woman with short black hair and a string of pearls smiled at me and pointed me to a pew at the back. I slumped down.

By chance it turned out to be the Flying Father's church. He came walking up the aisle, wearing a black jacket over his usual poloneck, and a silver cross on a chain, shaking hands and murmuring greetings, then took his stand at the front. "Where there are no oxen," his deep voice boomed, "the crib is clean." He went on to explain the proverb, but I found it hard to listen. It had something to do with not being able to make an omelet without eggs. I didn't take much of the service in, but it seemed full of the resigned Old Testament wisdom of Amos and Ecclesiastes. The cross and the mass were mere afterthoughts, while the real message was of the acceptance of suffering. "Vanity, vanity, all is vanity": he was a preacher in that tradition.

Afterwards he stood in the doorway, offering solace to the departing congregation, blessing them both with his words and with the fine matutinal incense of his bacon-scented breath, which rose up in clouds into the cold. When my turn came he recognized me and gave me an encouraging smile.

"All well?" he asked.

"Not really," I answered. I told him my girlfriend had just left me.

He listened, paused and said softly, "Put hand to the plough. You're an educated fellow. Enough summer-jobbing." He chuckled quietly. "I'm sure they're waiting for you back home."

I walked back to the Jeep feeling numb and dazed. But I was also aware of a little question mark resting like an uncertain smile on my breast.

I saw him the next morning at the airport, as he was leaving. He performed a cursory pre-flight check, stopping under the wings of his Mooney, then clambered into the cockpit and sent me a wave before he slid the glass shut. Then he did a clearance take-off, whether out of pure exuberance or because he guessed I was still watching I never knew. Either way, it brought a smile to my lips to see him get the nose up, level off at ten feet and scream along the runway with the undercarriage tucked up like a fighter plane, then suddenly yank the Mooney into a banking climb. He did a barrel roll and disappeared into the next valley on his quest.

New Mexico. The next day or the day after he might be there. I thought of him alone in his cockpit, his cropped suntanned head, his grip stowed on the back seat, just him and his wings high above the desert. It made my heart beat faster. He had a life to aspire to.

Eventually, over the following days, I realized that I had two choices. Either I went out to New Mexico and tried to find Frankie, in the hope of winning her back, or I went home. Then gradually it became clear that the Flying Father was right and I really only had one choice. A month later I left America.

Six years passed, during which I moved through a variety of jobs in England. But I never gave up on my hope of one day going to New Mexico, perhaps even of living there, and although I sometimes took time off to go travelling, in the hope that it might calm my dim craving, it didn't work.

I hadn't ever heard from Frankie again, but what finally decided me was coming upon the remains of an old T-shirt she had given me. It was on a Sunday night in London, after I had spent a rainy weekend elsewhere, while I was unpacking my bag. All that was left of the shirt was a square of cotton the size of a handkerchief, printed with a design of a Navajo rug, which I had cut from the front. I thought I had lost it years ago, but it had rolled itself into a tight scroll and lain in hiding in a seldom-used compartment of the bag. I opened it out on the bed.

It came from Taos, New Mexico, and had long been my favorite shirt, till it split along the seams and in order to save the design I cut the rest of it away. The rug was a weaving of amber and brown stripes with a row of tassels at the bottom, just below which the words "Navajo Serape by Bigfoot Walker" has been handwritten in slanting capitals.

I had had other mementos of my time in America with Frankie—an eagle feather from the Delaware woods, a finger-pull from a Manhattan manhole, a misshapen grey pearl that I extracted from an oyster caught in a trawling net off Maine—but I lost all of them. As the years went by I thought I had lost this one too. The sight of it, and the feel of the fine cotton, seemed to knock me to my senses like a cold shower. My pulse quickened. I thought of the Flying Father, of Joel, of Frankie, and wondered what had happened to them all. There was a world across the ocean that I had once been on the verge of entering. Just then I could not understand why I hadn't entered it back then, six years ago, when I had wanted to. I still wanted to.

I rolled the cloth up and went to the window. A flyover below stretched away to the south-west, and somewhere down that way, beyond the orange-grey smudge of London sky, the desert of America was just now basking in a strong morning sun, and a man with cropped silver hair was surely sliding shut the cover of a cockpit over his head, preparing to launch himself into the sky.

Born in Oxford, England, Henry Shukman is a regular contributor to GQ, Condé Nast Traveler, *and* Islands *magazines.* Savage Pilgrims *is his third book. He and his wife currently live in New Mexico.*

*

Like many another of my generation, I had dreamed of the place always. I dreamed of it romantically because where I grew up, on the Bristol Channel, the fact that no land stood between us and New York afforded me, at sunset especially, tantalizing visions of Manhattan's towers and palaces. I dreamed of it in an entertained way, like every-one else, at the cinema; even in the 1930s, when I imagine not one in ten thousand inhabitants of the British Isles had ever crossed the Atlantic, we were all strangely familiar with American scenes and id-ioms. Finally, when I was much older, I began to dream of it actually in my sleep. I dreamed repeatedly of a particular kind of office door, opening upon a street: Not at all a modern or glitzy door, but sur-prisingly homely, perhaps the door of some old-fashioned family es-tablishment, with varnished wood, and lots of brass about. Outside this door the street life of America, as I saw it in my sleep, proceeded with none of the Hollywood flash, but solidly and respectably.

—Jan Morris, *Pleasures of a Tangled Life*

$\star \; \overset{\star}{} \; \star$

Good People

Are you tough enough
for Minnesota?

A BIRCH TREE GROWS ON THE SHORE OF MOOSE LAKE. A CANOE lies on the bank beside it.

From that birch tree, you could paddle the canoe up to the end of Moose Lake and camp overnight and put the canoe in another lake the next morning. You could cross that lake, and camp for the night, and paddle across another lake on the third day. You could keep this up, visiting a different lake every day, for *a hundred years*, and you still wouldn't get to all the lakes.

Henry David Thoreau wrote, "A lake is the landscape's most beautiful and expressive feature. It is earth's eye."

I sat on a rock beside the birch tree, looking into the eye of the earth. I was watching the sun go down on Moose Lake and thinking about the universe of green forest and blue water I had come to in a day's drive north from Minneapolis-St. Paul. Loons called to each other out on the lake. Thunder rumbled away to the north in Canada. I stayed there until the night came on.

This was not the Moose Lake down there south of Kettle River, and not the Moose Lake west of Nashwauk, and not the Moose Lake that the Bigfork River flows out of. God knows how many Moose Lakes there are in Minnesota. This was that other Moose

Lake, the one east of Ely where the roads run out and the Boundary Waters begin.

The Boundary Waters Canoe Area is a million acres of wilderness with no roads, no buildings, no sign that human beings have ever been there, except for Indian pictographs on some of the rocks and footprints on some of the portages and signs of old campfires on some of the islands. Motors are barred; no outboard motors, no airplanes, no generators compete with nature's sounds. No cans or bottles are permitted. It is unlawful to cut down a tree, or even to cut off a bough or chip away bark. Groups of more than nine canoeists must split up and go in different directions.

If it is absolute solitude you want, you have only to paddle far enough. If the vast and glaciated U.S. wilderness isn't big enough for you, a Canadian wilderness of equal size awaits across the border. Without a topographic map and a compass, there's no way to tell which country you're in, anyway. In two or three days of paddling and portaging, you can be reasonably assured of reaching the beautiful lake of your fondest dreams, where you can set up camp for a week or two without hearing another human voice.

I had not come to Moose Lake to embark on an arduous wilderness trip, not this time. I've done it in years gone by, and I remember how long those uphill portages can be with a canoe and a backpack to carry. I thought it would be enough to wait until July when the black fly season is over, go as far north in Minnesota as I could, find a cabin on the last point of land where cabins are permitted, and just look at the wilderness and think about it.

The cabin came close to qualifying as a log mansion. I was planning to stay in a sparse outfitter's camp, but Linda Fryer, the energetic woman who runs the Ely Chamber of Commerce, called Chet and Nancy Niesel, friends she'd heard were planning to be away, and next thing I knew, I was ensconced in the Niesels' house. Or rather, in part of it. I occupied the spacious kitchen, a bedroom facing the lake, and the more extravagant of the bathrooms, without needing to venture into the rest of the dwelling, which was filled with the furniture and collections of an obviously well-lived life. I never met the Niesels, but I feel I know them. Sleeping in somebody's bed will do that to you.

The birch tree and the canoe belonged to the Niesels, and the shoreline where I sat to watch the sunset that first night and most of the nights that followed. How I envy them! Any time they want, they can drive twenty miles out of Ely nearly to the end of the Fernberg Trail, turn on the road toward Moose Lake, pass through groves of pine and stands of aspen, ash, and maple for a mile or two, bump along a few hundred yards of fire trail, and pull into the dirt driveway of their own utopia. It was my good fortune that the owners were away. If it were my house, I think I would never leave.

My trip from the Twin Cities took me north past Duluth, past the piles of tailings from the great days of the Mesabi Range iron mines, some of the heaps of red earth sprouting scrubby pines now. Around Eveleth, the music on the radio turned heavily to polkas, the favored music of the miners who came from the Old Country to the Minnesota north. I crossed the Laurentian Divide, beyond which all waters flow north to the Arctic. I was getting close. Between Tower and Ely, I counted seventy-one cars with canoes tied to their roofs. The guidebooks list twenty canoe outfitters for this general region, and the guidebooks don't list them all.

Ely's main street has the shops and cafes and gas stations you'd expect at the place where the road runs out, but it would be a lonesome street without the outfitters. Their front windows in every block, full of fishing gear and lifejackets and ice chests and freeze-dried food, remind you where you are. You can arrive in Ely in a coat and tie with no baggage and push off in a canoe an hour later, properly dressed and fully equipped for two weeks in the wilderness.

Ely is a town full of good people. I know all towns are, but Ely has always seemed to me especially rich in neighborliness and good nature and the salt-of-the-earth virtues. It's hard to be a stranger there. If your name is Charles, everybody in Ely calls you Chuck.

Minnesotans are different from the rest of us to begin with, as I was reminded on the trip in. Minnesotans don't smoke; the

Minneapolis airport was the first in the nation to ban smoking, even in bars. Minnesotans recycle; there are separate containers at the highway rest stops for cans, bottles, and plastic. Minnesotans return the grocery cart to the store. Minnesotans do not consume butterfat; at the supermarket in Virginia, Minnesota, where I stopped for groceries, they had abundant gallons of skim milk, one percent milk, two percent milk, and some kind of healthy milk substitute. I had to look a long time to find real milk, on a side shelf. Minnesotans bike with their helmets on. Minnesotans fasten their seat belts. Minnesotans hold the door for you. Minnesota men don't leave the toilet seat up. Minnesotans do not blow their horns behind you when the light turns green; they wait for you to notice. Minnesotans are nicer than other people. The farther away from the big cities you go, the nicer they are. Ely is about as far away as you can get.

I don't mean that there is anything bland or insipid about Ely. The town wasn't founded by canoe paddlers who came for the beauty. It was founded by miners who came for the iron. They were tough Swedes and Finns and Norwegians, durable Irishmen and muscular Slavs. The rough mining camp they staked out late in the last century was an ugly little place on the edge of a scenic paradise. The streets were so muddy in spring, somebody wrote, that they were "not passable, not even Jackassable." When Billy Sunday, the evangelist, passed part of a summer vacation nearby, he said the two worst places he'd ever heard of were Ely and hell, the difference being that there was a railroad out of Ely.

"Ely was hard on everybody," Bob Cary told me. He's a square-jawed outdoorsman of the old school in a flannel shirt and felt hat, "Jackpine Bob" to the readers of his stories in the Ely *Echo*.

"It was especially hard on the women, what with the mud streets and the brawling menfolks. There was all this beauty at the edge of town, but no beauty in their lives.

"Some of them tried to homestead, poor souls. They had always dreamed of a little farm, and the land was cheap. If you could prove it up in five years, it was yours. So some of them tried to grow something in these rocks. It was just impossible, of course."

This reminded me of Garrison Keillor's explanation for why so many Scandinavians located in northern Minnesota. They'd been brought up in a hard, rocky land with a short growing season, their lakes frozen solid most of the year, and they'd heard about the rich farming country of America. So they crossed the Atlantic and headed west. When they reached Minnesota—a hard, rocky land with a short growing season and the lakes frozen solid most of the year—it made them so nostalgic that they settled down, forgetting why they had left home in the first place.

The hard land bred strong characters. I was lucky enough to know some of them in years gone by, and now, in the evenings, sitting beside my birch tree and looking out at the lake, I thought about them.

> *L*ike many western Americans, especially the poorer kinds, I was born on wheels. I used to think that I was shaped by motion, but I find on thinking it over that what most conditioned me was the two places where we stayed long enough to put down roots and develop associations and memories and friends and a degree of self-confidence.
>
> ◆
>
> —Wallace Stegner, *Where the Bluebird Sings to the Lemonade Springs: Living and Writing in the West*

There was Bill Magie, who lived in a shack just around the bend on Moose Lake with his springer spaniel, Murphy. As a young man, Bill spent years mapping the country. "I'm the only man alive," he said to me, "who's walked from Lake Superior to Lake of the Woods on the ice and carried a transit on his shoulder all the way. You could tie me up right now, blindfold me, fly me into some lake and drop me off, and I'd know right where I was and find my way back, damn right, and without any help, either." Bill took Knute Rockne and Grantland Rice on a long canoe trip back in the Twenties, and guided Margaret Mead into the wilderness, and drank his bourbon straight, and told great stories, like the one about the night he crawled inside a moose he had shot to keep from freezing. People told Bill he'd become too old to be a canoe guide. He said, "The canoe country is where I want to die. If the old Reaper is going to catch me, let him catch me on a portage. Let it be the long portage to the happy hunting ground!" He laughed. When the Reaper caught him, that's about the way it happened.

There was Bill Hafeman, who was eighty-three when I met him. He had lived over on the Bigfork River since 1921, when he and his wife, Violet, moved into the woods. He said, "I wanted to live in a wild country like the Indians did. I thought, now that would be a free life. I could work as I wanted to, and nothing holding me back. I didn't want to live in a city where you go to work by a whistle, come home by a whistle. I didn't like all that stuff. So I told Violet we'll go live in the woods. And we done it. We learned how to live. We picked berries, we had wild rice for our grain, we had venison, fish, fruit. This is a Garden of Eden. Everything grows here." Bill made his first birchbark canoe with nothing but a knife and an ax so he and Violet would have some way of getting to Bigfork, the nearest settlement, fifteen miles down the river. Every canoe he built after that was a little better than the one before. I watched him build one of his last, with "all its mystery and its magic, all the lightness of the birch tree, all the toughness of the cedar, all the larch's supple sinews," to quote from the *Song of Hiawatha*, and when the buyer he expected never showed up, I bought that beautiful canoe from Bill Hafeman myself. Bill is gone. I try to take good care of one of his last masterpieces.

There was Dorothy Molter, who lived on an island in Knife Lake for more than fifty years, harvesting ice in the winter to see her through the summer, making friends with the mallards and chipmunks and chickadees, if never quite the troublesome bears, and selling her homemade root beer to thirsty paddlers who came calling. I portaged and paddled the long trail into Knife Lake one long-ago summer and spent an afternoon with Dorothy on her island. She told me her life story while I helped her wash out her root beer jars. Bob Cary, who wrote a book about her, helped win Dorothy special permission to go on living in the Wilderness Area until she died. A few years ago, in the winter, alone on her island, she did. They hauled her cabin all the way back to Ely by dogsled and set it up as a Dorothy Molter memorial and museum.

Those three I met, and others I heard about:

Chief Black Stone, the Ojibwa from Kawa Bay, who snowshoed a hundred miles through unbroken snow to seek help for his people during a flu epidemic. He made it to Ely, but never made it home. He died on Agnes Lake and was buried there in a rabbit skin blanket with his beds and his calumet, a great hero whose name is still honored.

There was Uncle Judd Cleveland, who had a little mining claim near Moose Lake, an old prospector who spent his life looking for the mother lode, sure he was going to find it any day. He left nothing behind when he died, except his name on Uncle Judd's Creek, which I crossed whenever I went back and forth from Moose Lake to Ely.

And Mike Kelly, who lived on boiled potatoes, salt pork, and bannock in a little shack on Birch Lake. He had a crooked arm from the time he was chased up a white pine by a bear, and fell and broke his arm on the way down. He set it himself and tied it to his body, and it set crooked. He never complained.

The old-timers were tough.

In thirty-seven years with CBS News, Charles Kuralt won a host of honors, including thirteen Emmys and three Peabody Awards, for his work both "on the road" and on Sunday Morning. *He was the author of five previous books, including the bestselling* A Life on the Road *and* On the Road with Charles Kuralt. *He passed away on July 4, 1997.*

*

My wife and I arrive in the spring, like Canada geese, sometimes taking off again but intermittently visible until the fall. The postman and the garbage collector have hard information about our comings and goings. There are, however, other mysterious underground channels of information, for when Jack Nicholson, accompanied by William Kennedy, the Albany novelist, and his wife called on me a couple of years ago, advance word got around. Nicholson, then filming Kennedy's *Ironweed* in Albany, had come to chat about a film based on one of my novels. His white stretch limousine could not make the narrow turn between my gateposts. Silent neighbors watched from a distance as the chauffeur maneuvered the long car with its Muslim crescent antenna on the trunk. Then Nicholson came out, observed by many. He said, "Gee, behind the tinted glass I couldn't tell it was so green out here." He lit a mysterious-looking cigarette and brought out a small pocket ashtray, a golden object resembling a pillbox. Perhaps his butt ends had become relics or collectibles. I should have asked him to explain this, for everything he did was noted and I had to answer the questions of my neighborhood friends, for whom Nicholson's appearance here was something like the consecration of a whole stretch of road.

—Saul Bellow, *It All Adds Up: From the Dim
Past to the Uncertain Future*

JIM HARRISON

✦ ✦ ✦

Going Places

*There are so many reasons
to hit the road.*

EVERYONE REMEMBERS THOSE KINDERGARTEN OR FIRST-GRADE
jigsaw puzzles of the forty-eight states, not including Hawaii or
Alaska, which weren't states when I was a child and perhaps for
that reason are permanently beyond my sphere of interest. I'm not
at all sure at what age a child begins to comprehend the abstrac-
tions of maps—Arthur Rimbaud's line about the "child crazed
with maps" strikes home. Contiguous states in the puzzle were of
different colors, establishing the notion that states are more different from one another than they really are. The world grows larger
with the child's mind, but each new step doesn't abolish the previous steps, so it's not much more than a big child who finally gets
a driver's license, certainly equivalent to losing your virginity in
the list of life's prime events.

It is at this point the pathology enters; out of a hundred drivers
the great majority find cars pleasant enough, and some will be
obsessed with them in mechanical terms, but two or three out of
the hundred will be obsessed with going places, pure and simple,
for the sake of movement, anywhere and practically anytime.

"You haven't been anywhere until you've taken Route 2 through
the Sandhills of Nebraska," they're liable to say, late at night.

"Or Route 191 in Montana, 35 in Wisconsin, 90 in West Texas, 28 in the Upper Peninsula of Michigan, 120 in Wyoming, 62 in Arkansas, 83 in Kansas, 14 in Louisiana," I reply, after agreeing that 2 in Nebraska is one of my favorites. To handle Route 2 properly, you should first give a few hours to the Stuhr Museum in Grand Island to check on the human and natural history of the Great Plains. If you don't care all that much about what you're seeing, you should stay home, or if you're just trying to get someplace, take a plane.

There is, of course, a hesitation to make any rules for the road; the main reason you're out there is to escape any confinement other than that of change and motion. But certain precepts and theories should be kept in mind:

Don't compute time and distance. Computing time and distance vitiates the benefits to be gotten from aimlessness. Leave that sort of thing to civilians with their specious categories of birthdays, average wage, height and weight, the number of steps to second floors. If you get into this acquisitive mood, make two ninety-degree turns and backtrack for a while. Or stop the car and run around in a big circle in a field. Climbing a tree or going swimming also helps. Remember that habit is a form of gravity that strangulates.

Leave your reason, your logic, at home. A few years ago I flew all the way from northern Michigan to Palm Beach, Florida, in order to drive to Livingston, Montana, with a friend. Earlier in life I hitchhiked 4,000 miles round-trip to see the Pacific Ocean. Last year I needed to do some research in Nebraska. Good sense and the fact that it was January told me to drive south, then west by way of Chicago, spend a few days, and drive home. Instead I headed due north into a blizzard and made a three-day back-road circle to La Crosse, Wisconsin, one of my favorite hideouts. When I finished in Nebraska, I went to Wyoming, pulled a left for Colorado and New Mexico, a right for Arizona, headed east across Texas and Louisiana to Alabama, then north toward home. My spirit was lightened by the 35 days and 8,000 or so miles. The car was a loaner, and on deserted back roads I could drive on cruise control, standing on the seat with shoulders and head through the sunroof.

Spend as little time as possible thinking about the equipment. Assuming you are not a mechanic, and even if you are, it's better not to think too much about the car over and above minimum service details. I've had a succession of three four-wheel-drive Subaru station wagons, each equipped with a power winch, although recently I've had doubts about this auto. I like to take the car as far as I can go up a two-track, then get out and walk until the road disappears. This is the only solution to the neurotic pang that you might be missing something. High-performance cars don't have the clearance for back roads, and orthodox four-wheel-drives are too jouncy for long trips. An ideal car might be a Saab turbo four-wheel-drive station wagon, but it has not as yet been built by that dour land without sunshine and garlic. A Range Rover is a pleasant, albeit expensive, idea, but you could very well find yourself a thousand miles from a spare part.

A little research during downtime helps. This is the place for the lost art of reading. The sort of driving I'm talking about is a religious impulse, a craving for the unknown. You can, however, add to any trip immeasurably by knowing something about the history of the area or location. For instance, if you're driving through Chadron, Nebraska, on Route 20, it doesn't hurt to know that Crazy Horse, He Dog, American Horse, Little Big Man, and Sitting Bull took the same route when it was still a buffalo path.

By careful about who you are with. Whiners aren't appropriate. There can be tremendous inconveniences and long stretches of boredom. It takes a specific amount of optimism to be on the road, and anything less means misery. A nominal Buddhist who knows that "the goal is the path" is at an advantage. The essential silence of the highway can allow couples to turn the road into a domestic mudbath by letting their petty grievances preoccupy them. Marriages survive by garden-variety etiquette, and when my wife and I travel together we forget the often suffocating flotsam and jetsam of marriage.

If you're driving solo, another enemy can be the radio or tape deck. This is an eccentric observation, but anyone under fifty in American has likely dissipated a goodly share of his life listening to music. Music frequently draws you out of where you belong. It is hard work to be attentive, but it's the only game in town. D. H. Lawrence said that "the only true aristocracy is consciousness," which doesn't mean you can't listen to music; just don't do it all the time. Make your own road tapes: start with cuts of Del Shannon, Merle Haggard, Stravinsky, Aretha Franklin, Bob Seger, Mozart, Buffett, Monteverdi, Woody Guthrie, Jim Reeves, B. B. King, George Jones, Esther Lammandier, Ray Charles, Bob Willis, and Nicholas Thorne. That sort of thing.

If you're lucky, you can find a perfect companion. During a time of mutual stress I drove around Arizona with the grizzly bear expert Douglas Peacock, who knows every piece of flora, fauna, and Native American history in that state. In such company, the most unassertive mesa becomes verdant with possibility.

Pretend you don't care about good food. This is intensely difficult if you are a professional pig, gourmand, and trencherman like I am. If you're going to drive around America you have to adopt the bliss-ninny notion that less is more. Pack a cooler full of disgusting health snacks. I am assuming you know enough to stay off the interstates with their sneeze shields and rainbow jellos, the dinner specials that include the legendary "fried, fried," a substantial meal spun out of hot fat by the deep-fry cook. It could be anything from a shoe box full of oxygen to a cow plot to a dime-store wig. In honor of my own precepts I have given up routing designed to hit my favorite restaurants in Escanaba, Duluth, St. Cloud (Ivan's in the Park), Mandan, Miles City, and so on. The quasi-food revolution hasn't hit the countryside; I've had good luck calling disc jockeys for advice. You generally do much better in the South, particularly at barbecue places with hand-painted road signs. Along with food you might also consider amusements: If you stop at local bars or American Legion country dances don't offer underage girls hard drugs and that sort of thing. But unless you're a total asshole, *Easy Rider* paranoia is unwarranted. You are technically safer on the road than you are in your own bathroom or eating a dinner of unrecognizable leftovers with your mother.

Avoid irony, cynicism, and self-judgement. If you were really smart, you probably wouldn't be doing this. You would be in an office or club acting nifty, but you're in a car and no one knows you, and no one calls you because they don't know where you are. Moving targets are hard to hit. You are doing what you want, rather than what someone else wants. This is not the time to examine your shortcomings, which will certainly surface when you get home. Your spiritual fathers range from Marco Polo to Arthur Rimbaud, from Richard Halliburton to Jack Kerouac. Kerouac was the first actual novelist I ever met, back in 1957 or 1958 at the Five Spot, a jazz club in New York City. I saw him several times, and this great soul did not swell on self-criticism, though, of course, there is an obvious downside to this behavior.

Do not scorn day trips. You can use them to avoid nervous collapse. They are akin to the ardent sailor and his small sailboat. You needn't travel very far unless you live in one of our major urban centers, strewn across the land like immense canker sores. Outside this sort of urban concentration, county maps are available at any courthouse. One summer in Michigan's Upper Peninsula, after a tour in Hollywood had driven me ditzy, I logged more than 5,000 miles in four counties on gravel roads and two-tracks, lifting my sodden spirits and looking for good grouse and woodcock cover (game birds literally prefer to live in their restaurants, their prime feeding areas). This also served to keep me out of bars and away from drinking, because I don't drink while driving.

> *W*e were all delighted, we all realized we were leaving confusion and nonsense behind and performing our one and noble function of the time, *move*. And we moved!
>
> ♦
>
> —Jack Kerouac, *On the Road*

Plan a real big one—perhaps hemispheric, or at least national. Atrophy is the problem. If you're not expanding, you're growing smaller. As a poet and novelist I have to get out of the study and collect some brand-new memories, and many of our more memorable events are of the childish, the daffy and irrational. "How do you know but that every bird that cuts the air way is an immense world of delight closed to your senses five?" asked Blake. If you're currently trapped, your best move is to imagine the next road voyage.

I'm planning a trip when I finish my current novel, for which I had to make an intense study of the years 1865 to 1900 in our history, also the history of Native Americans. I intend to check out locations where I sensed a particular magic in the past: certain culverts in western Minnesota, nondescript gullies in Kansas, invisible graveyards in New Mexico, moonbeam targets in Nebraska, buffalo jumps in Montana, melted ice palaces in the Dakotas, deserted but well-stocked wine warehouses in California. Maybe I'll discover a new bird or animal. Maybe I'll drive up a gravel road that winnows into a two-track that stops at an immense swale, in the center of which is a dense woodlot. I'll wade through the bog into the woods, where I'll find an old, gray farmhouse. In this farmhouse I'll find all my beloved dead dogs and cats in perfect health, tended by the heroines in my novels. I'll make a map of this trip on thin buckskin that I'll gradually cut up and add to stews. Everyone must find their own places.

Jim Harrison lives with his family on a farm in northern Michigan. He has written two collections of novellas, Legends of the Fall *and* The Woman Lit by Fireflies; *six novels,* Wolf, A Good Day to Die, Farmer, Warlock, Sundog, *and* Dalva; *and seven books of poetry. His work has been translated and published in nine languages. This piece was excerpted from* Just Before Dark: Collected Nonfiction.

✳

Only the other day, taking the night train from Chicago to New York, I felt myself all but overcome by the sheer human grandeur of the United States. After dinner in the restaurant car I walked back through the darkened coaches to my sleeper, as the great train labored across the continent toward Cleveland, Toledo, Buffalo and Albany, over many a gleaming river and through many a slumbering hamlet. Lurching and swaying I made my way back, coach after coach, and as I went I saw to right and left of me, exposed in the innocence of sleep, the faces of young America. They were black, and brown, and white, and yellow, some more handsome than others, some scrunched up against seat backs, some thrown back with open mouths; but seen as a whole that night, as we plodded on across the continent, they moved me with a most poignant sense of beauty—the beauty of the American idea, really. Few of those travelers were old, none of them were rich, or they would not be traveling coach class on Amtrak; some lay in each others' arms and one had a pet turtle—sleeping, too—upon his chest; sentimentalist that I am, it brought the tears to my eyes to see them.

—Jan Morris, *Pleasures of a Tangled Life*

⋆ ⋆ ⋆

Dose!

It is good to honor that
which sustains us.

PREPARING TO HUNT IN THE OLD WAY, DADDY AND I BUILT A SMALL
fire down behind the barn that evening. The flames painted
Daddy's dark face with deeper shadows, alternating with dancing
bright orange. And orange glinted off his straight black hair.

As a part of our hunting ceremony, we "smoked" ourselves,
sparks reaching up into the night when Daddy placed "medicine"
in the flames, a mixture of leaves and bark from a variety of trees
and shrubs. His brown eyes flashed orange as he looked deep into
the fire. Then, after putting the fire out we went into the barn to
sleep under the hay. This was so the *dose* (deer) could not smell
the human odor very well. Outside, the black sky was almost
white with millions of stars. Inside the barn, sweet dust floated
in the old air. *Suk'ahow* (owl) in the rafters returned a call from
suk'ahow upon the hill.

Now that we were somewhat "cleansed," Daddy said to sleep
and to dream about the *dose* we would get tomorrow. "Dream and
'see' them tonight just as they will appear tomorrow. To dream
and not see the *dose* is a sign that we should not go hunting. We
could go hunting, but we never would come close."

I was almost seven and thought that I was a great warrior.

Maybe like Straight Arrow. He taught everybody how to hunt and survive by leaving instructions on a big card in the cereal box. I could read every word, so I learned a lot from Straight Arrow. And I bet I could do everything he said.

But still there were some things that worried me. I knew the contents of the old barn. There were pigeons and hawks, owls and crickets. There were spiders and ants. There were lizards and *how'ta* (rattlesnakes). Some things still frightened me. At those times I was not a warrior after all.

Daddy seemed to go to sleep quickly. Under the hay, I did not rest because I could feel a *how'ta* sliding silently toward me, drawing nearer and nearer. I knew he was there, staring at me. Even though I could not hear or see him, I could "feel" his presence, like a ghost. He was planning to strike me, to poison me to death, then swallow my blood. I was a warrior. I could not wake Daddy talking about a little thing like *how'ta*, even if it was twenty feet long, and hungry!

> When you first go to the wilderness alone, it is best to have a purpose. This will be both a knife and a defense for the first challenges that you will encounter: family, friends and interior inertial reluctances.
>
> Our culture acknowledges, understands and respects "the purpose," "the task," "the goal." Unless you have one of these, a reason, it will be difficult to leave: expect this and you will probably actually succeed in getting away.
>
> ◆
>
> —P.K. Price, "Navigational Information for Solo Flights in the Desert," *Solo: On Her Own Adventure,* edited by Susan Fox Rogers

I did not sleep for a long time. *Suddenly* dose *appeared, breathing and studying its world with huge eyes that seemed to be made of black glass. It was alert, and puffs of steam came from its nostrils. It was a beautiful doe with huge ears, but it seemed like it did not make any difference if we killed her or not. It was a feathery dream.* Dose *just kept walking away, deeper into the forest and over the hills, then vanished.*

It was still dark when Daddy woke me up. As quietly as we could, we made our way out of the old barn and into the early darkness. At first light we moved toward Lake Britton. Silver shimmered upon the horizon, yet darkness wrapped all around us, thick. We stopped and gathered skunk berries and leaves, rolled them between our hands, crushing the odor out of them, then rubbed the mixture all over our Levi's, hands, shirts, and hair. Daddy always wore Levi's. I did, too. He liked to wear his gray sweatshirt, but I didn't have one, so I wore my long-sleeved, black-checkered shirt with a tear near the pocket.

"Daddy, we smell like *ha'yanna* (skunk)!"

"Shh. In the quiet, everything can hear the human voice."

Obeying the rules of the hunter, silently, without breaking a branch or turning a leaf, we melted into the thick darkness, sneaking west through trees and buck brush. Daddy made no noise. But I often stepped on a dead branch that cracked in the silence of early morning. We stopped, waiting for nature to resume its composure. Then, after tiptoeing for what seemed to be a hundred miles, we heard the wind moving in the forest near Lake Britton. Daddy knew the trail that the deer used as they came early to water from the high country, following the backbone ridge and dropping down the chalk bank. Then the trail skirted the lake.

If I breathed too hard, steam came from my mouth, wisping up into the darkness. Better stop breathing. Creeping now, like two shadows, a big one and a little one, we eased into our position between the sleeping lake and the deer trail. "Get comfortable, son. We may have a long wait."

Silent and motionless, we waited. Long we waited. It seemed like years instead of hours. Still we waited. I was uncomfortable and wanted to change position just a little, but was afraid I would make a noise and everything would hear me, and the deer would run away.

Then Daddy tensed slightly. *"Dose,"* he whispered softly. The urgency in Daddy's voice was a command, signifying several very important things. It meant for me to be quiet, like stone. It meant that the *dose* we dreamed of and were waiting for had arrived. It meant that I must use all of my hunting and warrior power to remain silent, now that we were within reach of our game. It meant that now the family would eat, and if I made a noise, if I breathed, if I in any manner spooked the *dose* and they took flight, I would be responsible for our family having no food.

His rifle was aimed at the target. Daddy was set.

In the dim light I stared hard, eyes riveted on the place where Daddy's rifle was aimed. Then my heart leaped! I went dizzy and thought I was going to faint. There, magically, almost at the end of Daddy's gun, appeared the *dose* that I had dreamed about last night! It stood motionless, its ears alert. Its eyes peered into tomorrow. Two small mists wisped from its shiny black eyes reflecting the whole morning world.

My spirit screamed, "Shoot! Daddy, Shoot!"

Then, as magically as it appeared *dose* disappeared. It simply vanished, like the mist from it nostrils, like the *dose* in my dream.

I was confused. We came here to kill a *dose*, and Daddy let it get away without a single shot! I wanted to scream, but remained mute and motionless. I had to. That is the way of the hunter, they always said. Daddy's rifle was still aimed at the target.

Then! The *dose* appeared again! No, this was another one. I thought I had blinked, and the first deer was still standing there. But this one held its head differently. "Shoot! Shoot!" cried my tormented spirit, again and again. In this manner many *dose* passed through the target, none breaking a branch.

Finally, for two reasons, I gave up on Daddy ever shooting. First, I had cramps everywhere. Second, I knew the *dose* would all pass by, and Daddy would not shoot. All the deer would be gone before he decided to kill one. My worried spirit and my aching body both decided that I should adjust my position, just a little. However, my will and the laws of hunting would not allow the slightest movement.

BOOM!

A thundering explosion shattered the quiet of morning. A red splotch came out of my consciousness and turned black, trimmed with silver. Faintly, I heard the rifle report echoing across the lake. The sweet, fresh air was filled with the pungent odor of smoke from the burnt gunpowder.

That BOOM! knocked me back into the thick brush, almost unconscious. I had been numb from waiting, numb from seeing the *dose* of my dreams; now I was numb from the report of the rifle. In the darkness of the brush, I lay there as if I were the one shot and not the *dose*. I tried to move my finger. It worked! Then my arm. Then my legs. Slowly I gathered myself together, and with a loud ringing in my ears, got up and looked around in the early light.

By the time I had recovered my senses and my balance and found Daddy and the *dose*, he already had the animal's stomach open with the hunting knife. Like skinny, dancing ghosts, steam wisped up into the early chill. A salty smell permeated the air. Daddy had blood on his hands, and dark blood clots lumped nearby. And pink blood foamed from its lungs.

Shivering from fright and excitement, and from sitting in one position forever, I stumbled around to the *dose's* head. I saw the painful blue-silver glitter of death in its eyes. I felt very sorry for the *dose*. Only a few moments ago it was alive and traveling with its family. Now it was food for our family and for the earth. To kill seemed like committing a crime, a bad one. Especially killing something so pretty. My stomach shook silently. I knew Straight Arrow would not cry, so I didn't either. But I wanted to. Still, again.

I thought about the deer's spirit. Eyes that only a few moments ago had seen the whole world shining now—maybe—saw shadows of memories. Upriver, *ma'ka'ta* (coyote) forlornly yapped to a departing night.

As is the custom of our mountain people, Daddy took out the purple liver from among the mounds of entrails and cut off a small piece for me and one for himself. He called upon *Kwaw* (the Wonder Power that created the universe) to forgive the injury to the family of the deer, and the injury to the silence of morning. Daddy licked the blood from the liver, then, in ceremony, ate it, for now his family could eat.

I looked at my piece of liver. It seemed to be looking back at me. With some hesitation I tasted the blood. I questioned my warrior-spirit, and wondered how Straight Arrow would react. Then I remembered that my grandfather might be nearby, studying me as I grew a little more this morning. Yes, Grandfather was watching me from somewhere secret in the shadows. I could feel his presence. So, in the manner of my people, I put the squishy piece of blood-warm liver in my mouth. A sharp taste (which I have always remembered) attacked my tongue with vengeance. Saliva flooded my mouth as if I had just bitten a hundred lemons. The soft flesh slipped and slid and did not want to go down my throat. I wrestled with it, and my spirit wrestled with it. Then, finally, it squiggled down. It almost got stuck, then kind of swam toward my stomach. I needed water, quick!

I ran to the lake, flopped down on my belly, and took a big swallow. Then, after waiting a few minutes to make sure the liver stayed down, I returned to Daddy and the *dose*. He had picked the carcass up and wrapped it around his neck so he could hold both front feet in his right hand and both back feet in his left. The head flopped down and the dry tongue hung out.

On the way home we stopped to rest, Daddy leaning against the fork of a tree to support the weight of the deer. He saw my tears.

"Son?"

"'Cause of...*dose*..."

Daddy gave me a pat on the head.

"There are many things you must learn. As hunters, we must kill so our family will live. All of nature knows this, and the hunter must obey all the laws of nature. One of those laws, the most important, is to talk with *Kwaw* and set things straight with the Great Powers of the world.

"In a herd that is in a following pattern, one after the other, the first *dose* is always the leader, strong, young. Do not kill this one. It is in nature that the old ones follow last. This is because the last one is the one ready to be taken; its life has been lived.

"*Maya'ki, piriki, wer'ak'mita* (Wolf, Grizzly Bear, Panther) know of this law, and they obey it. They wait beside the trail just as we did this morning. When the last *dose* passes, they spring to kill, just as we did.

"Don't worry son. It is a great law that you have obeyed. *L'hepta* (let's go), the family is waiting."

Daddy rocked the deer back to the balance of his body and turned toward home. I was one step behind him, carrying the rifle and the knife that still had blood on it. I felt very important. After all, I had just obeyed a great law, although I didn't quite know which one. Yet something about the *dose* was not settled in my heart. Maybe it was supposed to have another baby? I could not tell.

After walking for a while, Daddy had to rest again. He saw in my eyes the emotions that had broken through to the surface of my being.

"Remember, it is because of nature that the barren doe, the one that can no longer have babies, follows behind the herd. She is a decoy. When we, or the mountain lion, take the last *dose* that moves along the trail, we are taking only one from the world. If we take the first ones, the ones that are still having babies, we do not know how many *dose* we have killed, and we upset the way of life all around us."

"…But, Daddy, *jamal* (a fawn)."

"No, son, no more fawns. Because this deer is old and it was last. It was not as frisky as a younger doe and its neck is longer. The ears were not as alert and are large and floppy. And since *dose* moved slowly, I knew it was barren. It could not have babies."

Daddy could see all of that in the almost dark? Somehow I understood. And somehow I knew that I had just taken a big step toward becoming *It'jati'wa* (a genuine man).

Darryl Babe Wilson is a member of the Achumawe and Atsugewi tribes. His books include Surviving in Two Worlds *(written with Lois Hogle) and* The Morning the Sun Went Down, *from which this piece was excerpted.*

✳

Up ahead I see a grouse that has stopped by the side of the road to fill its crop with clover and gravel. It is an easy shot. I brace myself, legs apart, boots planted firmly on the road, raise my shotgun, take aim and pull the trigger. When I get to it, my ears still ringing, the grouse is dead. Some of its feathers are spread around on the colored leaves, and its blood has marked this spot. I put the feathery, warm bundle into the back pocket of my canvas hunting vest and keep walking.

I walk for thirty seconds and I wait for thirty more. As I walk I pick up more leaves. This time a maple leaf that is yellow and speckled with red. And the perfect, warm, brown leaf of an oak. I think of the veins in my mother's hands, like the veins in this leaf, except hers are blue and pink; blue and pink and covered with white dish soap or bread dough, her wedding band almost hidden by swelling.

Craig and I take the grouse we have each gotten back to our car. While we are skinning them Craig tells me the story of a man with whom he once hunted, who when he shot a grouse would put it down on the ground, put a boot over each wing and then with one swift motion, rip the breast right off the bird, leaving the carcass there on the forest floor.

Craig takes the liver from the grouse he shot and he walks way back into the woods and places the small dark red of it in the crook of two branches of a red maple. "It's silly," he says to me, coming back, wiping his bloody hands on his jeans. He is asking me if putting the liver in the tree is all right, asking me to reassure him this is a good thing to do. "No, it's not silly," I say. "It's a good, serious thing."

—Gretchen Legler, *All the Powerful Invisible Things:*
A Sportswoman's Notebook

DUBRAVKA UGRESIC

✶ ✶ ✶

L.A. Post–Modern

You better enjoy your meal.

ONCE, A COLLEAGUE OF MINE—ONE OF THOSE WHO PRONOUNCE
the words Foucault, Derrida, Lacan and Baudrillard with the same
familiarity as the words mum, dad and granny—took me to a
restaurant. It was in Los Angeles.

"There are only four restaurants like this in the whole of
America right now," he said as we made our way to the restaurant.
"Now at last you'll understand what postmodernism really is," he
added, with the kind of enthusiasm he might have used for, say,
lobster in orange sauce.

The restaurant was large and noisy. And it really did resemble a
postmodernist classroom crammed with objects of visual instruction. It was a museum of Americana and everything was there: real
and fake quotes from American films and television series, from
American history (which we know, of course, from American films
and television series), from American everyday life, American
painting (pictures which reflected that everyday life hyperrealisti-
cally). Everything was there: quote by quote, quote on quote;
everything was mixed up with everything else in a kind of vast
American salad. American everyday life was formulated a long
time ago, and it produced the American myth, then the American

myth—the stereotype—produced American everyday life, and everyday life—perpetuating that same stereotype—permanently produced that same myth, just as it was there, in that restaurant, transforming it into a life-myth show…Or something like that…

The menu offered naked quotations as well: we obediently ordered hamburgers and Coke. Waiters dressed as clowns entertained the customers zealously. They might lie on your table holding the plate and grin into your face while they spun the plate over their head as though they were about to spill the contents into your lap. Clown-photographers strutted about, taking pictures of customers with cheap Polaroid cameras, and then obliging them to buy the proof of their own enjoyment. One group of merrymakers had ordered a huge cake; they were throwing cream at each other, enjoying themselves like the actors in old comic films.

There was general uproar in the restaurant. It was an aggressive synopsis of American happiness, that image of happiness the American media—films, series, advertisements—had been producing for years; an image of happiness which life itself now zealously imitated. The model proved its efficacity for the thousandth time: people were enjoying themselves.

A stout woman, a camp-commandant in a clown's costume, some kind of supervisor, was carefully surveying the level of happiness in the restaurant. At one moment she caught my eye. Like an accurate camera the Ring Mistress recorded my inner dissatisfaction. She immediately pointed at me and summoned the whole room to do the same.

"There, in the corner, there's a face that's not smiling. Yes, take a good look, that woman there, in the black dress," she shrieked into the microphone.

Then, grinning at me, she playfully wagged her finger. The whole room did the same, enjoying the collective repetition of the gesture. The orchestra struck up "Don't worry, be happy" (what else) and they soon forgot about me. I tugged my postmodernist colleague by the sleeve and we went out. My indoctrinated European brain started to run the familiar images of totalitarian happiness, images of parades, happy masses acting as a collective body…

"America has imposed the dictatorship of happiness," I mumbled in a feeble voice.

"It's only a restaurant you can enter and leave whenever you feel like it," said my colleague, bristling slightly. At that moment he was defending American democracy more than he was soothing my sudden dread. And, of course, he was right. It was only a restaurant. And, besides, only one of four similar ones in the whole of America.

Dubravka Ugresic is a journalist from the former Yugoslavia, and the author of Have a Nice Day: From the Balkan War to the American Dream, *from which this piece was excerpted.*

★

The antidote to my spiteful if short-lived impulse to leave L.A. was the self-righteous Third World response to the civil disturbances—even to the earthquakes, seen in some Middle Eastern quarters as a further scourge of God. Thanks to the translating I did to earn my living, I knew that Egypt, Iran, Nigeria, and Lebanon had had riots or demonstrations around the same time as the L.A. riots. Some were for almost the same reasons. In Mashhad, Iran, thousands of Afghani refugees rioted the same week as the L.A. riots to protest economic and ethnic discrimination—three hundred people were killed, six times as many as in Los Angeles. No one said that Iran was going to hell in a handbasket, because the dishonest Iranian government did not broadcast the events. Los Angeles was the opposite, one of the world's most watched and least known places, frantic to understand and to market even its bad news. In this it was the opposite of a Third World city. Who knew which sort of place was the city of the future— what mattered to me was that L.A. was the city of my future.

—Peter Theroux, *Translating L.A.: A Tour of the Rainbow City*

JOSEPH O'CONNOR

* * *

One Too Many Dublins

In the Mid-Atlantic states, two Irishmen
do not feel at home.

WE DROVE PAST ANOTHER SIGN THAT SAID "DUBLIN MARYLAND"
and thus—I think reasonably—we began to entertain serious
expectations of finding ourselves in a town before too long. But
no matter where we went, we seemed to keep missing it. We drove
up and down the highway and kept seeing more signs that said
Dublin and following them. Each sign seemed to lead to another
sign, and after a while I began to get the uneasy feeling that
Dublin, Maryland was a place that did not really exist.

After about an hour and a half of this we pulled up in a gravel
car park on a country lane. A guy in a tartan shirt was shovelling
muck into the back of a little dumper truck. I got out of the
Thunderbird and approached him cautiously.

"Afternoon," I said.

He stood up slowly, like a gunman in a Western movie, and
turned to face me.

"Hep yew?" he said.

"I'm from out of town," I said.

"You don't say," he grinned.

"I was looking for Dublin," I said.

"Well," he said, pointing. "Yew just go down that way and follow the signs." He got down on his hunkers and started doing something to the wheel of his truck.

"I suppose it's a small place," I said.

"I suppose you could be right there," he said, without turning.

This was clearly not going well. "I was wondering," I said, "what's there to see around here?"

He shrugged. "What'd you have in mind?"

"I don't know," I said. "What do people do for fun?"

He stood up. "Fun," he said. "Oh yeah. Fun."

He turned to me again and grinned so disturbingly that I suddenly began to fear that the local idea of fun might be giving a naive tourist a ten minute headstart into the woods before getting a posse of hayseeds together, tracking him down and bludgeoning him to death with farming implements.

"You mean like sights?" he said.

"Exactly," I said.

He scratched his head and jammed his finger up his nose with such force that I thought he might do himself a mischief. "Hur's a air fawce base just south of here," he said. "They gotta whole lotta tanks and shit there. From the Gulf War, y'know? Planes and shit. Gut 'em all in a lawng line down

Say "Southerner" and you say worlds, conjuring up everything from Faulkner to football, Memphis to magnolia, juleps to jazz. Ditto for "New Englander": Frost and frappes, Boston and beans, town meetings and Transcendentalism. But say "resident of the Mid-Atlantic," and not merely have you said a mouthful, you haven't evoked a single image, except perhaps that of Interstate 95 making its noxious course from Rowland in southeastern North Carolina to the town of — yes!—Yardley in northeastern Pennsylvania. Say "Southerner," and in some places you've still said fighting words; say "resident of the Mid-Atlantic," and you've put your audience to sleep.

◆

—Jonathan Yardley, *States of Mind: A Personal Journey Through the Mid-Atlantic* there, y'should see it, it's about as long as mah dick." He scratched his head again. "I dunno what else I'm gonna say," he beamed. "S'kinda quiet around here."

"You must have a bit of fun sometimes," I said.

He considered this for a moment or two. "Not rully," he said, then.

I took this as my signal to go back to the car. I got into it, feeling heavy of heart. Sean asked me what this guy had said. I told him. He looked out at our new friend. "Bogtrotter," he said, with contempt in his voice. As we started up and pulled away, I noticed that our man had got into his dumper truck, and pulled on a lever and started dumping the dirt which he had just been shovelling into the truck back out on to the ground. I wanted to stop the car and ask him why he had done this, but Sean said he didn't think this was a good idea. "The guy's a fucking woolyback," he said. "He'd ate us for dinner if we let him. It's best not to get involved."

We drove around for another hour, desperately trying to find Dublin. This was really not going well. I kept getting out the map and trying to come up with a better route, but every single turn we took seemed to keep bringing us back to where we had been before. Finally, we came to a tiny little building in the middle of nowhere. It had a glass front and it looked like a store of some kind, so I got out with the intention of asking the shopkeeper for directions. The place was not a shop, as it turned out. It was a bail office. I asked the guy behind the desk how the place worked. He explained that the state was inundated with requests from criminals for bail. If you waited for your request to be processed through the official channels, it could take ages. But if you were prepared to go private and pay a little more, a bail office could speed things up for you. In other words, if you or one of your loved ones ever get locked in a Maryland jail, there are people who will be only too happy to make a fast buck out of getting you out again. I don't know. Call me a bleeding heart liberal, but is that not the weirdest and most unfair thing you've ever heard in your life?

Anyway, the guy in the bail office gave us directions and even drew us a little map—I guess there weren't too many serious

82   Travelers' Tales ★ America

crimes being committed in Maryland that afternoon—and after a
while we did manage to find Dublin.

At least, I think we did. Because Dublin, Maryland is small.
Indeed, it is so small that you would need a hell of a nerve to describe it as a town at all. It is more of a crossroads, really. In fact,
there is absolutely nothing in Dublin, Maryland except a church,
a lot of trees, and a very large high school. That's it. My father, who
had driven several hundred miles to get me to this epicentre of
total nothingness, was in a remarkably philosophical mood, all
things considered.

"Bit of a one-horse town," he said. "And the horse is fucking
well dying."

Sean and I got out of the car. He wandered off with his camera, no doubt pondering the fact that a mere seventy-two hours
ago he had been on the Concorde, sipping champagne and nibbling canapes, whereas now
he was in Dublin, Maryland,
at least a hundred miles away
from the nearest hamburger
stand. I walked around the
school playground taking
photographs of the building.
After a few minutes, the
school librarian came out and
asked me rather shortly what
I was doing.

"I'm from Dublin,
Ireland," I said.

Her face brightened up
considerably.

"Dublin, Ireland," she said.
"Oh imagine. Dublin, Ireland.
Gee whillakers."

I had never in my life met
anyone who would actually
say something like "Gee

*It is in the colonies,
and not in the mother
country, that the old life of the
country really exists. If one
wants to realise what English
Puritanism is—not at its worst
(when it is very bad), but at its
best, and then it is not very
good—I do not think one can
find much of it in England, but
much can be found about
Boston and Massachusetts. We
have got rid of it. America still
preserves it, to be, I hope, a
short-lived curiosity.*

◆

—Oscar Wilde

whillakers," but I was delighted to do so now. She brought me in and showed me around the school.

High schools in certain parts of New York are like something out of Dante's *Inferno*. To get in you have to be searched by security guards, and then pass through an airport-style X-ray gate. Then, when you have finally proved that you do not have any weapons with you, the security guards kick the shit out of you. Here in Dublin, Maryland, however, things were a lot more relaxed. There were cute little drawings of spacemen and animals on the walls. There were photographs of basketball and baseball teams. It looked like the kind of American high school you would see in *The Wonder Years*.

"You got a really pruddy accent," the librarian said.

"Thank you," I replied, blushing. "So do you." There was an awkward silence at this stage. "And you have a very nice school too," I added.

"We try to concentrate on educating the whole person," she beamed. "We like to think we raise decent people here."

Much as I liked the school, I told her, I was also interested in learning a little more about other aspects of life in Dublin. Her face went a little blank at this stage. "Like what?" she asked me. "I don't know," I said, "what about the history of the town?" She smiled again, so extremely that her eyebrows almost disappeared into her hairline. "Oh," she said. "If you want history, you just hold on there one second." She went into her office and telephoned the woman who ran the local history society.

"You're really going to too much trouble," I said. "I'm just passing through, you know."

"It's no trouble, dear," the librarian said. "You just hold on there, and we'll give you all the history you can handle."

A few minutes later a car pulled up outside the school. Out stepped Mrs. Smith, the history society's head honcho, and also a lady called Ruby, who was the oldest resident of the town. I was incredibly touched that they had made the effort to come and see me. I was also terrified, because now I would have to ask them some intelligent questions. Through the window of the school I saw my father wandering around the car park absent-mindedly taking photographs of the trees, with a plastic K Mart bag on his head to ward off the rain. How in the name of God would he ever forgive me for this?

"Now, Ruby," the librarian said, "wait till you hear this feller's voice." She turned to me, smiling.

"Say somethin, honey."

"Like what?" I said, feeling myself blush.

"I dunno. Say the Lord's prayer or somethin."

"Seriously?"

"Yeh. Why not?"

"Our Father who art in heaven, Hallowed be thy name, Thy kingdom come, Thy will be done…"

"Ain't he got a pruddy voice, Ruby?" the librarian said.

"He sure does," Ruby confirmed. "Why, it's jest softer than a new dishcloth."

Ruby was in her late eighties. She had attended Dublin High School as a girl. Indeed, she had met her husband there. Apart from this highly interesting fact, she seemed to know nothing else about the town at all. Was it settled by Irish immigrants, I asked Ruby and the lady from the history society. They looked at each other vaguely, as though what I had just asked was the most ridiculous question anybody could imagine. "Why do you think that, dear?" Ruby asked. "Well," I said, "it's just a small thing, but Dublin is the capital of Ireland, you see, and this town is called Dublin, and so, I just thought maybe…."

The lady from the history society shook her head. "I never

> When Joyce's Stephen Dedalus said, "History is a nightmare from which I am trying to awake," he summed up Irish history. And the United States was to be the place of awakening.
>
> ◆
>
> —Daniel J. Boorstin, *The Americans: The Democratic Experience*

heard of anybody Irish around here," she said, "did you, Ruby?"

"No," said Ruby, "I don't really know how it came to be called Dublin, do you, dear?"

"No, I don't," said the history society lady. "I guess that just never occurred to me."

I was beginning to sense that this had all been a terrible mistake. Desperate, I decided to kick for touch. Was there anything of interest in the locality that I should see?

The lady from the history society pursed her lips and began to think. "I'm sure there is," she said, "it's just that at the moment I can't really…" Her voice trailed off.

"There's a big nuclear shelter here," Ruby said, so suddenly that it made me jump. "If there's ever an attack we gotta go over there and get in the shelter. That's what it said in the paper. They have cans of food in there, and toilets, and, you know, mineral water and everything. They have everything a person would need in there."

"Really, Ruby?" I said.

"Oh yes," she said. "It's beautiful, but of course it's closed up right now."

I had the distinct impression Ruby would have quite liked Saddam Hussein to bomb Dublin, Maryland right that minute so she could show me the nuclear shelter.

"Apart from that," she said, "it's pretty quiet around here."

We stood in the school corridor simpering at each other for some time while everybody thought of something to say. Finally it got too much for me. I said I really had to go.

Ruby looked delighted at this news. She didn't mean to be rude, she said, but she had to go too. She was on her way home to start preparing the Thanksgiving dinner for herself, her children, her grandchildren and her seven great-grandchildren. She was cooking everything herself, and she hadn't even started on the pumpkin pie.

"I've never had pumpkin pie," I said.

"Oh Jeekers, you're joking," Ruby said.

"We don't have Thanksgiving in Ireland," I said.

"You don't have Thanksgiving in Ireland. Good Lord. You don't have pecan pie?"

"No."

"Pumpkin pie?"

"No."

I told Ruby that not only did we not have pecan pie in Ireland, but that I had never actually seen a pecan in my life. I would not know a pecan, I confided, if it walked up to me in the street singing "God Bless America."

"What a shame," Ruby said.

We agreed that Ireland was a barbaric and completely uncivilized kip of a country, not to have pecan pie, and I left them still standing in the corridor and discussing this gastronomical atrocity while I made my excuses and ran. As I stepped out into the rain, I reminded myself to write away and become an honorary member of the Dublin, Maryland History Society some time. I'm sure the meetings are really wild affairs.

Out in the yard, two teenage boys were playing basketball. One was very tall and gangly. He had on a baseball cap and a tracksuit with the words "Brooklyn Dodgers" on the back. The other was short and pudgy. He was wearing a t-shirt which announced "My Baby Left Me," and a pair of lurid luminous green shorts which went all the way down to his knobbly knees.

"Hi," said the fat one.

"Hi," I said.

"What you doin?"

"Nothing," I said.

"S'whut I thought," he said, and tittered.

I asked if these two fine fellow went to school here, and they nodded. What was it like, I enquired. They said something unprintable. And what was living in Dublin like? They said something unthinkable.

"And what are you going to do when you leave school?" I asked.

"I'm goin in the army," the tall one said.

"Why?" I wondered.

"Cos you don't have to work too hard," he said, "and you get to blow seven kinds of shit out of Ay-rabs."

Fatso snuffled with laughter.

I said I had heard, on the contrary, that hard work was very much an essential part of army life. And that blowing the shit out of Ayrabs was not. At least, not very often.

"Well see, I'm real good at sports," he said. "If you're good at sports you don't have to work so hard in the army."

I asked what kind of sport he was good at.

"Football, basketball, baseball."

"Anything with balls," Fatso said.

"Shut your mouth, Retardo," said the elongated one.

"Do you have a good football team in Maryland?" I said.

"In my dick we do," said Fasto.

I took this to be something of a negative.

"So who do you support?" I said.

"Miami Dolphins," he said. "Best deefence in the NFL."

"I like the Dallas Cowboys," his lanky friend said.

"You like my dick," he said.

"No, I donut."

"That your car?" said the aspiring soldier, nodding in the direction of the Thunderbird.

"Yeah," I said.

"Nice," he said. "That a rental?"

"Yes," I said.

"Where you from anyway?" he said.

"Ireland," I said.

"Where?"

"Ireland."

"In Europe, right?"

"Yeah."

"Near Germany, right? And Poland?"

"Not really, no."

"Not near Germany?"

"No."

"It ain't near Germany, you dork," said Chubby. "Snear Scotland."

"That right? Is it near Scotland?"

"Well, it's quite near there."

"Like how near. Like Maryland-New York near or what?"

"Do you know U2?" I said.

"Sure," they said.

"They're from Ireland," I said.

"No way," they said.

"Way," I said. "They're from Dublin, Ireland. That's where I'm from. The same town."

"You live in Dublin, Ireland," said Fatso.

"Yes."

"The same town as U2."

"Yes."

"You know U2, right?" he said.

"I don't know them," I said. "I've met them once."

"Yeah, right," they both said. "In my dick, you have."

"I have," I said.

"Bullshit."

"Have you?"

"Yes," I said. "But only once."

Another young fellow appeared at the entrance to the car park, riding an expensive-looking bicycle. He was doing wheelies.

"Hey, Jimmy," he bawled. "There's a guy here say he knows U2."

Jimmy leaned down low to his handlebars and pedalled hard. When he got off the bike he threw back his head, made a hawking sound with his throat, snuffled hard and spat on the ground.

"Oyster for lunch," he said.

"Oh God you're so gross."

"Shut up, pussy."

He looked up at me, his round teenage face a veritable symphony of florid acne and semi-healed scars.

"So anyways. You know U2."

"Look, I didn't say that. I just—"

"You know U2."

"Well, no. I—"

"You know 'em or not?"

"I met them once."

"In my big fat juicy dick you did. Where?"

"In New York. I only met them once. Very briefly."

"Really?"

"Truly."

His mouth opened and closed a few times in the manner of a goldfish.

"Fuck me backways with a chainsaw," he said. "You met them."

"Well, I—"

"What were they like?"

"I don't know," I said. "They seemed very nice."

"Nice? Nice? You met U2 and they were nice? What kind of a fucken word is nice?"

"I mean they seemed very friendly, but, I mean, I didn't talk to them for very long or anything."

"You ever met any other celebrities?"

"No," I said. (I had, actually. I just didn't feel like going into it right now.)

"Me neither," said Jimmy. "But my brother met Oprah Winfrey once."

There was silence for a few moments. I could hear the birds croaking in the fields. I could see my father, enthusiastically photographing a fence-post.

"He wants to meet Madonna," said Fatso.

"I do not," Jimmy scoffed.

"You do too."

"Do not."

"Tell him what you said, you know, about what you wanted to do to Madonna."

"No."

"No way."

"I'll tell him if you don't."

"You do that and I'll rip your arms off and beat you to death with the wet end."

Sadly, Jimmy didn't ever tell me what he wanted to do with Madonna. Give her singing lessons, I was hoping.

"You never met anyone else famous?" asked Lanky.

"No."

"My dad met Joe Namath once," Jimmy said.

"Oh yeah," tittered Fatso. "Well your dad met my big fat dick once too. OK?"

"Fuck you."

"And you."

"And your mother."

"And your dog."

"Retardo."

"I know you are."

"Thalidomide."

"I know you are."

"Pussy."

"I know you are."

"Homo."

"Douchebag."

"Pizzafeatures."

At this point, I decided I'd leave the lads to their merry banter. And so I departed, to a final fanfare of fucks.

Desperate for inspiration, I went off to look around the Dublin graveyard. There was a John Connor buried there, and there was a woman whose surname was Ward. These were the only two Irish names I could find. I took photographs of the two tombstones. I took photographs of the grass. And then I walked around for a while looking for something else to photograph. But there really wasn't anything else. I had the sinking sensation that I done Dublin, Maryland.

On the way back to the Thunderbird, I passed the three lads still hard at it in the playground.

"Scumbag."

"Shitstabber."

"Your grandmother sucks cocks in hell."

"You know the difference between your grandmother and the bus to Philadelphia?"

"No, Spazzo, what?"

"Not everyone's been on top of the bus to Philadelphia."

"Toilet-head."

"Testicle-face."

"Worm-dick."

"Shrimpfucker."

Shrimpfucker? I thought.

I got into the car. Sean was dripping all over the driver's seat, shivering and looking at the map.

"Well, where'll we go now?" he asked.

"Anywhere," I said, "just let's burn rubber."

"Anywhere like where?" he asked, reasonably.

I took the map from him and looked at it. "Baltimore?" I said.

He started up the engine and pushed the accelerator to the floor. "Outta me way," he said, "and bury me fucking decent."

Joseph O'Connor was born in Ireland in 1963. His debut novel, Cowboys and Indians, *was shortlisted for the Whitbread Prize, one of Britain's most prestigious literary awards. His work includes the novel,* Desperadoes, *a collection of short stories,* True Believers, *a play,* Red Roses and Petrol, *and non-fiction books,* The Secret World of the Irish Male *and* Sweet Liberty: Travels in Irish America, *from which this story was excerpted.*

✳

As I listen to people speaking that foreign tongue, English, I can hear when they stumble or repeat the same phrases too many times, when their sentences trail off aimlessly—or, on the contrary, when their phrases have vigor and roundness, when they have the space and the breath to give a flourish at the end of a sentence, or make just the right pause before coming to a dramatic point. I can tell, in other words, the degree of their ease or disease, the extent of authority that shapes the rhythms of their speech. That authority—in whatever dialect, in whatever variant of the mainstream language—seems to me to be something we all desire. It's not that we all want to speak the King's English, but whether we speak Appalachian or Harlem English, or Cockney, or Jamaican Creole, we want to be at home in our tongue. We want to be able to give voice accurately and fully to ourselves and our sense of the world. John Fowles, in one of his stories in *The Ebony Tower*, has a young man cruelly violate an elderly writer and his manuscripts because the legacy of language has not been passed on to the youthful vandal properly. This seems to me an entirely credible premise. Linguistic dispossession is a sufficient motive for violence, for it is close to the dispossession of one's self. Blind rage, helpless rage is rage that has no words—rage that overwhelms one with darkness. And if one is perpetually without words, if one exists in the entropy of inarticulateness, that condition itself is bound to be an enraging frustration. In my New York apartment, I listen almost nightly to fights that erupt like brushfire on the street below—and in their escalating fury of repetitious phrases ("Don't do this to me, man, you fucking bastard, I'll fucking kill you"), I hear not the pleasures of macho toughness but an infuriated beating against wordlessness, against the incapacity to make oneself understood, seen. Anger can be borne—it can even be satisfying—if it can gather into words and explode in a storm, or a rapier-sharp attack. But without this means of ventilation, it only turns back inward, building and swirling like a head of steam—building to an impotent, murderous rage.

—Eva Hoffman, *Lost in Translation: A Life in a New Language*

LINDA NIEMANN

✦ ✦ ✦

Iron Horse Blues

For an itinerant brakeman, the
challenge is to stop moving.

SWEET HIGHWAY, HEADING NORTHEAST. I COULD FEEL SOME OF the problems blowing off my shoulders, hope on that center line, a new town, new place, towards more unmarked canvas, an un-written page. Toward a meeting with myself at track's end, coun-try's end, as far in the future as I could push it.

Afternoon rain slicked the highway as I passed through small Mormon towns. I could feel the family closeness, knew that everyone was watching and being watched. A live soap. It got to be dinnertime, and I found myself at an intersection staring at Mom's cafe, a tawny brick building with a square Western facade and pickup trucks parked everywhere. Home cooking, the sign added gratuitously. I tried to remember the three warnings of the West: never eat at a place called Mom's, never play cards with a man called Doc, what was the third? I ate at Mom's anyway. What the hell. The place was filled with families and men coming in after work. I stare at the local paper and wonder if I want to drive all night. One of the fringe benefits of being a brakeman—turning day into night. It's like living near the Pole; it's always daytime for a rail. On the map I find Moab, like the name, and mark it for my destination for today.

What I really want is to derail somewhere, not to go on with this pursuit of work, to come to rest so that the babble can stop, so that an overwhelming beauty can color me. There could be no further beauty than this country here, chocolate mesa fingers washed in lavender distances, streaks of green and rose, the grey highway following the contours of the land. Navajo sandstone bluffs turned on a lathe, saturation of color dependent on the changing light, a landscape continually repainting itself. I could have just stopped here, let the railroad find me, let my careening mind go on alone. I could have just stopped, but instead drove on, pushed the curtain of evening through the deeper canyonlands courting the swollen rush of the Colorado River. Hearing her now in the dark, I take only one breath of her swift presence, and then I flee. I inhale the icy ideas of her, get close to the great geographical imperative, the defining arterial fact of the Western states, feel her power, her tumbling mist on my face, and I turn away to the south. Like my own power, my own river of strength within, it is too mysterious and frightening now. Drawn to it, I turn away when I feel its presence near me.

The town of Moab appeared out of the silence of canyonlands like the neon blaze of Reno out of the high desert. Motels and hotels, kayak rentals and four-wheel trips, Americans playing hard in their two-week vacations. Ghetto blasters raging in the campgrounds till after midnight, sounds of drunken arguments centering on concepts of manhood, fights over fender benders in overcrowded trailer parks. I put in my brakeman's earplugs and sleep next to my car. I still feel peeled. Way too vulnerable to be in a herd of yahoos

---

*I*n other parts of the world desert rivers are sources of civilization and life; the Tigris and Euphrates of the Middle East; the Nile of Africa. Here, however, they are barriers to travel and communication.

♦

—Kenneth A. Brown, *Four Corners: History, Land, and People of the Desert Southwest*

having fun. I want a library-like silence stretching from the Rockies to the Sea of Cortez. I find such a haven in Tucumcari, home of 2,000 motel rooms and 4,000 souls.

Tucumcari stands at the beginning of the panhandle and the end of the canyonlands, where the erosions and canyons are shallow but still rust-colored, where there is more flatland and grasses and less gorge and riverbed. The Canadian River borders the town, forms amiably into man-made lakes, and continues as a warm desert stream, spending most of its energy underground. Cottonwoods and humidity mark its presence in the landscape. It being summer, the sky is dominant with thunderheads and dark slanting bridges to the earth, seen a few miles off but gone when you get there. Only a transitory dampness sinking into the fragrant sand. It can rain a few feet away, as you stand dry in the raincloud's cool shadow. The rattlesnakes thrive and grow long and fat with eating prairie dogs and mice.

Everything in the town was falling down: paint peeling, adobe crumbling, phones broken and unrepaired since Mountain Bell moved to Clovis. I found the dusty station and ghostly freightyard baking in the 100-degree heat and met the new trainmaster, a huge man bumped to this outpost as punishment and marking time until he could take his pension. His look was long suffering, but he was trying to change it into the hostility trainmasters were supposed to project. It didn't quite come off. It was just too hot. He went through the usual harassment interview and handed me the two-hundred-question rules exam. After I had sweated through it one more time, I marked up as a Tucumcari brakeman on the extra board.

For the first time in my life I was really alone. I checked into a seedy motel and paid by the week. The manager was an alcoholic who had come out here with his wife to try to make something work out. This was their retirement move, and they had taken on the motel sight unseen, with just as assurance from the owner that Tucumcari's fortunes were on the upswing. The second week I was there, a drunk driver drove his car into their living room while they were eating breakfast.

"It's a good thing it happened when it did, because any other time I'd a been sitting there on the couch watching the TV, and he'd have hit me sure as taxes."

The manager looked at me resentfully as if all this was somehow my fault. If only he had charged me more rent, his life might be better. I thought they were ripping me off as it was. My room was a dump, and I only spent two nights a week in it anyway, but I could tell that they resented my being there at all, using the swamp cooler or turning on a tap. They probably resented my being young and having a good job and having the freedom to turn up in a place like Tucumcari and leave again.

I didn't have a phone and couldn't get one unless I was willing to wait a month and pay an outrageous fee. And so I used my trainman's right to be called by a callboy who would knock on my door an hour before they needed me. I phoned Naomi every week from the only working pay phone in town, outside the 7-11 store. It was kind of beautiful sometimes, talking outside when summer thunderheads would come sweeping by in the late afternoon and dump a few feet away, filling the air with the smell of wet dust and static. Since there were three phones in a row you could also eavesdrop on other people's lives—one of the only sources of amusement in Tucumcari. The eavesdropping was different here than in Utah, however. There wasn't that disapproving edge, that stiffening moral cloud hanging overhead. Folks here were just plain nosy. They didn't want to be the only ones with their laundry hanging out to dry. The Tucumcari laundromat or beauty parlor was a hotbed of information.

"Did you say you worked for the railroad, honey? Why that other girl that does—you know Sandy Burnett—just bought a house on the eastside, you know the one. I gave her a perm just the other day, looks right nice on her. Look good on you too. Say I heard she had some trouble the other night, was drinking and driving that car of hers too fast through town, gave the trooper some lip, too, I heard. Don't tell her I said so, but you know this is a small town and not much gets by. Not much at all. Where you from, honey? What does your boyfriend think about you bein' way out here?"

The railroad small world did me one favor out here, though, when I recognized Cadillac, the old head I worked with in El Centro, climbing off a caboose in the Tucumcari yard. Although I hadn't realized it then, he had impressed me because he was a sober man. Impressed me and made me feel slightly uncomfortable. Now I was just glad to see him, as if a cobweb feeling had been brushed away.

"I saw your name on the extra board. I figured it was you."

"Well you look right at home here. I thought you had a horse ranch and everything in El Centro."

"Decided to move it on out here. Say, I heard one of them Louisiana boys talking about you, saying women don't belong on the railroad. I told him the way it was. That he ought to be glad we got one that does her work. And that's just the truth."

"Well, these old boys here don't seem to want me to do any work. I had a conductor the other day order me to sit on the caboose. Said his wife would kill him if she heard he made me walk the train. I wanted to get off that crummy and get away from his foul cigar."

"Yeah, I know the one. God I hate a cigar."

The mainline run from Tucumcari was to Carrizozo, a distance of 180 miles. The tracks ran along the ridges of the Sacramento Mountains, averaging 6,000 feet. It was a roller coaster run, a hoghead's show to handle the air on a long train over such undulating territory. A lot of the new engineers weren't up to it, and it was common for trains to break in two because of problems with slack. This provided the train crew with their only exercise on this run—changing knuckles. There were no industries to spot, no cars to pick up, and the snakes were so bad that trainmen didn't usually walk their trains at every siding. They just wandered off a little into the desert and turned off their light, or hunkered down behind a tumbleweed and smoked. When the slack started to run, signaling she was starting to pull, the rear man would appear about twenty cars up the train, and swing aboard. When they had the Navajo track gangs in to replace the ties on this run, they spent more time killing rattlers than they did laying rail.

For a trainman, this run was a twelve-hour stretch of trying to stay awake and keep the hoghead awake. Since business was booming, you often got only eight or ten hours off between runs. As soon as you had your "rest" you were back on a train. Never the same hours of sleep, no pattern from day to day, week to week, month to month. Once on the train, there was no place to take a break, no stopping for coffee or meals. And nothing but darkness and desert to look at. Under these circumstances, people doze off occasionally. I was having additional problems with the schedule. I used to use alcohol to get to sleep immediately after a run, but now my body was on its own. Often I couldn't sleep and would end up having to stay awake two days or nights at a stretch, until I could collapse at the appropriate time for the railroad's needs. Railroad accidents get blamed on alcohol, but the true culprit is lack of sleep. The newspaper never reports whether the engineer tried to lay off and was refused, or how many twelve-hour days in a row he had put in. It was not uncommon for crews to work steadily for months with no days

> It was in that field that I met the snakes. There were green ones five feet long, and coal-black ones a yard long, and little grey ones with yellow livery stripes down their sides. Once I spotted one of the big green ones just as it heard me. It lay very still right across the path three feet ahead, its head and tail hidden in the long grass. It thought I couldn't see it. Very slowly I took a step backwards. Just as my cowboy heel came down it snapped around and darted towards me. I jumped back into the air and landed seven feet away. The snake then changed its mind and slithered away into the field. The next day I could still see the heel prints in the grass where I had landed, and tried to reproduce the spectacular backwards leap I had performed. I couldn't cover half the distance.
>
> ◆
>
> —Henry Shukman, *Savage Pilgrims: On the Road to Santa Fe*

off—no time to get fully rested, pay bills, do laundry, put gas in the car. Legally, you die on the federal Hours-of-Service law after twelve hours, but there is no regulation about how many of those days can occur back to back. Twelve hours from midnight to noon is a long time after a month of it with short sleep at the home terminal and disturbed sleep in the substandard company dorms at the change point.

The company lodging at Carrizozo was a case in point. The buildings had been thrown together in two weeks, using the cheapest possible materials. The walls were so thin you could hear trainmen snoring in adjacent rooms, and when a crewcaller came to pound on a door to give someone a call, the whole row of rooms shook. Since this was happening at intervals all day and all night, it was hard to get undisturbed sleep. They had located the dorms, moreover, four hundred yards from the mainline which was on a grade. All day and all night you heard ten units of power opening up to pull out of town, it often seemed, directly through your room. The walls would vibrate with a continuous diesel throb, chug-a-chug-a-chug-a whirr, chug-a chug-a chug-a whirr, hmmmmmmmmmmmmm, varoom. Objects would dance on the window baseboards. There were two ways to sleep through it—get dead drunk or get completely exhausted. The union complained about the noise level, and the Feds came by with a noise-o-meter and pronounced the levels acceptable. I couldn't imagine when they had done the testing. When there were no trains around, obviously. Or did this say something about all the levels the Feds say are unharmful?

At any rate, I wasn't drinking, so I had to get frazzled before I could sleep. And other than sleeping, there wasn't much for a sober person to do in Carrizozo. It was a mountain town of about 2,000 people and four eating establishments, two of which weren't open much. The other two catered to rails and were primarily bars. One of these was subsidized by the railroad to provide an open restaurant for crews at any time of night. The owner took the money and invested it in enlarging the bar. He was no dummy. He made a lot of money off the rails. Well, what were the choices? No moviehouse, no library, no gym, no twenty-four-hour coffeeshop, no bookstore, no pleasant place to hang out in at the dorms—just one big rec room with one TV set tuned to a sports or soft-core violent porn movie channel. No place to store bicycles or play an instrument or work out. Of course people went to the bar. You couldn't even listen to a radio in your room without waking up the whole row. And when the railroad decided to get punitive and crack down on drinking, did they stop subsidizing the bar? provide recreational alternatives? open a decent meals-only restaurant? Hell, no. They just hired spotters to hang out in the bar they subsidized to turn people in. The owner provided both the finks and the booze. Sober in Carrizozo, I sat in my room and read. I took up jogging and ran the dirt trails leading towards the base of the mountains. I played my flute over the hum of the laundry machines, sat

> *E*very railroad station exists in a dream. There is no way to avoid that. Now we can even imagine the railroads themselves ceasing to exist. What will stand then where the stations are now? If there should be any people in those places by then, what would they dream, perhaps many storeys up in what is now air? They will not know that a station was ever there, the trains coming and going below them where they sleep. In a dream people still get on a familiar train, and the doors close, and they know where to look for the first field. When they see it, already the station is far behind, and each of them is in a different green afternoon.
>
> ◆
>
> —W.S. Merwin, *Houses and Travellers*

on the fresh towels and tried to carve out some good space for myself, space that would bring my strength back, something that seemed far away and long gone.

The only benevolence around was what came from New Mexico itself, the landscape I passed through at different times of day or night. I can only say that it was never the same picture. I never got tired of it, I never felt I had been there before. It was the quality of the light and its constant subtle changes. I got lost in it the way I got lost in Monet's *Water Lilies* in its serene room at the Museum of Modern Art. Here ranchos needed thirty acres to feed one cow, and the land was for the most part undivided by fences, and the fences themselves were only wire stapled to mesquite posts, collecting tumbleweeds and blown debris. The small towns we ran through—Santa Rosa, Vaughn, Corona—were poor. But commonly a run-down stucco house or beat-up trailer would have a brand new horsetrailer in the yard, and beautiful animals munching hay under a lean-to. Their houses weren't much, but the horses traveled first class. The air was filled with the scent of pinyon, juniper, and mesquite, sometimes in bursts of fragrance released by a sudden rainstorm. A high-moving cloud would darken the greens of the trees, and the red-stippled soil would saturate and blacken. Then patches of light and dark would dance on the amphitheater of the rounded mountaintops.

It was looking out on this panoramic emptiness from the window of a moving train that I began my slow understanding of what serenity could be. My mind was a whirlwind, a spinning vortex of resentments, anger, and fear. These psychic tornadoes could spin themselves out here without encountering traffic jams or social relations. The other rails thought of me as antisocial. Aside from the small twelve-step meetings I attended in Tucumcari, this was true. It seemed like Tucumcari only had about six people in the program, and a lot of them were as new at this as I was. I went places with these people occasionally, and once I went out on the town with the other woman brakie, Sandy. The bar scene, however was too overpoweringly unattractive. No beautiful people in the fast lane here. Just balls-out, roaring, fighting drunks. Sandy and I tried to be sociable and picked up some construction workers from the project out at the dam. Like everyone else in the bar, however, they were too drunk to dance or talk. I got vertigo, wondering if I was going to get puked on in the middle of a two-step. And so I mostly visited the library or drove maniacally up and down Tucumcari's main street between its two poles of commerce, K Mart and Thrifty's. Peace came sometimes on those long mainline runs into the desert or when I was too exhausted by the crazy hours to have insomnia. Peace did not come naturally. Not for a long time.

I also developed a strange compulsion to buy things. I got fixated on what *Texas Monthly* refers to as the crowning achievement of Western civilization—the cowboy boot. I made a mental connection between this obsession and quitting drinking, but I thought of it uncritically in terms of expense.

"Well, I'm saving two hundred dollars a week not drinking, so I can spend that money on boots."

I didn't think, "Well, I gave up one obsession, so I better replace it fast with another so that I don't have to look at what's really bothering me." I hadn't gotten that far yet in self-understanding. So I bought boots.

Linda Niemann was born in Pasadena, California, in 1946. She has taught literature at the University of California at San Diego and at Santa Cruz, and has been a brakeman/conductor on the Southern Pacific railroad and AMTRAK. She has written Boomer: Railroad Memoirs, *from which this was excerpted, and her latest book is* Railroad Voices. *She currently lives in Santa Cruz, California.*

★

The last Broadway Limited rumbled out of New York's Penn Station and into history one Saturday afternoon in 1995, closing the book on yet another railroad legend.

Charlie Chaplin rode it. Dwight Eisenhower rode it. Millions of other world leaders and business moguls and just plain folks rode it.

When it started in 1902 as the Pennsylvania Special, renamed the Broadway Limited in 1912, it was one of the nation's most famous and luxurious trains, plying the Pennsylvania Railroad's main line to Chicago.

It took its name not from New York City's Broadway but from the Pennsy's broad right-of-way, which was four and even six tracks wide. And the "Limited" indicated it was an express, with limited stops.

Back in the Roaring '20s, the whole train was first class, with barbers, a library, maids and valets. Even as late as 1967, every car was a Pullman sleeper....

Resignedly, railroad buffs gathered around the engine beneath Penn Station to watch engineer David Haggerty attach two American flags for the last ride.

In the passenger waiting area upstairs, families going home from vacation and elderly folks going to visit relatives in Pennsylvania shook their heads sadly as they talked about the passage of another bit of Americana....

"It's a sad day," Haggerty said as he prepared to close the door of the cab. "Ninety-three years, and this is the end of it."

He waved and moved a lever, and the long train began to move. It stopped briefly to pick up one latecomer, then slowly started off again.

It seemed to diminish in size as it passed into the tunnel, and soon the blinking red light on the back of the last baggage car faded from sight.

A grizzled old railroad man turned and walked slowly up a stairway.

"Too many last runs, not enough inaugural runs," he muttered.

—Don Singleton, "Broadway Limited Chugs Into History,"
New York Daily News

✦ ✦ ✦

Volcano

Come to where the land is made.

ONE NIGHT, AROUND THE THIRD WEEK WE'D SPENT IN THE CABIN, I was annoyed awake by a rumbling I sensed underneath the futon. I heard a whining moan like water rushing through a big pipe, a groaning like a big bus cranking through a gearshift or going up-hill. It made the floorboards of the cabin shake a little. It made the windows rattle. It was sometime past twelve o'clock and it should have been nearly completely dark, but as I popped up, hugging the bedcovers against the chill of night, I saw the sky behind the back windows of the cabin illuminated with an infernal, fiery red light that cast the stand of forest trees nearby into silhouette, black and skeletal against its glowing. The sky had gone entirely red outside except for the stark fringing of 'ohi'a trees. Kilauea was erupting full force from a vent about nine miles away from us.

In the sleepy fog of my mind, I thought, *Oh, an eruption,* and I laid myself back down, trying to fall back asleep. I guessed the vibrating to be lava moving through the rift zone, its huge earthen conduit miles below us. I was happy in a dumb sort of way. I thought, *Oh, an eruption, and I'm here for it.*

Geologists had been expecting a new outbreak. I'd been read-ing the papers and hearing news bulletins and volcano updates on the car radio. There had been reports of seismic activity coming from Puʻu ʻOʻo, a new vent site about nine miles from the summit of Kīlauea and about a quarter mile from the site of the last outbreak at Kamoamoa. Lavas from a flow emanating from Puʻu ʻOʻo had oozed along the line of cliffs that had once made up the coast of this island some thousands of years ago, and ran down to burn a few homes near the ocean-side village of Kalapana. Pele, the Hawaiian goddess of volcanic creation, had decreased her activity somewhat after that, restricting herself to fuming, steaming, and a little shaking at a spot along the East Rift Zone on old Campbell Estate land just outside the boundary to the National Park.

The East Rift was a vague line of recent activity running in a northeasterly direction from the summit of Kilauea near Volcano Village down to the sea near the village of Kapoho. It was as if a huge underground conduit had been laid from Kilauea Summit (where most of the nineteenth-century activity had been centered in the lava lake of Halemaʻumaʻu) easterly down to the sea. It was believed that magma came up below Kilauea and filled a gigantic storage chamber under it about a mile deep, then, once filled, it ran out along this East Rift Zone until it simply overstrained the leaky plumbing and burst out in red blossoms of molten rock. The Kapoho eruption in 1960 had happened this way—a fountain of fluid *pahoehoe* first breaking out in a papaya patch, rupturing the earth and sending up small, attractive fountains; then it erupted in a huge and terrifying curtain of fire a hundred feet high and forty yards long behind the village stores; finally, it evolved into a huge cinder and spatter cone that sent flows of *ʻaʻa*, that clinkery rubbled lava, enough to bury the entire village and surrounding farms. Kapoho—a cluster of houses, agricultural buildings, and a string of shops along the highway—was entirely lost.

One of my uncles had land out there then, planted in vanda and dendrobium orchids—the fleshy purple-and-yellow ones—and my eldest cousin remembers running through the orchid fields, grabbing flowers, shoving them into buckets in the back of a running jeep, and smelling the sulphur fumes of the flow heading his way. All the recent activity had been along this line, from

Kilauea Iki in 1959 and Kapoho in 1960 to Mauna Ulu (the Darth Vader of all spatter cones) from 1929 to 1974. Since January of 1983, the eruption had been at Puʻu ʻOʻo, another site along the East Rift Zone, and episodes of fountaining had been occurring there about once a month. I knew this from having read up a little, from having had conversations with relatives, from remembering stories from my own childhood. I'd never witnessed an eruption, but I vaguely knew how it would go, or so I thought. In my drowsiness, I wanted to sleep a little more.

My wife, sitting up and gazing at the red glow in the windows, was aghast. She saw my sleepy nonchalance as pure foolishness. She thought I was irresponsible.

"I'm calling the neighbors," Cynthia said, prodding me with her knee.

My wife, from Oregon, and I, from Hawaii, had very different responses to volcanoes. Her knowledge came from the eruption of Mount St. Helens near Portland in 1980, an explosive and deadly, bomblike blast caused by the buildup of energy released in the collision between two massive geologic formations—the Pacific and the North American plates. Mount St. Helens blew the top off itself, knocked down forests, vaporized lakes and leveled towns. It killed. But, from the reading that I'd done, my idea of a volcano was Kilauea—a beautiful, almost continuous flowering of volcanic energy that, over eons, had slowly built this chain of islands. I'd read that eruptions here were fountains, lava displays, rivers of heaven. They were spectacles and illustrations of the world's splendor. And, given a good night's sleep, I felt completely ready to cherish them.

"Look," I said, calling after her, "if you have to call someone, why don't you call the Volcano Observatory? They'll have the news and you can ask them any questions."

The Hawaiian Volcano Observatory was a field station of the United States Geological Survey built during the early part of this century to monitor and study the activity of Kilauea. We'd been to a viewpoint adjacent to the observatory once. It was on a high bluff with a spectacular view of Halemaʻumaʻu, the remnant of the lava lake, and the old, gigantic caldera of Kilauea. I noticed then that there were geologists inside one of the buildings who seemed to be on observational duty around the clock.

She phoned through, getting a technician on the line right away. "What's going on?" she asked.

The technician, a local, explained that this was the nineteenth episode of the current eruptive phase of Kilauea that began in 1983, that this was an episode of "high fountaining—to one t'ousan' feet at leas'," and that lava was geysering out of Pu'u 'O'o, the main vent site just upslope from the prehistoric cone of Kamoamoa. His explanation, Cynthia told me later, was fairly technical, his delivery almost deadpan, except that he seemed to be suppressing excitement, as if he were speaking to her while staring through binoculars at the eruption. I imagined him to be a local guy dressed in rubber beach sandals, jeans, and a t-shirt while manning the hotline, stirring a cup of coffee with a wooden stir-stick, checking seismographs and jotting measurements, spotting the eruption through binoculars fixed on a metal stand, holding conversations with Civil Defense and USGS headquarters, and talking to my wife all at the same time.

"Where should we go?" Cynthia asked finally, getting to her point.

"Where are you?" the technician asked.

"In Mauna Loa Estates, twelve streets in from the twenty-sixty-mile marker," she said, citing our coordinates.

"Oh," he said. "You're only a few miles from the vent. All you have to do is get in your car, drive out to Volcano Highway, go down *makai* [seaward] about five miles to Glenwood. There's a turnout there across the highway from Hirano Store. Drive up to the horsegate and park. Guarantee you can see it real good from there."

"See it? I don't want to *see* it," she exclaimed, "I can *already* see it. From my window. The sky's all red. All the windows are red. The forest is *glowing*. What about the danger? Where should I take my family? I want to get them *away* from it!"

The technician laughed. He asked her where she was from. She told him. He laughed again. "There's no *danger*," he said. "I thought you were calling to find out the best place to *see* it!"

"Oh," Cynthia said, and she hung up, a little mad and a lot

relieved. "I guess it's no big deal," she said, turning to me. We hugged each other.

"Let's go look at it," she said.

I drove us according to the technician's directions, then downslope along the highway to the turnout in Glenwood, pulling up alongside the horsegate he spoke of. We looked out from the car and saw only a veil of overcast tinged red from the erupting volcano. It was vapor from the eruption that made the clouds that hid its light.

I drove us still farther downhill, hoping another, clearer vantage point, a little turnout along the highway where a crowd of locals might be gathering to witness the emergence of Pele. At Kea'au, a crossroads town only a thousand feet from sea level, we spotted a car pulled over near a power-switching station, and a local-looking man, heavyset, bearded, dressed in shorts and a flannel shirt, leaning over a guardrailing, was gazing fixedly over fields of sugarcane at a point nearly on the horizon. I parked the car, we got Alexander out of his baby seat, and we walked over to where the man leaned against the metal railing.

Nearly back to sea level, the air there was much warmer than in Volcano, the obscuring fog high above us. We were on a slight

---

*W*hy did not Captain Cook have taste enough to call his great discovery the Rainbow Islands? These charming spectacles are present to you at every turn; they are common in all the islands; they are visible every day, and frequently at night also—not the silvery bow we see once in an age in the States, by moonlight, but barred with all bright and beautiful colors, like the children of the sun and rain. I saw one of them a few nights ago. What the sailors call "rain dogs"—little patches of rainbow—are often seen drifting about the heavens in these latitudes, like stained cathedral windows.

◆

—Mark Twain, *Roughing It*

overlook above a field of lands cultivated in orchids, black plastic and white cotton sheets of curved awning and canopy in neat rows below us. Beyond this was old caneland, abandoned to flowering, and stretching out for acres and acres in the distance on the long lava plain of Kilauea. The man gestured with a lift of his chin, we turned to look, and we saw a thin wire of red fire lifting itself from under white and graying clouds out almost on the edge of all that we could see. Far away, from where we could make out the bare outline of a small cone, there was the rose-colored stem of light that illuminated a plume of white vapor billowing out into a sea of cloud cover spreading over the land. This was the eruption, the fire-fountain of lava, a tiny jewel of a glimpse into dread and delight.

The man was friendly. He explained he'd been watching the eruption from there for nearly an hour, how the fountain had been higher earlier on, how there had been less cloudiness, wider spreading of the lava as it spumed out from the vent. We stayed there only a short while, though, since there wasn't that much to see, and it seemed to me as if we were breaking in on the man's peace, his meditation. We drove back home, no longer excited, but feeling something else, all of our foolishness gone.

Garrett Hongo attended Pomona College, the University of Michigan, and the University of California at Irvine, where he received a Master of Fine Arts degree in English. He is a professor at the University of Oregon, where he was Director of the Program in Creative Writing from 1989 to 1993. He is the author of two books of poetry, Yellow Light *and* The River of Heaven, *as well as the non-fiction book,* Volcano: A Memoir of Hawaii, *from which this story was excerpted. He lives in Eugene, Oregon.*

*

After convincing myself I would have been among the lucky survivors (a typically Californian attitude toward seismic risk, although I did not know it at the time), I felt strangely disappointed at having missed the experience. After all, earthquakes are the Bigfoot of natural disasters, resistant to prediction, manipulation, or control, the only ones still defying both the imagination and the photograph. A hurricane's giant waves and black skies send witnesses dashing for cameras, but the first tremor of an earthquake sends them running for their lives. Earthquake photographs show an aftermath of fissures, landslides, and pancaked expressways—but those of the event itself are invariably disappointing, just blurred buildings or panicked shoppers caught by a security camera. People say their refrigerators danced and their palm trees kissed the ground, but where is the proof? The National Geographic Society has installed video cameras aimed at bar stools and couches in earthquake-prone Parkfield, California, setting them to begin filming at the first nudge, but film what? Crashing gin bottles and falling chimneys? And how will this help anyone imagine an earthquake?

—Thurston Clarke, *California Fault: Searching for the Spirit of a State Along the San Andreas*

DAVID LAMB

* * *

Peoria Baseball

The umpire cometh.

THE CLASS-A MIDWEST LEAGUE STRETCHES THROUGH FOUR states named for long-vanquished Indian tribes (Wisconsin, Iowa, Indiana and Illinois) and links a cluster of towns that ring with the echo of the American heartland, among them Peoria, Cedar Rapids, Rockford, Kenosha, Appleton. I was back in the minors. The free meals and large crowds and million-dollar salaries of Milwaukee's County Stadium were quickly forgotten and I returned, not unhappily, to a hot-dog diet and little ballparks where I could park free and wander into the clubhouse without a pass and order fast-food lunches with players who always insisted on paying their share of a five-dollar tab.

Each league and each team I had seen had taken on its own identity, but the players themselves were cut from a universal mold. They talked about the same things in Stockton as they did in Elmira, they dressed in El Paso as they did in Harrisburg. No one wore earrings or long hair or outrageous clothes, and I never heard any white-powder jokes or had any hint that cocaine was in vogue. I often felt as though I were back in the fifties and everyone around me had grown up in the Midwest.

The Middle West—which I suppose would have been known

111

as the Near East had we settled the Pacific coast first—was the perfect setting for baseball. Amid fields of corn and long summer nights and steepled white churches that filled to capacity every Sunday was the bedrock of a nation, broad-shouldered, sweaty-browed, fingernails lined with dirt. No one in New York or California paid much heed to the voices that came from this land, yet I knew with certainty that long after crack barons had taken over our cities, long after zealots had shot all the smokers and flag-burners and gays, and the urban family had become a relic studied in high school sociology classes, the Midwest would still stand out here on the plains, as square as it was sensible, feeding us and reminding us of who we were.

At a distance the Midwest had always seemed bland, but with my feet planted on its deep, black glacial soil—soil that "looks good enough to eat without putting it through vegetables," Robert Frost said—I thought it to be the most distinctive region I had found in the United States. The Midwest had a beauty that was unstartling, a way of going about its daily chores that was unspectacular. Yet everything about the place was reassuring: the sense of community, the closing of deals on a handshake, the unabashed expressions of hats-off patriotism (people glared at you in the Midwest League if you talked during the singing of the national anthem), the belief that a day's labor was an honorable pursuit. I even saw whites washing dishes, scrubbing floors and performing other menial jobs in the Midwest, a sight that would strike Californians as peculiar.

Being "average" is seldom a complimentary label, but that, in the kindest sense, is what the Midwest is. Des Moines, for instance, is the most frequently surveyed per capita market in the country by telephone researchers who want to know what the "average" American does and thinks. Milwaukee is second, Indianapolis third. In Peoria I ran across a statistic that reflected what the Midwest had kept and many of us were losing: 75 percent of the city's households were occupied by families, 41 percent had children and 65 percent of the parents were married. Back home in Los Angeles, 47 percent of the households were occupied by families, 22 percent had children and 34 percent were married. Take away the family as a cohesive unit, and the spread of drugs, crime, teenage pregnancy and truancy seemed easier to explain.

There is a feeling in the Midwest, as on Huck Finn's raft, that "nothing ever happened to us at all," and Peoria itself has come to epitomize all that is ordinary about this unordinary region. "If it plays in Peoria, it'll play in America," they still say, referring to the tough vaudeville audiences before which Jack Benny, Fibber McGee and Molly, Fanny (Baby Snooks) Brice and others performed before taking their acts on the road. When veterans of the battleship USS *Iowa* wanted to have a reunion, Peoria is where they came to hold it. Among the choice of dining spots they found downtown was the Chat and Chew Restaurant.

> The prairie is a community. It is not just a landscape or the name of an area on a map, but a dynamic alliance of living plants, animals, birds, insects, reptiles, and micro-organisms, all depending upon each other. When too few of them remain, their community loses its vitality and they perish together. The prairie teaches us that our strength is in our neighbors. The way to destroy a prairie is to cut it up into tiny pieces, spaced so that they have no communication.
>
> ◆
>
> —Paul Gruchow, *Grass Roots: The Universe of Home*

Peoria's minor league team was the Chiefs, an affiliate of the Chicago Cubs, and it drew nearly twice as many fans each season as the city had residents. I drove out to Meinen Field and parked Forty-niner, as I always did, with its nose facing away from the diamond to protect my windshield from foul balls, and went looking for the umpire's room. It was huddled in a dark corner under the grandstand and had a green door bearing the warning, UNAUTHORIZED VISITORS NOT ALLOWED. I knocked.

The room was about the size of a pantry, with a shower and toilet in the back, and two folding metal chairs set up by a pair of wooden lockers. Brian York and Bryan Wilber—who pursued their major league dream through the Midwest League in a battered '77 station wagon with two hubcaps and four colors—were stripped to their shorts, rubbing beautiful white shiny baseballs with mud and tobacco juice. They were happy to have a visitor, authorized or not, because umpires are so ignored in the low minors that their names often aren't even included in box scores. The reason: the official scorer didn't bother to ask them who they were.

I had once prized a new, unmarked baseball more than anything, and the mud ritual that all professional umpiring crews performed before every game mystified me. Good "working mud," York and Wilber said, takes the gloss out of a ball so it doesn't slip from a pitcher's grip. The mud must have just a touch a grit, though not enough to scar or discolor, and should be sufficiently slimy to spread easily. Sometimes it is mixed with tobacco juice, spit, shoe polish or other concoctions that umpires fuss over like chefs, each believing he has created the finest recipe for delicate morsels of earth, lightly moistened with Copenhagen or Bull Durham.

The mud used in the majors was discovered in 1938 by a coach for the Philadelphia Athletics, and comes from a New Jersey tributary of the Delaware River. Once a year the family-owned Lena Blackburne Rubbing Mud Company packs the mud into coffee-can-sized containers and ships it off (at twenty-four dollars a can) to big-league stadiums. But minor league umpires must find their own mud, unless they have a friend in The Show who can scrounge them some, and they spend a surprising amount of time checking out riverbanks and rain-soaked golf courses and roadside ditches. Brian York had packed his great find in peanut butter jars and he told me how he got it:

"My grandfather had come over from Ohio to see me umpire. He came into the locker room after the game and I said, 'Come on. We got to go out and find some mud.' My grandfather said, 'Who would want to rub mud on a white ball and make it brown?' He's so laid-back you wouldn't believe it. He's from Kentucky, the smartest man in the world, but he doesn't know anything about baseball. He never had the luxury of playing because he worked in the coal mines and got married when he was sixteen. His wife was fifteen. I just love telling stories about him because he's my best friend, and one of the toughest things that's happened to me in my brief career is that I had to umpire the night of his fiftieth anniversary and couldn't be there.

"So anyway, I wanted him to be part of my experience umpiring and we went down to the stream by Rockford Park. There's a bridge there and the river's right nearby. We pulled up in the car and walked down the hillside to the edge of the water. I stick my hands in up to my elbows, and my grandfather, he's just kind of watching. The first stuff I came up with was sewage. Really gross. But I figured if I found some rocks, there might be good mud there.

"Pretty soon my grandfather's taking all this very seriously. He's found an old headlight cover and he's scooping away, trying to dig down to good mud. I tell him we need grit and mushiness, and he yells out, 'Come here! Come here!' I run over and he's found the greatest dirt in the world. We mixed it up and put it in four containers and brought it back to the motel. I spread the mud out in the parking lot to mix in some other stuff I had. The visiting team's manager comes out of the motel and sees me there, like a kid playing in mud and says, 'How old are you anyway?' My grandfather really laughed. I just thought it was great he got to be part of all this."

York and Wilber were in the only profession I knew where a man was expected to be perfect his first day at work and get better as time went by. They, along with 200 other umpires in the minors, were competing for 60 major league jobs—a journey that could take ten years to make, and few completed—and their lives reminded me of those of desert nomads. They traveled at night to elude the prairie heat, avoided bars and motels frequented by players whose performance they had to judge, and lived a spartan existence, spending virtually every moment together from a season's first pitch to the last. Each earned $1900 a month, from which he had to pay all his road expenses.

Sometimes fans would see managers giving them a terrible

lashing. Their arms would wave and point in exasperation, their heads would bob and their feet would tap-dance in the pattern of a little boy who had to go to the bathroom. It was good theater, but as often as not the manager was speaking in a calm voice, saying something like, "You called that play right, I'm just protecting my player. Give me fifteen seconds out here." Then he would wheel, kick some dirt in disgust and stomp off to the dugout.

The mud having been applied, York and Wilber changed into their blue uniforms with padded shoulders and creased pants. They suddenly looked older and sterner. York stuffed the game balls into his pockets and Wilber flicked some lint off his jacket. "It's seven of," Wilber said, looking at his watch. "Time to go." Shoulders straight and heads back, they moved together down the concourse and with deliberate strides walked onto the field to a chorus of boos.

Meinen Field, filling quickly, had the feel of a shopping mall where people came to socialize and wander. Chuck Lewis, back home in Peoria on vacation, was standing with his kids down the left-field foul line, pounding his baseball mitt. "Isn't this what the world's really all about?" said Lewis, the Washington bureau chief for the Hearst newspaper chain. Dick Dutton, a business executive and president of the Booster Club, which provided players with towels, pillows, sheets, silverware and small appliances when they first arrived in Peoria, was recruiting fans for the trip to the Chiefs' upcoming series in Burlington, Iowa: box seat and bus transportation, ten dollars. The mayor's secretary was at her customary place in the concession stand, dishing out hot dogs even faster than she typed.

"Striiike!" yelled Brian York as the first pitch of the game went by the Beloit Brewers batter waist-high, and the crowd roared.

Peoria had been a wounded town in the early '80s, when minor league baseball returned after a 25-year absence. President Reagan, who grew up 85 miles away, had ended U.S. support for the Soviet Union's gas pipeline and Moscow had shifted its purchases of earth-moving equipment to Komatsu of Japan, costing Peoria's biggest employer, the Caterpillar Corporation, $90 million in lost contracts. Caterpillar laid off 8,000 workers. The Pabst brewery and the Hiram Walker distillery closed. Huge farms went belly-up. Merchants fled downtown, and even the Elks and the square dance clubs no longer considered Peoria a good place to hold their conventions.

It may have been only co-incidence, but not long after the Chiefs came home, they were bought by Pete Vonachen, a crusty local with an owlish face and a quick tongue, life took a turn for the better in Peoria. The farm-belt recovery started, the restoration of downtown got under way with the building of a convention center and a new hotel, and everyone seemed to get caught up at once with civic enthusiasm. When 76-year-old retired truck driver Charles Harshbarger found himself with more volunteer work than he could handle— he tended flower and veg-etable gardens at fire stations and nursing homes around town— the Bellevue Senior Citizen Center came through with a crew of helpers.

> *S*imultaneous industrial and agricultural decline wrought severe hardship throughout the Middle West. In factory and farm communities, cases of human suffering multi-plied, and the Middle West's unemployment rate was twice that of the national average. America's central region became a place apart from the prosper-ous America of East and West coasts. Funds to provide basic services were scarce, and thou-sands of jobs had been lost per-manently from the area. Young people were moving away, leav-ing behind an aging population less able to provide for itself.
>
> ◆
>
> —Haynes Johnson, *Sleepwalking Through History: America in the Reagan Years*

"You wouldn't expect women in their seventies and eighties, with hip transplants, backaches and knee problems, anticipating heat, sweat and bugs, to come out at seven a.m. and pick beans," he said, "but they do."

Peoria started believing in itself again, and the symbol of that
rekindled confidence was the Chiefs. They became winners and
set league attendance records two years in a row. Harry Caray, the
Chicago Cubs' announcer and Vonachen's best friend, talked about
Peoria often on his national
broadcasts, turning the
Chiefs into something of a
cult. Vonachen installed an
exploding scoreboard, baby-
sat for his players' children
when asked and let any fan
wander into the PA an-
nouncer's booth to sing

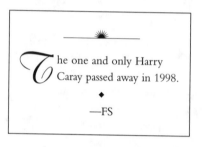

*T*he one and only Harry
Caray passed away in 1998.

◆

—FS

"Take Me Out to the Ball Game," in the seventh inning. Vonachen
was a Peoria nationalist. He had spent the winter eating ham and
potato salad off paper plates and promoting the Chiefs anywhere
he could get a dozen people together, from the Methodist Church
to the Elks Lodge and Boy Scout meeting halls. He understood
exactly what played well in Peoria and he ran his baseball business
the way he would have a neighborhood tavern. He was, I thought,
testimony to the strength of what the minor leagues have less and
less of—local ownership. His arm was wrapped in a sling the afternoon I met him in Sullivan's saloon. Vonachen had locked
himself out of his home and, trying to crawl through a second-
floor bathroom window, had fallen fifteen feet off a ladder. He
was full of painkillers and not very happy to have to order some
damn yuppie soda drink instead of his regular V.O. whiskey. "I
can't drink because I've got all kinds of shitty medicine in me," he
said. "I guarantee this seltzer is going to make me puke."

Vonachen was 64, his round face anchored by a sharp chin and
creased with smile wrinkles. His great-grandparents had emigrated
from Germany, and his grandfather had run an Illinois saloon, the
Big Foot, that served free lunches but not women. Saloons, he
thought, were where all the most interesting people still met.
Vonachen had what he called "that old Midwest gut feeling"
about when to get in and out of a business and he had gone from

owning the best restaurant in Peoria to running a $23 million-a-year blacktop construction company to operating a couple of motels. "You sit down to talk about a deal in the Midwest, and no one throws each other curves," he said. "You start from a position of trust." The sports editor of the local paper had talked him into buying the recently returned Chiefs in 1984 from a Florida group that was running the team into the ground.

"I like to say I'm streetsmart, but you know what?" he said. "I'm obsessed. I get into something and I'm obsessed with making it the best. I didn't know a damn thing about running a baseball team, but I got obsessed with making the Chiefs the best franchise in minor league baseball. I just can't stand to lose."

One night at Meinen Field, when Peoria was losing, umpire Mark Widlowski made several questionable calls. The rattled Chiefs started arguing. By the ninth inning manager Jim Tracy and four of his players had been ejected, and Pete Vonachen couldn't take it anymore. "Play 'Howdy Doody Time,'" he told the PA announcer and, appropriately inspired, the owner bolted the fence and raced onto field, screaming every obscenity he knew at Widlowski. The fans cheered wildly.

"Get out of here, or there's going to be a riot," the umpire said.

"You're going to have to throw me out," Vonachen snapped, falling to his knees in a position of prayer. "Go ahead. Do it. I'm praying for you to throw me out."

"You're gone!" ordered Widlowski, a stiff right arm pointed toward the yonder. The owner stomped off the field, pondered the dugout for a moment, and was struck by a TV image of how Billy Martin would have reacted to banishment. In a flash he was raging through the dugout like a tornado, uprooting helmets, gloves, bats and balls. The projectiles flew onto the field and Widlowski deftly danced and hopped his way clear of amputation and castration.

"Here, Pete, you forgot one," said a Chiefs pitcher, running over with the last helmet.

"Thank you, son," Vonachen said, flinging that one, too.

Vonachen knew immediately he had made a bad mistake, and

started plotting how best to capitalize on it. "It was a dumb, dumb thing I did," he said. "A guy in my position shouldn't be running on the field. It showed no class." He apologized to the umpires and sent them flowers and a box of Hersey chocolate Kisses. But the damage had been done. George Spelius, a Beloit florist and the Midwest League president, suspended Vonachen, banning him from the park for nine games, and assessed the largest fine in league history, one thousand dollars.

The next night a large crowd showed to see if Vonachen would defy the ban, but he was abiding by the order to stay out of Meinen Field. Just beyond the left-field fence, 335 feet from home plate, was a little equipment shed and on its roof he had built a platform and there he sat, in a lawn chair, next to his hibachi grill. "And now from the new owner's rooftop box...here's Peoria Pete!" boomed the PA man. Vonachen, holding a portable microphone, led the crowd in singing "Take Me Out to the Ball Game" and used a portable phone to call the Cubs' Harry Caray, who told the world of the happenings in Peoria.

Radio station WMBD got caught up in the spirit of rebellion and offered dinner in the "owner's box" to the person who called each morning with the best poem or song about Peoria Pete's dilemma. The nightly winner was escorted across the field by the Chiefs' marketing director, then climbed up onto the platform for dinner with the boss. One woman said she didn't like hot dogs, and Vonachen sent out for lobster tails. The crowds grew larger each night. Five thousand. Six thousand. Then standing room only. The only troublesome moment came when a spark from the grill set the roof afire, but Vonachen extinguished the flames with beer.

The ban ended on the tenth night and Vonachen returned to Meinen Field, wearing an orange jumpsuit and riding in a police van that was led by a motorcycle escort as it circled the field to cheers and applause. "Pete," league president Spelius said, "I knew I shouldn't have let you sit on that roof." The Chiefs estimated Vonachen's suspension had been worth ten thousand dollars in increased revenue.

Vonachen and the Chiefs were as Midwestern as a John Deere

tractor, and I was sorry to leave them. My last night in Peoria the Chiefs beat Beloit 10-6, and Vonachen brought a load of hamburgers and potato chips into the clubhouse for the players. "Pete, can you spare twenty till payday?" one of them asked. He rolled his eyes and reached into his wallet. I mentioned that his relationship with the team seemed unusual, especially since I had met some club executives who didn't even let players into their office without an appointment. "Nah," Vonachen said, "I don't do anything special. I just try to be decent."

I left Peoria at dawn the next morning, sipping coffee from my plastic mug and listening to the radio: "November beans are down a dime at five-ninety a bushel. Midwest cash hogs today are anywhere from a dollar lower to fifty cents higher. In Peoria they're getting forty-eight even. August hogs are down two, October hogs up twenty-five cents." The murderous heat and humidity came up early and would, I knew, hang about all day. My cab was a sauna. The land flew by unnoticed, hypnotizing in its flatness and sameness. I yearned for a bend in the road, the sight of hills, a cooling breeze.

David Lamb has traveled the world as a correspondent for the Los Angeles Times *and has lived in Egypt, Kenya, Australia, Vietnam, and a dozen American cities. He is the author of several highly acclaimed books and is an eight-time Pulitzer Prize nominee. This story was excerpted from his book,* Stolen Season: A Journey Through America and Baseball's Minor Leagues.

⁕

I am standing on the corner of Fourth and Broad [in Grinnell, Iowa], turning slowly and generally gawking, entirely unaware that before me stands an architectural landmark, a bank designed by Louis H. Sullivan, the man Frank Lloyd Wright called "the master." As I rotate slack-jawed and, apparently, befuddled-looking, a kindly woman inquires, "You look confused. Can I help you?" "Oh, uh, no, thank you," I reply, because however confused I appear, I am no more puzzled than is normal for me. I am just taking in the scenery, wondering if I can absorb some small bit of this town, thereby sparing myself the necessity of having to rely entirely on reason to figure out what makes it especially Grinnell. Then, as I amble up Broad Street on an unseasonably warm spring day, the first two people I pass on the sidewalk smile and say, "Hello." They do not merely nod or mutter an unintelligible greeting: they offer a genuine, articulated salutation. Perhaps it is the warm spring weather. Perhaps knowing everything about everybody else in town, they save their good wishes for strangers. But I doubt it.

They are friendly. They are open. They want to help.

Welcome to Grinnell. What can we do so we will not someday have to mourn its passing?

—Thomas H. Rawls, *Small Places: In Search of a Vanishing America*

ANDREI CODRESCU

Memphis: The City of Dead Kings

America responds in peculiar
ways to greatness.

MEMPHIS IN EGYPT WAS THE CITY OF DEAD KINGS, AND SO IT IS with Memphis, Tennessee. Our Memphis boasts two dead kings, Elvis, king of rock and roll, and Martin Luther, king of the poor. Between these two kings there stretches the outlandish spectacle of the American mind, which swings like a yo-yo between frivolity and concern.

You get to the house of King Elvis after you pass the giant rat on top of Atomic Pest Control, the Little Guns Motel, a huge milk bottle, and a Graceland Dodge dealership. You turn off Bellevue onto Elvis Presley Boulevard, and then you're there, at Graceland, where they unload a bus tour every three minutes to take gaggles of folk with awestruck bouffants and greased ducktails through the mirrored chintz of a white American nightmare. It's a good place to pick up decorating hints for your trailer. There is shag rug on the ceiling, window curtains gathered over a pool table, and one to three TVs in every room, including the dining room, where Elvis would have dinner with up to twelve people and never miss his favorite shows. One whole room, the proud guide says, was bought by Elvis right off the showroom floor of a downtown furnisher. That's the one with the mirrors, the huge neo-Hawaiian

123

hairy chairs, and the waterfall. And then, in a connected building, are endless rows of gold and platinum records interspersed with trophies, movie posters, honorary deputy badges, and even an ID card proclaiming the stoned-looking Elvis in the photo a captain of the Memphis police. There are full-sized dolls of Elvis and Priscilla in their wedding clothes, and a plaque from the local Cadillac dealership with thirty-one names inscribed on it to commemorate the famous "night of the Cadillacs," when a generous Elvis gave away thirty-one of these to friends and relatives. There are his numerous guns, and the bullet holes in the door Elvis used for target practice, right next to his father-in-law's office who, wisely, stayed inside during the fusillade.

Elvis is buried in the backyard between his mother and father, and some of his family lives upstairs, peering through drawn curtains at the 3,000 to 5,000 visitors who stream through every day at about ten bucks a head. The graves are in a semicircular walkway past a statue of Jesus with his arms in the air, and the visitors read the names on the tombstones carefully, moving their lips. One such gravesite visitor asked the guide, "Is this a relative of Elvis? Where is Elvis buried?" "That *is* Elvis, ma'am," said the guide politely. Several visitors expressed the same kind of doubt. It seemed impossible to them that the actual Elvis, not an impersonator, was buried in there. For them, Elvis was an idea and Graceland only the temporary stopping place for this idea. But they love Graceland, because it's their idea of how to live it up if they became kings somehow....

Later at the Groundhog Café, I ordered Elvis's "favorite," the peanut butter-and-banana sandwich. It came grilled, oozing a blended substance the consistency of baby doo-doo. It was one of the most vile things I ever laid a tongue on, but there was something about it at the same time, something *eerie* and *total*, as if I'd touched an electric icon (a sore on the Devil's eyelid, to be more precise), and I realized that I had reached an apex, the Grand Sum of White Trash Cooking. Elvis had these sandwiches made for him by his mum and flown to his stoned dressing room in Vegas where a legion of aides labored to pull him into his performing suit. They were, these baby-doo-doo sandwiches, his last sad link to reality.

The Lorraine Motel, on the other hand, is an abandoned shell with a heap of rubble in front. The sun beats mercilessly down from the cloudless sky on the abandoned asphalt and cement of downtown Memphis. There is a sign on one of the few doors left among many gaping holes on the second floor, a sign that alerts the passerby that his was Martin Luther King's room. From the balcony hangs a wreath. This is the spot where King stood when he was shot. A high, wire fence surrounds the desolate ruin. Camped in front in a small tent is Jacqueline Smith, the last tenant of the Lorraine. She has vowed not to move until the city builds a free civil-rights learning and cultural center there. But the city, which owns the expensive real estate, envisions a paying "museum of civil rights" displaying Martin Luther King's trophies with tour buses coming and going every three minutes. No way, says Ms. Smith, handing the rare visitor a sheet with Martin Luther King's last sermon, which says, in part: "I won't have the fine and luxurious things of life to leave behind. But I just want to leave a committed life behind."

I browse through the few but essential clippings and newspaper photos that Ms. Smith has laid on a makeshift table. The hot sun is melting the plastic on the cheap frames. Her seemingly hope-

---

The National Civil Rights Museum opened in 1991, housed in the partial remains of the Lorraine Motel. Each year, over 100,000 people view the museum's nineteen permanent displays commemorating many of the seminal events in the struggle for civil rights from 1960 to 1968—with particular emphasis placed on the work of Dr. Martin Luther King. Exhibits include material on the bus boycott in Montgomery, Alabama, the desegregation of public schools in Little Rock, Arkansas, Freedom Summer, and the March on Washington.

◆

—FS

less battle with the city has not made her bitter. She sees herself continuing Dr. King's struggle, her cause no different from her daily chores. Between answering questions, she goes in and out of her tent with a pan of water for her tea. Even ten years ago she would have had many friends and supporters around her, perhaps a whole street full of tents. But it is 1990 now, and this lone protester's cause is about something that makes us all very uncomfortable. Graceland, on the other hand, makes us feel safe and cool because it, too, is about something, namely money, pathos, cruelty, and bad taste.

Graceland has an army of keepers to keep the business going, The Lorraine has only Jacqueline Smith. Memphis has two dead kings. America has two minds.

Andrei Codrescu, a Romanian-born poet, arrived in the United States in 1966 penniless and without knowledge of the English language. Within four years he had learned to speak English well enough to publish his first poetry collection. Today, he has more than forty works to his name, including The Blood Countess, Hail Babylon!: In Search of the American City at the End of the Millennium *and* Zombification: Stories from National Public Radio, *from which this story was excerpted. He lives in New Orleans.*

⋆

After interviewing Martin Luther King, one magazine estimated his annual travel at 780,000 miles—a staggering total, which, even if only a quarter true, put him on propeller-driven commercial airplanes steadily enough to circle the globe eight times a year. He acquired a reputation as the complete evangelist, who could preach integration to the humble as well as the elite, to the erudite and the ignorant, to the practical and the idealistic. As he did so, however, he contracted the evangelist's curse. No matter how many cheers he received or how many tear-streaked faces assured him that lives were transformed, tomorrow's newspaper still read pretty much like today's. Segregation remained in place. People listened wholeheartedly but did nothing, and King himself was surer of what they should think than what they should do. Under these conditions, oratory grew upon him like a narcotic. He needed more and more of it because he enjoyed the experience, yet was progressively dissatisfied with the results.

—Taylor Branch, *Parting the Waters: America in the King Years 1954–63*

KATHLEEN NORRIS

Dakota Godot

Imagine Beckett in Fargo.

EASTERN NORTH AND SOUTH DAKOTA HAVE ENOUGH RAINFALL and population density to hang on at the western fringes of the Midwest, having more in common with Minnesota and Iowa than with Montana. But in western Dakota, the harsh climate and the vast expanse of the land have forced people, through a painful process of attrition, to adjust to this country on its own terms and live accordingly: ranches of several thousand acres, towns that serve as economic centers 40 or 60 miles apart. Taking the slow boat to Dakota, driving in from the East, the reality of the land asserts itself and you begin to understand how the dreams of early settlers were worn away.

Heading west out of Minneapolis on Highway 12, you pass through 150 miles of rich Minnesota farmland, through towns that look like New England villages with tall trees well over a hundred years old. These are sizeable towns by Dakota standards: Litchfield (pop. 5,900), Willmar (15,900), Benson (3,600). South Dakota is visible, a high ridge on the horizon, long before the crossing a few miles past Ortonville (pop. 2,550. elev, 1,094).

Your first town in South Dakota is Big Stone City (pop. 630, elev. 977) at the southern edge of Big Stone Lake, named for huge granite outcroppings in the area. Here you begin your climb from the broad Minnesota River Valley to what French trappers termed the "Coteau des Prairies" or prairie hills of eastern South Dakota. This is the beginning of the drift prairie of eastern North and South Dakota, named for the glacial deposits, or drift, that make up its topsoil. The road narrows, twisting around small hills and shallow coulees. You pass by several small, spring-fed lakes formed by glaciers and several good-size towns: Milbank (pop. 3,800), Webster (2,000), Groton (1,100).

After Groton you cross the James River Valley, its soil rich with glacial loam deposits. By the time you reach the city of Aberdeen, South Dakota (pop. 25,000, elev. 1,304), one hundred miles from the Minnesota border, you are in open farm country with more of a gentle roll to it than eastern Kansas, but basically flat and treeless except for shelterbelts around farmhouses and trees planted and carefully tended in the towns.

Driving west from Aberdeen you find that the towns are fewer and smaller, with more distance between them: Ipswich (pop. 965), Roscoe (362), Bowdle (590), Selby (707). One hundred miles west of Aberdeen you come to Mobridge (pop. 3, 768, elev. 1,676), on the banks of the Missouri River.

What John Steinbeck said in *Travels with Charley* about the Missouri River crossing 120 miles to the north is true of the Mobridge crossing as well. He wrote: "Here's the boundary between east and west. On the Bismarck side it is eastern landscape, eastern grass, with the look and smell of eastern America. Across the Missouri on the Mandan side it is pure west with brown grass and water scorings and small outcrops. The two sides of the river might well be a thousand miles apart."

The boundary is an ancient one. The deep gorge of the Missouri marks the western edge of the Wisconsin ice sheet that once covered most of north central America. Passing through Mobridge and crossing the river you take a steep climb through rugged hills onto the high plateau that extends west all the way to the Rockies. Lewis and Clark marked this border by noting that the tallgrass to the east (bluestem, switch grass, Indian grass) grew six to eight feet high, while the shortgrass in the west (needle-and-thread, western wheat grass, blue grama grass, and upland sedges) topped at about four feet. You have left the glacial drift prairie for a land whose soil is the residue of prehistoric seas that have come and gone, weathered shale and limestone that is far less fertile than the land to the east but good for grazing sheep and cattle. Here you set your watch to Mountain time.

Here, also, you may have to combat disorientation and an overwhelming sense of loneliness. Plunged into the pale expanse of shortgrass country, you either get your sea legs or want to bail out. As the road twists and turns through open but hilly country, climbing 325 feet in 22 miles to the town of McLaughlin (pop. 780), you begin to realize you have left civilization behind. You are on the high plains, where there are almost no trees, let alone other people. You find that the towns reassuringly listed every 10 miles or so on your map (Walker, McIntosh, Watauga, Morristown, Keldron, Thunder Hawk) offer very little in the way of services. All but McIntosh (pop. 300) have populations well under a hundred. You climb imperceptibly through rolling hayfields and pasture land punctured by wheat or sunflower fields for another 80 miles or so before you reach another town of any size—Lemmon (pop. 1,616, elev. 2,577).

You should have filled your gas tank in Aberdeen, especially if you're planning to travel after dark. For many years there was no

Eisenhower wanted the highways as a part of his overall Cold War program. Throughout the Formosa Straits crisis, he had worried about how to evacuate Washington in the event of a nuclear attack on the capital, and on other cities too. Four-lane highways leading out of the cities would make evacuation possible; they would also facilitate the movement of military traffic in the event of war.

◆

—Stephen E. Ambrose,
*Eisenhower: Volume Two,
The President*

gasoline available at night (except in the summer) between Aberdeen and Miles City, Montana, a distance of nearly 400 miles. Currently there are two 24-hour stations in towns nearly 200 miles apart. On the last stretch, the 78 miles from Baker, Montana, to Miles City, there are no towns at all, just a spectacularly desolate moonscape of sagebrush. Farmers will usually give or sell a little gas to stranded travelers, and small-town police forces often have keys to the local service stations so they can sell you enough to get you on your way. But the message is clear: you're in the West now. Pay attention to your gas gauge. Pay attention, period.

But it's hard to pay attention when there is so much nothing to take in, so much open land that evokes in many people a panicked desire to get through it as quickly as possible. A writer whose name I have forgotten once remarked, "Driving through eastern Montana is like waiting for Godot." I know this only because a Lemmon Public Library patron brought me the quote, wanting to know who or what Godot was. It struck me that the writer may as well have been talking about the landscape of Dakota from Mobridge or Mandan west. And it seemed appropriate that the good citizen of the region wanted to know if her homeland was being praised or put down. Had he lived here, I wonder if Beckett would have found it necessary to write the play.

But people do live here, and many of them will tell you in all honesty that they wouldn't live anyplace else. Monks often say the same thing about their monasteries, and get the same looks of incomprehension. People who can't imagine not having more stimulation in their lives will ask, "How can you do it?" or, "Why do it?" If those questions are answerable for either a monk or a Plains resident, they can't be answered in a few quick words but in the slow example of a lifetime. The questioner must take the process of endless waiting into account, as well as the pull of the sea change, of conversion.

Often, when I'm sitting in a monastery choir stall, I wonder how I got there. I could trace it back, as I can trace the route from back East to western South Dakota. But I'm having too much fun.

The words of Psalms, spoken aloud and left to resonate in the air around me, push me into new time and space. I think of it as the quantum effect: here time flows back and forth, in and out of both past and future, and I, too, am changed.

Being continually open to change, to conversion, is a Benedictine ideal: in fact, it's a vow unique to those who follow Benedict's *Rule*. This might seem like a paradox, as monks, like farmers, stay in one place and have a daily routine that can seem monotonous even to them. But the words spark like a welder's flame; they keep flowing, like a current carrying me farther than I had intended to go. At noon prayer we hear the scripture about "sharing the lot of the saints in light," and in the afternoon I read in a book about quantum physics that some scientists believe that one day everything will exist in the form of light. At vespers the text is from I John: "Beloved, we are God's children now; what we will be has not yet been revealed."

The sun is setting and a nearly full, fat-faced moon is rising above the prairie. We have time on our hands here, in our hearts, and it makes us strange. I barely passed elementary algebra, but somehow the vast space before me makes perfectly comprehensible the words of a mathematician I encountered today: it is easy to "demonstrate that there are no more minutes in all of eternity than there are in say, one minute."

The vespers hymn reads: "May God ever dress our days/in peace and starlight order," and I think of old Father Stanley, who said not long before he died: "I wish to see the Alpha and the Omega." He'd been a monk for over fifty years, a Dakotan for more than eighty. It's a dangerous place, this vast ocean of prairie. Something happens to us here.

Kathleen Norris is a writer whose books include: The Cloister Walk *and* Dakota: A Spiritual Geography, *from which this story was excerpted.*

*

"The Zunis believe in four stages of life. In this life, we are only in the first stage. The people buried in these sites are still on a journey. The journey is over when all the bones and all the grave goods are completely dissolved into the earth. So, wherever burials are, people are on journeys. It's going on now. It's in the present, not in the past."

—Roger Anyon, quoted in *When the Land Was Young: Reflections on American Archeology* by Sharman Apt Russell

ANTHONY WALTON

* * *

Mississippi

A northerner returns to
his family's south.

HAVING BEEN THROUGH, ONCE, WHAT WAS FOR ME THE ABSTRACT
Mississippi of history, imagination and legend, I thought it was
time to approach the state from another direction. Mississippi
wasn't only a place; it was also a way of being that had defined
and circumscribed the lives of millions of black Americans, my
antecedents and relatives. Inside the grander themes I'd been exploring were the threads of common lives whose experiences told
the story. The proper noun "Mississippi" carries in the American
language an incredible amount of weight, a complex of emotion
and belief, and I hoped to get closer to its meaning through the
stories of my family. My mother, Dorothy, and I were southbound
on Interstate Highway 55, traveling through the shallow rolling
fields of central Illinois, when we saw an exit sign for U.S.
Highway 24 and the small town of Chenoa. Interstate 55 is one of
the two main automobile routes—lifelines, really—between
Chicagoland's 1.5 million blacks and the "ancestral" home of the
vast majority of them, Mississippi. Highway 55 traces the route
coursed by old U.S. 66, southwest over the black loam of central
Illinois, skirting the farm towns of Willmington, Dwight, Pontiac,
Bloomington and Lincoln on its way to the state capital (and

Abraham Lincoln's hometown) of Springfield, continuing on past Litchfield and Edwardsville south and west to East St. Louis, where its four lanes of asphalt cross the Mississippi River and bear a hard left, paralleling the river due south to Arkansas and Memphis, Tennessee.

On the trip to Mississippi, choosing between 55 and the alternative, Interstate 57, is a matter of taste and circumstance: 55 is a winding scenic route; 57 is straighter and thus more boring, but its lack of curves can save two or more hours of travel.

The October day my mother and I chose to set out on the twelve-hour trek "home" was a day of beautiful clear fall weather, Indian summer. We'd decided on Interstate 55 because we were in no special hurry; we thought the ride would be pleasant, and it was. We passed by hundreds of miles of harvested corn and soybean fields standing beige-brown against green prairie grass; regular intervals of deciduous woods with trees just starting to turn; inevitable tributaries winding to the big river every few miles; and overhead a big, clear and cloudless sky made the horizon seem limitless. On either route you can see a mileage sign—ST. LOUIS, 263 or CAIRO, 312—and, looking at that horizon, feel that you'll never arrive. In that landscape, distance becomes a function of time, not landmarks, and the question is how to fill the time: in my childhood, we whiled away the hours playing games, singing, making up stories about the people in other cars, sleeping. Today my mother and I were talking, and, about two and a half hours into the trip, the large green sign for Chenoa called up memories.

In 1972, several members of a family from Aurora, our hometown, were killed here at a railroad crossing on old 66. Their station wagon had stalled and was hit broadside by a freight train; the mother and a daughter, one of five children, survived. They were coming back to Illinois the Sunday after Thanksgiving, returning from holidays with relatives in Mississippi, and I remember my seventh-grade friends and I were alarmed and upset because that accident could have happened to any of us. I'd passed through that crossing many times myself (it couldn't be avoided in the pre-I-55 years). When I reminded my mother of this story, she sighed and said, "A lot of things have happened on these roads. There's been a lot of traveling back and forth, most of it in tragedy."

Dorothy spoke of a trip she remembered more than any other. "I'm remembering when I went back with Papa in 1959, the year before you were born. We were carrying Mama home to be buried."

"Grandma died in Illinois?" I'd always thought that my mother's mother, Annie, had lived all her life down south.

"She came north for surgery—we thought the doctors might be better—but it was too late. She died a month after getting to Illinois. We buried her in New Albany, at Beaver Dam, that's what she wanted. Papa and I rode the Illinois Central, trying to cheer each other up. We talked to the other people, too. You know, it's funny how you see people going places, flying, driving, on the train, and you think it's a pleasure trip. But many times they're traveling in

It was in June I began my chain-bound journey to Alabama, where I eventually reached. Our journey was long and tiresome. Imagine yourself chained to a long chain to which men, women, and children were also attached. The roads were dusty or muddy the June I walked in such a convoy. We met other groups going in the same direction under the same circumstances. Some of the slaves were sullen, others gay and happy, others were mere animals. As for me, I was designing, hateful, and determined. Ragged and barefooted, I was resentful of the freedom of nature.

◆

—Stuart Seely Sprague, *His Promised Land: The Autobiography of John P. Parker, Former Slave and Conductor on the Underground Railroad*

tragedy. On that train when we took Mama home, there was a young man on his way to Arkansas to bury his grandmother, another lady going to Memphis to look after her mother who was dying, another going to Mississippi to bury an aunt. And this was just on one car." She hesitated and caught her breath. "When we got to New Albany it was dark, but the streets were crowded. People had come out, lined up at the depot to meet us. Everybody had come out to meet Annie Modena."

This sense of community was the other half of the black experience in Mississippi, the palliative to the difficulties of Jim Crow, and the unifying glue—the larger, self-contained and self-sustaining bond—that some felt had been lost with the advances of the civil rights age. The trip we were on was itself touched with a sense of both community and tragedy. Our cousin Mary Dilworth was riding along with us because her daughter Debbie, who'd returned to live in Mississippi after growing up on the South Side of Chicago during the sixties and seventies, had taken ill and entered the hospital in Tupelo. Mary heard through the family grapevine that Dorothy and I were headed out that morning, and literally caught us as we were walking out the door.

Later, well into central Illinois, over a lunch of chicken wings and soda, Mary reminisced about simpler times. "Dorothy, remember being on the train, everybody eating chicken?"

"Oh yes." Dorothy smiled. "I remember how the porter would walk around and just automatically pass out these garbage bags to everyone, saying, 'Put them bones in here.'"

"Them was some good old days," Mary said. "You'd get on the train, get settled, and them brown bags would come out—in those days people wanted to share. Sometimes the train wouldn't even be out of the station and people would be saying, 'You want some chicken, a piece of this cake?'"

Dorothy was born on July 10, 1936, in New Albany, widely known as the birthplace of William Faulkner and the site of de Soto's battle with the Alibamu during his last expedition. Dorothy Cannon Visor was born at home in a black neighborhood called the Flats, near what is now the center of town. She was delivered by the midwife Ludie Cooper, who presided over the parturition of most of the town's black children. Dorothy was the first and, as it turned out, the only child of Annie Modena Edwards, who was young, just twenty years old, and single, two grave liabilities for a black mother at that time. Annie, who was then working as a cook in a New Albany hotel, has been described to me as fiery and headstrong, traits that mellowed into vigilance, determination and faith as she grew older.

Dorothy and I had driven through New Albany so that she could introduce me to the quiet, dusty town. I had, of course, been there many times before, but hadn't then cared about its history or present. An uneventful collection of half-empty two-story buildings and low-slung, leaning houses, New Albany stands at the junction of Highways 15, 30 and 78. Every structure seems tired and half covered with clay, the washed-out pinks and greens and yellows sprinkled with ocher. The population, according to the town sign, is 7,072.

Our first stop was the cemetery at Beaver Dam Baptist Church, several miles north of New Albany proper. As a crossroads town, New Albany has several communities of blacks within its larger population, and I am direct kin to a least two of them: Little Zion, south of town on the road to Oxford, and Beaver Dam to the north. In the latter is the church to which Annie Modena was required to bring the infant Dorothy, to stand in front of the congregation and ask forgiveness for breaching, egregiously at that time, the mores of the community. She had insisted on being buried there.

The current brick church at Beaver Dam sits on a slight rise, in a clearing of standard north Mississippi forest of maple, live oak and pine. The church is a nerve center for Union County blacks, and for clans that spill north into Tippah, east into Lee, and south into Lafayette. The cemetery is a short walk from the church, on a gently sloped hillside of clay falling into woods. This red clay is perhaps my strongest childhood memory, its color a deep, rich red with a tint of orange, its texture thick, clumpy, unlike the even, fine black dust of northern Illinois. The clay seemed to get all over everything—shoes, pants, bicycle gears and, especially in my memory, cars. Bouncing around northern Mississippi as a kid, I could easily tell social rank—that is, who lived in town, who in the country—by the amount of red dust on the lower half of vehicles.

We found my grandmother's grave without any trouble, marked by a large, contemporary stone: OCT. 27, 1913—MAR. 20, 1959. Many of the graves in the cemetery had crude, homemade markers, sparse information scratched in home-mixed concrete; some of the markers, years old, were the plastic kind placed there by the undertaker immediately after burial. Other graves had no markers at all; people knew who was where from memory, aided by general family groupings.

"She was born up in Tippah County, just north of here," Dorothy said. "I believe there was a Beaver Dam up there, too. But this is where Annie considered herself as being from, and when she grew up she moved to town—New Albany—and she worked at different jobs, in various people's homes. She worked in particular for this doctor and his family, then at the hotel as cook." Dorothy smiled happily. "My uncle used to bring me down to the hotel and my mother'd let me sit in the kitchen with her while she worked. She couldn't keep me with her at that time, so I stayed with my grandmother until she got married."

"What happened after Annie Modena and Mr. Visor married?"

Dorothy smiled again, remembering. "I'll never forget it. They pulled up in this big, black car, one of those old cars with a trunk on the back of it. My mother got out and said, 'I come to get my baby.' She and Grandma talked about it for a while and then they carried me out to that car and we went out to Little Zion. It was another world out there."

She turned and pointed northeast, into the forest. "Grandma stayed out at what we called Connersville, about three miles over there."

I looked out over the trees and into the high pale sky. The only things moving around us were crows, cawing and walking along the ground, and insects that revealed their presence with buzzes and shrills.

"I was proud of my mother," Dorothy continued, "because she taught herself so much. She had to go out on her own quite early in life and get a job. It was a big family and she was the eldest girl. The oldest boy was already gone, and Grandma needed her help to take care of the other children. So my mother had to work and do what she could."

"Did she finish school?"

"No. She didn't get to go. I think she finished eighth grade, she was what we call a good eighth-grade scholar, because whenever they needed a substitute in the little country school out at Little Zion they'd come get her. She wanted to be a schoolteacher, and that was special to her when she got to help out a little bit at the school."

"You could teach with only eighth grade?"

She chuckled. "Most of the teachers had only eighth grade in the grammar school. They knew enough to teach reading and writing. I think they were better than some of these you got today."

The thought of my grandmother standing firm in front of a classroom brought something else to mind. "Everybody says she was so proud, how could she be like that in Mississippi back then?"

Dorothy laughed out loud, then quieted. "Even in Mississippi I was never raised to think I was second class, even when I was walking behind the white folks' bus. They used to ride past us every morning while we walked, but it didn't occur to us that we weren't as good as those kids riding. It was just a myth of white folks. They were mean and they wouldn't let us ride, but we were taught we were as good as them, and so, to me, that meant that I could have gone to Ole Miss if I'd wanted to, which was the ultimate achievement.

"My mother would not allow people to put her down. Most white people would call older black people 'auntie' and 'uncle' and names like that; Annie Modena never allowed it. She would say, 'I ain't your aunt.' The white people would look at her like 'This woman's crazy.' But she was forty-six years old when she died and certainly wasn't old enough to be called anyone's 'auntie.'" Dorothy's face was stern. "We had this thing called a rolling store, a truck that came up through the country with all the different things that you would need to buy: yarn, material, various dry goods. We needed it because we didn't often get to town. It would have candy, baked goods, it seemed like everything. The rolling store came by one day and we went out to get some stuff, and the man came around the side, smiled and said, 'What can I do for you today, Auntie?' Annie Modena said 'I ain't your aunt,' turned around and walked back into the house. He wasn't going to make no sale that day. What I'm trying to say is, that's how we were brought up.

"I remember when I started to realize that black people were considered to be different from white people. White people would say to your parents, 'Why you sending them any farther in school? They can be working here on the farm or they can help Miss So-and-So clean up the house.' Gradually you realized that they didn't intend for you to do anything in life. We were living on these people's place when I was in high school and the lady said, 'Why is she'—she meaning me— 'still going to school? She could be here helping you help me keep house.' Annie Modena, being who she was, looked at her and said, 'My daughter isn't going to be cleaning your house. She's not going to school for that.' It kind of broke up a little friendship between them, but I did finish high school."

We walked farther into the cemetery, looking at names on gravestones: Bryson, Crayton, Simpson, Foster, Stone and Berry, names I'd known in Illinois as well.

J went into the slave market, a place which the traveler ought not to avoid to spare his feelings. There was a table on which stood two auctioneers, one with a hammer, the other to exhibit "the article" and count the bids. The slaves for sale were some of them in groups below, and some in a long row behind the auctioneers. The sale of a man was just concluding when we entered the market. A woman, with two children, one at the breast, and another holding by her apron, composed the next lot. The restless, jocose zeal of the auctioneer who counted the bids was the most infernal sight I ever beheld.

◆

—Harriet Martineau (1834)

Many of the graves, I was surprised to see, were marked by government-issue stones commemorating service in foreign conflict: World War II, Korea, even a few from World War I. I couldn't help but think of the irony surrounding these men who had gone, willingly, to defend the United States that considered them at best three-fifths human. I mentioned this to Dorothy, who only pointed down the hill, just below the section that held Annie Modena's grave. Down there lay veterans of a more recent conflict, and one stone in particular stood out for me:

CHARLES M SHUMPERT

MISSISSIPPI

SGT CO B 506 INF ABN DIV

VIETNAM BSM-PH

OCT 28 1948 FEB 11 1970

I had never met Charles, by his last name a distant cousin of mine. I couldn't imagine his death in a jungle half a world away, a 21-year-old fighting for neighbors who had yet to fully acknowledge his worth as a citizen. Was he sorry to be fighting for a racist America, or glad to be out of Mississippi? What was he thinking in his last moments? Perhaps in those moments he was just a soldier trying to hang on to life and didn't have time to reflect upon the philosophical implications of his predicament. That, I realized, was left to me.

Anthony Walton studied at Notre Dame and Brown University, and currently lives in Brunswick, Maine. This piece is excerpted from his book, Mississippi: An American Journey.

✻

I feel somehow lucky that in all my years in America, I can't think of a single personal encounter that I would describe as racist. I say "lucky" because I know friends whose cars have been vandalized or graffitied with "Go Back to Asia" or other such stupidities. But looking back, I realize I had been alerted to more subtle forms of racism during a trip I took through the South three months after arriving in America. I was with a friend from Thailand, who had already spent four years in America and was sensitive to nuances of behavior.

In a coastal Florida town, we entered a pizza parlor for lunch. It was not crowded, perhaps a half dozen patrons. We ordered and sat down. America was very new to me, Florida even more so, since we had arrived early that morning. So I was busy observing, comparing and contrasting the Florida sights from what I had already seen in Louisiana, Georgia, the Carolinas.

Fifteen minutes and no pizza. My Thai friend had stopped chatting and was looking around. He commented that some others who had arrived after us had already been served. When he tried to get the server's attention, he looked at us and nodded noncommittally.

After five minutes, my friend got up abruptly and almost ordered, "Let's go!"

I was still busy being the wide-eyed tourist and exclaimed, "Why? What about our food?"

"They're not going to serve us. Come on, let's get out of here."

He strode out before I could say anything more. I followed, and realized the server was watching us but made no move to stop us.

"Racists!" my Thai friend exclaimed. "Did you see that? We were there for a half hour and they never brought our food. Man, America is a funny place. You got to be careful. Sometimes you dance with blondes, and sometimes with bastards. Today, we got the bastards."

We drove for a long time silently.

—Rajendra S. Khadka, *The Hovering Hindu:*
An Education on Two Continents

DENNIS COVINGTON

Under the Brush Arbor

God takes strange forms in Alabama.

THE CARD HE PRESSED INTO MY HAND READ: "CHARLES McGlocklin, the End-Time Evangelist." "You can have as much of God as you want," he said. His voice was low and urgent. "These seminary preachers don't understand that. They don't understand the spirit of the Lord. They're taught by man. They know the *forms* of godliness, but they deny the *power*."

Brother Charles was a big man in his early fifties with a full head of dark hair and hands the size of waffle irons. He didn't have a church himself, and he didn't particularly want one. He'd preached on the radio, he said, and at county fairs and trade days. In years past, he'd driven all over the South, conducting revivals under a tent he'd hauled in the back of his '72 Chevy van. He said he had even stood on the road in front of his house trailer in New Hope, Alabama, and preached at passing cars.

"I get a lot of stares," he added, and then he put his big hand on my shoulder and drew me toward him confidentially. "I have received visitations by angels," he said. "One of them was seven feet tall. It was a frightening experience."

I said I bet it was.

"And I'll tell you something else," he said. "One night I was

143

fasting and praying on the mountain, and I was taken out in the spirit. The Lord appeared to me in layers of light." His grip tightened on my shoulder. "He spoke a twelve-hour message to me on one word: *polluted*."

"Polluted?"

"Yes. Polluted. Now, you think about that for a minute. A twelve-hour message."

I thought about it for a minute, and then decided Brother Charles was out of his mind.

In time, I'd find out he wasn't, despite the fact that he kept four copperheads in a terrarium on his kitchen counter between the Mr. Coffee and the microwave. He said God moved on him one night to handle a big timber rattler right there in the kitchen. His wife, Aline, showed me a photo of him doing it. Aline was thirteen years younger than Charles, childlike and frankly beautiful, a Holiness mystic from RaceTrack Road who worked the night shift weaving bandage gauze. "I had just got up, getting ready to go to work," she said, "and my camera was just laying there." She pointed at the photo. "You see how the Holy Ghost moved on him?"

In the photo, Charles is standing in the kitchen in his white t-shirt and jeans. He has a rattlesnake in one hand, and he appears to be shouting at it as though it were a sensible and rebellious thing. "There's serpents, and then there's *fiery* serpents," Charles said. "That one was a fiery serpent."

Another time, Charles said he wanted to take up a serpent real bad, but he didn't have one on hand. The Holy Ghost told him, "You don't have a snake, but you've got a heater." So Charles ran to the wood-burning stove in the living room and laid his hands on it. "Baby, that thing was hot," he said. But his hands, when he finally took them off the stove, weren't a bit burned. Instead, they were as cold as a block of ice, he said.

Aline reminded him that he did get a blister from a skillet once, but Charles said, "God wasn't in that. That was in myself. That's why I got burned."

"You were just thinking about that corn bread," Aline added with a knowing smile.

Long before I was a guest in their home, I'd seen the McGlocklins at services at The Church of Jesus with Signs Following in Scottsboro. We became friends, and then something more than friends, but that is a long and complicated story that began, I think, on the afternoon of my first brush arbor meeting on top of Sand Mountain, when Aline was taken out in the spirit, and I accompanied her on tambourine.

I had never even heard of a brush arbor until J.L. Dyal built one in a field behind his house near the Sand Mountain town of Section in the summer of 1992. Brother Carl had invited me to the services, and J.L. had drawn a map. "You take a left at the Sand Mountain Dragway sign," he said. "We'll get started just before sundown."

I was pleased the handlers had felt comfortable enough to include me. It meant the work was going well. The relationship between journalist and subject is often an unspoken conspiracy. The handlers wanted to show me something, and I was ready to be shown. It seemed to me that the [attempted murder] conviction of Glenn Summerford was not the end of their story, but simply the beginning of another chapter. I was interested in what would happen to them now that Glenn was in prison and The Church of Jesus with Signs Following had split. But I had a personal agenda

*G*lendel Buford Summerford was the pastor of The Church of Jesus with Signs Following. A man given to fighting, drinking, and philandering, he was arrested and charged with attempting to murder his wife Darlene by making her stick her hand into a cage which contained a canebrake rattlesnake. Summerford, though drunk, had the presence of mind to force his wife to write a suicide note at gunpoint. She survived. As author Dennis Covington covered the trial, he discovered the bizarre and compelling world of holiness snake handling. Summerford was later sentenced to 99 years in jail.

◆

—Sean O'Reilly,
The Road Within

too. I was enjoying the passion and abandon of their worship.
Vicki didn't seem to mind. She encouraged me to go. So I told
Brother Carl and J.L. I'd be there for the brush arbor services,
although I couldn't visualize what they were talking about. "Brush
arbor" seemed a contradictory term. The word *arbor* suggested civilized restraint. The word *brush* didn't.

I did know that outdoor revivals had once been commonplace
in the rural South. The most famous occurred in 1801, when
thousands of renegade Presbyterians, in their rebellion against
stiff-necked Calvinism, gathered in a field near Cane Ridge,
Kentucky, for a week-long camp meeting. They were soon joined
by Methodists and Baptists, until their combined ranks swelled to
more than 25,000, a crowd many times greater than the population of the largest town in Kentucky at the time. Something inex-
plicable and portentous happened to many of the worshipers in
that field near Cane Ridge. Overcome by the Holy Spirit, they
began to shriek, bark, and jerk. Some fell to the ground as though
struck dead. "Though so awful to behold," wrote one witness, "I
do not remember that any one of the thousands…ever sustained
an injury in body."

Cane Ridge set the stage for the dramatic events at a mission
on Azusa Street in Los Angeles in 1906, when the Holy Ghost
descended in power on a multiracial congregation led by a one-
eyed black preacher named William Seymour, and the great
American spiritual phenom-
enon of the twentieth century, Pentecostalism, began in
a fury of tongue speaking
and prophesying and healing.

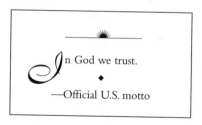

In God we trust.

—Official U.S. motto

Cane Ridge had been the
prototype of revivalism on a
grand scale. The crowd at J.L's
brush arbor was somewhat smaller—thirteen of us altogether,
plus a gaggle of curious onlookers who hid behind Brother Carl
Porter's Dodge Dakota pickup. But the facilities at J.L.'s were
top-notch. Traditional brush arbors had been small and temporary,

primitive shelters usually built at harvest time from whatever materials might be at hand. Willow branches were especially prized because of their flexibility. Thick vines added strength. The idea was to give field hands a place to worship so they wouldn't have to leave the premises before all the crops were in. But J.L. had constructed his brush arbor out of sturdy two-by-fours over which he had stretched sheets of clear plastic so that services could be held even in a downpour. The vines and brush piled on top of the plastic appeared to be decorative rather than functional, yielding the impression of a brush arbor without all its inconveniences. J.L.'s father-in-law, Dozier Edmonds, had helped string electricity to the structure and had installed a length of track lighting. The place was perfect, except for one thing. There weren't any snakes.

"I thought you were going to bring them," said Brother Carl to Brother Charles.

"I thought Brother Willie was going to bring them," Charles replied. He was getting his guitar out of the car, an instrument the Lord, he said, had taught him to play.

"Brother Willie got serpent bit last night," Carl reminded him.

"I know, but he said he was going to be here today."

"Maybe I need to check on him after the service," Carl said. "It was a copperhead," he confided to me. "Over in Georgia. Bit him on the thumb, but it didn't hurt him bad."

"Well, we don't *have* to have serpents to worship the Lord," Charles finally said. He put his boot up on a pine bench that would serve as the altar and began strumming the guitar. When everyone had gathered around, he started to sing. *"He's God in Alabama. He's God in Tennessee. He's God in North Carolina. He's God all over me. Oh, God is God...and Jesus is his name..."*

The service had begun at five o'clock to avoid the midafternoon heat. The light was low and golden over the field, and Charles's voice rose above it like a vapor, unamplified, snatched away by the breeze. Aline was there; Brother Carl and the old prophetess, Aunt Daisy; J.L. and his wife, Dorothea; one of their daughters-in-law and her baby; and Dorothea's father, Dozier, and her mother, Burma, who had a twin sister named Erma. Both

Burma and Erma, 68, attended snake-handling services, usually in identical dresses, but only Burma actually handled.

I'd also brought photographers Jim Neel and Melissa Springer with me, and they moved quietly around the edges of the arbor as the service picked up steam. The choice of photographers had been simple. Jim was one of my oldest friends. In addition to being a sculptor and painter, he'd worked with me as a combat photographer in Central America during the 1980s. Melissa, whose work I'd first noticed when it was censored by police at an outdoor exhibit in Birmingham, had been documenting the lives of men and women clinging to the underbelly of the American dream—female impersonators, dancers with AIDS, women inmates in the HIV isolation unit at Alabama's Julia Tutwiler prison. When I told her about the snake handlers, she said she had to meet them, but unlike most people who say they want to, she kept calling and insisting that we set a time. She and Jim were an interesting study in contrasts: he was moody, private, and intense; Melissa was warm, expansive, and maternal. But both were obsessed with their work, easy to travel with, and open to possibilities.

Melissa had worn an ankle-length dress this time. At her first service in Scottsboro, she'd gotten the message when Aunt Daisy prophesied against the wearing of pants by women. Outsiders are bound to get preached at a little in Holiness churches. But the same Holiness preachers who draw attention to unorthodox details of behavior or dress inevitably hugged us after the service and invited us back.

Some preachers didn't take the Holiness prescriptions about dress quite as seriously as others. Charles McGlocklin's theory was simple: "You've got to catch the fish before you clean them." His wife, Aline, didn't wear makeup or cut her hair, but she occasionally allowed herself the luxury of a brightly colored hair ornament. "God looks at the heart, anyway. He doesn't look on the outside," she said. She also drove a white Chevy Beretta with an airbrushed tag that read "Aline loves Charles." Charles's pickup had a matching tag, with "Charles loves Aline." Both sentiments were inscribed in the middle of interlocking hearts, like the brightly colored hearts on Aline's hair clasp.

Despite the empty chairs and the lack of electric guitars or serpents, the worship at J.L.'s brush arbor followed the same pattern I'd experienced in Scottsboro. Without church walls, it seemed more delicate and temporal, though, and Brother Carl's sermon echoed the theme. He talked about the flesh as grass, passing in a moment, of earthly life being short and illusory. He talked about the body as "fleshy rags" that he would gladly give up in exchange for a heavenly wardrobe. But at the center of Carl's sermon was the topic of God's love, which he seemed to first discover fully even as he talked his way into it.

"It's got no end," he said, "no bottom, no ceiling. Paul says nothing can separate us from the love of God through Jesus Christ. And let me tell you, sometimes we find His love in the little things. The fact that we're here today is a sign God loves us." *Amen.* "The fact that we got a brain to think with, and a tongue to speak with, and a song to sing. I just want to thank Him for waking me up this morning," he said. "I want to thank Him for giving me food to eat and a roof over my head. Sometimes we ask Him to work big miracles, but forget to thank Him for the little ones." *Amen.* "But he's a great big God, and He never fails. His grace is sufficient to meet our every need. He's a good God, isn't He?" And everybody said amen.

Then Carl invited Brother Charles to give his testimony. In Holiness churches, a testimony is a personal story that reveals God's power and grace. It's not meant to exhort or instruct the congregation—that would be preaching—but simply to praise the Lord. In practice, though, the line between testifying and preaching is not so clear-cut.

Brother Carl and Brother Charles hugged, and after a few introductory comments about the beauty of the afternoon and the love he felt from everybody gathered there, Brother Charles began to testify. It was a story, both lurid and familiar, that could only have come from the South.

"Up until I was five years old," Charles said, "I lived in a tent on the banks of the Tennessee River at Old Whitesburg Bridge. Y'all know where that's at. Then my mother got remarried, and we moved to a houseboat at Clouds Cove."

Clouds Cove.

"My stepdaddy was drunk."

"Amen," said J.L., who knew something about drunks himself.

"My real daddy lived to be eighty," Charles said. "He died in the Tennessee penitentiary, where he was serving a life sentence for killing his second wife. I was like a lamb thrown into a den of lions when we moved to Clouds Cove," Charles said. "In 1948, when I was six, we lived on nothing but parched corn for three weeks, like rats. We slept on grass beds. We didn't even have a pinch of salt. Now, that's poor."

Amen. They all knew what it was like to be poor.

"By the time I was eight, I'd seen two men killed in our house. I was afraid to go to sleep at night."

Help him, Jesus.

"I made it to the eighth grade, but when I was just shy of turning thirteen years old, I got shot in the stomach with a twelve-gauge shotgun. That was the first time I heard the audible voice of God."

Praise His holy name!

"There I was, holding my insides in my hands. Then things, they really colored up funny, I thought to myself. Then I had the awfullest fear come up on me," Charles said. He was pacing back and forth by now, a loping, methodical pace, his huge, dog-eared Bible held loosely in one hand like an implement. "I saw a vision of my casket lid closing on me, and the voice out of heaven spoke to me and said, 'Don't be afraid, cause everything's gonna be all right,' and I felt that shield of faith just come down on me!"

Hallelujah!

"God's been good to me!"

Amen.

"He's been good to me!"

Amen.

"Doctors told my mother I had maybe fifteen minutes to live.

'There's no way he can make it,' they said. 'Almost all his liver's shot out, almost all his stomach.' I was on the operating table sixteen to eighteen hours. They had to take out several *yards* of intestines. I stayed real bad for forty-two days and nights. I was one hundred twenty pounds when I got shot and eighty-seven when I got out of that hospital. But just look at me now!"

Praise His name!

Brother Charles was standing with his hands clenched at his side and a wild look in his eyes. He was a big man, an enormous man. It was not the first time I'd noticed that, but it was the first time I had considered the damage he might do if he ever had a reason.

"God's been good to me!" he said as he started pacing again.

Amen.

"I said He's been good to me!"

Amen!

He suddenly stopped in his tracks. "But I wasn't always good to Him."

"Now you're telling it," Brother Carl said.

"When I was sixteen, I went to live with my real daddy in Tennessee," Charles said. "He was one of the biggest moonshiners in the state, and I wanted to learn the trade. I dabbled in it a good long time. I was bad. I went up to Chicago and did some other things I shouldn't have."

Tell it. They'd all done things they shouldn't have.

"When I came back South, I drove a long-haul rig twice a week to New York City. Then I bought me a thirty-three acre farm in Minor Hill, Tennessee. Two-story house. Fine car. I had a still upstairs that could run forty to fifty gallons of whiskey, and in another room I stored my bales of marijuana. Pretty good for a boy who'd grown up picking cotton."

Amen. They knew about cotton.

He raised his Bible and shook it at us. "I don't have to tell you that's the deceitfulness of riches talking, boys."

Preach on.

"One day, things had really got bad on me. I had just got under so much that I couldn't go no further, and I was getting ready to kill myself. The devil spoke to me and said, 'Just go ahead and take that gun and kill yourself and get it over with.'"

No, Lord.

He walked to the edge of the arbor and pantomimed picking something up from the grass. "I went over there and got the gun and was fixing to put a shell in it, and when I did, this other voice came to me and said, 'Put that gun back down and walk back over in front of that wood heater.'"

Amen.

"I walked back over there in front of the wood heater, and suddenly that power from on high hit me in the head and knocked me down on my knees, and I said six words. I won't never forget what they was. I said, 'Lord, have mercy on my soul.'"

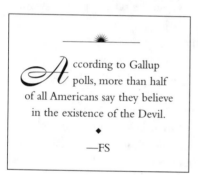

According to Gallup polls, more than half of all Americans say they believe in the existence of the Devil.

◆

—FS

Amen. Thank God.

"He took me out in the spirit and I came back speaking in other tongues as the Spirit gave utterance. The devil said, 'Look, look now. Now what are you going to do?' He said, 'Look at all that moonshine, all that marijuana you got. What are you going to do now? Ain't you in a mess now? Here you are, you've got the Holy Ghost, and you've got all this in your house.' And the Lord spoke to me and said, 'Just set your house in order.'"

Bless him, Lord!

"He said, 'Just set your house in order!'"

Amen!

"So that's what I did. I set my house in order. I got rid of that moonshine and marijuana. I told the devil to depart that place in the name of Jesus, and within a year I'd taken up my first serpent."

Amen.

"We've got to set our house in order!" Charles said, and now he was leaning toward us, red-faced, with flecks of white spittle in the corners of his mouth. "We're in the last days with the Lord, children! He won't strive with man forever! He's a merciful God, he's a loving God, but you better believe he's also a just God, and there will come a time when we'll have to account for these lives we've led! We better put our house in order!"

Amen. Thank God. Bless the sweet name of Jesus.

There were only thirteen people under that brush arbor, but it seemed like there were suddenly three hundred. They were jumping and shouting, and pretty soon Brother Carl was anointing Burma and Erma with oil, and Brother Charles had launched into "Jesus on My mind" on his guitar, and J.L. and I had our tambourines going. There was so much racket that at first it was hard to hear what Aline was doing over in the corner by a length of dog wire that the morning glory vines had twined around. Her back was to us. Her hands were in the air, and she was rocking slowly from side to side, her face upturned and her voice quavering, "Akiii, akiii, akiii. Akiii, akiii, akiii…"

It was the strangest sound I had ever heard. At first, it did not seem human. It sounded like the voice of a rare night bird, or some tiny feral mammal. And then the voice got louder, mounting up on itself, until it started to sound like that of a child who was lost and in great pain. But even as the hairs on my arm started to stand on end, the voice turned into something else, a sound that had pleasure in it as well as torment. Ecstasy, I would learn later, is excruciating, but I did not know that then.

"Akiii, akiii, akiii…" The singing and praising elsewhere in the brush arbor had started to diminish. Brother Charles had stopped strumming his guitar. Brother Carl had put away his oil. Burma and Dorothea kept their hands raised, but except for an occasional amen or praise Jesus, the air fell silent around Aline's voice. Everyone was listening to her now. I could not disentangle myself from the sound of her voice, the same syllables repeated with endless variation. At times, it seemed something barbed was being pulled from her throat; at other times, the sound was a clear stream flowing outward into thin air. Her voice seemed to be right in my ear. It was a sobbing. A panting after something she could not quite reach. And then it would be a coming to rest in some exquisite space, a place so tender it could not be touched without "Akiii, akiii, akiii…" The sun had set and the electric lights were not yet turned on, but the arbor seemed filled with a golden light. We were swaying in it, transfixed, with Aline silhouetted against the dog wire and the morning glory vines. All but her trembling voice was silent, or so it seemed, until I realized with horror that my tambourine was still going, vibrating against my leg, almost apart from me, as if it had a motive and direction of its own.

My hand froze. It was as though I had been caught in some act of indecency. But Aline's voice reacted with renewed desperation, "Akiii, akiii, akiii," and so I let the tambourine have its own way, now louder and faster, until it almost burst into a song, and then softer and more slowly, until it resembled the buzzing of a rattlesnake in a serpent box. It anticipated every move that Aline's voice made, and vice versa. The intimacy was unnerving: her voice and the tambourine, perfectly attuned to one another and moving toward the same end. I was unreasonably afraid that Charles would be angry with me. I didn't yet know the full dimensions of passion. It was much later that I would come to understand what had gone on in that moment. The tambourine was simply accompanying Aline while she felt for and found God. And I mean "accompany" in its truest sense: "to occur with." And nobody could predict when something like that might happen. Through the tambourine, I was occurring with her in the Spirit, and it was not of my own will.

I cannot say how long the episode lasted. It seemed to go on for a very long time. J.L. turned the lights on at the end. The men hugged the men. The women hugged the women. Aline and I shook hands. If the snake handlers found anything unusual about our curious duet afterward, they never spoke directly to me about it. But I do know one thing: it was after that brush arbor meeting on Sand Mountain that they started to call me Brother Dennis.

Dennis Covington teaches creative writing at the University of Alabama at Birmingham. He writes on the South for The New York Times *and is*

the author of the award-winning novel Lizard *and* Salvation on Sand
Mountain: Snake Handling and Redemption in Southern
Appalachia, *from which this story was excerpted. He lives in Birmingham
with his wife, novelist Vicki Covington, and their two daughters.*

※

It was late in the afternoon of a hot dry day in the eastern Cascades when
I staggered, bleary-eyed, from the shack. A loud hissing broke my reverie,
and I looked up to see a Serpent of Yore coiled and ready to strike not
five feet away. I seized a stick and set about to slay him. I progressed from
stick to rocks and boulders, scoring impressive strikes only to have the
Serpent bounce, coil, and hiss again. Our struggle took on a Biblical cast
(I, Cain, slaying Abel), though I suspect this was only the case in my own
mind and not the Serpent's. By the time I lofted a boulder worthy of
Conan, my adversary had slithered away into a maze of brambles.

The next day, out for a stroll with wife and daughters, the Serpent
was spotted in a bed of pine needles not far from the shack. He had a
distinctly Gary Larson look, with a crooked "neck"—so I had good reason to believe he was the same one I had encountered and injured the day
before. I set upon him with a stick and rocks, and finally lopped his head
off with an ax. Headless, he wriggled toward the girls, who were under-
standably concerned at his approach. We buried the head, which has
been known to confer a bite hours after death.

We took the body home, lamenting the fact that our friend Richard
hadn't sent us his recipe for Rattlesnake Piccata. My mother-in-law then
deftly showed us how to dissect *Crotalus viridis oreganus* and how to preserve the skin. The Serpent was just over three feet long, with twelve
rattles, which in this climate meant he was anywhere from six to ten
years old. His skin will make an excellent hat band or picture frame.

I marinated him in lemon juice, white wine, soy sauce, and tomatoes
from the garden, pan-fried him for a few minutes, and then baked him for
an hour. I served him coiled on a plate with a wedge of lemon and a sprig
of parsley. How did he taste? To paraphrase another friend, "Taste is a
function of hunger"—and we were not overwhelmingly hungry. I would
characterize rattlesnake as a poor man's calamari. Long strings of chewy
meat embedded in an amazing architecture of bones.

Fortunately for all at the table, there was also chicken.

—James O'Reilly, "Encounters with the Serpent,"
Travelers' Tales Food, edited by Richard Sterling

PART TWO

SOME THINGS TO DO

JAN MORRIS

⋆ ⁎ ⋆

Mr. Lincoln's
Neighborhood

Allow the hometown of a
great soul to soak in.

AT A LOOSE END FOR A FEW DAYS IN THE UNITED STATES OF
America, I decided to go to a very epitome of Americanness—
Springfield, Illinois, which is situated in the heart of the Midwest
prairies at 39.49° north, 89.39° west—more or less on a line, that
is to say, with Lisbon one way, the Galapagos Islands the other.

I offer this detail because the American prairies have always
seemed to me less an actual place than a geographical notion—a
sprawled and unenticing plain, sometimes icy cold, sometimes
appallingly hot, over which combine harvesters perpetually grind
their way through illimitable fields of corn, and in which very
slow-speaking raconteurs swap laborious anecdotes in provincial
and all too likely teetotal saloons.

Springfield was just the place to go for a short immersion
course in prairiedom; and having sorted out which Springfield it
was I wanted to visit—there are at least fourteen Springfields in
the United States, not to mention three in Canada and one each
in Kenya and New Zealand—I found myself one morning on the
train called the *Ann Rutledge*, which stops at the Prairie Capital on
its daily way from Chicago to Kansas City.

On the train? Of course. Who would not wish to take the train

159

on such an expedition? It was the train that enabled these prairies to grow rich, and made it possible for Springfield itself, situated more or less in the middle of nowhere, to become the capital of Illinois—still, with its 106,000 inhabitants, the political superior of Chicago up the line.

It was winter when I made the journey, and Amtrak itself would not claim that there was much to see through our windows. The prairies may look wonderful in the summer, when the tall grass waves and the wild flowers blossom, but at my time of the year it all looked pretty dismal out there. The towns we passed through reminded me of Albania, so run-down seemed to be their railside factories and warehouses, and the wide prairie itself, speckled with farmhouses and windbreaks, was like some stretch of wartime ocean, in which the masts and superstructures of sunken ships protruded here and there from the swell.

The man across the aisle from me, who took his jacket off the better to cope with the mass of papers and correspondence he took from his briefcase, was also bound for Springfield, and the very look of him cheered me up. Surely he was a state senator, or at least an influential political lawyer, and was a portent of the vivid political goings-on that I was going to find in the capital, the *sotto voce* conferences in smoke-filled corners of the Sangamo Club, the politicos intriguing arm-in-arm as they strolled up to the state capitol. I watched him with professional satisfaction as he resumed his jacket and his expensive overcoat, gathered his papers and looked out of the window expectantly, I thought, for his waiting limousine.

But no, he stumbled out of the train like everyone else, and I last saw him wandering rather helplessly around the station yard looking for a taxi. I had forgotten it was a holiday season. The Illinois Legislature was not in session, the Sangamo Club proved to be anything but smoke-filled, the governor was out of town and there were remarkably few people about.

"Which hotel would you suggest," I asked a chattily home-spun bystander as I waited for my own cab to appear, "the Hilton or the Renaissance?" "Six of one, half a dozen of the other," he said, metaphorically spitting out his tobacco chaw, "and there'll be plenty of room in either."

He was right. I chose the Hilton, the only skyscraper in town, towering even over the dome of the state capitol, which is itself, so the man told me, higher than the capitol in Washington. It seemed to be entirely empty of guests.

I found a clutch of tourist publicity material in my room on the 22nd floor, and tried to identify, in the vast melancholy expanse outside my window, some of the tourist sites it recommended. Could I see, for example, the site of the Old Tyme Tractor Show at Hillsboro, or the Two-Story Train Depot Museum at Greenup, or Taylorville where Kay the Circus Elephant is buried—only the second elephant, as my brochure winningly told me, to die in Illinois?

But a veil of cloud and mist lay low over the prairie, and if these varied marvels were ever visible from the Hilton, I could not see them that day. On the other hand I could make out, close beneath the lee of the skyscraper, a little cluster of clapboard houses which was identified on my map as "Mr. Lincoln's Neighborhood." I hastened there at once—down my 20 floors on the elevator, past the municipal parking garage on 7th Street and the First Presbyterian Church on the corner, turned left and lo! all my supercilious feelings about Springfield and its prairies evaporated.

The streets might be empty, the mist lay low, the restaurants were deserted, the doors of the First Presbyterian Church were locked, but there before me stood one of the best-known and best-beloved houses in all America at 8th and Jackson Street, Springfield, Illinois, the only house that Abraham Lincoln, Esquire, ever owned in his life. Oh Captain, my Captain! O sweetest wisest soul! From that moment on I saw Springfield through new eyes, and every symptom of its prairie origins, every dismal wisecrack I pretended to laugh at, the very silhouette of the Springfield Hilton Hotel, looming apparently lifeless above me, I saw as emblems or products or origins of the Gettysburg Address.

Of course Springfield never lets you forget that Lincoln was the most famous of all its citizens. There are Abe Lincoln markers all over the place, an Abe Lincoln Garage; an Abe Lincoln hair-dresser; Lincoln's tomb, of course; Lincoln's law office; the railway station where Lincoln set off for the Presidency in Washington, D.C. For me, though, skeptic that I was about the attractions of prairie culture, what made the place so marvelous was the fact that out of an environment so fustian, so fascinating a hero should have emerged. Like it or not, when we consider Springfield and all it represents, we must remember that for 25 years Abraham Lincoln was part of it.

I bumped once again, for instance, into that man from the train, who did indeed turn out to be a lawyer, and I realized now that he was just the kind of man Lincoln might have had as a partner long ago. I thought again about that philosopher of the station yard, and easily imagined the two of them outdoing each other in prairie anecdote. At the Caffe Capitol one day I introduced myself to the assembled Poetry Society of Springfield, a very hospitable crew, and could easily imagine old Abe, holding an awful ode of his own, unfolding his lanky limbs to greet me. In Downtown News & Books I swear I saw him dropping in for the day's *State Journal Register* (which has his portrait at its masthead).

A day or two later several hundred adolescents, attendants at some kind of church convention, unleashed themselves upon the Springfield

The possession of land is the aim of all action, generally speaking, and the cure for all social evils, among men in the United States. If a man is disappointed in politics or love—he goes and buys land. If he disgraces himself he takes himself to a lot in the West. If the demand for any article of manufacture slackens, the operatives drop into the unsettled lands. If a citizen's neighbors rise above him in the towns, he takes himself where he can be monarch of all he surveys.

◆

—Abraham Lincoln,
speech in Springfield, Illinois
(January 26, 1838)

Hilton, monopolizing the elevators, sitting in corridors eating pizzas, laughing and shouting and ringing random telephones in the small hours. But even as I swore at them and resolved to claim my money back from the management in the morning, it occurred to me that young Abe, visiting the big city from his log cabin home down the Sangamo River, might perhaps have let off his American high spirits in rather the same way....

I will be frank with you. I was not altogether at a loose end when I went to Springfield. Actually I went there because I was having trouble with Lincoln. Somehow I could not reconcile his historical presence with the United States that he, more than any- one, bequeathed to us. His gentle character seemed incompatible with the style of modern America, or for that matter with the style of the prairie society he sprang from. The more I read about him, the more I saw of the United States today, the more it seemed to me that he must have been some kind of historical freak, one of those prodigies who appear to have no connection with their own origins, but are flung into the world at God's whim.

My few days in Springfield taught me otherwise. Late one night I went wandering around Mr. Lincoln's neighborhood all by my- self. So inescapable is his presence still, even in the imagination, that over the years countless people have reported seeing his ghost down on 8th Street. I cannot claim a similar experience—the whole neighborhood has been prettified, sanitized, and made suit- able for tour group experiences by the National Park Service— but I did most powerfully sense his influence lingering there. And when I pottered somewhat aimlessly toward Capitol Avenue, just around the corner I looked up and saw, magnificently floodlit, the not very beautiful dome of the Illinois State Capitol, which is said to be considerably higher than—oh, but I told you that before.

I was greatly stirred, despite myself. Lincoln never even set eyes upon that structure (it went up after his time), but for all the shenanigans that, I do not doubt, go on inside it—for all the rogues and scoundrels who have been, at one time and another, elected to its membership—for all the corruptions that it has witnessed, and the conspiracies that it has fostered—still as I looked at it, that night in Springfield, I remembered that out of that very milieu, his genius recognized if not cherished by those very people, Honest Abe went off to Washington and the possession of the ages.

I returned to Chicago again myself on the *Ann Rutledge*: which is named, by the way, for Mr. Lincoln's original girlfriend, probably one of those screaming harpies who kept me so furiously awake all night in Room 2212.

Welsh essayist Jan Morris is currently writing a book about Abraham Lincoln. She is the author of more than 30 books, her most recent being Fifty Years of Europe.

★

The summer heat of Washington held, and again President Truman was alone in the great white jail, as he had begun calling the White House. Some of the servants had been telling him how the ghost of Abraham Lincoln had appeared over the years. Truman became convinced the house was haunted:

> Night before last [he reported to Bess] I went to bed at nine o'clock after shutting my doors. At four o'clock I was awakened by three distinct knocks on my bedroom door. I jumped up and put on my bathrobe, opened the door, and no one was there. Went out and looked up and down the hall, looked into your room and Margie's. Still no one. Went back to bed after locking the doors and there were footsteps in your room whose door I'd left open. Jumped up and looked and no one there! Damn place is haunted sure as shootin'. Secret service said not even a watchman was up here at that hour.

—David McCullough, *Truman*

MICHAEL RAY TAYLOR

* * *

Tight Spot

It's a struggle to get beneath
the surface of America.

WHENEVER I FIND MYSELF TALKING ABOUT CAVING WITH A GROUP of strangers, a question that always comes up is "Don't you ever get claustrophobia?" I generally answer that the human body can fit into some fairly small places, and in caves small places often lead to big ones. Wriggling through a squeeze is part of the total experience, I say. Successful cavers think of the goal beyond. They've learned to calmly ignore the panic that might otherwise set in when one is compressed between tons of rock. No, I tell people, I don't feel the least bit claustrophobic underground.

Of course, I'm lying. Squeezes scare the hell out of me. (*Squeeze*: any crawlway whose passage requires the removal of gear, clothing, or skin.) Some of the less pleasant squeezes I recall include the Agony, the Back Scratcher, the Claustrophobia Crawl, the Gun Barrel, the Eighteen-Hour Girdle, the Crisco Crack, and, of course, the Grim Crawl of Death. All involved a few anxious moments. But the only time I've ever known—and been forced to overcome—true subterranean panic was at a small, allegedly easy place called the Devil's Pinch, deep beneath the limestone hills of West Virginia.

The Devil's Pinch connects two very different caves named

Bone and Norman. Norman's damp ceiling bristles with calcite formations in a dozen hues of ocher and umber. The mazelike tunnels of Bone are colored a uniform pale gray. Beads of water glisten on Norman's walls, and dripping stalactites dig tiny craters in the mud-slick floor. Bone stays dry as a you-know-what. A river runs through Norman, filling blue pools and chirping happily over small rapids. Its course has determined the twists and turns of the arched corridor that forms Norman's central trunk. Bone's floors are covered with a loose powder similar in color and consistency to the stuff Apollo astronauts once kicked up on the moon.

The only thing these two caves have in common is a chance connection at the Devil's Pinch, an undulating tube about three body lengths long, a yard wide, and seven to ten inches high. It's the height that gets you. That and the sloping floor, and a ceiling lined with knifelike ridges that can dig at your chest like an excited cardiologist. Hence its name.

After Bone and Norman became a single cave, Bone-Norman, by virtue of the connection, it became popular among West Virginia cavers to take recreational through-trips, entering at one and exiting through the other. An experienced team that knows the route can pretty well see both caves in four hours. When my longtime caving partner Lee Pearson and I found ourselves in West Virginia with an afternoon to kill, we decided to try the through-trip ourselves.

Our guide was Miles Drake, a wiry and powerful Washington, D.C. window washer whose underground prowess is something of a legend in caving circles. I had met him two years before while exploring vertical pits in the Cockpit Country of western Jamaica, and found him to be—like so many of the best American cavers—a competent climber, obsessive about his gear, and more than a little eccentric. Along with the three of us were three novices, new members of the D.C. caving club to which Miles belonged.

It had been a few years since Miles had been through the Devil's Pinch. He couldn't quite remember which of Bone Cave's myriad stoopways and belly crawls led to the connection. He knew we had to crawl "about fifty feet" to a steeply sloping chamber, at the bottom of which would be the Devil's Pinch.

Normally, you expect to spend some time finding the proper route in a rambling cave like Bone. You expect whoever's leading to occasionally say things like "Okay, that rock is familiar. We turn left at that hole underneath and it should open into a stoopway." You expect the hole to lead nowhere, and the guide to say things like "Well, it's a rock just like that one, only now that I think about it, it should be on the right. Yeah, that's it. Check the *right* wall." Getting a little bit lost is part of the total experience.

While Lee and I weren't exactly happy after crawling 500 feet down five different "this is the one" holes, we weren't exactly discouraged either. We were underground, among friends, and seeing a cave that we had never seen before. The novices, however, were not so generous. Two in particular, women I'll call Fran and Hannah, were not entirely comfortable spending an hour on their hands and knees, lost, squirming

There is no way to describe the mixed feelings of hopelessness, fear, and anger when a man realizes he is lost. Finding the way out is uncertain at best, and there is a sickening realization that your civilized skills are useless. The physical discomfort is exacerbated, at least, by the potential embarrassment of impending search parties and publicity. You imagine the headlines: JIMMY CARTER LOST IN THE WOODS. At worst, there is the vision of a dead, frozen body lying in the swamp. Rational thought is difficult. For some reason, you want to crash frantically ahead even though the right direction is unknown.

◆

—Jimmy Carter, *An Outdoor Journal: Adventures and Reflections*

through dust that filled their boots, powdered their hair, and sifted its way through their underwear.

They were making increasingly loud noises about heading back for the entrance—if Miles could find it—when suddenly we emerged into a steeply sloping chamber above a rocky crawl that had to be the Devil's Pinch. Miles went through first. "Oh, this is it all right," he said. "You don't forget a nasty place like this." Miles was, by far, the smallest member of the group.

He made it through, then turned to coach the novices. Lee and I took up the rear. All I could see of the passage ahead was the soles of Lee's size 12 boots. I could hear Miles shouting that if Fran slid one arm forward and dragged her packs behind, she should be able to wriggle through the tightest spot without any problem. Her muttered curses made me a little nervous, but I reasoned: Hey, she's a beginner. If she makes it through, I can make it through.

In twenty minutes, both novices were standing in Norman Cave.

I'm six feet tall and weigh about 195. Lee was a few pounds lighter, but three inches taller, and big-boned. When I saw his boots push ahead, and heard him grunt and power his way to the other side, I breathed easy. He was *nearly* as big as me. "Coming through," I said.

The floor sloped downward and to the left, with a trench a few inches deep running along the left wall. Floor and ceiling were solid limestone. They hugged my chest and back, but I could push with my toes. I tossed my cumbersome helmet ahead of me in such a way that the lamp was pointing back, lighting my way.

I had forgotten to remove a backup flashlight from my shirt pocket. It dug painfully into my chest as I inched forward—but the ceiling dug into my back, and the floor sloped downward, helping me slide along. I exhaled to remove the friction from my rib cage, and slid through.

With a short hands-and-knees scramble, I was standing in Norman with my companions, in a comfortable tunnel the size of an airplane hangar. "Thank God I don't have to try that bastard uphill," I said. That was when I realized something was wrong. Fran breathed so heavily she had nearly hyperventilated. Hannah was in tears. Miles, Lee, and the other novice, a man who had barely spoken all day, stood looking discouraged. We had been underground perhaps three hours. Clearly, the extensive crawling and the uncomfortable pinch were more than Hannah and Fran had bargained for. They were ready to go home.

Miles admitted that he had forgotten just how much crawling was involved in Bone. He apologized for leading inexperienced novices through such an unpleasant place. "But look at the bright side," he said. "It's all walking passage from here. We'll be out in an hour or two."

"Do you know the way?" asked Hannah, her tears subsiding.

"I'm sure I can find it."

Poor choice of words. Hannah and Fran started arguing that we should go back the way we knew. Lee and I argued for pressing ahead. Miles just looked embarrassed. The other novice resolved the argument by saying, "I've had enough," and scrambling back into the Devil's Pinch—uphill.

We had no choice but to follow. Again Lee and I took up the rear. This time, the others took a good hour to pass through. Their echoed groans and curses were far more pronounced. Lee and I slipped out of the crawlway and walked around in Norman, briefly enjoying the river and formations. Every few minutes, we'd hike back to see how they were doing. At last they all had made it through. I remembered to slip my flashlight into my pack, and fell in behind Lee, who quickly gained distance up the crawl.

By dragging one arm and reaching forward with the other, I narrowed my shoulders, but lost one hand for pulling. While pushing with my toes had worked coming in, I made little progress against the slope. I would move forward and feel the ceiling press me into the blades beneath my chest. A knifelike fin of rock that ran from below my left foot to somewhere well beyond my left shoulder seemed far more pronounced than it had coming in. And the trench that had helped me earlier was now in my way.

I pushed with my toes, slid forward another inch, and felt the ceiling press me that much more into the knife. I could see Lee reclining comfortably in the passage ten feet ahead, waiting for me. Another yard and I'd be through the worst. But I couldn't move.

I felt panic rising and paused to breathe deeply—but I was in too far. As I inhaled, my ribs swelled against the constriction and stopped. I could take only half breaths, could move forward only when I exhaled. What if I exhaled too much? What if I reached a point where I couldn't inhale at all?

I closed my eyes, lay my face on the cool rock, and fought the idea. Even if I passed out, Lee could pull me through from the other side. But what if my coveralls snagged, trapping me where I couldn't breathe?

I decided to take off my coveralls. I used my right hand—the one I could see—to slowly push myself back down the inches I had gained. Exhale, move, pause, inhale. Exhale, move, pause, inhale. At last I stood and stripped off my coveralls, wadded the coveralls into a ball, shoved them ahead of me with my helmet, and lay down on the bedrock in my boots and Fruit of the Looms.

The limestone blade—a mere irritant before—now tore at my bare chest, not deeply, but enough to open the skin. But with a few more millimeters of room, I moved uphill a bit more easily. Soon I was to the point where I had turned back. I called Lee toward me, and tossed him my coveralls and helmet. After he moved them out of the way, I asked Lee to slide in close enough to grab my arm.

"Pull when I tell you to," I said. I took four slow half breaths, then tried to relax fully as I exhaled, "Pullll." I moved forward six inches, tried to inhale, and could not.

My heart beat in my ears. I made no sound, hoarding the scant oxygen left in my lungs. I had a sudden vision of black lake water closing over my head—the time at age eight I jumped off the old wooden high dive at my uncle's lake in Illinois. The water had stretched on forever as I kicked my way toward distant summer light. There in the Devil's Pinch I remembered the

> *N*ature is excessively fond of drapery in America. I have never yet fallen in with a naked rock.
>
> ♦
>
> —Capt. Frederick Marryat,
> *A Diary of America* (1839)

panic, the kicking, and suddenly gulping heavy air. By the time I swam back to the dock, I had pushed the moment of fear to the back of my mind, and dove again, and again. By the end of the day, I had forgotten the black water that had tried to hold me down. Until now.

My arm felt as if Lee were yanking it out of its socket. I desperately dug both toes into the rock and pushed. The knife scraped my chest once more, I slid forward an inch, and I could breathe again. My ribs were free of the Devil's Pinch. I gasped at Lee to let go of my arm. I closed my eyes and lay again on the bare rock, waiting for my breathing to return to normal. I worked the pinch from belly to hips to thighs, and I was out.

"Well, that wasn't much fun," I said to Lee. "But it was better than law school."

A native of Ormond Beach, Florida, Michael Ray Taylor holds graduate writing degrees from the University of South Carolina and the University of Arkansas. He has written for Outside, Audubon, Sports Illustrated, *and has led expeditions for the National Geographic Society, the Smithsonian Institution, and the National Speological Society. Currently an assistant professor of journalism at Henderson State University, he lives with his family in Arkadelphia, Arkansas.* Cave Passages: Roaming the Underground Wilderness, *from which this story was excerpted, is his first book.*

✳

All summer long Grandpa remains in the basement, two pounds of cremated ash in a plain cardboard cylinder. I can't get used to the idea of this odorless beige powder as the guy who taught me how to land brook trout with a hand-tied fly, the son of a Montana mineral chaser, the teller of campfire tales about hiding from the Jesuits with his schoolboy chum, a jug-eared kid named Bing Crosby. He had smoked himself to death, and near the end Grandpa couldn't even take a pee without falling down and gasping for breath. He'd be lying on the bathroom floor of his house in Seattle, a plastic-tipped cigar clenched between his teeth, all that loose skin draped over a shrinking body. Fifty years of two packs a day, that's what did it. Finally, the emphysema literally asphyxiated him. He was as old as the twentieth century when he died.

My job is to bury him. Something appropriate, my Granny says, handing me the cylinder after the funeral. "Just throw him off the ferry or dump him into the Yakima River," she says. "Whatever you think is best."

—Timothy Egan, *The Good Rain: Across Time
and Terrain in the Pacific Northwest*

ADAM NICOLSON

⋆ ⋆ ⋆

Mall Walking

Walk a mile in another man's
shoes—and then buy them.

ALWAYS HAVE A GUIDE IN THE U.S.; IT'S A MUCH MORE FOREIGN place than you think. In this expedition to the new heart of the New World (there are now more shopping malls in the States than either post offices or secondary schools), I was lucky enough to have with me Doug Stumpf, the immensely handsome and brilliant young editor at William Morrow, the New York publisher. He made only one condition in return for abandoning his desk: that I should describe him as "the immensely handsome and brilliant young…"

At six-thirty on a sunny spring morning I met up with Doug outside his apartment far up on the upper west side of Manhattan. His car, for the second time in two weeks, had had a window smashed in overnight, by crack addicts, he said, looking for anything they might use or sell. So it was a windy drive out into Connecticut, which was looking new and beautiful, the drifts of white and pink dogwood, the colours of ice cream, flowering among the new green of the leaves.

Past Greenwich and Stamford, in the unhurried courtesy of American traffic, we drove out to the small, middle-class dormitory town of Trumbull, and more particularly to Trumbull

Shopping Park: not merely a shopping centre, more like a haven from the world.

The mall resembles an airport terminal building, a cluster of blocky, windowless shapes, covering about 15 acres, surrounded by a 55-acre sea of car-parking. The building makes no effort to be beautiful outside. The outside does not matter. This, first and last, is an interior space, a climate-controlled cocoon, where the occupants turn away from the world outside towards a neat and un-frightening vacuum, where trees are somehow persuaded to grow, where birds in bird shops sing in their cages, and where people go for long walks in the most comforting landscape they know.

In through the double doors, to the world of de-nature. It was eight o'clock in the morning, well before opening time. The mall is on two levels, connected by escalators, with a large department store at each of its three corners and about 200 boutique-style shops filling the spaces between them.

Inside the avenues of the mall, the light was neither bright nor dim, the air not cool nor warm, the fittings neither plush nor tawdry, the place neither crowded nor empty, but gently animated by the slow, plasticated pad-padding of the mall-walkers, old people in loose walking suits perambulating along the seamless tiling of the floor. The mall is unobjectionability itself, perfect pap.

Doug and I had an appointment to meet the manager of the mall who could tell us about Trumbull's role in the new phe-nomenon of mall-walking, but he had decided not to come for the day. We met his assistant, Ann Marie Sultzbach, and the di-rector of security, a super-groomed ex-FBI man called William B. DiFederico, who had a moustache that stood out at an angle from his upper lip and chains hanging from his waistcoat pockets.

This was a perfect environment, he said, for those with heart or respiratory conditions. It was far better than the streets of Trumbull itself, which were impossible for peace of mind. It was safe here, and even if Trumbull wasn't exactly the most crime-ridden place in the U.S., there was a perceived threat. It never got too hot or cold here; it was relatively social. There weren't any ups and downs. It was more fun than the treadmill.

I thought he was joking, but no. Doug explained how the instrument of self-improvement at the moment is the high-tech treadmill, probably the purest form of walking one can imagine, walking for its own sake, the mileage clocking up on a dial in front of you, without the bother of going anywhere.

DiFederico had 235 registered mall-walkers on his books, all of whom had signed a release to say that it would not be the mall's fault if they dropped down dead. No one yet had, but he had to be careful. DiFederico saw something beautiful in mall-walking. "This mall has got a rhythm to it," he said. "You can go round and round and round. The corridors are beautiful. This is where people can get happy. Many people come to do it here every day, religiously. And if they want to do it, may God bless them."

I approached a couple sitting down in the Food Court, eating Dunkin' Donuts. Robert and Mildred Giannini (he an ex-school principal, she an ex-lab technician) bore the safety factor in mind. They read about muggings in the papers. There was the curse of drugs on the streets. "We are being cautious in the backs of our minds," Robert said. The Gianninis confessed that there was no talking whatsoever during the walk itself. It was a serious four miles every day. It was a job that had to be done.

Another group was more promising—men only, chatting and giggling. And here we chanced on the hero of the Trumbull Shopping Park. Vincent Testani is famous. Articles have been written about him in newspapers. DiFederico had mentioned him. He is 70, is a great one for the girls, still talks English with a monstrous Italian accent, despite having been here since 1937 ("because I don't pay any attention"), and walks and runs between twelve and thirteen miles every day around the mall. This was the real thing. Could I go for a walk with him around the corridors? "Of course, of course!"

It wasn't a walk; it was an obsession. Vinnie, as he's known, skipped up the escalators in a gym instructor way and immediately homed in on the corridor walls like a cruise missile, flicking his torso in and out of every nick and indentation of the shopfronts. "You have to keep to the edge, otherwise you don't get the yardage," he explained. Past I Can't Believe It's Yoghurt, Vinnie broke into a stiff-torsoed trot, grinning up at me to show, yes, he could trot too. Quicker and quicker, Diet Swirl, Maison du Popcorn, Vinnie's tense old little body, flicking out the familiar path.

A female missile came the other way. The two of them dodged niftily apart at the meeting only to return to the comfort of the measured wallside path. Quick, quick, he knew every tile, Denby's Tobacco Barrel, Doktor Pet, as I jogged parallel to him in the easy middle of the mall corridor, bemused by the distortions to which this man had subjected all the graces and pleasures of walking.

Quick, quick, Complete Athlete, quick Cosmetics a la Carte. Vinnie grinned as he skipped sideways, first one way, then the next, his chest held out, his arms almost motionless at his side. "There are no holes in the path here. I cannot trip," he explained.

Back to the escalators and down to the lower level. Fredelle, Naturalizer, Underground, every shop the same. Personally Yours, Mr. Store, Body Accents, Vinnie's grin was clamped shut. "I am going to Norwalk, Connecticut," he said through it, "to visit a young lady, very nice. You?" "I must go back to Manhattan," I said.

We reached the Food Court again. Doug had been sitting there patiently while Vinnie demonstrated his prowess to me. We thanked Vincent and his friends for their time and instruction and walked out of the place, into the slightly windy real air where a slight and real sun shone on the tarmac, and where Doug's car was waiting with its broken windows to take us back to the city.

Adam Nicolson is the author of Long Walks in England, Scotland and Wales *and* Long Walks in France. *He is the grandson of Vita Sackville-West and Harold Nicolson and the son of Nigel Nicolson. He lives in Cambridge, England.*

✳

It was in 1956 that the first enclosed shopping center, Southdale, opened in Edina, a suburb of Minneapolis.

But the biggest mall event of 1996 was not this happy birthday. It was instead a rude development that occurred in September at the most mega of American malls, also outside Minneapolis. The Mall of

America—4.3 million square feet of retailing—joined less fabled peers in declaring a curfew for teenagers on weekend nights in an effort to curb juvenile violence.

It was also this fall that a bank robbery and fatal shootout at Tysons Corners Center in suburban Washington prompted a *Washington Post* reporter, Doug Struck, to investigate crime at other area malls. When he inquired about the level of criminal activity at the Annapolis Mall, he was told "zero"—only to discover that police records showed scores of crimes there in the past two years, many of them violent. Though mall crime is sometimes too glaring to escape the local 11 o'clock news—remember the outbreak of shooting and stabbing at Long Island's Green Acres Mall two years ago?—there is, amazingly, no national collection of mall crime statistics.

What does it say that a country so obsessed with "inner-city" pathologies spends so little time examining its outer cities, the malls? Chalk it up to the great America religion: escapism. In a nation where the middle class more often gravitates to malls than to urban centers, we'd rather worry about other people's problems than our own.

In his classic 1985 history of suburbia, *Crabgrass Frontier*, the historian Kenneth T. Jackson aptly summed up the mall ideal we still want to believe in—a refuge containing "no unsavory bars or pornography shops, no threatening-looking characters, no litter, no rain, and no excessive heat or cold." Malls, which first appeared the year after Disneyland opened, were designed to be brightly lit, poverty-free theme-park versions of the darker, less savory old downtowns they would soon usurp (and helped destroy).

—Frank Rich, "The Mall Pall: Trouble in the
Outer City," *The New York Times*

SUE HUBBELL

* * *

Hey, Presto!

Is Colon, Michigan, the trickiest
town in America?

COLON, MICHIGAN, IS THE MAGIC CAPITAL OF THE WORLD. YOU know that's true because the sign at the village limits says so:

WELCOME TO

COLON

MAGIC CAPITAL OF

THE WORLD

1832 SESQUICENTENNIAL 1982

1989 CLASS D

STATE BASEBALL CHAMPIONS

Colon is a village of eleven hundred people in southwestern Michigan, in flat prairie farmland. It is a village of two-story Victorian houses and smaller, modest ones, each nestled into an ample, well-tended yard, and there are gardens big enough to grow sweet corn two blocks from the intersection of the two main roads, State Street and Blackstone Avenue. The avenue is named for Colon's most famous past resident, Harry Blackstone, the magician: Blackstone the Great, né Henry Boughton, who came there in 1926, and for whom it was home, as much as any place could be for a traveling entertainer. It has more parks than anything else, and maple trees—big, overarching ones—really do grow on Maple Street. And there is not a place in the village where you can't hear the cooing of mourning doves on a summer day.

Colon is also the home of Abbott's Magic Manufacturing Company, founded by Percy Abbott, an Australian magician, in 1934, a few years after a Blackstone–Abbott magic company, started in 1927, failed, and Blackstone and Abbott had a falling out. With a million dollars in annual sales, made mostly through a three-pound mail-order catalog, Abbott's is the biggest magic manufacturer in the world, according to the present owner, Greg Bordner. And for a time in late summer of each year since the 1930s there have been more magicians around Colon than anywhere else on earth. The occasion is the Magic Get-Together, cosponsored by Abbott's and the Colon Lions. Magicians are a clubby lot and hold other meetings, but those are usually in big cities. According to Harry Blackstone, Jr., a magician in his own right, the Get-Together is the meeting that all magicians look forward to, because of the rural setting and the air of sociability. A thousand magicians, perhaps a few more—some full-time performers, the rest part-timers and amateurs—come to Colon from around the world, and take over the village. For twenty years now, Blackstone himself has been coming back to his hometown (he went to school here for a year or two, and still owns a bit of land on what is called Blackstone Island, in Sturgeon Lake).

I grew up in Kalamazoo, about twenty-five miles to the northwest as the crow flies. I was the easiest kid in the world to fool;

> *A*mericans of all ages, all conditions, and all dispositions, constantly form associations. They have not only commercial and manufacturing companies, in which all take part, but associations of a thousand other kinds—religious, moral, serious, futile, general or restricted, enormous or diminutive.
>
> ◆
>
> —Alexis de Tocqueville,
> *Democracy in America*

for a while, I cherished the notion that I had a head full of nickels, because my father could produce them so easily from my ears. In those days, I was a pushover for the public performances held in Colon in the evenings during the Get-Togethers. I can remember the aura of those evening shows, shows that I attended forty years ago and more: the dark stage, the bright colors, flowers, floating scarves, capes in black and red, and the daring, slightly wicked quality of dying vaudeville.

This past August, I decided to pay a nostalgic visit to Colon to see what happens when a thousand magicians come to town. It was the 53rd Annual Magic Get-Together. Colon may be only twenty-five miles from Kalamazoo, but in order to get there I had to take out a map and look up which turns to take on state and county roads—a process lending substance to a conceit that Bordner and Blackstone like to maintain in interviews, that Colon is like Brigadoon, a hard-to-find place that disappears except during Get-Together time. I had known Harry Blackstone when we were both eighteen, and, seeing him recently in California, where he lives, I had asked him what growing up in Colon was like. "Shades of gray," he said, with a sigh. I knew what he meant. When I was growing up, I was under the impression that the sun vanished in October and was not seen again by humankind until May. The weather, blowing in from Lake Michigan, was bleak, cold, damp, and dark for much of the year.

On the first day of the 53rd Get-Together, however, Michigan was at its winsome best. It was a clear, sunny, high-pressure day, with blue skies and fluffy white clouds, and the corn was greening in the fields. In the village, I parked under a shady tree, because Tazzie, my dog, was with me. I walked over to the Abbott plant, a low cement-block building that would look like a radiator-repair shop if it were not painted black with white skeletons dancing across its front. I passed a knot of people on the street. "How d'ya like this?" a man was asking. He shook his wrist, and bright-red carnations bloomed from his fingertips. The members of his tiny audience nodded, smiled, and applauded. Inside the Abbott office I picked up my registration papers. I've never quite recovered from

being fooled about those nickels, so I had paid the full professional fee, seventy-five dollars, to be allowed to attend not only
the four public evening shows but also the dealers' showrooms and
the workshops, lectures, and demonstrations. In my envelope of
materials I found a plastic badge with my name on it and a cord
attached, and I hung it around my neck to separate myself from the
ordinary citizens of Colon. I peered inside the Abbott showroom.
It was a dark room with creaky wooden floors, and its walls and
ceiling were covered with magicians' posters, including one of
the senior Blackstone, backlit to emphasize his aureole of white
hair. The room was lined with glass cases that looked like old-
fashioned candy-display counters but were filled with magic
tricks, and in the center of the room an Abbott employee was
putting on a magic show, mostly for children.

It was only ten in the morning, but magicians were already arriving in town, many of them in vans and oversized campers.
Colon has no hotels, no motels, no inns. Some of the magicians
camp out in the parks, but more rent rooms or houses from the
residents. And many pairings of guest and landlord have stayed
the same over the years, giving the Get-Together a mixed quality,
of friendship and cash crop. Yard sales were springing up all over
town, and I talked to the proprietor of one. She told me she was
renting out a room to a magician couple who had been staying
with her each August for the past ten years. "When my husband
was alive, we used to rent out nearly every room in the house,
and all our outbuildings, too," she said. "Haven't done that since
he's been gone. But I've been thinking about all the campers that
come these days. I guess I'll get me a batch of Porta Potties next
year and set them up and rent out the yard."

I walked up State Street, where all the merchants had stenciled
signs in their windows that said WELCOME MAGICIANS alongside
posters for a circus that was coming to nearby Three Rivers later
in the month, and out along the creek, past the dam that makes
Palmer Lake. Beyond the dam I found the elementary school,
where many of the activities were to take place. Just inside the
school door, a uniformed security guard with a big smile was

checking every plastic badge. The school gym and a couple of classrooms were filled to overflowing with magic wares and books, in odd contrast to the little desks and sober blackboards, and magicians were busily taking over rooms for workshops, demonstrations, and sales booths.

The magicians—most of whom were men—talked magic, passed out business cards, did magic, passed out business cards, bought magic, passed out business cards, demonstrated gimmicks, passed out business cards. "Gimmick" is a magicians' word that has entered everyday language. It refers to that device or object—that invisible wire, false fingertip, hidden lever—which makes the magic possible. Magicians use other words specially. Scarves are called "silks." "Disappear" and "vanish" are transitive verbs, as in "I vanished the ball" and "He disappeared the girl." "Tricks" are small pieces of magic—the silk that turns into a dove, the cut and knotted rope that mends itself. "Illusions" are big pieces of magic. Illusions are pricey; they can cost many thousands of dollars. Abbott's has made many of them over the years, some to order: Houdini's underwater torture box; Blackstone's buzz saw; David Copperfield's straitjacket; the device that disappeared an elephant, for which Abbott's furnished everything except the elephant. One whole wall of the gym was covered with a display of books: *How to Sell by Magic*, *Nite Club Illusions*, *Conjurors' Psychological Secrets*, and so on. Heaped on shelves along another wall were Abbott's offerings: Dove Through the Glass ($135), Elusive Bunny Box ($100), Mirror Tumbler ($5), Disecto ($90), and more objects in Day-Glo colors and shiny metal than I could take in.

I was thoroughly disgusted with the life of an itinerant show-man; and though I felt that I could succeed in that line, I always regarded it, not as an end, but as a means to something better in due time.

◆

—Waldo R. Browne, *Barnum's Own Story: The Autobiography of P. T. Barnum*

Greg Bordner was standing near the Disecto, expansive, cheerful, busy. A handsome, athletic-looking man in his late thirties,
he is a political-science graduate of Michigan State, and the son of
Recil Bordner, a magician who was Percy Abbott's partner after
Abbott broke with Blackstone. Versions of the cause of the split
vary, but all agree that the two men, both strong-willed, clashed
over the financial end of the business, and that Blackstone, the bigger of the two, came over to Abbott's house one night, beat him
up, and stalked out. According to Bordner, Abbott called the police, and when they arrived Blackstone walked back in and greeted
Abbott like an old friend—"Hi, Percy, it's been a while. Good to
see you"—thus flummoxing the police. But, Bordner said,
Blackstone stayed so angry that whenever he saw Abbott in the
grocery store he would pull canned goods off the shelves and hurl
them at him. He also tried to start a rival magic show and manufacturing company, and refused to perform for the Abbott Get-
Together until 1961, when he was seventy-five. Though his skills
were failing, he came from California to perform in a sentimental
return; when he died, in 1965, his ashes were buried in the cemetery at Colon, where they lie under a stone that appears to be part
flower, part flame. According to Bordner, more magicians—
around a dozen—are buried in that cemetery, along with
Blackstone, than anywhere else in the world.

I asked Bordner about the Disecto, and, confiding that he was
only a fourth-rate magician, he got it out. It looks like a simple
wooden stand with a big hole in the center and two little holes
above and below. At the top is a sharp-looking knife that raises
and lowers like a cleaver. The cleaver slices through carrots placed
in the little holes. Bordner put his arm in the big hole and dropped
the cleaver. His hand was just fine when he pulled it out. I gasped.
I couldn't help myself. "How did you do that?"

Bordner grinned and said, "The trick's told when the trick's
sold." He invited me on a tour of his empire, and we went back to
the Abbott building. Behind the display room was a dark,
Dickensian stockroom lined with drawers bearing labels like
RABBIT WRINGER and FLOWER SURPRISE. There orders were being

filled for Sweden and Japan. We walked past a set of sinks where silks are dyed and the staff makes coffee, then went downstairs to a room where a woman was making magical silk flowers, stitching away and listening to country music on the radio. Outside again, Bordner put a big box of outgoing mail in the back seat of his Chevy ("The magic business isn't what it used to be. My father drove a Buick") and drove me over to the workshop, a nondescript blue-and-white metal building on the edge of town, next to the supermarket. Except for a preponderance of rabbits, it looked like an ordinary wood-and-metal shop. Tacked to the walls were snapshots of magician customers, including one of a Nigerian prince who once came, with an entourage, to the Get-Together. He placed a big order for illusions and had them shipped home. Bordner shook his head over the prince. "He billed himself as someone who had Powers." he said. Bordner doesn't approve of Powers; he doesn't like to associate magic with the paranormal. He made a face. "Hey, this is just a business. We manufacture tricks and illusions. I know the U.P.S. rates anywhere."

I very much wanted to buy a trick. Back at the elementary school, I asked around about the gimmick used for one of the world's oldest recorded magic tricks. In the Bible, in Exodus, we are told how Aaron so impressed Pharaoh with wonders and magic that Pharaoh let the people of Israel leave Egypt. Aaron showed Pharaoh a rod and changed it into a snake. Pharaoh called his magicians, and they also turned rods into snakes, but then Aaron caused his snake to eat up theirs. Bordner laughed when I asked him about it, and said he didn't have a trick like that. "Maybe one of the snake handlers could help you," he added. He looked around the gym-salesroom, but couldn't spot a snake handler at the moment. I moved on to another salesman, who was doing impossible things with what looked like a solid hoop of gleaming metal. It became a square, then a flat strip. "Oh, yeah, I know that trick," he said when I asked. "I got a wand that turns into a snake, but it's not a very good snake. I mean, it isn't a python or a cobra, or anything." I watched a New Age magician, Jay Scott Berry, who was dressed in black and had long, curly blond hair, produce a brilliant flash of light from his fingertip: "Uses no batteries." Then he transformed a rainbow-colored bar into gold.

"Ummm!" said a watching magician. "That's smooth."

"Ye-ahh," said Berry, changing from entertainer into salesman. "I worked a long time to get it so smooth." He was monopolizing the crowd, to the chagrin of a Japanese magician at the next booth, who smiled bravely as he plucked fire from the air and lit a fire in the palm of first one hand, then the other.

I settled for a trick called the Amazing Keybender ("Yes, you can bend keys and spoons"), which I bought from Abbott's for five dollars. It is a small, simple gimmick, and comes with three pages of directions which include the plea "All we ask is that you do not claim to have supernatural powers," and adds archly, "One doing that is enough"—a prim reference to Uri Geller. I practiced the trick at home after the Get-Together, but no one applauded. "What do you have up your sleeve?" my stepson asked at my first and only family performance. That brings me to the basic secret of magic: the gimmicks are simple, but the tricks are hard, and require im-

Burning Man [an annual gathering in the Nevada desert] is an art gig by tradition. Over the longer term it's evolved into something else; maybe something like a physical version of the Internet. The art here is like fan art. It's very throwaway, very appropriated, very cut-and-paste. The camp is like a giant swap meet where no one sells stuff, but people trade postures, clip art, and attitude.

People come here in clumps: performance people, drumming enthusiasts, site-specific sculptors, sail-plane people, ravers, journalists, cops. I'm a journalist and a newbie, but even I can tell the pros from my fellow newbies. The veterans have brought their own pennants, bicycles, flashlights, and tiki torches, plus enough water for anything.

◆

—Bruce Sterling, "Greetings From Burning Man," *Wired*

pressive skills and dexterity, and a keen sense of psychology for misdirecting the audience's attention. Every evening during the Get-Together, there was a public show, and during the day spontaneous shows never stopped: a thousand magicians showing off to a thousand magicians, receiving and giving applause and appreciation. They all knew the gimmicks. What they were applauding was the skill in their use, the quick hands and sly diversions, the breaking apart of cause and effect, forcing the senses to trick the brain.

Colon grows weirder and weirder. Everywhere magicians' vans are parked. Magicians nap in folding chairs. Magicians sell magic to one another. Magicians sit on curbs and throw their voices, so that trash cans begin to twitter like birds. At the counter of the M & M Grill, a stocky man in glasses hits his hand on the counter—*whack? whack?*—disappearing fuzzy balls every time. His companion nods appreciatively while he eats his cheeseburger. There would be applause from the booth behind them, except that one of the six magicians sitting there has the attention of the rest, asking them to pick a card from the fan of cards he holds in his hand. Jugglers fill the parks. I talk to a young juggler named Steve. "I do magic, too, but I prefer juggling," he says. "There are lots of jugglers around these days, because we had parents who were hippies who took up juggling; it was supposed to represent psychic balance, or something. We don't go in for that stuff, but we learned how to juggle from them. I'd like to get a job on a cruise ship or work in a theme park." Theme-park magicians, I learn at an afternoon workshop, are paid seven hundred dollars a week, and must do five shows a day, six days a week. Cruise ships pay from four hundred dollars a week to eighteen hundred; the occupational hazard is weight gain from good food.

Waiting for the evening performance, in the high-school auditorium, I take Tazzie out for a romp in the meadow behind the high school. She leaps from the car and begins running joyous circles around a young, sinister-looking man with punked hair dyed flat black, who is wearing black pants, slightly pegged, and a black shirt—the preferred dress of young magicians. With him is a savage-looking girl with purple makeup and a mane of black hair, who is wearing a black leather miniskirt. They squat down and scratch Tazzie on the belly, transforming themselves into teenagers. A clown is working out on a unicycle in the school-bus parking lot. Tazzie finds gopher holes to dig out, and I lie down in the clover, listening to the doves and the katydids. Overhead, swallows circle and swoop. How do they do that?

Later, inside the auditorium, women in sequined gowns float in the air. One, to the amusement of the audience, refuses to be sawed in two and forces the magician to take her place inside the specially designed box. Ropes cut and heal themselves, and knots in them slide and disappear. Needles are stuck into balloons with-out popping them. Coins multiply. Cards are chosen and told. Silks appear from nowhere. A thousand magicians and six or seven hundred other spectators cheer and applaud under a banner cele-brating the Class D Baseball Championship. (The team is called the Magi; its mascot is a white rabbit coming out of a hat.) The seats are hard and cramped, the sound system crackles and occasionally fails, but the performances are slick, smooth, very Big Time, paced for television. Last year's young-talent-contest winner has been invited back for a segment of an evening show: he presents a display of leggy girls, dancing, and other flourishes that looks as though he had MTV in mind. Other magicians use backdrops with their names in flashing lights and work to a rock-and-roll beat. Blackstone's segment is filmed for a TV show to be broadcast next spring. Magicians from Switzerland and Czechoslovakia are featured, calmer and wittier than the Americans, who are from a vaudeville tradition. A contingent of Indians comes into the audi-torium, the women dressed in saris. I ask a gray-haired matron with an empty seat beside her if it is taken. "It's my husband," she says. "I vanished him."

One morning, I dropped in on the Vent-O-Rama. Ventriloquists call themselves "vents," and the Vent-O-Rama is a workshop for them. Ventriloquism has long been a part of the Get-Together. Edgar Bergen was born in nearby Dowagiac, and sometimes attended the Get-Together with Charlie McCarthy and Mortimer Snerd. "The *Pythonists* spake hollowe; as in the bottome of their bellies, whereby they are aptlie in Latine called *Ventriloqui*," Reginald Scot wrote, in 1584, in *The Discoverie of Witchcraft*, which is said to be the oldest surviving text on magic tricks. Not only does Scot discuss ventriloquism; he says that if one is not a "sluggard," a "niggard," or a "dizzard," one can learn to perform "Magicke," and proceeds to give detailed directions. While reading that 400-year-old handbook, I was pleased to note that my father had been no dizzard: his nickel-from-the-ear trick is detailed by Scot under the heading "Of conveiance on monie." It is done by "palming," the word that magicians use to describe the way to hold a coin, card, or other small object hidden between the fingers or on the back or front of an apparently empty hand. You and I don't have muscles trained to do that, but they do. ("This is hard," said Doug Anderson at an afternoon workshop, as he demonstrated how to make a coin appear to jump straight up from his motionless hand. "It was painful to learn how to squeeze my palm muscles. Broke some blood vessels, too.")

Scot's may be the oldest handbook of magic tricks, but conjuring, or trickster magic, has an even older history. Aaron and the Egyptian magicians with their wand-snakes were not the only ones in antiquity to use gimmicks. (Aaron's most famous trick, making a rod bloom with flowers—by which he established the preeminence of the tribe of his brother, Moses, over the eleven other tribes of Israel—can be found in the Abbott mail-order catalog: the Flower Wand, under "Flowers that bloom with a spring, tra la!" for four dollars.) What is thought to be the first self-moving vehicle

> *I*n desperation, Harry set up "Professor Harry Houdini's School of Magic." "Do you want to learn an act?" inquired the flyer. "If you want to go on the Stage, travel with a Circus, play Variety theatres or Museums, you must first learn to do something to attract Attention."
>
> ◆
>
> —Ruth Brandon, *The Life and Many Deaths of Harry Houdini*

was designed by Hero of Alexandria, an engineer who flourished around the beginning of the first millennium. It was used to make gods and goddesses move upon their altars, revolve, and produce milk and wine as if by miracle. Egypt, Greece, Persia, Rome, China, and India all had magicians, and some of their tricks—Cups and Balls and the Hindu Rope Trick, to name two—are part of modern magicians' stock-in-trade.

The morning I was at the Vent-O-Rama, the principal vent had a cold and a sore throat, so he asked the vents perched on tables and chairs around the classroom to volunteer. Almost before the words were out of his mouth, a young woman with red hair called out "Me…me…me!" and ran to the front of the room with two oversized stuffed toys. (Magicians are not shy. Boffo routine in the evening show: the MC says, "Tonight, we have the world's greatest magician with us. Will he stand up, please?" A thousand magicians leap to their feet, and everyone applauds.) I watched the red-haired ventriloquist as her stuffed toys carried on a lunatic conversation with her. Her mouth didn't move; her throat muscles didn't even quiver. How does she do it? When she returned to her seat, amid applause, to give way to the next performer, she regained our attention momentarily, and received some appreciative chuckles, by throwing her voice to the front of the room.

In the village, the good people of Colon were busily turning goods and services into dollar bills. In the general store, a troupe of young magicians was buying cotton balls. "Gonna have a new opening tonight," one of the women said. And, sure enough, that evening I saw those mundane cotton balls deftly appear and disappear between outstretched fingers.

I talked to Bob Kolb, the owner of Magic City Hardware, who is active in the Chamber of Commerce.

"You bet the Get-Together is good for the economy," he told me. "People rent out their houses. Some people even leave town for vacation and turn their houses over to the magicians. There are some real little houses here, and I've seen maybe ten magicians in a single one of them. Then, there are the fund-raisers. The Lutherans put on a big lunch, and the magicians like it, because

they don't charge big-city prices. I sell the magicians nuts and
bolts to fix their campers, and some big-ticket items, too. And
then there are the merchants' sidewalks sales—how am I going to
put this? We all have some stock…Now, it isn't bad merchandise,
it's just that folks in Colon haven't bought it all year. These magicians come from all over—California, New York, Canada—and
their tastes are, um, different, so we sell it to them. We unload a
lot of stuff that way."

Craft sales began to appear among the yard sales. Soon it
seemed that every third house had something for sale: wrought-
iron trivets, odd dinner plates, hand-painted ceramics, little
wooden benches, children's outgrown clothes, plastic purses.
Curbside-parked cars had FOR SALE signs in their windows.
Amish had driven in from farms in their buggies and were racing
around town to snap up the best bargains before the magicians
could get to them.

Having attended the Vent-O-Rama, I had missed the magicians'
buffet lunch at the Lutheran church, a handsome, new, sprawling
building on the outskirts of the village, right next to the
Enchanted Glen Apartments. Instead, I went over to the Grange
Hall, on Blackstone Avenue, for the Pig Roast. Inside the hall
were long tables covered with oilcloth. A motherly-looking
woman served me barbecue, baked beans, two homemade molasses
cookies, and a cup of iced tea, for three dollars and ten cents. This
was a fund-raiser. It was the first time the Grange had put one on,
she told me. "Some years back, the Lutherans used to serve dinner
every evening during the Get-Together. That's the way they raised
the money to build the church." The church that magic built.

After a whole day of magic and a three-hour evening performance, the magicians, their attention sharpened, tingling from
their own applause, are high on magic, and reluctant to end the
day. When the tourists (some three thousand of them paid to see
the public shows during the week) have driven away, the magicians
return to the Abbott showrooms for auctions of magic equipment,
or they go over to the American Legion Hall, on State Street. I
drop in at the hall about midnight. It is stuffed with magicians

drinking beer, eating fries, laughing, and showing off. A t-shirted magician moves from table to table performing what I have learned to call closeup magic. He is applauded as he moves a safety pin from one corner of a square of red flannel to another without unpinning it. I find a place at a table with a group recalling their days on the road.

"D'you remember the night at the motel when we took the ice out of the ice machine and stuffed Ed inside?"

"Yeah, remember the look on the face of that little old lady when she opened the machine door and he handed her a bucket-ful of ice?"

"Hey, how about the time in the hotel in Kentucky when we took the furniture out of our room and put it in the elevator, so that it looked like a sitting room, and rode up and down in it reading newspapers and watching the faces of the guests when the door opened for them?"

"Where was it that we filled up the motel swimming pool with Knox gelatin?"

The laughter grows louder; the air is thick with cigarette smoke, magic, and fellowship. At 2:00 a.m., the American Legion will close its doors and force the magicians out onto the street. They tell me about the young Doug Henning, seventeen or eighteen years old and unknown, who wandered around town one night after the hall closed until he found a twenty-four hour Laundromat, the only public building with lights still on, and did magic tricks for his friends until dawn. His later fame has assured that it will forever be known as the Doug Henning Laundromat. Some years ago, they tell me, there was still enough of a crowd on the streets at 3:00 a.m. to respond to the request "Pick a card any card." And, just as someone in the small audience did so, and looked expectantly at the magician to identify it, a heavyset man lurched toward the spectators, stumbled on the curb, and fell. Several men reached out to help him up, and as he regained his feet his pants slithered to his ankles to reveal baggy undershorts with the card printed large upon them.

As the week progresses, there is far more magic on and off the streets of Colon than I can take in. The wild mourning doves are reproduced onstage in the white doves that flutter from silks, flowers, hats. A man balances 135 cigar boxes on the end of his chin. Wands shoot confetti, and it settles in our hair. White bunnies are everywhere. Street musicians play. A lank-haired man in a polo shirt walks down State Street tossing up balls, and they vanish high in the air. "Hey, I like it. I like it," his companion says, slapping his knee. One evening, Harry Blackstone recreates one of his father's most famous performances. Taking a lighted lamp, with a stagily long electric cord, offered to him by his assistant—his wife, Gay—he removes the bulb. On the dim stage, the bulb remains shining eerily in his hand. He then apparently releases it, and it hovers dreamily about him in the darkness. He sends it, glowing, down to the front rows of the audience, where he invites spectators to touch it and reassure themselves of its substance. When a doubter farther back in the auditorium calls out, Blackstone says, with a smile, that he will send the bulb out to him. Luminous, spectral, the bulb—a mere light bulb, made lovely and strange by behaving in a way that no mundane light bulb should—drifts gently out over the audience and then soars back to its master, who returns it to the lamp. And I understand that I have never really seen a light bulb before.

---

*A*n oft cited but undoubtedly epiphanic moment occurred while visiting mining sites in the Sierra Nevada and Rocky Mountains during his western tour. Overlooking the mighty Platte River, witnessing the laborious process of drilling ore by hand, Edison turned to his colleague, Professor Barker (or "Barky," as he was fond of calling him) and exclaimed abstractedly, "Why cannot the power of yonder river be transmitted to these men by electricity?"

◆

—Neil Baldwin, *Edison: Inventing the Century*

One hot afternoon, I take Tazzie down past the dam to a little creek that runs from it. Tazzie wades into the water while I sit on the grassy bank and watch a pair of tiger swallowtails circle in the air above me. A pretty little girl with curly chestnut-colored hair comes walking down the bank from one of the houses nearby. "What's your dog's name?" she asks.

"Tazzie. What's your name?"

"Jessie. You know what?"

"What?"

"I'm four years old. Can Tazzie do tricks?"

"Not really. She likes to take rocks out of the water, though." I point to Tazzie, hard at work loosening from the bottom of the stream a rock much too big for her.

"Well, I can do a trick."

"You can?"

"Yes, I can put my head under water." And—hey, presto!—she does. Carefully pinching her nostrils, Jessie puts at least half an inch of her face into the water and very quickly pulls it out. She looks at me, expectant, proud. I applaud.

Sue Hubbell was born in Kalamazoo, Michigan. She splits her time between the Ozarks of southern Missouri, where she keeps bees, and Washington, D.C., where her husband works.

✷

I entered the old pink stucco house in the Vieux Carré at nine o'clock in the morning with the parcel of needed things. Turner placed the new underwear on the big Altar; prepared the couch with the snake-skin cover upon which I was to lie for three days. With the help of other members of the college of hoodoo doctors called together to initiate me, the snake skins I had brought were made into garments for me to wear. One was coiled into a high headpiece—the crown. One had loops attached to slip on my arms so that it could be worn as a shawl, and the other was made into a girdle for my loins. All places have significance. These garments were placed on the small altar in the corner. The throne of the snake. The Great One was called upon to enter the garments and dwell there.

I was made ready and at three o'clock in the afternoon, naked as I came into the world, I was stretched, face downwards, my navel to the snake skin cover, and began my three day search for the spirit that he might accept me or reject me according to his will. Three days my body must lie silent and fasting while my spirit went wherever spirits must go that seek answers never given to men as men.

I could have no food, but a pitcher of water was placed on a small table at the head of the couch, that my spirit might not waste time in search of water which should be spent in search of the Power-Giver. The spirit must have water, and if none had been provided it would wander in search of it. And evil spirits might attack it as it wandered about dangerous places. If it should be seriously injured, it might never return to me.

For sixty-nine hours I lay there. I had five psychic experiences and awoke at last with no feeling of hunger, only one of exaltation.

—Zora Neale Hurston, *Mules and Men*

∗ ∗ ∗

Washington, D.C.
for Beginners

The citizen sees his home through
the eyes of strangers.

TOURISTS HIT WASHINGTON IN TWO GREAT WAVES. IN THE springtime come the high school students, for their class trips and civics programs. They jam the fast-food restaurants; they form unruly lines outside the Capitol and the White House; they buy souvenir t-shirts. In the summer come the families—the Americans by van and station wagon, the foreigners in mammoth tour buses lumbering through the main streets.

I find myself smiling when I see the students. Some are goggle-eyed at the monuments and famous buildings. Most are flirting with each other and disobeying their teacher-chaperones. The town's spring foliage looks fresh at this time of year, and so do the kids.

I try not to notice the families, because when I do, I wince. They may later tell themselves that they had a great time in the capital, but most of them look miserable. The city is hot, they are hot, and they move around in sweating herds. The foreign tourists (you can pick them out instantly by their nicer clothes) move in organized groups—Japanese groups following tour guides with flags. Europeans clustered around guides speaking German or French. The Americans—dad and mom in tank tops, junior in backwards baseball cap—form one great mass trudging from the White House to the Air and Space Museum across the dusty Mall.

I sometimes wish I could take some families aside and say, "Look, this doesn't have to be so hard." Often my wish comes true, when friends from Europe or Asia visit my family in Washington and ask for advice on sightseeing. In return for our help we get a vicarious sense of what is surprising, impressive, and alarming in a city whose quirks we rarely notice anymore. Occasionally we're jolted into seeing Washington through foreign eyes.

When the visitors are Japanese, we beg them to come in the spring. That is the best time for anyone to visit Washington, despite the teenagers' assault, because the flowering trees make the city into one big arboretum. It is especially important for Japanese visitors because of the cherry blossoms. The blossoms that count are not on the famous trees along the Tidal Basin, near the Jefferson Memorial. Those trees were donated by the Japanese government before the First World War and are the stars of the annual Cherry Blossom Festival, but somehow that festival never works out. It's too cold and the buds freeze off, or it has been too warm and the blossoms are gone, or a big wind has roared through and blasted the petals into the Chesapeake.

The special cherry blossoms are several miles away, in the ritzy district of Bethesda called Kenwood. This is the kind of district that has its name on a plaque by the entrance gate, and an accompanying country club. Also, William Safire lives here. But I forgive Kenwood a lot because of its dense stands of *sakura*, Japanese flowering cherry trees. The trees are so old, so large, and so thickly planted that when they bloom, in March or April, their branches form a pinkish-white canopy over the road, obscuring the sky. In several seasons of *o-hanami*, or "blossom-viewing," in Japan, I saw nothing as breathtaking. Two springs ago, while having a tedious argument about trade policy with a visiting Japanese official, I said, "Let's not spend the day this way. I've got something to show you." We drove out to Kenwood, and I let him walk for an hour under the trees. As I had hoped, he felt both comforted (about this bond that transcended politics) and overwhelmed (by America's power—even to produce cherry trees!). "We—we do not have this," he finally said.

My family has not yet had visitors from rural China, but when we do, I will take them to the downtown and suburban avenues that are lined with gingko trees. In the fall thousands of gingko fruits litter the ground near each tree. Most Washingtonians hate the trees then, because when trod underfoot, the fruits reek like vomit. Early in the morning these same trees are surrounded by peasant-looking Asians, collecting fruits (their hard kernels are apparently a delicacy) from

> "*W*ashington is a Scorpio city, and Scorpio is about things that are hidden. Whatever is interesting in Washington is hidden; power is hidden; its most interesting people are hidden."
>
> ◆
>
> —Caroline Casey, Washington astrologer, at the time of much ado about Nancy Reagan and Joan Quigley, in *The Washington Post*

the branches and ground before they can be squashed. Visitors from Germany perk up when sent on healthful Sunday walks in Glover-Archbold Park, with trails that run for miles through northwest Washington. The better-known walking routes, on the C & O Canal towpath and in Rock Creek Park, are less enjoyable, because they are also jammed with bikes. If I could identify a group of Swiss mountain folk among the tourist throngs, I would urge them to escape the Mall and drive fifteen miles up the Potomac to Great Falls. This is a surprisingly scenic gorge, with trails on both the Maryland and Virginia sides. A "Billy Goat Trail," on the Maryland side, takes several hours of jumping from rock to rock to negotiate.

Visitors from Northern Europe should arrive in the dead of winter. The weather is mild by their standards, but every two or three years it is cold enough in Washington to freeze the same C & O Canal into a marvelous Brueghelian skating course that leads for some twenty miles alongside the Potomac, from Georgetown well past Great Falls. I rarely think of Washington as charming, but it is exactly that on bitter February mornings by the canal. As we sit on the bank lacing up our skates, the only sounds are the *click, click* of long speed skates and the bursts of chatter in Dutch or Russian from happy groups whooshing by.

These attractions are ways of showing foreigners transplanted versions of cultures they already know. Of course, it is also valuable to show them slices of life quite different from what they would see at home. Even a city as display-conscious as Washington offers several unselfconscious revelations about American ways.

Everyone comes to Washington prepared for one of these revelations: the clichéd contrast between power and misery, with drug pushers operating in the shadow of the Capitol. Actually, most visitors see less of this contrast than they expect. The worst areas of New York and Chicago look terrible. The poorest and most dangerous areas of Washington, like those of Los Angeles, don't look as ominous as they are.

Movies and TV documentaries have prepared most foreigners to see bombed out neighborhoods. Nothing has prepared them for vast middle- and professional-class African-American neighborhoods, like those of upper Sixteenth Street and Rhode Island Avenue. Washington's most interesting sociological journey is a drive (or long walk) straight up Sixteenth Street, starting at Lafayette Park and the White House and ending at the very northern tip of the District of Columbia. The mansions and civic buildings along the way are virtually a fossil record of successive ethnic and religious waves—the huge Masonic temples, the synagogues, the enormous African Methodist Episcopal churches. On either side of northern Sixteenth Street is perhaps the most extensive mainly black luxury-housing area in America. (As a bonus, the Walter Reed Army Medical Center is also just off Sixteenth Street. Its National Museum of Health and Medicine contains an amazing assortment of ghoulish specimens and displays, the sight of which you may try to forget but never will.)

Some white residential areas of Washington also surprise many visitors. (Only a few of the city's neighborhoods are integrated.)

Suburbs like Potomac and Chevy Chase, in Maryland, and McLean, in Virginia, fit a pre-existing picture of what nice suburbs are like. The big houses on leafy streets off Foxhall Road—white Washington's more bucolic counterpart to upper Sixteenth Street—are surprising because they are less than three miles from the White House. I was driving an intense European scholar through these areas at a time when politicians in Washington had just taken an unusually frivolous step. "This is why Americans cannot be serious," the European exclaimed as he saw a mansion in Spring Valley, surrounded by graceful tulip poplar trees. "You live in a park!" In fairness, these same sylvan dwellings have housed many Americans notable for their seriousness, from Richard Nixon to Ira Magaziner....

Having done my share of guiding visitors around town through the years. I thought recently that I should let myself be guided by them. I signed up to join two groups of foreigners as they went on Gray Line's special multilingual tour buses. One group was Europeans and West Africans who listened to French as they rode around town. The other was visitors from Japan. I was hoping to overhear some embarrassingly biased narration—bragging about Lafayette and l'Enfant, for instance, in front of the French-speakers. In this I was disappointed: the narrations were faithful translations of Gray Line's English tour. But the tours showed me the city in a completely new way.

The Gray Line tours, which leave from Union Station, near the Capitol, are either four-hour or all-day bus rides through Washington and Arlington. The multilingual bus has headsets with a choice of narration in English, French, German, Spanish, Italian, Japanese, Chinese, or Korean. As a resident, I had long resented the huge buses, preferring the more picturesque Old Town Trolleys that take visitors around the Mall and embassy areas....

My attitude changed once I climbed aboard a bus. Inside, it was spacious, cool, and comfortable. Most important, it was high. I could see over the tops of jammed-up cars and the heads of bustling pedestrians, straight to the buildings and monuments. The tours pointed out only one thing I had never seen before—a tiny monument to Franklin Roosevelt near the ugly headquarters of the FBI. But for the first time in years I looked at the city's famous structures and the story they were telling foreign visitors.

Much of the story, as with any set of monuments, concerns war. Washington has many equestrian statues, nearly all of generals. The U.S. Marine Corps War Memorial, better known as the Iwo Jima monument, lists all the campaigns in which leathernecks have fought—followed by an impressive amount of empty space. (The French-speakers talked as if they were impressed. The Japanese visitors took pictures of each other with the monument and the Potomac in the background.) Maya Lin's design for the Vietnam Memorial seems more a work of genius with each passing year. Monuments—it becomes clear, when you see dozens in a day—are touching attempts to grant immortality, by preserving names to be seen when their bearers are dead. The Vietnam memorial is the only one to immortalize all who died for their nation on the battlefield.

> $\mathcal{A}$lice Roosevelt Longworth, Theodore Roosevelt's daughter, spanned the Washington scene from T.R. to Ronald Reagan. Late in life she described Washington as "a small, cozy town, global in scope. It suits me." Such superior raillery was unknown to New York, Boston, Chicago. In Los Angeles it would not have been understood at all. Mrs. Longworth understood, as did Henry Adams, that the romance of Washington was the show it put on. In a way totally unlike the development of other American power centers, Washington *looked* consistent, all of a piece along its white Roman fronts. It was what the founders had hoped for, perhaps the only thing that the wildly heterogeneous America of the late twentieth century could look up to—a *center*.
>
> —Alfred Kazin, *A Writer's America: Landscape in Literature*

Yet the message that struck me more, as I tried to see what the foreigners were seeing, was how much work over how many years has gone into holding the country together. The challenge that faced Lincoln during the Civil War is only the most extreme example. Apart from the generals, almost everyone honored with a plaque, a statue, or a building in Washington devoted his or her life to building the institutions through which self-government operates. The institutions didn't grow by themselves. The statue of Albert Gallatin outside the Treasury, of A. Philip Randolph inside Union Station, of Teddy Roosevelt on Roosevelt Island, in the Potomac—these and dozens of other symbols on the tour were reminders of architects and builders whose best efforts had allowed a functioning national structure to arise. Perhaps the new congressmen arriving in Washington should take an outsiders' tour of the city, to get an idea of the structure's history before they begin taking the thing apart.

James Fallows is a contributing editor for The Atlantic Monthly. *He is the author of* More Like Us: Making America Great Again, Looking at the Sun: The Rise of the New East Asian Economic & Political System, *and* Breaking the News: How the Media Undermine American Democracy.

✳

The fact is I gravitate to a capital by a primary law of nature. This is the only place in America where society amuses me, or where life offers variety. Here, too, I can fancy that we are of use in the world, for we distinctly occupy niches which ought to be filled....

Literary and non-partisan people are rare here, and highly appreciated. And yet society in its way is fairly complete, almost as choice, if not as large, as in London or Rome.

One of these days this will be a very great city if nothing happens to it. Even now it is a beautiful one, and its situation is superb. As I belong to the class of people who have great faith in this country and who believe that in another century it will be saying in its turn the last word of civilisation, I enjoy the expectation of the coming day, and try to imagine the first faint rays of that great light which is to dazzle and set the world on fire hereafter....

—Henry Adams, in a letter to Charles Milnes Gaskell (1877)

The Minnesota State Fair

*About to venture the length of the
Mississippi, the author takes
in a side show.*

THE STREET HAD MERGED INTO AN EXPRESSWAY, AND THE EX-
pressway was jammed solid. We were elbow to elbow in the crush,
a grumbling herd of dusty pickup trucks, all windows down, all
radios turned full up. I spoke to my nearest neighbor, a colossal
jellyfish in a plaid shirt and a cowboy hat with a wide curly brim.

"Where's everybody going?"

"You goin' to the Fair, man. Hey, Butch—guy here don't know
where noboby's goin'."

"He's goin' right to the Fair," Butch said from the driver's seat.

"I just told him that. Hey, where you from? You ain't a
Norwegian, are you?"

"I'm from England."

"England. Shit. Guy's from *England*. Reason I asked if you was a
Norwegian fella is because I'm a Norwegian myself. Got a
Norwegian name. Olen. That's Norwegian, Olen—ain't that right?"

"Sounds right to me."

"Hey, you talk just like one of them Norwegians. That kills me.
Yeah, I come from those parts. From way back. Wanna beer?"

He passed me a can of cold Budweiser clad in a sheath of poly-
styrene foam.

"That's *Bud-weiser*, that beer." Remembering that he was talking to a foreigner, he carefully separated every syllable for me, and started shouting. "That's a *German* name. Don't come from Germany, though. Comes from the *Yew*-nighted States."

We rolled forward in consort for a few feet, and stopped.

"I'm looking for the river," I said.

Olen's jellyfish face squinched up, then expanded again.

"*Lookin'* for the *river*."

"The Mississippi."

"The river's back," said Butch. "He just come over it."

"The river's back," Olen said. "Ain't no exits now, not till the Fairgrounds."

"Shit," I said.

"You gonna have a real good time at the Fair, man. They got all kinds of things there. They got freaks. You know what we all call the Fair? It's the great Minnesota get-together."

"That's right," Butch said. "The great Minnesota get-together."

"I wanted to find the Mississippi."

> Each tourist took notes, and went home and published a book—a book which was usually calm, truthful, reasonable, kind; but which seemed just the reverse to our tender-footed progenitors. A glance at these tourist books shows us that in certain of its aspects the Mississippi has undergone no change since those strangers visited it, but remains today about as it was then. The emotions produced in those foreign breasts by these aspects were not all formed on one pattern, of course; they had to be various, along at first, because the earlier tourists were obliged to originate their emotions, whereas in older countries one can always borrow emotions from one's predecessors.
>
> ◆
>
> —Mark Twain,
> *Life on the Mississippi*

"*Mississippi*? That ain't nothin' much. Any road, you gone past it. It's way back."

With the sole exception of Olen's ten-gallon affair, everyone in our crowd was wearing a plastic cap with a long shovel-brim. The caps gave the cavalcade a vaguely military air, as if we were off to sack a city. The fronts of the hats were decorated with insignia and slogans. OH BOY! OH BEEF! advertised a kind of cake that cows ate. Others peddled farm machinery, Holsum Bread, chemical fertilizers, pesticides, corn oil, cement and root beer. Under these corporation colors, the owners of the caps looked queerly like feudal retainers riding around wearing the arms of their barons. A few self-conscious individualists wore personalized caps announcing I'M FROM THE BOONDOCKS and you CAN KISS MY…followed by a picture of an ass in a straw bonnet. Butch's cap said JOHN DEERE; I took this for his own name, and only gradually noticed that several hundred men at the fair were also called John Deere, which turned out to be a famous brand of agricultural tractor.

The state fair sprawled across a hillside and a valley, and at first glance it did indeed look like a city under occupation by an army of rampaging Goths. I'd never seen so many enormous people assembled in one place. These farming families from Minnesota and Wisconsin were the descendants of hungry immigrants from Germany and Scandinavia. Their ancestors must have been lean and anxious men with the famines of Europe bitten into their faces. Generation by generation, their families had eaten themselves into Americans. Now they all had the same figure: same broad bottom, same Buddha belly, same neckless join between turkey-wattle chin and sperm-whale torso. The women had poured themselves into pink stretch-knit pant suits; the men swelled against every seam and button of their plaid shirts and Dacron slacks. Under the brims of their caps, their food projected from their mouths. Foot-long hot dogs. Bratwurst sausages, dripping with hot grease. Hamburgers. Pizzas. Scoops of psychedelic ice cream. Wieners-dun-in-buns.

Stumbling, half-suffocated, through this abundance of food and flesh, I felt like a brittle matchstick man. Every time I tried to turn my head I found someone else's hot dog, bloody with ketchup, sticking into my own mouth.

On either side of us, the voices of the freak show barkers quacked through tinny loudspeakers.

"Ronny and Donny. The only living Siamese twins on exhibit in the world today. Now grown men, Ronny and Donny are joined at the breastbone and the abdomen, facing each other for every second of their lives."

"We carry the most deadly and dangerous of any in the world. Don't miss it. All alive!"

"Can you imagine being permanently fastened to another person for your entire life?"

"You see the deadly Monocle Cobra from Asia, the Chinese Cobra and the Black-Necked Spitting Cobra. All alive."

"Ronny and Donny, the Siamese twins, are fascinating to see, interesting to visit, and completely unforgettable. The Siamese twins are alive, real and living."

"You'll see the giant, one-hundred-pound pythons. They're alive, and they're inside. Don't miss it. Everything's alive."

"You will remember your visit with the Siamese twins for the rest of your life—"

Crushed between the bust of the woman behind and the immense behind of the man in front, I did not find it hard to imagine what it might be like to be Ronny or Donny. There was no chance of visiting with them, though. As the sluggish current of the crowd passed them by, I was carried with it, deep into the heart of the state fair.

I was going down fast. The air I was breathing wasn't air: it was a compound of smells, of meat, sweat, popcorn, cooking fat and passed gas. Wriggling and butting my way out of the crowd, I found myself in the sudden blessed cool of a vaulted cathedral full of cows. They stood silently in their stalls with the resigned eyes of long-term patients. The straw with which the stadium was carpeted gave the whole place a ceremonious quiet. Grave men, whom I took for bulk buyers from the burger industry, padded from stall to stall. The cattle stared back at them with profound incuriosity. I wondered what they made of the smell of charred beef. Soon they'd be minced, ground up with cereal and soybeans, and turned into Whoppers and Kingburgers. For now, though, the animals had a lugubrious dignity that put the people at the fair to shame. They were the real heroes of the day. Washed sleek as seals, they were the scions of the finest stock of Minnesota, aristocrats in their world. They looked temperamentally unsuited to the garish democracy of the fast-food business.

I was trying to make contact with some kind of pedigreed shorthorn whose face had reminded me of the late Zero Mostel when I noticed the man standing at the next stall along. He was wearing a stripy one-piece pajama suit which hung on him in loose folds. Once, perhaps, he too had had a Minnesotan figure, but he had shrunk inside his peculiar garment until his pajamas flapped like rags on a stick.

He also was attempting to strike up a relationship with a cow. He was dabbing at her ears with a liver-spotted hand as if he'd short-sightedly mistaken her for a dog.

"Lady...Lady...Lady..." he pleaded. The cow regarded him with ageless stupid skepticism. "Hey, Lady—"

He turned toward me. His cap said, HAPPINESS IS BEING A GRANDPARENT.

"Know about stock?"

"Nothing at all," I said.

"Me neither. That's you and me both. You and me both." His twiggy fingers went dandling away in the fur of the cow's neck. "You ain't from around these parts."

"No—I'm just passing through."

"I could tell. You from the East? From New York? You from New York?"

"No, England."

"England. Oh, yeah. England." His tone was forgiving. He was letting me off the incriminating hook of coming from New York. "I was there once. In the days of wrath. I went all up Italy in the days of wrath."

"In the war—"

"The days of wrath." He looked at the cow and spoke to it in a cracked, erratically remembered parody of a British accent. "Wot yer! Yer bloomin' bloody bloke!" He wheezed with pleasure at this performance. "We had English out there with us. Days of wrath. Yeah. I was there. You ever hear of Monte Cassino?" He made the place sound like a Chicago gang leader.

"Yes. My father was there."

"I was there. Him and me both." He gave his cow another friendly scratch. "Englishman, eh, what? What ho, old bloke!"

I couldn't find more than a feeble snicker to answer him with, but my silence seemed to please him more than any words could have done. He left his cow, pulled excitedly at the folds of his pajamas, and launched himself into speech like a parachutist hurtling out of a plane.

"Know somethin', old bloke? You come out here in the summer, huh? Hot enough, ain't it? Hot enough to boil your brains. Boil your brains. That's Labor Day for you. Up in Minnesota here, Labor Day she really means something, you better believe it. Last day of summer. Know what folks are at all over this state right now?"

He allowed himself a thunderous, dramatic pause. His dried crabapple face was about six inches away from mine. His eyes were wet.

"Eating and drinking and pig roasts and partying! Every kind of partying you can think of! They got barbecues like you never seen…and pool parties…and euchre…Hell, every sonofabitch is having himself the finest goddamn time he can. And you know why, sir? The Minnesota Winter! Now, that is something else. That is really something else. You come here Thanksgiving, old bloke, *that's* when you ought to be up here in Minnesota. Cold? I'm telling you. It'd freeze your nuts off. Freeze your nuts off. Snow? There's whole cities underneath the snow there. Ain't nothing that ain't froze right over. You go out there in that air, that is *cold*, I'm telling you. Twenty below, thirty below—that ain't *nothing* in Minnesota. Hell, we got it worse than the Eskimos here. And that's why when folks in this state go partying on Labor Day, we put on the best goddamn show in the whole United States. You hear what I'm saying? I been to state fairs, and there ain't none like the Minnesota State Fair, because there ain't nobody who knows how to party like the Minnesota people do. And it's all because of them goddamn freezing winters—"

This breathless oration was accompanied by a frantic series of clockwork nods and jerks. The brim of the old man's cap wagged an independent emphasis at the end of each sentence. Happiness, it kept on announcing, was being a grandparent. The whole performance came to a sudden stop when a woman's voice called, "*Hatfield!*" across the cattle stadium.

"*Hatfield!*" It was a blowtorch of a voice, and the old man was being roasted in it. He shrank even farther back inside his pajamas.

"Hatfield! I been looking all over!"

The man gestured, flutteringly, at me. I clearly was not much of an alibi.

"I had to leave Doug and Mo. They're eating popcorn and wieners. You know Jo-Ann hates to have the kids left *any*place!" Hatfield's spouse was wearing Bermuda shorts. The varicose veins on her thighs were so intricately blue that they looked like the willow pattern on a Chinese plate.

"Beatrice…this gentleman is from England—"
I got a brief once-over from behind a pair of clip-on dark

> *I* 'd been living in San Francisco two years before it occurred to me that I routinely walked out into the December night air wearing only a light jacket and a smile. The catalyst for this realization was a Christmas trip to Minnesota, where I knew it would be different. But I'd forgotten how different. When I boarded a plane in San Francisco the temperature was 63 degrees; when I stepped out of the terminal in Minneapolis my first breath was almost my last. Ice appeared in my nostrils and my lungs screamed for mercy. The temperature was 16 degrees below zero, a drop of 79 degrees. My friend Lou just smiled inside his woolens and said, "Welcome back to Minnesota."
>
> ◆
>
> —Larry Habegger,
> "A Minnesota December"

glasses. Beatrice could tell a rotten tomato when she saw one.

"Well," she said. "Is. That. So."

"Hello," I said.

"We, uh, kind of got talking…" said Hatfield, but I could see that the words sounded improbable in his own ears. Talking was not an area of life for which Hatfield carried a license. He plucked at the knees of his pajamas. Beatrice studied the rows of cows in their stalls. "Cattle," she said, identifying them as if they were a species hitherto unknown to her.

"Been nice talking to you," said Hatfield sadly. I hoped that he was going to muster up one of his cracky tags of wartime-British, but he glanced across at Beatrice, thought better of it, and let the brim of his cap sink down over his face, forestalling further communication. He was led off, silent, rainbow pajamas flapping, to join his grandchildren, in the wiener-and-popcorn corral.

I'd never been much good at being one of the crowd. Now, feeding myself back into the flow, I tried to settle in, to feel part of the blood being pumped through the fair. Be a corpuscle. Let go. We oozed down a long sickly tunnel of cotton candy, came up against some invisible obstruction, and were channeled into a mass of separate thread veins and arteries. The going was hot and smelly, the pace jerky, as if the whole coronary system were clogged and subject to frequent breakdown. All nerve ends and elbows, I kept on getting stuck.

I was shown a selection of snow blowers. A lady dog handler demonstrated the latest psychological technique for dissuading Ajax and Hercules from leaving piles of poopie on the rug. I found her frank, instructive, but a bit too academic for me. I nearly bought some vitamin pills. I looked at a display of swimming pools, custom-designed to suit my yard; I did my best to covet a threshing machine; I moved fairly swiftly through the extensive exhibit of chemicals that promised to enhance the nutrient values of my poor soil. I did pause, in mute assent, in front of a placard which asked me: DO YOU SUFFER FROM THE LITTLE PAINS USUALLY ASSOCIATED WITH ARTHRITIS? The handsome orthopedic vibrator, on which I might have massaged all my little pains away, was both expensive and rather too large to carry on a small boat. The demonstration model was being put to heavy use by a line of sweating agribusinessmen. I came upon a stack of illustrated encyclopedias. Their grained plastic bindings were a deep episcopal purple, the color of seriousness. Their salesman had been got up to look like everyone's idea of a proper scholar. Close-cropped, in chunky tortoiseshell glasses, he was the only man in Minnesota who wore a necktie on Labor Day.

"If I may ask, sir, would you have children of school age?"

"Oh, yes," I said. I like purely hypothetical questions, and have always found it a treat to be singled out by Gallup pollsters.

"Would they have ready access to encyclopedia sources in the home?"

"I very much doubt it."

The salesman brightened up no end. I began to ferret through the volumes. They stank unpleasantly of a mixture of gasoline and lavender.

"…outstanding aids to education…indispensable in the home, school or college situation…no article longer than seven hundred words…" His voice ran on like a leaky tap. The language of encyclopedia selling is an Esperanto; I imagine that every phrase is duplicated word for word in China, Persia or Peru.

I found LINCOLN–PACIFIC.

"…world's foremost scholars in their fields…expert communicators…selected vocabulary…uniquely commissioned from leading illustrators and artist…"

MISSISSIPPI, I skimmed the entry. Nothing new.

…principal waterway in the U.S., draining all or parts of 31 states in the heartland of the nation. Its name derives from Chippewa, *mici zibi*, or "large river"…

I copied out those two sentences and returned the book to its rank.

"Thanks, I was just looking something up."

"May I ask the ages of your children, sir?"

"I haven't got any."

The salesman stopped looking like a scholar. *Jerk. Smartass.* But there were other, real parents about, trailing visible children of genuine school age, and I watched the salesman reminding himself that his own imposture was of more immediate importance than mine. He gave me a cold, waxy, very scholarly smile. The lenses of his spectacles were plain glass.

Ebbing and swirling, we drifted from tent to tent. At every bend there was another pagoda selling brats or franks or dogs or burgers. Church flags flew from their tops. The Lutherans specialized in bratwurst sausages, the Methodists in hot dogs, the Catholics in hamburgers. At each stall, there was a stack of giveaway devotional reading placed handily beside the ketchup squirt. Did all this eating have some sacramental significance? Could munching on an Adventist wiener be the first step on the ladder of conversion?

The crowd was wedged solid from horizon to horizon. There were no signs of an exit from this colossal Roman holiday. In a brief gap in the stream of overamplified country-and-Western I heard a faint familiar voice, and almost thought of it as a friend.

"We offer a reward of a thousand dollars if they're not real and alive, exactly as advertised. We could make it a million dollars, or a billion dollars, it doesn't make any difference, because we won't have to reward anyone a penny. Because the Siamese twins are real, human and alive."

Lucky Siamese twins. As each sticky, claustrophobic minute went by, I felt less real, less human, less alive. I thought how curious it was, this crowd. No nation in the world had ever put quite such a high value on privacy and space as the United States, and nowhere in the country did people live so far apart, in houses islanded in acres of sequestered green, as here in the Midwest. When Minnesotans got together on Labor Day, they did so with the fervor of people for whom being part of a crowd is a rare holiday luxury. The fairgoers were like children playing sardines.

We rolled slowly on past an amphitheater. They might have been feeding born-again Christians to the lions there, but no—it was just a late-model-stock-car race. On the public-address system, the commentator's voice was bawling over the top of the growling animal bass of the auto engines. He was getting the Amzoil Three

Hundred under way. Well, we certainly had a beautiful day here today in Minnesota, he said. Plus, we had some real beautiful cars and a lot of real super people.

"They're turning those engines at over seven thousand r.p.m.," he shouted. "So, gentlemen! Let's go racing!"

Please, I thought, please don't let's go racing. The thought was instantly smashed from my head by the noise of what sounded like an intercontinental bronchial hemorrhage, as the stock cars took off from their starting positions and went roaring around the stadium. Christians and lions must at least have been a great deal quieter.

I didn't want to go racing. I didn't want to stuff my face with meat, corn and cotton candy. I didn't feel like rolling dimes for the National Heart Foundation. I wasn't going to buy a snow-blower. I didn't care to ride the Big Wheel or goggle at the Black-Necked Spitting Cobra. I wanted out. I wanted to find my river.

Jonathan Raban's Old Glory: A Voyage Down the Mississippi, *from which this story was excerpted, won extraordinary critical acclaim. His other books include* Coasting, *the novel* Foreign Land, *and the collection* For Love & Money. *He lives in Seattle.*

✳

Being a city kid (well, suburban), I couldn't understand why anyone would want to go into a dark, dank hall that smelled of hay and manure to look at cows, when just around the corner was The Midway! It was a place where you could shoot mechanical ducks and win a prize, knock down lead milk bottles with baseballs, pick up treasures with a steam shovel, and spin till you puked on the "tilt-o-whirl." But my child's mind was most enchanted by the grotesque signs and the hoarse calls of the barkers at The Freak Show. Just inside, for the mere price of 50 cents (or was it a dollar?) lay unimaginable depravities: the bearded lady, the amazing reptile man with the skin of a lizard, the shocking donkey man with the body of an ass. I never had the nerve to ask my parents for the money, but one day my brother came home to say he'd gone in.

"What was it like?" I needed to know.

"Unbelievable," was all he could say.

And so it was. The State Fair was the biggest deal of every summer when summer meant heat and baseball and corn-on-the-cob. It was still a big deal when summer meant beaches and cars and girls, and no doubt it remains a big deal today for kids of all ages who will never forget the amazing reptile man.

—Larry Habegger, "It All Ends on Labor Day"

ROBERT LEONARD REID

* * *

The Mountain of Love and Death

When in doubt, do something
you've never done before.

I WENT WEST WITH MY FRIENDS LEON AND HENRY BILLS, AND there in the Tetons of Wyoming I saw my first high mountains. I knew that I had to climb them. I had no idea how I would accomplish that seemingly impossible task, but, camped at their base, gazing up each day at faraway summits drifting in and out of clouds, I somehow guessed at the intimacy that is available only to the mountaineer, and longed to share in it. I was spellbound by one peak in particular. Teewinot was a perfect snow-draped triangle that swept up and up, ever narrower and more thrilling, to a wondrous pinnacle piercing the sky. By day she quickened my pulse; by night she haunted my dreams. She lay so close to my campsite that I began to know her habits and moods. As though courting her, I wove a sinuous dance at the mountain's foot—exploring her circling paths, dipping at midday into her refreshing streams, pausing in her cool shadows, withdrawing to admire her from afar.

One fine day my friends and I rented ice axes, purchased a length of goldline rope, and set off to consummate the mad affair. We were quite impetuous all the way, I think. It was our first time; we were hale and determined, but lacked style. Several times in my eagerness I dislodged large, efficient-looking rocks that sailed harmlessly past my companions (but woe to anyone below!). On steep snow I came loose but was saved by the rope, a stroke of luck that cheered us greatly. It became clear that we were not to be thwarted, so excellent was our mission.

As we approached the top I saw to my horror that the summit was a smooth rock the size and shape of a very large almond. On all sides the drop-off was terrible. It was evident that the final act would be a desperate business. The three of us looked at each other with blank faces. I took a deep breath, said a heart-felt prayer, dropped to my hands and knees, and crawled to the summit like a turtle.

From far below came a thin sound of cheering that failed to encourage me. I lay there hugging that inadequate slab of masonry as though it were my dear mama. To distract myself I thought of other places I had visited, nice places, low places.

Slowly then, after what seemed like an interminable length of time, I began to gain confidence. Following careful and exhaustive planning, I rolled onto my back. Then I sat up and looked around.

My first impression was one of a curious drifting of time and space. I seemed to be moving. I know now that I was. I liked it. Summits, I quickly realized, are not the solid, precisely defined spots that are shown on maps. Rather, they are capricious, meandering places, whose locations, like those of elec-

The Teton Mountain Range is a group of Rocky Mountain peaks located south of Yellowstone National Park and stretching 40 miles long and 10–15 mile wide. The range's highest peak, at 13,770 feet, is known as the Grand Teton.

♦

—FS

trons and small children, are incapable of being pinpointed at any given moment.

My senses came to attention. Below I saw my friends snapping pictures. I felt the wind and the dazzle of the nearby sun. I felt the top of my head rubbing the sky. (I am now bald there; many climbers suffer this affliction.) I gazed across a choppy ocean of space at the mountain called the Grand Teton, a resplendent peak that reached even higher into the heavens than the point where I hovered. Suddenly, for the first time, I felt the terrible addiction of the mountaineer: *I wanted that one!* I wanted, more precisely, the east ridge of the Grand Teton, a steep, narrow, utterly bewitching buttress that sliced upward in one magnificent mile-long line from the glacier thousands of feet below me to the very summit of the peak. That long and elegant route introduced me to the aesthetic element of mountaineering: the east ridge of the Grand Teton (or the Grand, as we soon began calling it) was desirable not simply because it led to the top of the peak, but because it was so beautiful. From my lofty perch I studied it raptly: its explosive eruption in the glacier below, its urgent coalescence into great towers and gleaming black ice and rock tumbled on snow, its dark aprons and white cornices and inexorable upward thrust, now narrowing, now rushing, now only rock, now only snow, now only sky—

My eyes ran swiftly over the ridge, taking in more and more detail with each pass. I grew more familiar with my newfound beauty by the minute, more needful, and all I could think was...*to be there! to be there!*

It was beyond my present powers. But I vowed that one day, when I had perfected my skills, I would return to climb the ridge.

On the way down I fell. Descending a long and steep snowfield unroped, I slipped, dropped my ice axe (which I had no idea how to use anyway), and slid out of control for several hundred feet before crashing at an exciting rate of speed into a jumble of boulders at the bottom of the snow. I stood up, dusted myself off, waved triumphantly to my friends above, and continued the descent.

That was not our only near-miss. A few days later, as we approached the summit of Mount Moran, we were caught by a storm that leapt over the top of the peak at us. The morning had been beautiful; now freezing rain was pouring down and a wicked wind was whipping at our parkas. We were inexperienced but not stupid. We saw that our position on a tiny island of rock in the middle of a steep snow tongue was perilous. Quickly we crossed the snow to a more protected spot. A moment later a brilliant flash of light burst around us, followed almost instantly by an ear-splitting clap of thunder. Fifty yards away a bolt of lightning reached out of the mist and blasted our recently departed island of rock to smithereens.

Nor was that all. After descending a pinnacle called Cube Point on rappel, I disengaged on what turned out to be very steep ground. Afraid to move, I simply stood stolidly at the base of the rappel. A few moments later my partner came flying down the ropes quite magnificently and crashed into me like a sandbag from the rafters. Together we rolled merrily down the slope until we came to rest in a lovely meadow filled with wildflowers.

Perhaps it was madness. And yet those early days held a hunger for the full length and breadth of experience and a thirst for the limits of emotion that were preeminently human and therefore preeminently sane. They helped me define what it meant to climb mountains. Utterly naive, burning with desire and fear, I set off each day to quell my foolish passion, and sometimes I succeeded. It was adventure of the grandest sort, adventure that ranked with the seat-of-the-pants voyages of Vasco da Gama and the wonderful, preposterous search for the Nile. The nation was about to land a man on the moon, and I couldn't have cared less. I began to see how easy it is to confuse adventure with flash, and to suppose that astronauts supported by worldwide communications networks and millionaires in zircon-coated balloons are adventurers. They are not. An adventure is a voyage into the unfamiliar. If you know what you're doing, it isn't an adventure. An adventure is a baring of your soul, not your wallet, an agreement to trust your wits rather than your digital homing device. Gentle reader, here is how to have an adventure: breathe deeply, throw down your defenses, *and take a flyer!*

Robert Leonard Reid was a mountaineering leader for the Sierra Club. He edited A Treasury of the Sierra Nevada *for Wilderness Press and wrote*

Mountains of the Great Blue Dream, *from which this story was excerpted. He now lives in Corrales, New Mexico, with his wife and son.*

★

Many years ago I was working as an instructor at the North Carolina Outward Bound School, co-leading a group of 12 young men between the ages of 16 and 18 on a climb up Mt. Mitchell, the tallest mountain east of the Mississippi in the Blue Ridge Mountains. With heavy backpacks we were working our way up a trail with 2,000 feet to go to the summit. I kept hearing complaints of how hard and steep the trail was and how miserable everybody was feeling.

I thought to myself that what is difficult is all very relative, and I told the group that I heard their complaints and decided we needed to act on them. My co-instructor and I told them we would change their perspective on just how difficult climbing Mt. Mitchell could be by abandoning the trail and bushwhacking straight up the mountain.

For the next four hours we proceeded painfully and excruciatingly up, hacking our way through thick rhododendrons that ripped our legs, arms, faces. The comments from the group were passionate and invigorating, to say the least. After what seemed like an interminable hell through this rhodo jungle, we finally came to the top and the hooting and hollering that commenced was truly epic. These young guys had really accomplished a major physical and mental challenge. More importantly, however, they never complained again and had gained a new perspective on how delightful an actual hiking trail could be.

—David "Gorilla" Spicer, "Confessions of a Wilderness Lunatic"

✫ ✫ ✫

The Walt
"You Will Have Fun"
Disney World

In which Dave's world collides with Walt's.

I'M AN EXPERT ON VISITING DISNEY WORLD, BECAUSE WE LIVE only four hours away, and according to my records we spend about three-fifths of our after-tax income there. Not that I'm complaining. You can't have a bad time at Disney World. It's not allowed. They have hidden electronic surveillance cameras everywhere, and if they catch you failing to laugh with childlike wonder, they lock you inside a costume representing a beloved Disney character such as Goofy and make you walk around in the Florida heat getting grabbed and leaped on by violently excited children until you have learned your lesson. Yes, Disney World is a "dream vacation," and here are some tips to help make it "come true" for you!

When to Go: The best time to go, if you want to avoid huge crowds, is 1962.

How to Get There: It's possible to fly, but if you want the total Disney World experience, you should drive there with a minimum of four hostile children via the longest possible route. If you live in Georgia, for example, you should plan a route that includes Oklahoma.

Once you get to Florida, you can't miss Disney World, because the Disney corporation owns the entire center of the state. Just get on any major highway, and eventually it will dead-end in a Disney parking area large enough to have its own climate, populated by large nomadic families who have been trying to find their cars since the Carter administration. Be sure to note carefully where you leave *your* car, because later on you may want to sell it so you can pay for your admission tickets.

But never mind the price: the point is that now you're finally *there*, in the ultimate vacation fantasy paradise, ready to have fun! Well, okay, you're not exactly there *yet*. First you have to wait for the parking-lot tram, driven by cheerful uniformed Disney employees, to come around and pick you up and give you a helpful lecture about basic tram-safety rules such as never fall out of the tram without coming to a full and complete stop.

But now the tram ride is over and it's time for fun! Right? Don't be an idiot. It's time to wait in line to buy admission tickets. Most experts recommend that you go with the 47-day pass, which will give you a chance, if you never eat or sleep, to visit *all* of the Disney themed attractions, including The City of the Future, The Land of Yesterday, The Dull Suburban Residential Community of Sometime Next Month, Wet Adventure, Farms on Mars, The World of Furniture, Sponge Encounter, the Nuclear Flute Orchestra, Appliance Island, and the Great Underwater Robot Hairdresser Adventure, to name just a few.

Okay, you've taken out a second mortgage and purchased your tickets! Now, finally, it's time to…wait in line again! This time, it's for the monorail, a modern, futuristic transportation system that whisks you to the Magic Kingdom at nearly half the speed of a lawn tractor. Along the way cheerful uniformed Disney World employees will offer you some helpful monorail-safety tips such as never set fire to the monorail without first removing your personal belongings.

And now, at last, you're at the entrance to the Magic Kingdom itself! No more waiting in line for transportation! It's time to *wait in line to get in*. Wow! Look at all the *other* people waiting to get in! There are tour groups here with names like "Entire Population of Indiana." There sure must be some great attractions inside these gates!

And now you've inched your way to the front of the line, and the cheerful uniformed Disney employee is stamping your hand with a special invisible chemical that penetrates your nervous system and causes you to temporarily acquire the personality of a cow. "Moo!" you shout as you surge forward with the rest of the herd.

And now, unbelievably, you're actually inside the Magic Kingdom! At last! Mecca! You crane your head to see over the crowd around you, and with innocent childlike wonder you behold: *a much larger crowd.* Ha ha! You are having some kind of fun now!

And now you are pushing your way forward, thrusting other vacationers aside, knocking over their strollers if necessary, because little Jason wants to ride on Space Mountain. Little Jason has been talking about Space Mountain ever since Oklahoma, and by God you're going to take him on it, no matter how long the ...My God! Can *this* be the line for Space Mountain? This line is so long that there are Cro-Magnon families at the front! Perhaps if you explain to little Jason that he could be a deceased old man by the time he gets on the actual ride, he'll agree to skip it and...NO! Don't scream, little Jason! We'll just purchase some official Mickey Mouse sleeping bags, and we'll stay in line as long as it takes! The hell with third grade! We'll just stand here and chew our cuds! Moooo!

Speaking of education, you should be sure to visit Epcot Center, which features exhibits sponsored by large corporations showing you how various challenges facing the human race are being met and overcome thanks to the selfless efforts of large corporations. Epcot Center also features pavilions built by various foreign nations, where you can experience an extremely realistic simulation of what life in these nations would be like if they consisted almost entirely of restaurants and souvenir stores.

One memorable Epcot night my family and I ate at the German restaurant, where I had several large beers and a traditional German delicacy called "Bloatwurst," which is a sausage that can either be eaten or used as a tackling dummy. When we got out I felt like one of those snakes that eats a cow whole and then just

When my parents came from Nepal to visit they said Disneyland was on top of their "must-see" list. I tried to make excuses. It was a 7-hour drive, too expensive, there would be long lines under the hot sun that may not be good for their blood pressure or diabetes. And besides, it was for kids, not sophisticated, world-traveling adults. But Disneyland was not for themselves. It was for the grandkids, so they could tell them all about it.

So we went and I was glad, for my parents genuinely enjoyed themselves. They liked every ride, especially the large plastic "submarine" which took us " exploring" under the water of a vast swimming pool, a huge thrill for folks who live in a landlocked nation and had seen submarines only in movies. My own cynicism disappeared and I too found myself screaming in the Haunted House or cowering in fear as the cruel pirates of the Caribbean raided and pillaged.

◆

—Rajendra S. Khadka,
*The Hovering Hindu: An
Education on Two Continents*

lies around and digests it for a couple of months. But my son was determined to go on a new educational Epcot ride called "The Body," wherein you sit in a compartment that simulates what it would be like if you got inside a spaceship-like vehicle and got shrunk down to the size of a gnat and got injected inside a person's body.

I'll tell you what it's like: awful. You're looking at a screen showing an extremely vivid animated simulation of the human interior, which is not the most appealing way to look at a human unless you're attracted to white blood cells the size of motor homes. Meanwhile the entire compartment is bouncing you around violently, especially when you go through the aorta. "Never go through the aorta after eating German food," that is my new travel motto.

What gets me is, I waited in line for an hour to do this. I could have experienced essentially the same level of enjoyment merely by sticking my finger down my throat.

Which brings me to my idea for getting rich. No doubt you have noted that, in most amusement parks, the popularity of a ride is directly proportional to how horrible it is. There's hardly ever a line for nice, relaxing rides like the merry-go-round. But there will always be a huge crowd, mainly consisting of teenagers, waiting to go on a ride with a name like "The Dicer," where they strap people into what is essentially a giant food processor and turn it on and then phone the paramedics.

So my idea is to open up a theme park called "Dave World," which will have a ride called "The Fall of Death." This will basically be a 250-foot tower. The way it will work is, you climb to the top, a trapdoor opens up, and you splat onto the asphalt below like a bushel of late-summer tomatoes.

Obviously, for legal reasons, I couldn't let anybody actually *go* on this ride. There would be a big sign that said:

WARNING!

NOBODY CAN GO ON THIS RIDE.

THIS RIDE IS INVARIABLY FATAL,

THANK YOU.

But this would only make The Fall of Death more popular. Every teenager in the immediate state would come to Dave World just to stand in line for it.

Dave World would also have an attraction called "ParentLand," which would have a sign outside that said: "Sorry, Kids! This Attraction Is for Mom 'n Dad Only!" Inside would be a bar. For younger children, there would be "Soil Fantasy," a themed play area consisting of dirt or, as a special "rainy-day" bonus, mud.

I frankly can't see how Dave World could fail to become a huge financial success that would make me rich and enable me to spend the rest of my days traveling the world with my family. So the hell with it.

Dave Barry is a Pulitzer Prize-winning syndicated columnist at the Miami Herald. *His books include* Homes and Other Black Holes, Dave Barry's Greatest Hits, Dave Barry Slept Here, *and* Dave Barry Turns 40, *among others.*

Disneyland had its champions, too. The science fiction writer Ray Bradbury went to Disneyland in the company of the distinguished actor Charles Laughton (who later introduced Elvis Presley to America on Ed Sullivan's Sunday night TV show). They both loved the place, as much for the fact that the robot crocodiles were made out of plastic as for any other reason. Compared with the genuine article—dangerous and often invisible to the tourists—the toothy Disney version was new and improved: tireless, predictable, and benign, the very ideal of croco-tude on a sparkling clean Amazon in Anaheim, California, adjacent to the freeway. Disney's land as a whole was a lot like plastic crocodile. It was utopian, perfected—or perfectible. What is most important about the Laughton/Bradbury excursion to Disneyland, however, is the ripping good time the pair had "ducking when pistols were fired dead-on at charging hippopotamuses, and basking face up in the rain as we sailed under Schweitzer Falls." The Jungle Cruise was a visceral, sensual experience, like stepping, somehow, into the Technicolor confines of *The African Queen* and becoming a member of the cast, bound for some exotic coast in the company of Bogart and Hepburn.

—Karal Ann Marling, *As Seen on TV: The Visual Culture of Everyday Life in the 1950s*

DASHKA SLATER

* * *

Taken by Storm

Paddle to Georgia's barrier islands
before they blow away.

TROPICAL STORM GORDON GOT HIS NAME THE DAY BEFORE I flew to Georgia. I wasn't able to attend the christening, but I watched his progress on the Weather Channel from my sofa in California. The weatherman said there were small-craft warnings all the way from Savannah to the Florida Keys. This was not good news. I was going on a Sierra Club sea-kayaking outing off the Georgia coast, and even though I hadn't logged many hours in kayaks, I was pretty sure they qualified as small craft.

By the time my plane set down in Savannah, Gordon was growing stronger—and so were my doubts. On the flight I had pictured myself paddling through howling squalls and mountainous waves, and tried desperately to remember the rescue techniques I had been taught in my one and only kayaking class.

Still, everything looked fine as we got ready to put in at Tybee Island, a mass of beachfront houses, cheap motels, and seafood diners connected to Savannah by a causeway. The air was warm and moist, and the sky was veiled with a thin layer of pearly gray that seemed about to burn off any minute. Our first day's destination was the northern end of Little Tybee island (which, despite its name, is actually bigger than Tybee). More a complex of islands than a single land mass, Little Tybee is a green expanse of tidal marsh, populated by mink and sea otter and a vast array of birds. Scattered between the marshes are sand dunes and scrubby forests that become islands themselves at high tide, separated by creeks and channels and the spiky tops of the marsh grasses. We planned to spend the next five days kayaking in and around Little Tybee, moving progressively farther from civilization.

As we paddled out into Savannah Channel, bottlenose dolphins frolicked coyly around the boats, their black fins and tails blinking in and out of the waves. I yelped with pleasure at the sight of them. Fifteen minutes from the launch point I was soaking wet and the wind had whipped my hair into knots; nevertheless, I was feeling rapturous about nature, weather, and the Great Outdoors.

We hit Jack's Cut just as the tide began to turn, threatening to swamp our boats with insistent waves. A narrow inlet that snakes through the marshes of Little Tybee, the cut is only passable at high tide. Even at full spate it provided a substantial navigational challenge to those of us who were just getting the hang of steering a kayak. Jutting up from the water were "oyster rakes," sharp stalagmites of shells that can shear off the bottom of a boat. It seemed that whenever I swerved to avoid an oyster rake I ended up careening toward the opposite bank, causing a chain of kayak collisions to the rear as my tripmates paddled furiously to avoid me.

The cut opened into a wide expanse of water, and the green of the marshes was broken by a smooth mound of white beach. We pulled the boats up onto the shore and finished unloading them as the sun sank low over the horizon, spattering the sky with orange daubs as if from the hand of an unsubtle painter. A moment later the moon flared over the lip of the beach and we began looking for places to set up our tents.

The search for the perfect homestead can transform any group camping adventure into the Oklahoma Land Rush, but our trip leaders had cautioned us against trampling the vegetation because the sinewy railroad vines and feathery sea oats are all that hold the dunes together. This warning made the usual claim-staking a bit more decorous. Rather than stampeding through the dunes, we trotted along on tiptoe, hopping daintily over plant and shrub like ballerinas afraid of soiling their toe shoes.

The bad news came when we sat down for dinner. While the rest of us had been hunting for the perfect sleeping spot, our leaders had been listening to the weather radio. Tropical Storm Gordon was headed our way. By tomorrow night, our campsite would be under water.

There was just one other teeny problem. To get to higher ground we had to go back through Jack's Cut, and to go through Jack's Cut we needed a high tide. The next high tide was scheduled for the ungodly hour of 5 a.m., and if we wanted to be on dry land when the storm arrived, we had better be there to catch it.

Gordon hit a few hours later. He seemed to come all at once, in a rush of sound. I woke to a cacophony—the roar of the wind and the crashing surf punctuated by the twin percussions of the drumming rain and my rattling tent fly. As I lay awake trying to remember how securely I had staked my tent, I could hear the waves creeping up the shore, clapping against the sand as if applauding their own audacity.

At 5 a.m., I heard the soft drawl of Steve Braden, our kayak instructor.

*T*ropical weather, of continental violence, matching the landscape: the swamp of South Carolina running into the marsh of northern Florida, reeds green and brown, patches of water silver or black, a landscape impressive by its great size. And soon enough, from this tropical swamp, Charleston—which one had begun to take for granted: so perfect a creation—began to seem far away. It was hard to think of that town being set down here—as it was hard to associate all this coastal land with African slavery, land so much of the New World, so unlike any other, land one wanted to contemplate, to enter a little into its wonder.

♦

—V. S. Naipaul,
A Turn in the South

"Y'all awake?"

I was, but I didn't want to be. It was still dark out, and the rain was coming down in sheets. I knew I had to pack up my tent—if only I could figure out how to do it without getting out of my sleeping bag. Eventually I hoisted myself into a sitting position, only to be completely stymied by the question of clothes. Some sensible part of me knew that anything I wore in a kayak in a storm would be instantly soaked by saltwater and rain, but my skin recoiled at the thought of slipping into yesterday's sopping shorts and t-shirt. Succumbing to temptation, I put on every stitch of warm, fleecy clothing I had, and set out through the downpour.

Once we were on the water, being drenched to the skin seemed perfectly normal. Everything else in the landscape was wet, and there was no point in setting ourselves apart. I paddled alongside the marsh, listening to the *greet-greet-greet* of a clapper rail and wallowing in my discomfort. Carl Paulsen, the trip naturalist, had told me that clapper rails lay their eggs in featherweight nests that float when the tide floods the marshes. I pictured a sodden bird perched precariously on a damp, bobbing nest and felt a pang of kinship. A puddle of rainwater had gathered on my spray skirt and was slowly dripping into my lap and trickling down my thighs. My hands, after 24 hours of repeated soakings, were ter-rifying to behold. Thick coils of puckered white skin padded my fingertips, which were gloved by a fine coating of sand. The sand had also mysteriously found its way into my mouth, scalp, and the corners of my eyes. I felt as if I were being slowly transformed into a sand dune.

Carl and Steve wanted to keep close to home until the storm passed, so we set up camp on Buck's Hammock, not far from where we'd set out. When I looked across the channel I could see the snug little houses of Tybee Island. It felt a bit like camping in my parents' backyard, except that no one was bringing me any hot chocolate.

There was something about getting waterlogged in full view of people with roofs and hot water that made me self-conscious. I kept imagining some elderly Tybee Islander standing at the window of his warm living room and gazing at us through binoculars. "Honey," he'd be saying, "looks like there's some damn fools drenching themselves out on Buck's Hammock. Do you think they've lost their minds?"

"Don't worry dear," his wife would answer. "They're ecotourists. They like that kind of thing."

We finally got around to eating breakfast sometime after noon, following which most of us retreated into our tents to recuperate. A few, however, went for a walk along the beach with Carl, who promised that stormy weather was, in fact, ideal for learning about the geology of barrier islands.

"These islands are incredibly dynamic and fluid systems," he told us as we hunched against the wind. I could vouch for the fluid part, at least; the rain was still pelting down and the beach was racked with surf. All along the shore, we could see the contorted silhouettes of driftwood trees that were embedded in the sand. Wisps and swirls of sand skittered down the beach like a flock of ghostly sandpipers. If you were inclined to look on the bright side of things (I admit I wasn't), you could say we were seeing the island in its most characteristic mood.

Barrier islands first formed some 13,000 years ago, when the world was coated with glaciers and the eastern edge of the North American continent extended some 50 miles farther into the ocean. As the glaciers began to melt, the sea rushed over the continental shelf and onto the coastal plain, pushing forests, mud, and sand ahead of it. The wind, moving parallel to the land's edge, began arranging the sand in long ridges. Storms cut inlets through the ridges, and the sea flooded past them, turning them into islands. Then the ocean, still rising, began pushing the islands over the drowned coastal plain, closer and closer to shore.

Even now, the islands won't stay put. As winter storms and hurricanes strip sand from the islands' ocean side, the tides deposit sand and silt from the continental rivers on the landward side moving the islands gently west. At the same time, the prevailing northeasterly wind peels sand from each island's northern head and lays it down at its southern tail. In effect, the islands are rolling over themselves, imperceptibly somersaulting along the continent's edge.

As they move, barrier islands alternately erase and remake their own landscape. The trees we had taken for driftwood, Carl explained, were the bleached and gnarled remains of a forest of live oaks and palmettos much like the one directly behind us. As the island shifted, the old forest had been uprooted and then buried in sand.

Carl tapped his sneaker against a thick wedge of clay that lay on top of the beach. "This is a piece of old marsh," he told us. "The sand dunes rolled over it and it was covered for maybe ten years, and then became exposed again." He bent down to run his fingers along its sleek, brown surface. "This is beautiful to me," he said. "It's a perfect example of how dynamic this place is."

Once you become aware of the vagrant nature of these islands, it's hard to understand why anybody would build a town on one. But people do. There are nearly 300 barrier islands along the Atlantic Coast and most have been blanketed with resorts and vacation homes by those who believe that a beach is best admired from the front porch. Still, the islands refuse to honor the concept of private property, and eventually roll right out from under the houses and roads. Property lines stay fixed but the beach moves, sometimes bestowing an extra 500 feet of beachfront property, sometimes disappearing altogether and dumping a house into the sea.

> *I*slands have always fascinated the human mind. Perhaps it is the instinctive response of man, the land animal, welcoming a brief intrusion of earth in the vast, overwhelming expanse of sea.
>
> ◆
>
> —Rachel L. Carson,
> *The Sea Around Us*

The practice of building castles in the sand is encouraged by the federal flood insurance program, which bails out coastal residents whose homes are destroyed by sea or storm. "It's basically a subsidy for developing a fragile ecosystem," Carl told us. After Hurricane Hugo tore through South Carolina in 1989, 90 percent of the people who lost their homes rebuilt them on the same lots.

The ultimate effect of building houses on barrier islands is to take a natural process and make it into a disaster. If no one is living on the beach when a storm hits, no one is killed by flying debris and no one loses their house to flooding. It is only by insisting on stability in an environment where change is a constant that we put ourselves in danger....

Georgia is the one state that has left its barrier islands pretty well alone. Only three of its dozen barrier islands have been developed; the others are still wildlands of beach and dunes and marsh, where giant sea turtles come to lay their eggs and the occasional alligator stumbles through brackish swamp. This happy state of affairs is due more to luck than to planning, though. In the 19th century, these sea islands were a fashionable vacation spot for the families of northern industrialists like the Carnegies and southern planters like the Reynoldses; descendants of each of these families have passed their islands over to the state or federal park services.

Keeping barrier islands natural allows them to do what they do best: protect the mainland. As Steve Braden explained over dinner, barrier islands absorb the energy of Atlantic storms. Steve is a big fan of Orrin Pilkey, the Duke University geologist who has spent two decades crusading against thoughtless beach development. Pilkey has described a winter beach as a "battlefield filled with pitfalls." Each time the army of the waves advances over it, the waves lose a portion of their force. "So when people flatten out the dunes to build," Steve told me, "there's no defense against storms and hurricanes."

That night, the storm kicked up again. Gordon was now a hurricane and was doing his best to underscore all that Carl and Steve had been saying about the foolishness of trying to create permanence on barrier islands. In North Carolina's Outer Banks, 16-foot waves were toppling beach houses and pulling the carpet out from under part of Highway 12. The wind battered my tent with such force that I thought it was going to lift me up and carry me to Oz. When I poked my head out in the morning, I found that the water had risen almost to the front door.

The sea was too rough for us to travel anywhere, so we spent the day roaming the island. I ventured into a forest of pines and live oaks and amused myself dodging small thorny missiles launched by the jump cactus, which seemed equipped with a guidance system that sought out exposed flesh.

I blundered through a tangle of creeping vines and curtains of Spanish moss, until I burst out onto a vast expanse of red-tipped green cordgrass crossed by narrow saltwater creeks. Over the marsh, birds were wheeling and diving—snowy egrets, blue herons, and a pair of ospreys.

In the afternoon I sat on the beach and watched the sea birds. It was still raining, but by now I was so used to being wet and sandy that I scarcely noticed. In fact, I seemed to be taking the damp better than the great blue heron that was fishing apathetically by the edge of a creek. It stood ankle-deep, shoulders hunched like a reluctant swimmer, and raised first one foot and then the other as if shaking off the cold. Pelicans bobbed over the water wearing smug expressions that reminded me of fat restaurant patrons trying to settle on dessert. But my favorites were the skimmers, black and white sea birds with overlong bottom jaws. When feeding they fly low, dangling their oversized chops in the water in the hope that a fish will swim right down their throats. (I wondered how many cigarette butts and pieces of seaweed they end up swallowing in the process.)

Gordon began petering out by the end of the day, and the next morning we tried to get to an island called Petit Chou, nine miles away through a tortuous maze of channels. If we played the tides right, though, we could cut through on a creek with the unappealing name of Mosquito Ditch and shave off a couple hours of paddling time.

I was in a double kayak with a New Jersey naturalist named Douglas. We had paired up because we had discovered a shared fondness for the music of the '60s and '70s and had spent most of the past few evenings singing around what would have been a campfire if there had been any dry wood. Now we planned to sing all the way to Petit Chou, and had already drawn up a song list that included Janis Joplin, Simon and Garfunkel and the entire sound-track of *Godspell*.

Within ten minutes we had barely enough breath to hum. Both the wind and the tide were against us, and it seemed as if we had to paddle with all our might just to keep from going backwards. After an hour, we hadn't even covered a mile. Mosquito Ditch was still a ways ahead, and we had already missed the tide. There was no way to get to Petit Chou before dark. We were forced to turn back.

As we paddled toward our old campsite, the landscape that had been done up in shades of gray for the past three and a half days suddenly dissolved into Technicolor. The marsh turned an emerald green, the sea sparkled sapphire-blue, and a yellow ball of fire appeared in the sky. The sun was out.

The storm had turned on its heels and fled back down the coast, and for the remaining two days of the trip we had perfect weather. That night, as we ate dinner on the beach, the full moon ascended over the rim of the horizon and a single dolphin capered along the milky ladder of its reflection. Later, a few of us paddled up the creek deeper into the marshes. The night was perfectly still and the moon was so bright that we cast long shadows on the sand as we carried the boats down to the water. After the days of stormy chaos, the quiet was hypnotic. We spent an hour gliding through the marshes, hearing only the splash of our paddles, and the frantic flap of a great blue heron startled by our presence.

Even so, when the trip was over and I had returned home, I found that what stayed with me was the storm itself. Sitting in my house in California, a description of ocean waves that I had read in *The Beaches Are Moving* by Orrin Pilkey and Wallace Kaufman kept coming to mind. "A wave is like a bulge traveling across the ocean's surface," they write. "The bulge is not water itself racing from place to place, but energy traveling like a ghost through the body of the sea."

That energy, that ghost in the body of the sea, was the same spirit I had seen animating the shape-shifting coastal islands. In the sunshine, Little Tybee had been docile as a sleeping seal, a tropical postcard of white beach and swaying palmettos. But in the storm it had been alive and breathing, sloughing off its placid, sandy skin to reveal a wild and capricious soul.

Dashka Slater lives in Oakland, California, where she works as a staff writer for the weekly Express.

★

The sound of America was wild, and it was ear-rending. Listen:

Pelicans, ditzy wing-slappers, rising by the hundreds like a clatter of pots and pans over the river islands of places we know today as Kansas and Nebraska. Parakeets, shrieking flocks of them, in Virginia, Tennessee, and the Carolinas, tame, darting, pint-size rainbows swarming inches from the fingertips. Turkeys jabbering, jammed so thickly into trees along the river banks of Arkansas, Missouri, and Oklahoma that travelers told of turkey trees and likened the birds to apples. Whooping cranes tall as trombones, tooting their five-foot windpipes across Louisiana, Iowa, New Jersey, and Maryland. Trumpeter swans, elegant thirty-pound jazz bands, blaring down the Ohio and the Mississippi and south to the Gulf. Ivory-billed woodpeckers, monstrous wild-eyed things, red-crested, hard-hatted, jackhammering the forests of Georgia, South Carolina, Florida, and Alabama. Plovers and curlews, shrill-crying, roaming the Atlantic like storm clouds, pounding the mainland of Massachusetts, Rhode Island, Connecticut, and New York. And for nine million years, sandhill cranes, too high to be seen, too clamorous to go unheard, passing over Nebraska, over the Southwest and the Midwest, over all the Atlantic States.

—Robert Leonard Reid, *Mountains of the Great Blue Dream*

CATHY PETRICK

* [*] *

The Only Good Bear

Heed the ranger's warnings—
and enjoy the forest.

LAST SUMMER IN YOSEMITE NATIONAL PARK, BOY SCOUTS stoned to death a 100-pound black bear because it was stealing their dinner. Three bears, a sow and her twin year-old cubs, had wandered into the scouts' campsite, attracted by improperly stored food. Rangers speculated that if the troop had been able to accept its loss, no harm would have come to either the boys or the bears. But when the ursine raiding party refused to be scared off by human shouts, the troop leaders stepped up the attack until they nailed one of the cubs with a grapefruit-sized rock to the head. The bear died from its injuries. The scouts were allowed to continue their hike through the park.

As a park ranger in Yellowstone National Park, I think a lot about bears. In Yellowstone, we have grizzly bears as well as black bears, and we treat them all with respect. Of course, most people, in a panic, can't tell a grizzly from a black bear—so there's only one set of rules governing encounters with both species. Walk away— if you can. Or, if the bear attacks, play dead. Above the 45th parallel, we view bears as genuine threats rather than general nuisances—although the facts of their ferocity and proximity complicates things for many of us.

235

Most people would love to see a bear in the wild. Indeed, that's the number one goal indicated by Yellowstone tourists. But then, most visitors stick to their cars, scanning the forested hillsides through the tinted glass of their windshield. These same thrill-seekers, if they were to stop and secure a backcountry permit, abandon their vehicle, and buckle on a pack, would feel differently about their chances of meeting a bear.

Bears have made me feel all kinds of things.

I learned to backpack in bear country, in Yellowstone, where I first worked as a concession employee while in college, and then much later became a park ranger. Since then I've hiked other places, but whenever I think of sleeping out under the stars, I think of bears too. Experienced Yellowstone backpackers know enough to follow the rules and keep their fingers crossed. Bears are the last thing you want to see at your backcountry campsite. Suddenly, the bear drops to the bottom of the traveler's list, and even fleeting thoughts of the animal can prove unsettling.

The wisest visitors to Yellowstone follow the guidelines set forth in leaflets distributed by the National Park Service: Don't cook in the same place you plan to camp. Don't cook odiferous foods. Change your clothes after you cook and before you go to bed. Hang all food, along with scented cosmetics, toothpaste, deodorant, and the clothes you cooked in, at least one hundred yards downwind from camp. To accomplish this feat, you'll need to find a tree with an appropriate down-sloping limb, about 17 feet up. Throw the weighted end of a line over the outermost reach of the branch. Secure the food sack to the free end of the line and haul it up at least 12 feet off the ground. Tie the long end of the rope to the base of the tree.

In truth, it's almost impossible to exercise this degree of conscientiousness. In my experience, no limb exists in nature of the requisite height and configuration to secure food according to the textbook. After you tie the rock to the end of the rope and toss it, the rock usually falls off before the line has completed its arc to the branch—sometimes dropping down onto the heads of your unsuspecting companions. Most branches, if they are too skinny to support the weight of a bear, are also too slim to support the weight of a food sack. The branch bends and the sack dangles within batting distance from the ground. My husband, when he used to hike alone, would find himself worrying about his food to the extent that he would hike back two or three times from his tent to re-hang the food before retiring once and for all for the night. I have hung my food so far from camp that I was unable to find it in the morning.

Still, I've grown lazy and taken a risk from time to time. Yet I never stopped thinking about bears. Even in the bold light of day, the rare encounter is unforgettable.

During the very first backpacking trip I took as a ranger (I was supposed to set an example now), I saw a bear with cubs and I reacted badly. My sister Ellen had just explained to me that the last thing you want to do is run. If you run, you will only attract the attention of the bear, which otherwise may have been happy to ignore you. By "acting like dinner," the hapless runner triggers the chase response in the bear; the predator is then obligated to play out the equally instinctual pull-down-and-eviscerate response. When my friends and I saw the black bear and three cubs at the tree line at the far edge of the meadow, two hundred yards away, we knew enough to turn around. The last thing we wanted was to encroach upon the territory of a mother bear with cubs. We hastened to make room for her. Unfortunately, in my desire to appear non-aggressive, and fueled by adrenaline, my "hasten" got cranked up to a run. I wasn't aware that I was running. It was only when my sister, jogging alongside, screamed in my ear that I realized I had over-reacted. She wanted me to stop running because until I did, our companions, trailing calmly behind, would only appear to the bear as weaker and slower members of an otherwise nimble-footed herd.

When bears meet humans, they too usually choose to walk the other way. My brother-in-law, who often fishes in bear country, told me of a recent near-miss.

Ed and his camping buddies had canoed into the remote South Arm of Yellowstone Lake to spend Labor Day weekend. "Weren't you nervous?" I asked. "I mean, being so far from help?" I didn't say bears, but he knew what I meant.

"Wait," he said. "I'm getting to that part."

Ed and his two friends had beached their canoe, and were spending the afternoon exploring on foot, some thirty miles from the nearest road. Inland, they had located a backcountry geyser basin and had enjoyed exploring the curiously-shaped and multi-colored pools. While hiking back to camp, they stopped to rest, drank some water, and then continued on their way. Almost immediately, they came upon some tracks. Without speaking, they all recognized the tracks as bear tracks, although they couldn't see the toes or the claws clearly enough to identify the species. They all commented on the size of the prints, which appeared to measure about five inches across. They trailed it for a few yards, to a point where the bear's tracks intersected the hikers' own set of prints. At this point, the bear tracks told an interesting story. The bear had stomped out a circle in the dust. Apparently, having verified their presence, it had shaken off the steps of an agitated tarantella before veering off into the woods. Ed figures that the bear had executed its odd dance on the spot not ten minutes before—that it had, in fact, puzzled out their presence while they drank from their canteens not 50 yards away. "In retrospect," Ed says, "*all* of my experiences with bears have been positive."

We don't know what it is, exactly, that provokes the rare attacks, so it's hard to tell people what to do when faced with a bear. Statistically, it's a good bet to play dead. But this trick probably only works in sudden, surprise encounters at close range. If a bear is startled, its defensive reaction is to strike a quick blow. "And a grizzly's defense puts most good offenses to shame," notes Paul Schullery, a Yellowstone naturalist and writer who has long observed bears. Surprise encounters are especially dangerous if the bear is with cubs, or defending a kill.

Take the story of one of my fellow rangers. Naturalist Barb Pettinga and her husband had been hiking at Mud Volcano on a spring day, scouting out the trail for an interpretive hike. When they noticed a bison carcass they grew uneasy because they knew that bears feed on carcasses in early spring. Then they saw the bear. The bear charged. Barb recalls the moment with emotion even several years later.

Her ears were flattened down along her head and all of the hair was flattened. So she looked very streamlined. She was fully stretched out so she was coming fast.

"It's a terribly frightening.... It's a real jolt to see something coming like that and knowing that...it's happening."

The next thing Barb knew she was on the ground and the bear was on top of her. The bear was moving all over her body and Barb could feel her claws or her teeth (her eyes were closed so she didn't know which). Barb knew instantly that her only hope was to play dead.

> *M*onsters and marvels can inhabit empty spaces; but once spaces are filled—with rivers, lakes, and continents—the creations of imagination must move. Where? The Utopian lands, the Islands of the Blessed, could linger at the horizon. But when the horizon is pushed back, delineated, fixed and crowded with coordinates, then where?
>
> ◆
>
> —Sheila Nickerson,
> *Disappearance: A Map:*
> *A Meditation on Death and*
> *Loss in the High Latitudes*

Throughout the attack, Barb lay perfectly still. Mercifully, she felt no pain at the time of the mauling, but she was aware of the strength of the blows which knocked her about. Then the bear ran off. The bear stopped a short distance away, upslope from where Barb lay. Then she charged again. The bear rolled Barb over three times. Each time Barb used the momentum from the blow and her position on the hillside to roll back over onto her stomach in a protected position. Only when the bear was sure that the humans posed no threat did it leave them.

Barb and her husband hiked the mile-long trail back to the road, and all Barb could talk about was how she hoped they wouldn't kill the bear. The bear had reacted aggressively in the surprise encounter to scare the intruders off the carcass. It had left them alone once it was sure they posed no threat. Barb got her way and nothing was done to the bear. Her injuries healed (I was only aware of a long, seam-like scar the length of her jaw), and she continued to work in Yellowstone, talking freely about her experience, and educating people about bears.

My favorite book in my Yellowstone collection is Stephen Herrero's *Bear Attacks, Their Causes and Avoidance.* Herrero states that his aim isn't to horrify, but to sufficiently describe and explain attacks and suggest how to minimize the chance of their occurrence. Most people I know, however, have read only chapters 1–9, the attack chapters, and skipped chapters 10–17, the sections on bear biology and bear management. I, too, find the opening chapters most compelling. Some of my fascination is the thrill of pure horror. This is the book I pull off the shelf to read aloud and entertain Yellowstone house-guests after dinner. But, once the novelty has passed and I find myself fascinated still, I like to think that these stories nourish me in other ways. I wonder how many people have read them as I have: as morality plays, in which the bear metes out punishment for the human sins of sloth, vanity, and pride.

In the story of Julie Hegelson, a concessions employee in Glacier National Park, the bear doesn't really decide to do her in until she

---

They were picture-book grizzly tracks, slab footed, with the long claws, and for a moment—as when you first awaken from a dream—I could not make sense of the size of them. I could tell they were grizzly, but the size of them shut something down in my mind. My little twenty-gauge popgun, the little iron stick with the little cardboard shells in it, felt like a crooked twig in my hand. I felt as if I were suddenly filled with straw and existed for no other purpose than to have the stuffing knocked out of me.

◆

—Rick Bass, "My Grizzly Story," *Audubon*

breaks down and cries out in pain. "It hurts," she protests, and then she starts to scream. She continues to scream as the bear drags her down the hill and her voice fades away in the distance. Her companion, who remained stoic throughout the attack, survived. In this story, I also appreciated the details of the chewing gum in the backpack and the leftover sandwiches, which the campers had cached nearby, "under a big log."

Then there's the tale of Michele Coons, another Glacier Park employee—strangely enough killed on the same night as Julie Hegelson, but by a different bear. For some reason Michele was unable to react in time. A bear had been harassing Michele and her friends all night long, stealing their food, and chasing them from one campsite to the next. When the bear finally attacked, the boy sleeping next to Michele got clawed in the back. The bear tore off his shirt, but he managed to spring free and ran for a tree. Three other friends were also able to scramble safely into the trees. Michele either made no effort to get out of her sleeping bag or her zipper got stuck. Her friends called to her to unzip her bag, but by then the bear had the zipper in his mouth. The bear tore off Michele's arm and then dragged her away in her sleeping bag. Michele screamed, "Oh God, I'm dead," and that was the last sound anyone ever heard from her. "Michele was known to be a heavy user of cosmetics," Herrero writes—the scent of which could have drawn the bear to her. The teenagers had also brought cookies and Cheezits into camp with them.

In each of these stories, bears were killed shortly after the attacks. The night after Julie was killed, two adult grizzlies returned to the campground to feed on garbage. Both bears, possible suspects, were shot, though no direct evidence linked them to Julie's death. The next night a female with cubs appeared. She was known to be an old and experienced garbage feeder. She too was killed.

The day after Michele was killed, park rangers shot an old female grizzly bear two-and-a-half miles up the valley from the attack site.

It would be easy for a ranger to condemn Julie for her chewing gum and Michele for her mascara. Did they follow the rules? we ask. After all, education and enforcement are our jobs and we take our work seriously. We write pamphlets and distribute them at entrance gates, and we give lectures at the evening campfire programs. We tell people how to protect themselves. When they screw up we write tickets and confiscate their unattended coolers. We do these things for the campers' own good as well as for the protection of the bears. But, in the cases of Julie and Michele, chewing gum and mascara were probably not the key attractants.

My own occasional lapses in backcountry etiquette also cause me to bite my tongue. I recognize that Michele and Julie stumbled into their tragic encounters; they are not to blame. Nor, really, can I condemn the bears. Over time, and with repeated exposure to human garbage, the bears that killed the young women had lost their fear of humans. The bears were probably confused by the humans once they had been drawn into the camps. At some point, it seems, the bears began to think of the campers as possible prey, but the focus of the attacks was not killing for food. If it had been, death would have come quickly. And in neither case were the bodies consumed.

These stories are very different from the brief encounters that I and friends of mine have experienced. In Glacier Park, where the bear was bold enough to enter a campsite, playing dead would have done no good. In fact, the camper's best chances would have been either to flee or to attempt to intimidate the bear before it made up its mind to attack.

I feel sorry for Michele and Julie, but three bears were killed at the site of Julie's death, and two of them at least were totally innocent. The death penalty fell quickly upon the species as a whole, without a thought for the individual. It is only after a bear is killed, after all, and the contents of its stomach examined, that we can know for sure whether the animal is the actual perpetrator. The swiftness of the human reaction to the insult of death by a wild animal is what bothers me.

There are so few grizzlies left now that it's a wonder we pretend the fight has any punch left to it at all. Man has long ago established his dominion over all—the bears are doomed. When a bear takes a human life, we will insist on the last word with the blast of a gun.

The closest I ever came to a grizzly bear was to a dead one. A bear had been struck by a car and left to die shortly after sunrise along the road near West Thumb Junction—a hit and run. A ranger came upon the bear in the middle of the road just two miles into the morning's first patrol. When he laid his hand upon the bear's back, it was still warm. It took four men, a pick-up truck, and a stretcher to move the two-year-old grizzly from the road into the ranger station. Word spread, and park employees were encouraged to stop in at the station throughout the day to view the grizzly bear stretched out on the concrete floor of the garage. Most of us had never seen a grizzly up close, and it was a good opportunity to learn to identify the species.

It was dark and quiet inside the garage, and the awe I felt in the presence of the bear was undiminished even by its death. No one said much. We just walked around the bear to inspect it from all sides and then crouched down to get a closer look. There was no blood. Its coat was healthy and smooth. Apparently, it had been fishing for cutthroat trout in the nearby creek, and had been struck as it had attempted

Though we still try to see the wildlife in America as untrammeled, there is little left that is pristine. This is no exaggeration: the wilder, the more spectacular a creature is, the greater the likelihood in America that it is tagged or radio-collared, even surviving on dosages of medicine. Few wild animals are seen anymore except by the biologists who make it their living to chart—and save— these creatures' lives with all the paraphernalia of high technology. The reality is that much of our wildlife had been lost and most of what is left wears collars.

◆

—Charles Bergman, *Wild Echoes: Encounters with the Most Endangered Animals in North America* to cross the road. Its weight was later determined at 250 pounds—at the time I just thought it looked big—and its age was estimated by taking a cross section of a tooth and counting the rings.

After I had squatted next to it for a long time and my legs had started to cramp up, I reached out and touched its shoulder. The sadness I felt in that moment has become the strongest emotion I feel now whenever I think about bears.

Cathy Petrick works for the National Park Service in the Marin Headlands near San Francisco. She was a Yellowstone ranger from 1989 to 1995 and is currently writing essays about Yellowstone.

★

The alluvial plain of Yellowstone is dinosaur country. Some of the most spectacular beasts in East Coast museums happen to be *Tyrannosaurus rexes* from Montana. In recent years, the man who was leading the dig near Fonda's ranch, John ("Jack") Horner, curator at the Museum of the Rockies in Bozeman, had uncovered dinosaur graveyards composed not of lone *T. rexes* but of over ten thousand individuals. Some plant-eating dinosaurs evidently ran in placid herds, "the cows of the Cretaceous." This intrigued me mightily.

Like most people, I had always held to the *Dances with Wolves* view of what the plains of the Yellowstone were like before we—us white men and white ladies—arrived: that the grasslands were covered with countless herds of brown buffalo, so many that the members of the Lewis and Clark expedition were forced to wait for hours down-river for the animals to pass before they could proceed, and sometimes at night had to fire their weapons to keep from being trampled in their beds. But this vision of Montana, obviously, was fresh-painted. This morning I conjured not bison on the banks but, instead, giant, oddly shaped, scaly skinned, duck-billed *Maiasaura peeblesorums*, the "good mother" dinosaurs with which Professor Horner was revolutionizing the world's view on dinosaurs, perhaps our view of ourselves, and certainly my view of historical Montana. *M. peeblesorums* is now the official state dinosaur of Montana.

—Steve Chapple, *Kayaking the Full Moon*

SEAN O'REILLY

* * *

Diamonds!

High hope in Arkansas.

How many of you have dreamed of struggling through treacherous jungles, warding off fever and bellicose locals to finally come across a sun-swept clearing and a stream? Bending down to wash off the sweat and the mud, your eye catches a sparkle; you plunge your hand into the water and pull out a fistful of diamonds, glittering in the sun and conjuring up images of fantastic wealth.

You don't have to go to South America or Africa to find diamonds; they are here for the picking in Arkansas.

In the forests of southwest Arkansas near Murfreesboro there is a 40-acre field where diamonds can be found in their natural geologic matrix—the only diamond area in North America open to the public. There have been more than 60,000 diamonds found at the "Crater" (an eroded volcanic pipe) over the years, including the "Uncle Sam" (40 carats), "Star of Murfreesboro" (34 carats), "Star of Arkansas" (15 carats), and the "Amarillo Starlight" (16 carats). Most recently, in June of 1981, the near 9 carat "Star of Shreveport" was added to the roll call of impressive finds picked up at the site.

Although genuine diamonds are the major attraction, other semi-precious gems and minerals can also be found. Amethyst, agate, jasper, quartz, calcite, barite, and many others—over 100 different rocks and minerals altogether—make the area a paradise for rock-hounds. Nearby in Murfreesboro there is also an old Indian burial ground for those of a more archaeological bent. South of Murfreesboro on State Highway 4 is the historic town of Old Washington. During the Civil War this town became the state capital after Little Rock was captured by the Union. Here also, Sam Houston, Davy Crockett, and Jim Bowie met to gather a frontier army to fight for Texas in its battles with Mexico.

Since its discovery in 1906, the Murfreesboro Crater of Diamonds has been shrouded in mystery and intrigue. There were rumors in the past that the worldwide diamond cartel schemed to keep it closed or at least inactive. A South African baron is reported to have offered one of the American owners of the mine a bribe of $150,000 and boasted that he would spend one million pounds sterling to keep the Arkansas field from going into production. Gems from Murfreesboro, he feared, would mean a catastrophic break from the cartel's artificial prices.

The Crater of Diamonds story really began in 1899. That year a tall backwoodsman by the name of John W. Huddleston bought 160 acres, including four-fifths of the Crater, for $2000. He thought there might be some chance that it would contain gold. After a particularly heavy storm in August of 1906, he was prospecting, crawling along the rain-furrowed ground, when he saw a shiny pebble half sticking out of the dirt. He examined it quizzically and decided to take it home for a closer look. There he found that he could etch his window pane with the stone.

He saddled his mule with slow excitement, beginning to think that he might have found a diamond. He rode to the bank in town and showed the stone to a cashier.

"I think this might be a diamond," he said. "How much will you give me for it?"

The cashier inspected the steel blue stone; turning it over in his hand, he said "Fifty cents."

Huddleston was disgusted. "If that is all it's worth, I might as well throw it away." He stormed across the street to the office of

J.C. Pinnix, a Pike County bigwig. Pinnix listened carefully to Huddleston's story and told him that he would send the stone to S. Swift, a Little Rock jeweler whom he could trust. Swift later reported to Pinnix that the diamond was of the highest quality, on par with South Africa's best. What happened to John Huddleston from this point on remains lost in the lore and legend that has grown up about this place.

The diamonds found at the Crater today are of similar quality to Huddleston's stone and they are yours for the keeping.

The modern Crater area is beautifully situated in pine forests along the banks of the Little Missouri River. Coming down from the reception area to the Crater, I was filled with a sense of antic-ipation and adventure. I spent a great deal of time the first day on my hands and knees, clambering over the hillocks of the Crater, listening to the distant echoes of the dinosaurs, who 60 million years ago had surely walked this way.

I found many pieces of broken quartz—your heart leaps every time you see *anything* that shines. Diamonds have been found all over the field, so it is worth your while to pick a comfortable spot and work it with a trowel and sieve (both can be rented at the park center) for a couple of hours.

I was the only person in the field who had kneepads and be-lieve me, they are essential when you are getting eyeball close to the ground. I was told that one lady had found over ten diamonds by going through the tractor furrows (the fields are plowed weekly) on her stomach. I was unable to determine her profits, so perhaps this story too is legend.

The forty-acre field is roughly circular, with the remnants of old mining operations visible at three locations. At one end of the field is the "pig pen" where some good quality diamonds have been found. The mud is black and difficult to work through, so bring rubber boots if you want to examine this end of the Crater.

Three days later, while I still had found nothing, five small dia-monds were found by others. Their sizes ranged from under a "point" to four carats. I was not disappointed though, as the tall pines and rough-hewn beauty of the place made it a delightful visit; besides, I know that my forty-carat stone is lying out there in the Crater of Diamonds, just waiting for me.

Sean O'Reilly is editor-at-large for Travelers' Tales.

★

Practical Tips for Hunting Diamonds

Park authorities suggest the following practical tips for hunting diamonds:

1. Look for a small, well rounded crystal. A diamond weighing several carats may be no larger than a marble.
2. Diamonds have an oily, slick outer surface that dirt or mud will not stick to, so look for clean crystals.
3. If you think you have a diamond, hold it carefully in your hand. Experience has shown that once a diamond is dropped, it usually isn't found again that day.
4. Diamonds may be of several colors. The most common found at the Crater are brown, yellow, and clear white.
5. Bring any stone you think may be a diamond to the Visitor Center for free weight and certification. Anything you find is yours.

—FS

CALVIN TRILLIN

* * *

Enjoying the
Louisiana Rodent

You can watch, wear, or eat him.

I WAS, I'LL ADMIT, TAKEN WITH THE NOTION THAT LOUISIANA HAS a scheme to eat its way out of its nutria crisis. In south Louisiana people tend to discuss nutrias in more or less the same tone of voice that Texans might use to discuss armadillos. The tone of voice is not the one you'd employ for serious statements about grace and nobility in the animal kingdom. A nutria is about the shape and size of a small beaver—except for the tail, which is, I'm afraid, very much like the tail of a rat. There are other features that do not please. Nutria fur is used for coats, but the guard hairs that cover the usable fur are a snarl. The nutria's hind feet are webbed, which somehow does not make a nice contrast with its front feet. It has four clearly visible incisors, two up and two down—wide and curved and exceedingly long and, well, not to put too fine a point on it, orange.

The unsettling appearance of nutrias might cause less nervous laughter if they weren't so numerous. In the bayous and swamps and marshes and sugarcane fields a couple of hours south-west of New Orleans, an area settled in the eighteenth century by the people who became known as Cajuns, there are literally millions of nutrias. They are not shy. On a recent trip to Louisiana, I heard more than one person estimate the number of nutrias observed on, say, an afternoon's canoe trip as "so many that it was kind of scary." Nutrias are spotted near shopping malls in Lafayette and even in the drainage canals of Jefferson Parish, in suburban New Orleans. Last winter the New Orleans *Times-Picayune* carried a quotation from a trapper that sounded as if it had been snatched from a horror movie: "They're eating Jefferson Parish. It's out of control."

Most of Louisiana's nutria population can be traced to a hundred or so nutrias that escaped from the Avery Island spread of E. A. (Mr. Ned) McIhenny, the Tabasco mogul, around 1940: they were the descendants of thirteen he had imported from Argentina, the nutria's native habitat, a few years before. There is some indication that Mr. Ned, who was devoted to maintaining the coastal marsh of Louisiana in its natural state, may have been raising the nutrias with the intention of introducing them into the marsh anyway, as a way to broaden the trapping industry, then dominated by hunters of muskrat pelts, or as a way to keep down objectionable aquatic weeds—like the water hyacinth, another South American import that some people thought the nutria would just naturally gobble up.

*A*s for New Orleans, in springtime—just when the orchards were flushing over with peach-blossoms, and the sweet herbs came to flavor the juleps—it seemed to me the city of the world where you can eat and drink the most and suffer the least.

◆

—William Makepeace Thackeray (1852)

Whether by accident or by design, the descendants of Mr. Ned's nutrias did come to dominate the Louisiana fur industry. At the height of the boom, in the late seventies, Louisiana trappers brought in nearly two million nutria pelts a year, most of which were sent to Europe, where nutria has always been more popular as a fur than it is in the United States. In those days the nutria was often thought of as a successful transplant—an economic incentive to preserve vital marshlands. Given the amount of money coming in, some people had probably decided that the nutria was, in its own way, rather attractive.

Although the nutria industry was based almost entirely on pelts, some carcasses were ground up for mink food, and some were employed in a Department of Agriculture project as a medium for growing screwworms. (The uses of nutria carcasses have tended to be unromantic.) In Washington, Louisiana, I met a woman named June Lowrey who for a time was making jewelry out of nutria teeth—a business she launched by acquiring a hundred nutria heads and, after a long and frustrating afternoon with an ordinary pair of pliers, consulting her dentist for some advice on tools. Her jewelry business came to an end when she discovered that nutria teeth grow brittle with age. Until then they are striking—two-tone, because the back and the part beneath the gum are white. Lowrey referred to them as "swamp ivory."

In the eighties the price of nutria pelts began to fall, and trappers began to find that it wasn't worth their while to go out. The nutria birth rate, though, did not adjust to the shrinkage of the market. Rice and sugarcane farmers began complaining that their irrigation dams and crops were being destroyed by nutrias. Even more serious, evidence was mounting that nutrias, which destroy a lot more vegetation than they actually consume, were obliterating entire sections of the coastal wetlands. Scientists have a succinct term for the damage nutrias can do to a section of marsh: an "eat-out."

As evidence of marsh destruction was documented, the nutria joke often heard among conservationists was that Paul Prudhomme ought to be persuaded to invent a nutria recipe popular enough to bring the nutrias under control. The reference was to Prudhomme's impact on the redfish. In the late seventies, while working as a chef in a renowned New Orleans restaurant called Commander's Palace, Prudhomme decided that the method for cooking what was sometimes called an Indian steak—tossing a steak on a ferociously hot piece of cast iron known to chefs as a flat-top, so that the meat was seared on the outside and juicy inside—could work with firm-fleshed fish. He happened to try it with redfish, which is the name people in Louisiana use for red drum—a fish then popular mainly among sportsmen. The menu at Commander's Palace—and at Mr. B's Bistro, where Prudhomme went next—called it grilled redfish. When Prudhomme opened his own restaurant in the French Quarter, K-Paul's Louisiana Kitchen, he used a white-hot skillet instead of a flat-top and called the dish blackened redfish. It was an instant hit—so popular that he had to ration it to one order per table. Within six weeks of its introduction, he told me when I stopped in to see him in New Orleans, a customer reported having seen blackened redfish on a menu in Florida.

Partly owing to the impact of Chef Paul, a massive and magnetic figure, restaurants around the country began including on their menus a version of this dish, which they called Cajun—and which Prudhomme, a legitimate Cajun from Opelousas, described sadly as "burnt fish with a whole lot of pepper on it." It was immaterial that the only Cajuns

---

We decided to have breakfast before rather than after reaching New Orleans, which was about 70 miles away. At the roadside cafe, I said to the waitress almost pleadingly, "Please, no grits for me." After a week of traveling in the South, I had taken a violent dislike to grits, a white mound or barfy spread next to the eggs, sunny-side up.

The waitress, a woman approaching middle-age and a pro at her job, regarded me silently for a moment. Then she rasped, "No grits, huh? What are you, a Yankee?"

I had to suppress my surprise—and laughter. Here I was, a brown college boy, who was often mistaken for a Puerto Rican, now being told I was a damn Yankee. I have never felt more American.

◆

—Rajendra S. Khadka,
The Hovering Hindu: An Education on Two Continents

who had ever eaten blackened redfish were those who had traveled to New Orleans, a city where Cajuns had traditionally been ridiculed as ignorant country folk with funny accents, and had dined at Commander's Palace or Mr. B's Bistro or K-Paul's Louisiana Kitchen. Some commercial fishermen began going after schools of redfish with spotter planes. Although Prudhomme himself switched to blackened tuna early on, the national redfish craze continued. He felt guilty about the redfish, he told me, and guilty about the glop that was being passed off as Cajun food. ("This is my culture!") In 1988 Louisiana banned the commercial catching of redfish in its waters. The ban created a new crime: redfish laundering. In an ambitious undercover operation in July of 1993, wildlife agents arrested 45 people on charges of sneaking Louisiana redfish to Mississippi and then bringing it back to sell in Louisiana.

Getting Paul Prudhomme to do for the nutria on purpose what he had done for the redfish by accident did sound like a joke, but Robert Thomas, a biologist at the Louisiana Nature and Science Center, in New Orleans, thought Chef Paul might at least demonstrate what a nutria could taste like when it emerged from the pot of a master. A year or so ago Thomas asked Prudhomme to provide some demonstration dishes for a day of food and entertainment and education which the Louisiana Nature and Science Center had decided to call a nutriafest.

As if doing penance for all those redfish that were sacrificed so that Yankees could coat them with pepper and call them Cajun, Prudhomme showed up to serve nutria dishes that included cubed and deep-fried nutria, prepared more or less the way he prepares the crayfish appetizer that the K-Paul menu introduced as Cajun popcorn. The experience made him think that the notion of serving nutria in restaurants someday was not so far-fetched. Bob Thomas points out that nutrias are lean animals and are strictly vegetarian. ("You just have to get by the fact that it's a big old rodent-looking thing.") He says that in Eastern Europe, where raising nutria for both fur and meat caught on years ago, the meat, known as *ragondin*, is considered a delicacy. He says that nutria meat "accepts seasoning well," which sounds like a nice way of saying that it doesn't have a whole lot of taste. By the second annual nutriafest, Thomas had as a corporate sponsor the McIhenny Company—another penitent. The cookoff was won by a computer specialist who prepared what he called "apple-smoked nutria and wild-mushroom crepe in bourbon-pecan nutria sauce." Tacos came in second.

"I don't think we're going to solve the whole problem with Chef Paul," Greg Linscombe told me, when I called on him at the Louisiana Department of Wildlife and Fisheries office in New Iberia. "But he might be part of the answer." Linscombe, a biologist, is responsible for both the coastal marsh and the management of fur-bearing animals—interlocking portfolios that have made him into the state's resident expert on what to do about nutria proliferation. His strategy is based on the simple fact that the nutria's only predator—aside from the alligator,

> *eavers' primary enemies are humans. North American beavers were heavily trapped when the West was first explored and settled, exploited for their highly prized fur. Beaver pelts were even used as a form of currency in remote areas, and wars were fought over access to beaver habitat. From a population of millions, beavers almost became extinct by the beginning of this century; by 1900, only an estimated 100,000 remained in the wild. Though still hunted for fur and meat in parts of North America, they are now slowly recovering through reintroduction efforts.*
>
> ◆
>
> —Diana Landau and Shelley Stump, *Living with Wildlife: How to Enjoy, Cope with, and Protect North America's Wild Creatures Around Your Home and Theirs*

which spends part of the year in a sort of hibernating state that inhibits the appetite—is man. Linscombe figures that even if the method of control is spreading poison or offering bounties, several thousand human beings are going to have to be in the marshlands. He would prefer to have them there as trappers in a prosperous industry. To that end he is working on ways to enhance the price of nutria pelts: Louisiana now has a nutria-marketing consultant, for instance, and a campaign to distinguish its product from Argentine nutria by marketing it as Genuine Louisiana Bayou Nutria. He sees the use of the nutria carcass for human consumption as potentially a way to "put another dollar or dollar and a half into the trapper's pocket"—a supplement that could tip the balance toward persuading someone that trapping nutrias is economically worthwhile.

Linscombe envisions nutrias being offered as a sort of gimmick appetizer in certain restaurants in New Orleans and Lafayette, and eventually finding broader use—on the model of alligator meat, now a significant factor in the economics of both alligator hunting, which was once done strictly for hides, and alligator farming. Inquiries from Asia and Africa have already been received. He reminded me that people from different cultures have differing ideas of what appears appetizing. "Maybe some place in the Far East will want it with the tail on," he said.

"Or only the tail," I ventured.

And so to table. Linscombe had arranged to deliver a few nutrias to Enola Prudhomme, Chef Paul's sister, who runs a restaurant called Prudhomme's Cajun Café, just north of Lafayette. Enola Prudhomme, whose menu already includes "alligator sauce piquante" and wild-boar sausage, is, like her brother, optimistic about the appeal of nutria meat. ("People are going to eat it as a curiosity and then find it really tastes good.") One of her sons, Sonny, prepared three different dishes for a few of us novice nutria eaters—nutria chili, a sort of nutria fricassee, and panfried nutria tenderloins with a Creole mustard sauce. We cleaned our plates. I suspect that any one of Sonny's dishes could have taken the nutriafest cookoff hands down, if I may say that with no disrespect intended toward the apple-smoked nutria and wild-mushroom crepe in bourbon-pecan nutria sauce. If I had been pressed to say what nutria reminded me of, I would have said rabbit, although I may have been biased in that direction by the thought of a rabbit's nice fluffy tail.

After dinner Sonny took us back into the kitchen, so that he could use the nutria carcass he had left to explain a bit about nutria anatomy. He said that the meat is remarkably lean—both Paul and Enola Prudhomme have found they have to add some pork in order to make nutria sausage—and easy to work with, except for a membrane that has to be removed. I assume that Greg Linscombe would avoid mentioning the membrane in his meat-marketing schemes; it's one of those words, like "rodent."

The next afternoon I paid a visit to a friend named Barry Jean Ancelet, a folklorist who is the chairman of the modern-language department at the University of Southwestern Louisiana. Barry, assisted by his wife, Caroline, was preparing nutria sauce piquante. In Barry's view, the nutria probably would have joined other swamp critters in the Cajun diet long ago if it had been around when poverty and isolation enhanced Cajun inventiveness in the kitchen. By the time nutrias began to appear in the marshlands in any numbers, he said, the Second World War had already drawn a lot of Cajuns into the cities and to their first salaried jobs. Although Cajuns remain much more adventurous in their eating habits than most other Americans, the days when they were assumed to eat just about anything are gone. As someone I met in New Iberia said, "Why eat nutria when you can get frozen chicken breasts cheap at Sam's?"

One of the Ancelets' sons, Francois, put a nutria skull on the table as a sort of centerpiece, and we sat down. The nutria sauce piquante was terrific. Barry showed me the recipe. It had some instructions familiar to Cajun cooking, such as "make small roux, add onions, bell peppers, celery, and garlic" and "add parsley and onion tops just before serving." The nutria was a triumph, I told Barry, although I had to allow for the possibility that prepared in his sauce piquante the *Times-Picayune,* which presumably also accepts seasoning well, would have been a triumph. Putting both the tail and the membrane from my mind, I asked for seconds.

"I actually call it Nutria Caroline," Barry said, with a hint of a bow toward his wife. "I thought of calling it Nutria Cagney."

"Nutria Cagney?"

Barry stood and, holding his elbows close to his body and his hands pointed straight ahead, said, "You dirty rat."

"You dirty rat!" I was still thinking, as I arrived at the New Orleans airport for the flight home. I had spoken to a couple of other chefs in New Orleans, who thought that the notion of restaurants serving nutrias was somewhere between a pipe dream and an opportunity to use phrases like "free-range nutrias"—in other words, an excuse for more nutria jokes. Then I happened to pass the stand that sells Louisiana seafood to departing passengers. It had peeled crayfish tails, which seems natural—except that people in most of the country still won't eat what they call crawdaddies or mudbugs, and in the days before Paul Prudhomme opened his restaurant, crayfish were not easy to come by even in New Orleans. The stand also had turtle meat and alligator-tail meat and both fresh and smoked gator sausage. Why not nutria?

Would it really be impossible to develop someday one of those everything-but-the-squeal operations, which could harvest nutrias at a profit and protect the marshlands at the same time? The airport would sell gift packs of nutria sauce piquante and nutria étouffée and nutria gumbo. Deep-fried cubes of nutria would be on the K-Paul menu as swamp popcorn. The hind legs would be sent to Chinese restaurants in New York and San Francisco, where waiters could point to them on the *dim-sum* carts and say to Occidental customers: "You no like." The fur, brilliantly marketed by the fur consultant, would be what everyone in Paris and Milan was wearing. June Lowrey would have found someone who knows how to protect against brittleness in beautifully polished nutria teeth, set in silver. The tail? Well, we'd have to do something about the tail.

Calvin Trillin is a staff writer for The New Yorker *and a columnist for* Time *and* The Nation. *He is also the author of several books including* Deadline Poet, Travels with Alice, The Tummy Trilogy, *and* Family Man.

✳

Such talk led us to speak of New Orleans restaurants, those he liked and trusted and those he avoided. Among the former he mentioned Mosca's, a little roadhouse on the river's west bank beyond Westwego. I remembered it well: undistinguished in appearance both from the road and inside, but the food was superb. We both sang of Mosca's pan of fried oysters. Joe said that some years ago the Mafia don Carlos Marcello (believed by some to have been connected with the JFK assassination) was so taken with Mosca's that he made the owners an offer he thought they couldn't refuse. "He told them he'd give them the money to do whatever they wanted," Hero said, "travel, retirement, carte blanche, you might say. But they actually turned him down. They told him he could keep his money and go on doing the things he knew how to do, and they would go on doing what they knew best, which was running their restaurant."

—Frederick Turner, *A Border of Blue: Along the Gulf of Mexico from the Keys to the Yucatán*

MICHAEL AARON ROCKLAND

Philadelphia Stroll

The city is renowned for its cheese steaks,
chop shops, and brotherly love.

I HAD DECIDED TO TRAVERSE PHILADELPHIA AS I HAD EARLIER traversed Manhattan, only there wasn't one street, like Broadway, to take. And since Philadelphia spreads out over the land, isn't confined to an island, doesn't perceptibly descend from a height to the sea, my walk across would not be so driven by geography. It would have more of a desultory aspect than my Manhattan hike. I would simply diagonal across Philadelphia from its Bucks County border, pass through the center of town, and continue on out to its southwestern extreme at the international airport.

Poquessing Creek, a tired, littered stream with eroded banks, is not one of Philadelphia's major waterways, but it is the northeast boundary of the city and the place where I began. Patricia had driven me down to the city line with our son, Joshua, then four years old, along for the ride. When I got out of the car, Joshua said, "Where are you going?"

"I'm going to walk across Philadelphia," I said.

"Why?" Joshua said.

I didn't know what to say. As the car U-turned and headed back to New Jersey, Joshua looked worriedly out at me through the back window.

I nearly missed Poquessing Creek amidst the collection of road-side eateries and motels clustered about it—not to mention the distraction of the X-rated movie house, which that day was offering a triple feature: *Lip Service, Sizzling Seniors,* and *Eager Beavers.* The "Welcome to Philadelphia" sign assured me as to my whereabouts, but what was I to make of the huge legend a bit farther on, painted on a Roosevelt Boulevard overpass, that said, "God Lied to Me"?

To whom had God lied, and did this person still feel that way? Was there not something ominous about being welcomed to a city and immediately told that God had lied to one of its citizens?

Roosevelt Boulevard, despite such signs and being named for the ebullient Teddy Roosevelt, is dull—all nondescript row houses with pleated aluminum awnings and with a prodigious number of Burger Kings and weed-filled vacant lots where deer occasionally feed. More than once I've read in the Philadelphia newspaper of deer crashing through somebody's front window on Roosevelt Boulevard. Deer aren't supposed to come through windows in cities, but on Roosevelt Boulevard they do.

I soon quit Roosevelt and got on Frankford Avenue, which has no deer but a great deal more urban vitality—Palm Reading by Sister Ruth, the Hercules Restaurant, Original Bernies Cancellation Shoes, lots of ethnic food stores, and, straight out of *The Great Gatsby,* a billboard with the giant eyes of Dr. M. Falkenstein, optometrist.

At the bottom of the hill where Frankford meets the elevated train, a Kresge's five-and-ten-cents store was loudly blaring "Guantanamera" and there was a sprinkling of Philadelphia's peculiar sidewalk Ad-A-Benches, one offering "Free Foot Facts on Tape, 547-7800."…

Next to the bench was a brick building housing Norman's Bath Boutique, and just above the garbage cans in the wide alley alongside Norman's was a corroded bronze plaque that read:

Erected by the People

of Frankford

To Mark the Site of an Arch

Where on Behalf of the Citizens
And Assisted by a Choir of
Twenty-Four Young Ladies
General Isaac Worrell
Welcomed
General Marquis de Lafayette
September, 1824

I wondered whether Norman's customers ever notice the plaque and, if they did, whether their reactions fulfilled the tender hopes of those who had placed it there. A delivery truck pulled into the alley, and I asked the driver what he knew of the plaque. "Wasn't Lafayette some French guy?" he said. Opined his assistant: "All's I know is the country is filling up with these illegals."

The hill I had come down was a welcome interruption of the otherwise unrelievedly flat terrain. Most of Philadelphia's 129 square miles are a coastal plain more typical of New Jersey and Delaware than of mountainous Pennsylvania. The city averages barely one hundred feet above sea level and was once largely under the ocean, as workmen digging the subways who found sharks' teeth could attest; at its lowest point, the marshlands of Southwest Philadelphia, one can still encounter quicksand.

Frankford Avenue now carried me down into the Kensington neighborhood, which reminds one of Belfast, Northern Ireland— gritty, run-down, working-class white, embattled. The brick row houses are dingy, with busted marble stoops.

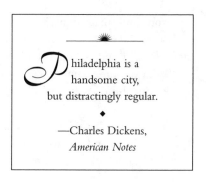

Philadelphia is a handsome city, but distractingly regular.

♦

—Charles Dickens,
American Notes

Signs in store windows offer The Paralyzer, an aerosol tear gas.

Suddenly I understood why the skies were so dark. It began to snow, first a few small flakes, then many large ones. The wind came up, blowing the rapidly increasing snow into my face with such intensity that I could not see and could barely catch my breath. In mid-March, wearing nothing but jeans and a wind-breaker, I was walking in a blizzard.

Through a break in the curtain of snow I spotted McGinty's Tavern and managed to pry the door open against the wind. I brushed the snow off my hair and clothes and decided to have lunch. Corned beef and cabbage and Irish soda bread were being served in honor of the holiday, and there was even green beer available.

Though it was a weekday and during working hours, McGinty's was packed with people, and a carnival atmosphere prevailed. A wizened man of indeterminate age was telling all who would listen that he was the 1943 pinball champion of Philadelphia. I sat at a bar and ordered lunch. On the next stool, a big, blond woman, a tattoo with the simple legend "Willie" emblazoned on that part of her right breast available for inspection, was shouting above the din, "So, I said to him, 'I don't care if you're Mick, Polack, or American. I keep a shotgun by the front door and a .45 by the back. You just *try* getting in. Nothing would make me happier than to blow your head off.'"

She turned and looked at me. "You think that's funny or somethin'?" she said.

"What?"

"You think that's funny?"

It's possible I had been smiling at her story. I wasn't smiling now. "No," I said, "I don't think that's funny."

"Whatya, some kind of fancy college guy or something? You think your shit doesn't smell?"

"I…"

"You think that's funny, this is what you can do," she said, thrusting her hand in front of my face with the middle finger raised. Clearly, I thought, Philadelphia, like New York, has more than one kind of wildlife.

This incident put a damper on the enthusiasm I often entertain for walking through cities, meeting "the people," and fancying myself one of them. I was definitely not one of the people in McGinty's, and the woman with the tattoo had told me so. I ate my lunch more quickly than I had planned.

When I emerged from the dark cave of McGinty's, it was as if the snow had never happened. The sun was out, the air warm, and spring had returned. I continued along a sparkling Frankford Avenue, which now angled toward the Delaware River into Center City. Center City, which is what Philadelphians call their downtown, is a peninsula, a tongue of land bordered by the Delaware River on the east, the Schuylkill River on the west, and the confluence of the two on the south. William Penn laid out Philadelphia where the Delaware and the Schuylkill are closest—guaranteeing a city with not one but two waterfronts. Thus, while Center City is not, like Manhattan, an island, it is just as much under the influence of its neighboring waters.

In the shadow of the bright blue Ben Franklin Bridge, at the corner of Front and Vine, I stopped to rest and watched a raft of ruddy ducks, who seemed to inhabit the cove created by two abandoned piers, struggle against the incoming tide. Although Philadelphia is 90 miles from the sea, the ocean visits twice every 24 hours, when five-foot tides sweep up the Delaware, salting the river and causing it temporarily to change direction.

It is always thrilling to encounter natural forces at work in the city, but the sun was going down and I needed a place to sleep. Easier said than done. Every hotel I came to as I walked away from the river and past Independence Hall and the striking colonial buildings of the historic district was either full, frightfully expensive, or run-down.

In the frightfully expensive category was the onetime Bellevue Stratford, now not only elegantly refurbished but renamed from the days when it became identified with a new human calamity: Legionnaires' disease. When it was later proven that the virulent virus that killed 29 American Legion conventioneers in 1976 was harbored in the hotel's air conditioning system, this confirmed my long-held conviction that there is something ultimately unhealthy, if not immoral, about air conditioning. My wife, champion of the great indoors, and I have discussed this idea of mine on more than one hot summer night....

I finally found a room in the Hotel Apollo, at 19th and Arch, price $49.99. I soon concluded the former Bellevue Stratford wouldn't have been such a bad idea after all. I'm not sure what I expected for my $49.99, but surely a room with a towel more absorbent than a starched shirt; a television set with more colors than pink and green; a water glass. One especially desires such amenities when traveling as light as I was; I wasn't even carrying a toothbrush, planned to keep my teeth clean with some Dentine that was in my pocket.

When I hiked downstairs—the elevator wasn't working—and asked for a water glass the desk clerk took me into his confidence. He winked and whispered, "They keep stealing them on us." I wondered who "they" were. He made a grand gesture of handing me a plastic cup and, as I mounted the stairs, called after me enthusiastically, "Enjoy!" Only when, back in my room, I raised the cup to drink and water dribbled down the front of my shirt did I discover the cup was cracked.

Breakfast the next morning largely made up for the hotel. At the corner of Chestnut and 19th I encountered The Donut Inn, where I sat at the counter and, for $2.09, had orange juice, two eggs, home fries, toast, coffee, and something called scrapple. I thought scrapple was a word game, but here I was eating an indeterminate, meaty substance the short-order cook had cut from a loaf, dusted with flour, and dropped sizzling onto the griddle atop a ladleful of grease. "What is this stuff?" I asked him.

"Scrapple," he said.

"Yes, but what's it made of?"

"Irving," the short-order cook called out to the man who stood stone-faced by the cash register, "tell this gentleman about scrapple."

Irving sprang into action. "Scrapple," he said with a shrug, "is…scrapple."

Would inquiring further be considered bad manners in The Donut Inn? I was about to give up the subject as a lost cause when the man on the next stool said quietly, "Pigs' lips and assholes."

"What?" I asked, astonished.

"Discarded pig parts. Everything but the squeal."

Philadelphia has other examples of regional cuisine, if this is not too fine a term for scrapple—which, by the way, I ceased eating immediately. The cheesesteak sandwich, greasy with onions, is a Philadelphia delicacy. So is the salt pretzel—well, not the pretzel itself but the way it is eaten. I learned about this after my visit to City Hall.

After breakfast I walked by Philadelphia's statuary-encrusted, Second Empire-style City Hall, the most impressive in America, the one institution in Philadelphia that dwarfs its New York counterpart. Next to Philadelphia's City Hall, New York's would look like a dollhouse. The largest masonry structure in the world—larger than St. Peter's in Rome—Philadelphia's City Hall squats like some great feudal castle in the metropolis's central square, leaving no question as to where power resides in the city.

One senses this not only in the massiveness of the structure but in all the whispered conversations taking place along its stone corridors and behind its smoky glass doors. Much more than in New York, power is centralized in Philadelphia. When Frank Rizzo was mayor, he commented on the CIA-sponsored, ill-fated 1961 Bay of Pigs invasion in Cuba by saying, "It would have been different if they'd sent in the Philadelphia police." When the MOVE cult refused to be extricated from their row house, Mayor Wilson Goode dispatched a helicopter with a bomb, and the result was the annihilation of an entire square block. Many New Yorkers do not even know where City Hall is; *everyone* in Philadelphia knows.

I wanted to get to the top of City Hall so as to see the whole city at once. Easier said than done. First I had to make my way through the advocates from various causes ringing the building, including two competing evangelists, each with his loudspeaker system. "Jesus!" one cried plaintively. "What does *he* know about Jesus?" the other shouted from across the square. Then I had to take a combination of stairs, an escalator, an elevator, and yet another elevator—a real rickety, slow one—to the top, with delays at each level.

Until recently, City Hall was the tallest building in Philadelphia. There had been an understanding that no building might surpass the Quaker hat atop the head of the giant statue of William Penn that crowns the tower. This understanding had now been violated several times, especially by two particularly brutal-looking blue towers, but the view, as I stood at William Penn's noble feet, still fulfilled my hopes. The city was laid out before me like a diorama. I could see the terrain over which I had walked the day before and my itinerary for the rest of that day, even out to where planes skimmed in over the misty far reaches of the city as they approached the airport.

Descending to the street, I encountered a Greek salt pretzel vendor, who said he had been selling his wares on Walnut Street ever since immigrating to the United States twenty years before. "A lot or a leetle?" he asked.

"A lot or a little what?" I responded. Was one expected in Philadelphia to buy several pretzels at a time?

He looked at me quizzically and said something that sounded like mustache, only he meant mustard. That's when I learned of a key gastronomic difference between Philadelphia and New York: Philadelphians eat their salt pretzels with mustard. Only one hundred miles away, New Yorkers would freeze in horror at such a prospect. It was nice to discover that all of America hadn't yet become McDonald's, that some regionalism was still alive on Walnut Street in Philadelphia.

Walnut Street. Philadelphia's main avenues are virtually all named for trees, for the Quakers considered naming streets for people unseemly if not blasphemous. In all, 150 of Philadelphia's streets are named for native plant life, beginning with Acorn and going all the way to Verbena. Such street names contribute to Philadelphia's small-town feeling. There is a world of difference not only in scale but in tone between Broadway in New York and Walnut, Chestnut, and Pine in Philadelphia.

Philadelphians like to say they have more trees than any city in the world and greater variety as well. The variety might be explained by the city being where North and South meet. Philadelphia is, for example, both the northern terminus of the Carolina hemlock and the southern terminus of the Canadian

hemlock. Philadelphians take as a matter of course the meteoro-
logical phenomenon of snow in the northeastern part of the city
simultaneous with rain in the southwestern. Indeed, as I was to
learn in a phone conversation with the United States Weather
Service a few days later, it was raining at the airport at precisely
the time I experienced the miniblizzard on St. Patrick's Day.

After leaving City Hall, I trudged down Broad Street for several
miles. Increasingly, the names and bell plates on the row houses
became Italian—Mesina, Giordano, Esposito. This was South
Philadelphia, scene of the *Rocky* movies. Statues of saints sprouted
in front yards, and there was a sprinkling of busybodies on the
top floors—systems of mirrors whereby you can see who's at the
front door from upstairs without showing yourself.

I was staring at one of these busybodies, above Delvecchio's
Grocery, when the proprietor came outside and asked, in what, at
first, seemed a good-natured way, "You planning to blow the
place up? Why not? We got insurance."

"What?" I said.

"Go ahead," he said, showing a lot of teeth, "be my guest.
Only don't rob me, okay? You blow up the place we both go to
Florida on the insurance, but rob me and we don't get *caca*."

"What are you talking about?" I said, but he abruptly went inside and I decided to just move on. In Philadelphia, people are local,
territorial. Everyone knows everyone else, and since Delvecchio
didn't know me, and thought I might be casing his grocery store,
he challenged me. At least, I think that's what happened.

The incident made me feel a little as I had felt in McGinty's
Tavern: like a stranger. New York is a world city, so everyone's on
an equal footing, everyone's a stranger. New York doesn't have
institutions like Philadelphia's Mummers—secret societies of
grown men parading about in feathers and bangles and beads each
New Year's Day. Philadelphia is a large small town. People either
belong or they're strangers.

At the corner of South Broad and Passyunk was the chrome-
and-glass Melrose Diner, where I had some Danish and coffee. I
needed the respite. I was shook-up from the conversation at

Delvecchio's Grocery, and I was about to begin the last, and least eagerly anticipated, part of my trip. Coming in from Philadelphia's northeastern outskirts the day before, I had felt some excitement as I approached Center City. Now I felt dispirited. It seemed stupid to be willfully abandoning the relative glamour of down-town for Passyunk Avenue and the grim further outskirts of Philadelphia.

Passyunk is the Delaware Indian word for level place, which certainly described the terrain thereabouts: level and boring. Approaching the Schuylkill, one might be tempted to add *ugly* to the list. Upriver, I knew, genteel oarsmen in tennis shoes and whites train for the Olympics in one-man sculls, but here the river was characterized by the hideous industry on its banks and, espe-cially for me, by the perilously rusted-out walkway of the iron bridge I was now attempting to cross. On the other side of the river was Eastwick, the largest and most sparsely settled section of Philadelphia. Eastwick is where yellow fever victims were quaran-tined during the epidemics of the eighteenth century, and it looked as if it might still be appropriate for such a purpose today.

This wasn't what William Penn had in mind when he envi-sioned Philadelphia as a "greene countrie towne." The largest oil refining complex on the East Coast stretched as far as the eye could see, while in the foreground was an endless array of auto junkyards, each with its colorful name. There was Smashy's and Spanky's and Ajax Late Model Auto Parts/"Ask for Pete" and Louie's Smart Parts. It looked like your car wouldn't remain intact half an hour if you made the mistake of parking outside one of these places. Indeed a few weeks after my hike, I was in my dentist's office glancing at an article on car theft in *Time* magazine, and it referred to Passyunk Avenue as "the chop-shop capital of America."

The article didn't mention the ferocious guard dogs—German shepherds, Doberman pinschers, pit bulls—who acted, as I passed, like no one on foot had gone by on Passyunk Avenue in ten years and were expressing their outrage on the matter. The dogs rushed about inside the chain link fences, persecuting me with their merciless fang-bared barking, as eager to chop me up as their masters were to chop cars.

I found myself thinking about the "God Lied to Me" sign. Was Eastwick what the lie had been about? Or was the lie inherent in my conceit that, by my mere presence, I could liberate even the most urban landscape? Trans-Schuylkill Philadelphia certainly looked deformed to me now—deformed and evil. There were even big For Sale signs posted about in the marsh that ominously boasted "Zoned Least Restrictive."

Passyunk took a curve, and now the street was called Essington. A sidewalk had been built along Essington, but it was obvious no one ever used it, for it was as overgrown as a two-thousand-year-old Roman road. The rank vegetation emerging through its cracks brushed against me uncomfortably and went up my pants legs. It was easier to walk in the street.

*T*he city [Bridgeport, Connecticut] resembled a bombed-out Bangladesh: deteriorating streets and buildings, shuttered stores, increased violence, and an air of palpable despair.

"From Portsmouth, New Hampshire, down to Norfolk, Virginia, maybe fifty miles wide, this is Uni-City," says Sam Marks, a third-generation businessman in Bridgeport. "It's one city, just one strip of millions and millions of people. And Boston is in trouble and New Haven is in trouble and Bridgeport's in trouble and New York's in trouble and Newark's in trouble and Philadelphia's in trouble, and we're all in it together."

◆

—Haynes Johnson,
Divided We Fall: Gambling with History in the Nineties

I heard a vehicle approaching behind me. I kept walking, trying to ignore it, but it pulled alongside, and then red, white, and blue lights flashed. An amplified voice challenged: "Whadya doing out here?"

"Just walking."

"Why?" the voice in the police cruiser bellowed. That was the same question my son Joshua had asked.

Why indeed? I thought. "I'm walking across the city. I'm trying to get to the city line."

Without another word, but with a look of severe disapproval on his face, the officer made a screeching U-turn and headed back to town. It appeared that even he, hermetically sealed in his mobile fortress, didn't care to go any farther along Essington Street.

Near the airport, Essington made a sharp turn to the right that wasn't on my street map, but old Essington was still there, so I took it because it seemed a more direct route. A reed marsh was encroaching on the abandoned Essington, and into it the concrete edges of the street were breaking off in chunks. There was garbage everywhere. A large brown Norway rat, oily and bushy, scampered across the road, looked at me, and continued on its way.

Seeing the rat in the near dark gave me the creeps. I wished I could have overcome my prejudice and appreciated it as just another life-form sharing the city. I tried telling myself that if animals survive in the city, there's a decent chance for people, but that isn't what I felt. What I felt was disgust. Maybe it was a combination of things: not only the rat but the assault by the tattooed blonde in McGinty's; the paranoid conversation with Delvecchio; the vicious dogs along Passyunk Avenue; and, of course, the "God Lied to Me" sign. Whatever it was, I was fast learning I wasn't as much the square-jawed Mark Trail of an urban outdoorsman as I pretended to be.

In conceiving the idea for this trip, I had ambitiously hoped I could find adventure, just as satisfying as the traditional kind, not where no one has been but where no one wishes to go. Now this notion seemed foolish. It occurred to me that there are perfectly good reasons for not going where no one wishes to go. I had also hoped that my story would be a love letter to my much abused land. But I wasn't feeling very loving as I stood among the degraded remains of old Essington Street. I was tired. I wanted to go home.

Yet I was still the same goal-oriented person who got depressed when Phil and I narrowly missed circumnavigating Manhattan. In my place, Phil could have quite happily quit this hike right then and there, and of course Patricia, with no remorse, would have quit the trip, assuming she had ever started it, five minutes after crossing Poquessing Creek the day before, or certainly when it began to snow.

Someday, a circumstance may arrive where the true adventure, given who I am, may be in quitting rather than persisting, but, right now, I couldn't stand having walked this far only to quit. So I plodded on, and soon I was skirting the great chain link perimeter fence of Philadelphia International Airport. It was a strange place to be on foot, what with jet airplanes roaring in over my head one after another like great winged beasts. When I got around the airport, I couldn't find the city limits sign in the dark, but I knew from my map that the airport's far side is Delaware County. So I had made it; I had crossed Philadelphia.

Skirting the perimeter again, I entered the airport terminal, where I felt like a swamp creature amidst the bright lights and hubbub of voices in the cavernous building. There was a half-hour wait for the next bus to Center City, so I bought candy bars and a copy of *People* magazine in the gift shop and found a seat in one of the waiting lounges. I simultaneously gorged on an Almond Joy, a Butterfinger, and the annual cover story in *People* called "The Sexiest Man Alive," disappointed once again to discover that the article was not about me. I was treating myself, nevertheless, after what felt to me then like two days of sensory deprivation. Patricia would be proud of me, I thought. I'm living a little.

Soon I found myself on the bus, seated among bewildered travelers and their belongings, rushing down some of the same streets I had trod by foot that very day. My dark mood was lifting. I took a certain satisfaction in knowing that, unlike the travelers who had been flown here from Los Angeles or London, I had walked twenty-six miles across Philadelphia for the privilege of taking that bus.

Michael Aaron Rockland is professor and chair of the American Studies Department at Rutgers University. Earlier, he had a career in the United States diplomatic service. Snowshoeing Through Sewers: Adventures in New York City, New Jersey, and Philadelphia, *from which this story was excerpted, is his seventh book.*

✳

The cold smell of broken stone trailed my family's drives from Long Island to Brooklyn. Exiting the Interboro Parkway for the surface streets of Brownsville, there was an eerie resemblance between the vast cemetery through which we had just driven and the urban burial ground that we were now negotiating. My parents almost immediately started complaining about the hollow streets and defeated architecture in this remote part of New York City. I'd be reminded that a vacant lot infested with ailanthus trees was once the site of romantic evenings at the cinema, or that the steel-shuttered storefronts on Pitkin Avenue were earlier filled with the latest fashions, or how my father met a long-lost friend from Europe standing in front of a shoe store while my mother shopped inside.

The climax of these drives to visit my relatives on the southern edge of Prospect Park was the rarely-fulfilled suggestion by my father that we first swing by Hopkinson Avenue and look at their old apartment, the first place they lived in America after arriving by boat from Germany in 1950. At this point, my mother would scream "what would be the point," and "why should I (and her children) be subjected to such nonsense and danger?" My father, on cue, would retort that the boarded-up building meant a great deal to him. It spoke about our family's history; he had studied there for the New York State Medical Exam. In those days it was a lively neighborhood where they had many friends.

In the early 1970s, while in high school, I was drawn to Brooklyn and particularly the old neighborhoods. Not coincidentally, many of the people where I grew up in Long Island had also fled from similar places a decade or so earlier. At times, I felt that the solidity of our large, detached, split-level house (built in 1963) was cemented by the vials of wrath cast against the new inhabitants and different tongues of the old neighborhoods, and the abuse hurled at their torn facades. In those days, the word Brooklyn signified failure to Long Islanders, a failure that legitimized their current suburban existence. They had escaped Brooklyn for a better life much as the Dodgers had abandoned Ebbets Field for sunny Southern California. Brooklyn's visible scars were a metonymy for

a past my parents (and many of their neighbors) were trying to forget—
a slow pedestrian life that took place in spaces of material limitation.

—Mitchell Schwarzer, "Ghost Wards: The Flight of Capital
from History," *thresholds 16: speed impact change*

PART THREE

GOING YOUR OWN WAY

Texas Heartache

The road to heartache ends in Austin.

I THOUGHT IT MIGHT HELP TO START SEEING SOMEBODY NEW, TO date again. I met the country singer in the airport in Denver, and he left me months later in the airport in Austin, Texas. One night in between, he phoned to sing me a song he'd just written. It was called, "This One's Gonna Hurt You for a Long, Long Time." You could say I was warned. By the time it was a hit on the radio, I got the cosmic joke.

Not long after we'd met, he suggested a road trip across the hill country to south Texas. We stayed in motels that had been decorated by taxidermists and ate in Denny's, where waitresses would ask for his autograph. He wasn't that famous yet, but he dressed the part anyway, making me think all the time of all those birds that have a drab female and a brightly plumed male. He was from the South, and he said things like, "What's time to a hog?" which, it turned out, had nothing to do with the town we stopped in that was the Home of the Swimming Pig. It was hot outside, and he would say, "I just saw a dog chasin' a rabbit and both of 'em were walkin'."

We stopped at both the Alamo and a replica of it called the Alamo Village, where John Wayne had made movies, and he'd suddenly whip out a notebook and write down lines he'd thought of for new songs, asking me what I thought of them. We traveled together for a week, and though it was very clear that what he wanted was not a relationship but some new material, I cried my heart out when he didn't call after I got home.

Not long after that, his record came out. There was a song called "Easy to Love (Hard to Hold)," which explained everything. But there was another called "Don't Leave Her Lonely Too Long," and one day he called again, like he'd never been gone. This sort of thing went on for a while, and it never occurred to me to ask what was going on. I guess I was waiting for more concrete evidence that this was not a perfect relationship, like when the girlfriend of one of my friends made an appearance on *The Tonight Show*, and she said she wished she could meet someone she could really care about.

I had a hard time letting relationships go, even the ones I didn't like. When it was finally over with the country singer, my friends tried to console me by pointing out how weird the country singer dressed, like he was Roy Rogers, but that had been one of his best qualities.

I decided to drive all the way from Montana to see the real Roy Rogers, who was in his eighties, at his museum in Victorville, California. Roy was never as rich as Gene Autry, the other big singing cowboy, and I knew there'd been tragedies in his life, like when one of his daughters had been killed in a church bus accident. His life had gone way up and back down, and still, he felt like putting on those fancy cowboy shirts. His story was inspiring: a good life doesn't necessarily go blithely along.

The museum was full of all of Roy and Dale Evan's stuff, like a big attic. Bullet the dog was barking at a critter in a diorama, and even Trigger was stuffed and doing a trick up on his back legs. Roy was waiting in his office when I got there.

Before we began to talk, he said he needed to call Dale. The line was busy, and Roy looked worried. "Who could she be talking to?" he asked. They have about a hundred grandchildren, and I suggested that maybe it was one of them. Roy started to tell me about his hunting trips years ago with Alfalfa from Our Gang, but he was staring at the telephone. "I better go home and see if she's okay," he said at last, and he left. I sat there awhile, realizing that though I sometimes thought a marriage like Roy and Dale's was the end-all, I could no more picture myself in one like that than I could see Alfalfa with a gun.

When the country singer and I were in south Texas, we crossed the border into Mexico. On the table in the café where we had dinner was a gallon jar of hot pickled vegetables. On the wall, there was a picture of Annie Oakley. She'd gotten famous when she won a big sharp-shooting contest when she was a teenager, and afterward, she'd married the man who lost. She looked really miserable. Lots of married people do. It's a fact you can sometimes console yourself with, when you're alone. Once I went to a massage therapist, who told me she'd felt devastated on her wedding day. "I looked at myself in the mirror," she said, "and I thought, Now I'll never get to join the army."

When I got back to my house, I figured out how to make Mexican relish. You can make it so hot it makes your eyes water, though I was beginning to feel like I'd cried enough.

Debby Bull is a former editor and writer for Rolling Stone *magazine. She grew up in St. Croix Falls, Wisconsin. She graduated from Northwestern University and has a master's degree in American Studies from the University of Minnesota. As a rock critic and popular-culture observer, her writing has appeared in many magazines. She now lives in Montana and northern Wisconsin.*

★

After awhile, the impassive waitress came back with my order. When I saw the sausage-looking items on my dish, I knew I might've done well to do some checking around beforehand. I took a swig of beer and cut into one of the sausages.

"What's that?" Susan asked with her nose wrinkled up.

"*Boudin*," I told her, as if I'd been putting the stuff away by the plateful since early childhood.

"I don't know French," she said. "What is it in English?"

Laughing, I said, "That's what I'm about to find out."

It turned out to be a spicy, bready mixture—a little like turkey dressing—stuffed into a sausage casing. It wasn't bad; in fact, it was awfully tasty—but, really, three dollars?

I forked up a bit of it for Susan to taste, then Lorenzo and Mike came back to the table.

"Look at you, Al Young," Lorenzo said in jest. "Sitting up here studying this stuff. I used to be like you when I first moved down here to Texas from New York, but now I've cut all that out. Now I've just fallen on off down into this shit."

With this, Lorenzo loosened his tie and hit the dance floor again. Once the music got going, some perky little woman, who looked sixteen at the most, actually walked over and asked *me* to dance.

What the hell, I thought, and proceeded to shed my coat and tie right then and there.

—Al Young, *Drowning in the Sea of Love: Musical Memoirs*

A Day in the Lake

Why would you want to
get there from here?

I HAD BUSINESS IN UKIAH BUT DECIDED TO SPEND THE NIGHT IN Lakeport, on Clear Lake, the biggest lake in California. I consulted my AAA map. Between Ukiah and Clear Lake loomed Cow Mountain. One highway looped to the north around it, another to the south. But a third road appeared to go right over the top, then to descend and bridge Scotts Creek. I decided that would be the scenic shortcut.

I swung onto Mill Creek road, following the gentle bends of the creek through green deciduous woods. An occasional cabin appeared through the trees. At 3,000 feet, the woods changed to scrub—manzanita, knob-cone pines and California nutmegs—and all signs of human life ceased. Soon, the paved road turned into a gravel road; soon after that, a dirt road. I bounced along, my Toyota's 1.8-liter engine propelling me over potholes and ruts.

After a while, I topped the mountain and could see Clear Lake in the distance. I was halfway home and sighed with relief.

Then—the road began to deteriorate. Bumps swelled into hillocks. Potholes opened into yawning abysses. Large rocks crashed against the chassis. Dust flew behind me. The cracks and fissures widened into ruts that bisected and trisected the road, erupting into fissures and troughs, which then proceeded to decussate the road, to crisscross it, to carve it up, to mangle and maim it, to divide and subdivide it into a veritable network of ditches and canals, of trenches and troughs, so that the ruts were sharing less and less of the road with the vehicle, and the vehicle no longer knew if that was road beneath it or some utterly new and terrible species of terrain.

Perhaps I should have turned back. But I had come eighteen miles over the houseless solitude of Cow Mountain, and Scotts Creek was only two miles away. Beyond it, I could see the first cottages on the outskirts of Lakeport. As I bounced along, I contemplated the majestic panorama of mountains and valleys below, the higher snow-clad peaks to my—*bang*! My stomach pitched. The Toyota had lurched into a rut.

Actually, two ruts. The car had planked down on a narrow ledge of road flanked by two gaping chasms. I would need a Chinook medium-lift chopper to get it out.

I pondered my surroundings—barren terrain, the sun dropping, the temperature plummeting. Okay. I began hiking down the mountain toward Clear Lake, shimmering in the distance. A pleasant early-evening jaunt, I told myself.

Then—I went into a rut. My ankle twisted amazingly around, like Linda Blair's head in *The Exorcist*.

I limped the remaining mile of rutted road in 40 minutes…and discovered that, contrary to my map, the road expired on the banks of roaring Scotts Creek. No bridge.

I contemplated the currents. Then I removed my boots, tied them to my belt, rolled up my pants and began wading across. The cool waters soothed my twisted ankle. The creek was fast but a mere six *inchhheeiieeeh*!—abruptly, the creek was six feet deep, and I was beating about with all my might to keep from being washed downstream and spit into Clear Lake.

I made it, though. I crawled onto the opposite shore and poured the water from my boots. I coaxed my swollen ankle back into its residence. Then I climbed the bank to where the road sprang back to life.

The man in the first cottage I came to took one look and offered to drive me into Lakeport. The manager of the motel where I was deposited dripping wet took one look and offered to throw my clothes in his dryer. And the next morning, a gentleman from the sheriff's office with a four-wheel-drive tow truck took me up the mountain and helped me extract my car. "Happens all the time," he said jollily. "Usually out-of-towners. Except this one guy and his wife. They should've known better. He's paraplegic. But, they thought, no problem. They had a Jeep and made it over the mountain. Halfway across Scotts Creek, the riverbed drops out and they're spinning downstream in the current, sinking. By the time we fished him out, the water reached his chin."

"Why the hell don't you put up a sign?"

The deputy gazed at me. "There's a thought."

Michael Covino was born in Brooklyn, grew up in the Bronx, and now lives in the San Francisco Bay Area. He is the author of The Off-Season, *a collection of short stories, and a novel,* The Negative. *His work has won numerous awards, including a National Endowment for the Arts fellowship and the* Paris Review's *Aga Khan Prize for fiction. He is completing his second novel.*

*

Mountains holy as Sinai. No mountains I know of are so alluring. None so hospitable, kindly, tenderly inspiring. It seems strange that everybody does not come at their call.

— *John of the Mountains: The Unpublished Journals of*
John Muir edited by Linnie Marsh Wolfe

* * *

Trucking the Distance

Call it truck or lorry, it's still named Mack.

WHERE WERE WE GOING?

California.

Via Laredo, Texas.

California: where they gave you huge fines for drawing the wrong line in your Log Book, and tickets for an unwashed trailer, and where you often holed up hanging around a truckstop for days, weeks, waiting for a decent back load.

A four-thousand-mile run: one of the longest continuous hauls you could do in the States. So I was going all the way across again—and via the Mexican border.

Tim Brown rubbed his eyes. "How do I get through Arizona?"

"You buy your way through," said George. Cargo's trailer fleet was registered in Maine, where the licences were cheaper. But states like Arizona objected to Maine undercutting them on trailer-plating business, and retaliated by refusing Maine reciprocal permit agreements, so we'd need to buy a special ticket on the border to let us through. "You buy your way through New Mexico too."

Mid-afternoon already: better be going. We stowed my bag in the back locker of the dark blue Mack and climbed in. Tim shook his head. "California, man—that scares me."

Another Cargo driver was pulling out of the yard just ahead of us. Neil was bound for Omaha, Nebraska, and had his daughter with him to drop off along the way at her grandparents' in Des Moines, Iowa. He came over the CB: "Where you goin', Tim?"

"I think I'm goin' to Hell, but first I gotta go to Texas!" "I'm an outlaw, man, a gipsy outlaw! I'm surprised they put me with you, man." Tim talked fast, with much bustling gesticulation and a deafening shout of a laugh. "They were going to put you with Ernie, but his parole don't extend beyond Mississippi."

"Who was the guy who looked like a wasted Willie Nelson?"

"Ah, that's Don. Yeah, then they were going to put you with him, but he's sick right now."

Tim had been driving for George for nearly nine years: "I used to have my own truck, but I went flat broke, got divorced and it all went to shit." He'd run a little "sub-shop"—a sandwich bar—in Nashua for a while, but he'd sold it when "it got to be a pain in the balls." Now he just drove—"I'm homeless, man. When I go home I stay with my grandmother." For a while he'd done a lot of deliveries for a company manufacturing waterbeds—hauled them all over the country. "They offered me one"—he waved an arm at the monastic cell of his cab—"but where the fuckam-agonna put it?" With a late start like today we were looking to put on about four hundred miles tonight—just get as far as Pennsylvania. "And then," shouted Tim, "we'll just ride, ride, ride!"

Our Mack was only four months old—George had paid half a million dollars for a fleet of six new trucks. Tim, as one of the senior drivers, had got one, and already clocked up 38,000 miles in his. Traditionally Macks, with their pugnacious bulldog mascot perched above the radiator, were America's workhorse trucks— the equivalent, if you like, of the British ERF, staple of tanker fleets and bread-and-butter motorway trucking work: "A bit of a gaffer's truck," as ERF's marketing manager had once put it to me, as the stereotype he'd had to overcome; "you know, 'I'd rather have a Scania, but the boss has given me this bloody ERF…'" Macks had been something similar: snouty and hulking, too often the first choice at the front of a coalbucket. Not pretty, not a style accessory: a brick shit-house on wheels. This CH600 wasn't as powerful as the Kenworths Bill and Earl drove—350 horsepower would have to work quite hard to pull a full trailer up a big hill—but neither was it a snowplough. It had a streamlined hood, a deep wraparound windscreen, cruise control, and it was Mack's state-of-the-art.

We had four loads aboard our trailer. There were two drops around Dallas: one skip—a pallet in the UK—of advertising brochures to go to a print finisher, and some faulty computer monitors for return to the supplier down in Grapevine, Texas, just outside the Dallas-Fort Worth conurbation. Then there were four vertical swing pumps built by a firm in Lawrence, Massachusetts, to go to Santa Clara, Mexico, which we were taking as far as the Mexican border at Laredo where they'd be transhipped on to a Mexican truck. Mexico had suffered tornadoes a couple of weeks earlier: these pumps would be used to disperse sewage overflows or restore drinking water supplies: together they made up $171,000-worth of equipment. The Lawrence manufacturer, said Tim, was a good customer, "because their loads have to go. Even if it's only half a load, they pay for the whole trailer. So Cargo makes its money by throwing all the other shit in on top." And to take us all the way to California we had another consignment of NEC computer monitors for the Tatung warehouse in Long Beach.

"I like runnin' Texas," Tim said. "You can really lay down some miles there, really stretch your legs. There's no hills to pull. Nothin' about. You just *ride*." Until a few years ago he'd done East Coast to West Coast regularly—Seattle in three days, California in three and a half, four, a thousand miles a day. "When I started working for this guy that's all I used to do—Seattle and Los Angeles. Coast-to-coast it's a sixty-hour trip, so if you do four fifteen-hour days you can still have eight hours' sleep every night. You just gotta keep up with the programme." California was the problem, though—notorious for its paucity of good back loads to the East Coast. This was the *rich* state, the consumer state: it sucked in goods from the rest of America. Freight went in: it didn't come out. All it had to send back was the seasonal harvest of fruit, and some canned food, from its produce growers. Truckers hated going to California—they never knew when they'd get to leave. When I'd ridden with Keith Derscheid he'd told me about the time he'd had to sit around for over a week waiting for a back load: that had been in California. It didn't sound very long compared to the way days lost in European border queues accumulated over a single trip—but this was antsy America. The other place truckers hated going, however, with its horrendous clogged traffic and mazy streets, was New York City. So at least if you were prepared to take a New York load you could put yourself at the head of the line to get out of California. "The only thing that saves my ass loading back to the house is New York City," said Tim. "If I see a load on the board sayin' New York City I say 'Yup, That's goin' on my wagon!'" But Tim hadn't done Shaky—in CB-demotic California was the earthquake zone—for four years. "Now I'm too old. I thought, fuck all that shit."

We were riding the same route down towards Pennsylvania that I'd come with Keith a while back, down 495 and 290 to Worcester, Massachusetts, then Interstate 90 and 84 to Hartford, Connecticut—but then Keith had headed west, and we wanted south. Just because Tim hadn't been to Shaky for a while didn't mean he wasn't putting miles on. A fortnight ago he'd managed 4,400 miles in a week. "I did Boston to San Antone and back in six days. I slept every night from midnight till the sun came up, but during the days, man, I was humpin' it. And as soon as I dropped my load I found another one a hundred miles away hauling trash bags. See, all the Chinese are movin' down to Texas and settin' up in business recycling plastics, all these food containers and things, and making them into trash bags, and then we haul them back up to the east coast. Got caught for speeding on the way, but this cop, he was kinda keen on us bringing the state business, so he even gives me directions to where the place is and lets me off with a warning! I got back from San Antone in two days—I was two days ahead of schedule. That pay check was a real good week!"

We hit the coast road at New Haven and followed it down towards Bridgeport and Stamford, and stopped for an early bite to eat with Neil and his daughter at the Milford Services at Bridge Haven. Tim told Neil how his daughter's dental brace was going to cost $1,200—he also had a teenage son. His wife now had two children with her new husband, who was going to go halves with Tim on the dental bill. "I was young," he reflected. "She was sixteen, I was twenty-one, just out of the service. I picked her out at a party, we spent a week at the Holiday Inn and I fell in love and I married her…"

"It happens," said Neil.

> *I*ndiana ranks No. 1 on that list of states said by truck drivers to have the best roads. No. 2: Ohio. No. 3: Georgia. Tied for No. 4: Florida and Virginia.
>
> ◆
>
> —L.M. Boyd, "Best Roads in the United States," *San Francisco Chronicle*

By eight o'clock, the dusk starting to fade the New York skyline into a charcoal-etched silhouette, we were crossing the George Washington Bridge across the Hudson and passing through the top of Manhattan. In the tunnel on the approach to the bridge a hubcap came off a pick-up truck in front and bowled through the traffic towards us; the driver of a private hire bus in the next lane was smoking a colossal cigar. Neil was supposed to be following us—we were going to ride with him until Pennsylvania, when he cut off westwards, but we'd already lost him. Tim called up "Cookie-Duster"—Neil's CB moniker; his own was "Mr. B."—in vain. "He's kinda slow," said Tim. "I like to ride wide open all the way. I don't like nobody on my front door…" We were due in Dallas Monday morning: that meant a thousand four, said Tim, to do today and tomorrow, and then two hundred to knock off on the morning we dropped.

On the radio Delbert McClinton and Tanya Tucker were singing their bouncy duet again about "Teardrops in the Dark."

"I like country music," Tim said. "Kenny Rogers, Willie

Nelson, guys like Garth Brooks. I don't know—country music and driving seem to go together. Makes the miles slip down easier."

The sun went down over New Jersey, and we drove into a deep pink sunset.

Sometimes, Bill had said to me, the miles just disappear, and sometimes you have to drive every single one of them. Today, despite the country music, felt like one of those times. Probably it was because we had no predetermined destination for tonight: we were just trying to get as far as possible. We weren't driving towards a winning tape: we were just driving away from where we'd started out. And also it felt as though we'd been bounced into this trip—you think you're going south to the Mexican border, and then you find you're going on from there and as far again. Your mind takes a while to come up to speed. In *The Songlines*, Bruce Chatwin passes on the story of the white explorer who paid his African porters for a forced march: within sight of the final destination they suddenly sat down and refused all inducements to walk any further—saying they had to wait to give their souls a chance to catch up.

For the first time in the States, too, the ride felt unexalted, attritional: this wasn't a proud owner of a chromium steed allowing his services to be hired; this time it was a tired guy being catapulted out on to another long, long road—three times as far as a European slog to Moscow—and we were still at the start. You can sense the exact moment when the wind goes out of someone's sails. The truck rolls on at exactly the same speed, the hands still rest across the wheel-rim, the posture shifts not at all—but suddenly the tiredness has broken out like a sweat, and the gaze is directed so much further into the distance ahead.

"This is another good song," Tim said. We listened in silence.

It was called, "A Thousand Miles from Nowhere." Over that long-loping, seven-league-boots rhythm with which the best songs fell into perfect stride with the wheels eating up the highway, Dwight Yoakam sang a simple, rueful lament.

I'm a thousand miles from nowhere
Time don't matter to me

'Cause I'm a thousand miles from nowhere
And there's no place I want to be...

A guitar engraved a crisp, pensive solo that soared slowly higher and higher, the reverb took Yoakam's voice out away into the distance—where was he singing from?—and he sang the words grave and solemn—he didn't need to put any sadness in them. In all the miles I rode I heard plenty of songs too many times, but I heard this one only once. Dwight Yoakam, I later discovered, had spent six years driving trucks.

And as he sang a flood of moments came out of recent memory: Keith talking in a half-whisper to his wife on the phone that late night in the truckstop diner somewhere in North Pennsylvania; the image of Bill taking his German shepherd Chrissie down to the river in Montana for a quiet walk to listen to the sounds; Earl stowing his golf clubs under his bunk for the prospect of a round of golf in Missoula, or Seattle, or wherever he found himself; and now here was Tim, driving like hell into the night with a bed at his grandmother's to do for home.

Graham Coster trucked across Europe and the U.S. to write A Thousand Miles from Nowhere, *from which this story was excerpted.*

✳

As good Eagle Scouts know, any big trip into the woods requires extensive planning and preparation, and this one was no exception. We spent the next two mornings researching one of the most important purchases for this ride, the car stereo. Sitting six weeks in a car, you have to have a pumping stereo. We tested many in the stereo stores down to Canal. Most weren't loud enough. We settled on a Sony deck with six-channel amp and a complementary-component speaker kit. It was costly, but when the man hooked it up and turned it on, it made the windows vibrate on the electrical store across the street and a man drop his lunch on the sidewalk.

—Simon Mayle, *The Burial Brothers*

* * *

Cincinnati Ho!

Belonging is good, and it builds
civilizations too.

OUR BUS TOUR OF CINCINNATI WAS MODAL RATHER THAN LINEAR.
The tour guide was in some sort of dreamspace. He repeated certain words and phrases without regard to the scenery passing outside. It was a reverie disguised as a lecture.

Throw in a score by Philip Glass, and you'd have a lovely evening of experimental theater—"Cincincincinatiatiati," it might be called.

Winston Churchill made an appearance—he called Cincinnati "the most beautiful inland city in America," which is impressive until you consider (a) the probable circumstances under which he said it, and (b) the competition. Procter & Gamble was mentioned frequently, and Crosley Field, and the mysterious phrase "many countries within one country."

As our bus ambled through a neighborhood called Over-the-Rhine, the tour guide brooded about juvenile crime. "Six hundred children a week," he said. "That's unacceptable." It was not clear what 600 children a week did exactly, but presumably it was linked to crime in the Tri-State area and was, it goes without saying, unacceptable.

The entire bus bounced in silence, the riders staring out at the

antique stores and small restaurants, assenting to the unacceptabil-
ity of the 600. It was a grim moment.

A little later, pointing to a prominent feature of downtown
Cincinnati, the guide said, "The Sky Walk has no beginning and
no end," and it was almost as if we were supposed to respond,
"Praise ye the Sky Walk."

It was pleasant to have some surrealism during the journey;
it made me feel more grounded. Cincinnati is a pretty city, tucked
into San Francisco-sized hills along the banks of the Ohio, a
bridge away from the fleshpots of Kentucky, lush, hazy, striving in
the way that American cities strive. It looks like America, too, in
a way California does not—lawns made green by local water,
large brick buildings indifferent to earthquakes, houses with
porches and porch swings, fireflies in the evening, steeples poking
through the trees.

It's nice for a Californian to visit America occasionally. It gives
him a sense of his roots.

I was there to attend the wedding of the grandson of the sister
of my wife's mother. Said sister had nine children; they have had
14 children, some of whom have had children themselves. Throw
in spouses at each generational level, and it's more than 30 humans.

I am an only child in a family in which almost everyone is childless or dead or both. Over the years, hearing tales of the great invisible tapestry in Cincinnati, the triumphs and failures, I had wanted
to put faces to names, to see the players and shake their hands.

So the trip to Cincinnati was sort of like visiting the set of
"One Life to Live." It was also…something else. I would not have
said "a longing" before I went; now I am less sure.

I went with Tracy and her mother, Ruth, who sees her sister
and all those nieces and nephews only infrequently. I met acres of
people, long tons of humans. The Harkins Family, much like the
Sky Walk, has no beginning and no end.

So this happened: I was at the reception, and Mike, one of the
Original Nine, told me I was needed in the lobby. There was a
family picture and I was in it. I had crossed some invisible line
when I had crossed the Ohio; I was now eligible for the group shot.

I stood in the back row between two strangers who were not strangers. It occurred to me that I had not posed with this many people since my high school graduation. I was the blurry face in the back row of a family photo. "That's Jon," people might say in 20 years. "He went mad."

And I report to you now, without knowing any more about it, that I was at that moment gripped by an inexpressible euphoria. I felt peaceful and small and attached. Another door opened. "What now?" I asked myself, and said cheese.

Jon Carroll writes a daily column for the San Francisco Chronicle.

*

All animal wants are supplied profusely at Cincinnati, and at a very easy rate; but alas! these go but a little way in the history of a day's enjoyment. The total and universal want of good, or even pleasing, manners, both in males and females, is so remarkable, that I was constantly endeavouring to account for it.

—Frances Trollope (1831)

SHERYL CLOUGH

✦ ✦ ✦

Icebergs in My Dreams

Alaska feels biggest when you travel alone.

I WATCH MATT'S BACK RETREAT, ACROSS THE FERRY TERMINAL parking lot and up the ramp; he reboards the ferry M/V *Columbia* under the black Southeast Alaska sky, dotted with dim stars whose light shines dully through the spaces among scattered clouds. Darkness provides cover for my tears. *The great adventurer has opened her big mouth once too often*, I think. *Now I have to follow through.*

My plan had seemed natural, even logical, at the time. Sitting on a driftwood log with Matt and Stan at our campsite on Kolosh Island, holding in my hands a cracked wooden bowl filled with rice, I listened to them plot their plans now that our four-week expedition together was almost over.

"I'd like to do some backpacking in the mountains around Juneau," Stan said. "I've heard a lot about that country."

Matt frowned. "My job starts soon," he said. "To make it back to Seattle in time, I have to catch the September 12 ferry from Sitka."

They both looked at me. Four weeks of their frequent unsolicited advice had taken a steep toll. I remembered Stan instructing me in how to hold my kayak paddle. I had been working as a whitewater river guide for three seasons; this was his first summer kayaking. I remembered both of them standing over my white sixteen-foot Chinook kayak, the *Ozzy*, and telling me how to arrange my stuff sacks. I remembered the morning I was cooking a huckleberry pancake, and Matt appeared and said I should turn it over now. I turned it, and Stan strolled over, peered into the pan, and pronounced that it had not been ready to turn over yet. That was the day I stopped cooking. After that, when either of the men began a meal, I wandered away from camp to read, pick berries or talk with the ducks and seals who live at the margins between beach and sea.

And I remembered Audrey Sutherland's talk at the Mountaineers Club in Seattle. She had autographed my copy of her new book, *Paddling Hawai'i* with these words: "For Sheryl: Paddle south of Sitka—down to Goddard. Aloha, Audrey Sutherland." Her advice had been followed: here we were, camped offshore of Goddard. It had been excellent advice. At both the beginning and the conclusion of her talk, Audrey told her listeners, "Go now, and go solo."

I flexed an arm grown hard and muscular through these many weeks of paddling and thought of my guide friends back home. "Arms like tree trunks" expressed the common standard we held to. I looked at Stan and Matt. "I don't have to go back yet," I said. "I think I'll get off at Petersburg and paddle solo down to Wrangell." Stranded without comment, they contemplated the steam swirling over their tea mugs.

Matt and I parted company with Stan in Sitka a few days later. I had not been sorry at the parting. I had known Stan only casually before joining this trip. A strong and experienced outdoorsman, he had nonetheless shown a penchant for cruising off alone, out of sight of the other two kayaks. During a storm in Windy Channel, Matt and I had stayed overnight at Goddard and did not see Stan for over twenty-four hours. The worry had kept us awake all night. "What do we do if he's missing, or dead?" we had asked each other. Tightwads ever, the experience even brought up a conversation about buying marine-band radios. Although Matt and I had argued over many other points during this trip, we agreed that Stan's non-team attitude was dangerous and put all of us at greater risk than necessary.

After Stan left, Matt and I cruised the Siginaka Islands for several days, savoring the fuchsia sun setting over Mount Edgecumbe's collapsed crater like rhododendron petals into a brandy snifter. As his remaining time in Alaska dwindled, Matt grew less argumentative, more meditative. He treated me to dinner, at twelve dollars apiece, too expensive by kayak bum standards. We sat at the windows in the Sea Glory dining room the night I was to disembark at Petersburg. The fact that the ever-thrifty Matt paid for my dinner indicated the depth of his concern over my solo venture. Gazing across the rims of our wineglass at the glow cast by the moon over low-hanging ice fields, we enjoyed each other's company almost as we had in the beginning, before our mutual insecurities surfaced and ground against each other like icebergs turning, abrading in their night channels.

Stuff sacks, paddles, ammo can: all are piled around my rubber-booted feet. *I'm alone, in the dark, in the rain.* I feel less alone, though, than the day I hollered a route question to Matt under the howling wind while rounding Povorotni Point in whitecaps. Flinging the chart and compass bag out of his cockpit toward me, over eight-foot waves, he yelled, "It's your chart; learn to use it!" Now the ferry horn blasts twice, a sound that usually churns the blood through my veins. Tonight, though, in it I hear a double death knell, and fix on the word solo as a saltwater mantra...*solo, solo, so low, here I go*. I plant my Therm-a-rest and sleeping bag under the ferry terminal overhang to wait for dawn's light. Despite the racket from the disco across the street, sleep falls like a river rapid descending its glassy tongue.

I wake to the sounds of bottle glass smacking pavement. "Muh' fucker," a man's voice yells. A woman mutters something incomprehensible, and the next sounds I hear are those of police sirens addressing the parking lot. A glance at the watch under my Capilene sleeve reveals that it's only 4:00 a.m. I shrivel down into my sleeping bag and hope the police won't notice me. My wide eyes stare at the stitching inside the bag. I long for daylight.

Dawn and rain arrive together, the drops making pock marks in the bay's leaden surface. I depart Petersburg's harbor as a cruise ship anchors. Resting the wooden paddle across my spray-skirted lap, I munch an apple and look at the people on the upper decks. A man trains his video camera on me, and I feel like a member of an endangered Alaskan species, captured on film before it's too late. *Time to get outta town.*

Paddling south along the east coast of Mitkof Island, I welcome the familiar rhythms settling in: push, pull, inhale, exhale. Shoulders, arms, wrists, waist: they move themselves like actors playing their parts for the thousandth time. Rain lightens to drizzle, then stops altogether. Strengthening sunlight reveals the whorls of my paddle blades reflected on the water. Birds wheel and call, brown kelp bulbs bob, sea swells cradle the boat and over all things the crusty pungency of salt. All afternoon I crawl alongside steep cliff walls which plunge unrelieved to the water line. After several hours, my muscles begin to tire; time to consider tonight's campsite. Another hour's paddling and my upper arms are jammed with lactic acid. The underpaid actors start to grumble. Around a headwall a long, gently sloping beach offers itself. I land the yak and disembark to look for the high water mark. The woods behind this beach are too densely overgrown to yield a tent space. I settle for pitching my tent as high as possible, but the encrusted rings of algae and kelp in this zone make me nervous. Scanning the tide table, I see it will be close, with the highest water due just after midnight. A pile of driftwood logs higher than my head looks like a stable stash for the *Ozzy*, and after hoisting her over my head into the log nest, I lash her bow to the trunk of an overhanging cedar tree. The whole assembly reminds me of the absurd osprey nests I saw in the Florida Keys, big batches of sticks with pieces of clothing and sometimes even towels cascading out, riding the random breeze.

As I cook rice over a tiny climbing stove, eight curious seals bob offshore, their smooth gray heads echoing the shape of beach rocks smoothed by tides. Ball-bearing-sized saltwater beads slide down their whiskers and drop into the sea. In the slanting rays of the day's last sun, I see random squirts from a clam colony. Far across Frederick Sound, a cluster of icebergs rides the tide out to sea. I don't need the chart to tell me that the ice exits from Le Conte Bay, melting pot for Le Conte Glacier, the southernmost tidewater glacier in the United States. The ever-lowering sun mutates colors on the berg surfaces: green, blue, pink. Through coffee steam, I gaze at the beautiful danger, feeling the pull of those crystal layers compressed by thousands of years of weight.

In that ponderous weight hangs the bergs' principal danger to kayakers. The portion of an iceberg visible above the water line may be less than one-fourth of its total mass, and its instability due to uneven melting creates the potential that it will roll suddenly. When a couple of tons of ice roll over, the motion generates a huge wave. Even larger waves follow the fall of a chunk of hanging ice, maybe as big as a house, into the water. The Tlingits, Southeast Alaska's aboriginal people, call the sound made by calving ice "white thunder." A sixteen-foot kayak riding into such thunder has about as much chance of survival as a toothpick tossed into a flushing toilet bowl. From such primitive physics flows the advice that a kayaker's minimum safe distance from a hanging glacier is one-half mile.

My musings about iceberg dangers and rapture over kaleidoscopic ice colors do not transcend my anxiety as to the camping spot. *What could go wrong? The tide could wash into my tent door while I'm asleep and soak all the gear, or wash it out to sea.* I cram everything except one foam pad and my sleeping bag into the boat. Sleep brings fitful dreams, in which I dance naked across purple icebergs that shift in time to the spouting of humpback whales.

Morning's heavy mist conceals the icebergs, so I content myself with watching the squirting clams, circling gulls and seals playing offshore. Frederick Sound is calm, the color of split shot. After brewing a cup of coffee, I settle onto a boulder to weigh the risks

of a solo crossing of Frederick Sound against my desire for closeness to those icebergs. The chart shows a three-mile stretch of
open water between me and Camp Island. The island forms a partial border between the Sound and Le Conte Bay. If I go, sooner
is better, as the stronger winds tend to whip up in the afternoon
in Southeast Alaska. The beings who camp in my brain begin
their debate.

*You told Matt you were taking the east coast of Mitkof. They'll never
find the body.*

The water is calm; there's no wind.

You don't have a rudder.

It's only three miles.

You've never tried an Eskimo roll with a fully loaded boat.

I may never be in this place again.

And so it goes for about
ten minutes, the conservative
versus the wild woman.
Ultimately I don't know why
I let them engage in battle; I
knew from the moment I
saw those icebergs that I
would alter my original route
plane and cross the Sound.

Decision made, the pack-
ing proceeds swiftly. I settle
into the cockpit and tug the
skirt around the coaming.
The paddle cuts through the
water as easily as a ski tip lifts
through new powder snow,
and soon I spy through the
lifting haze the tribe of ice
beings trekking toward me
on their journey from Le
Conte Glacier, where they
cleave from the mother ice,

*T*here are stories of women
who simply set out on
journeys; women confidently
stepping into a dazzling
unknown. I yearned to be that
type of woman but knew that
I was not. I wanted to let life
affect and deepen me through
pure immediate experience but
knew that I could not. I planned
my voyage: crafted an itinerary,
made reservations. The truth
was, I did not trust life to
provide me with experiences
to suit my liking.

♦

—Lydia Minatoya, *Talking to
High Monks in the Snow: An
Asian American Odyssey*

fall into the bay and slide through the outlets at either end of Camp Island into Frederick Sound, diminished by melt water as they go. They range in size from baseball-sized chips to freeform, sculpted chunks longer than my boat. Some carry seal mothers and pups, serving as nurseries secure from landlubber predators. The largest piece I can see is about the height of a one-story building. I keep my distance, even from the smaller ones. An abruptly flipping iceberg could swamp my boat.

Perhaps the most compelling feature distinguishing solo kayak travel from a group trip is this absolute zero margin for error. If my boat should roll or swamp, I cannot rely on an altruistic porpoise to appear at the right moment and carry me to a safe beach, although those stories appeal to me and even seem believable, from dry land. Other than this greater requirement for self-reliance, and the satisfaction that meeting it brings, I haven't figured out all the reasons why people travel alone.

Alone applied to travel seems a questionable idea when consideration is given to genetics, upbringing, friends, mentors, cartographers, boatmakers and equipment suppliers who all have contributed something to the journey. And, many travelers upon return from their solo journeys publish photos and articles telling other people all about their experiences. Do our adventures exist outside the zones of memory and imagination? Are our solo travels real if they are not told to others? The solo theme, after all, formed the basis for Sutherland's talk to a well-attended meeting of Seattle's Mountaineers and an inspiration for my being where I am right now.

Where I am: in a floating seal nursery, though smaller and less populated than the one in Johns Hopkins Inlet of Glacier Bay, where I once floated blissfully with two other paddlers in the iceberg-choked inlet. There, every other ice bit supported a group of mothers and pups. We laid paddles perpendicular to our yaks, across the spray skirts, and wordlessly watched the glistening seals. The Alaskan maritime sun blazed down onto our slightly bowed, hatless heads. To watch seals, one must look at them while aiming the eyes elsewhere, slightly off-angle. A mother seal alarms so easily that direct eye contact will cause her to plunge abruptly from her ice haven into the water.

The silent seal watching proceeded for about ten minutes. Then the fourth member of our group caught up. "Hey, you guys!" his voice boomed across the bay. Four seals plunged. "You hafta be really quiet in here—the seals are nursing." The other three of us exchanged glances, and picked up our paddles. The difficulty of even two human beings deliberately not speaking for any significant length of time often precludes wildlife sightings. The animals know we're coming long before we've turned the corner into their neighborhood. The solo traveler has much better chances to see animals, especially by the quiet kayak mode of travel.

I think about these aspects of solo travel while noting that I haven't seen another boat all morning, simultaneously an omen of a high-quality trip and a risky one. I can see Camp Island's shoreline clearly now, and the nearer I get, the faster and closer together the iceberg shards drift toward me. Also, the tide is ebbing fast, and I have to land soon or risk being marooned in the dreaded Stikine mud flats until the next tide change, a six-hour cycle, which would then require paddling after dark. When Matt and Stan got stuck in the Stikine mud flats, they just sat in their yaks and read books until the tide came up. But, they had lots of daylight.

I increase my paddle speed and point the bow for a landing just below a weathered gray cabin I see about a hundred yards back in the grassy clearing above the beach. After lashing the *Ozzy* to a huge driftwood log, I climb out of the cockpit. With the blue neoprene spray skirt and red life jacket still around my waist, I lurch toward the house in water-logged rubber boots. Maybe this is how walruses and seals feel when they have to navigate out of water.

Through the panes, a red-and-white checked tablecloth under several wine bottles welcomes. By custom, many Alaskan cabin owners leave their places unlocked for use by those in need of shelter; in turn, the travelers are expected to leave the place cleaner and/or better stocked than they found it. The vandalism that plagues modern times threatens this extended grace with extinction. The Camp Island cabin has not yet been so dishonored. A note written on the back of a dried-food label says the 1986 Vouvray was left by kayakers, so drinking it will not deplete the owners' supplies. Deciding the wine will taste better chilled, I unload my gear and then hike around the island in search of ice. On the east side, two dozen bergs lie on the mud flat under a bright rainbow, stranded by the outgoing tide. The icebergs talk, in a way. Like Rice Krispies popping, they spit and crackle as they melt. I bend my ear to a glistening surface to hear the story. The ice tells where it began, what icefields it calls family. How it was loosed from substrate to slide downhill. How it was dumped into the bay and landed here. Maybe this is a story only the solo traveler hears.

I stroll among the stilled ice chunks, choosing a whale-shaped one dripping fast. My pail placed into the sand under the icy head catches melt water for drinking. Glacier chips drop into my cup. I want to see these icebergs moving again, weaving and dancing to the tide's rhythm, but the smaller ones will not last for the next tide. I turn back to the cabin, where I light a candle on the front porch and lounge with my glacial wine, listen to the dusk music of owls, tiny frogs, soft wind and lapping waves and watch the sun go down over Frederick Sound.

The *tock* of a hand-wound clock on the kitchen table is the only human-made sound available here, other than noises I make myself. Maybe lack of human conversation is one of the misgivings people have about solo travel. "If I don't miss the sound of other people's voices," I ask the clock, "does that mean I'm anti-social?"

Tick-tick-tick. The clock won't commit.

Hunting magazines, bullet casings and duck decoys decorate the shelves and windowsills. In the cross piece of the front window hangs a little banner which says "Gateway Office of Aging." Wine or people? Hunting cartoons and a dart board add to the ambience.

On the living room wall over the sofa hangs a pair of men's jockey shorts. Tacks hold the shorts spread out like the pelt of a wild thing. In the center back, a large, brown liquid-fart spot is labeled with careful black felt-pen letters: "TYPICAL L.A. BRIEF."

The Camp Island cabin: so companionable that I spend a second day, lounging naked outdoors in the eighty-degree sun and writing poetry. Because the Vouvray is long gone, I drink vin rose sprinkled with Le Conte ice chips. The night is cold, though, so chilly I wear a wool watch cap to bed. Huddled in the narrow bunk, I know the weather gods will slap me in the face if I don't keep moving toward Wrangell.

In the morning I haul away a bag of trash for the duck hunters. I feel I know them now, the way I know my own siblings after years of being allowed to hang around in their rooms, snooping in their stuff: the marbles, comic books, zit medicine and gum wrappers that mark adolescence. "Thank you," I say to the walls and the clock, picking up the last load of gear and heading for the beach where the *Ozzy* waits.

Another beauty of paddling solo is that I don't need to time my departures around the readiness of companions. I have my loading routine down so precisely that today I eyeball the rate of the incoming tide, carry the empty boat down to where I think the tide will catch her, stuff all my gear in while the tide swirls over the toes of my rubber boots, position my body with my back to the sea, fasten the spray skirt, grab the paddle and grin; after less than two minutes, the draw is sufficient to carry me away. I hear the chewing of icebergs as they crowd Le Conte Bay. Small chunks already appear at the north and south channels, making their way into Frederick Sound. I paddle away fast because I can't bear the thought of waking up tomorrow without icebergs visible.

The usual contingents of birds and seals accompany my southward travel. I used to try to count the seals, but the moment I would make eye contact with one, she'd duck under. Another two or three would pop up on the periphery of my vision; if I turned toward them to get a count, they'd go under and others would pop up in a direction I wasn't looking. I don't try to count them anymore; now I sing or whistle. They stay above water longer for Beethoven than for Peter, Paul and Mary. Critics everywhere. The occasional drone of a distant motorboat syncopates the mix.

The sun's pulse throbs hard enough that for the first couple of hours I can paddle without a shirt under my life vest. As I cross the strait between Dry Island and Little Dry, wind whips the water like a hand mixer beating egg whites. I put my shirt on and maneuver hard to keep my bow pointed into the foamy crests of the waves. Off starboard, a long, brown barracuda shape barrels toward me—a log escaped from its boom. My eyes pick out another off port, about ten o'clock; then another. Huge logs have broken their cables and now race for the open sea. Maneuvering to avoid the mavericks, I look for the channel that will lead to the camp shown on Little Dry Island's chart. Wind shrieks around my head. Wind twists the paddle blades; I tighten my clutch. *Only about an hour 'till dusk, Koknuk Mud Flats stretch for miles, tide's going out too fast…*

The system of mud flats off the Stikine River mouth supports a marshy shoreline, swampy plains cut with deep channels. Reaching the forested parts where cabins and good campsites lie requires threading my way up twisting muddy channels until I find one that goes all the way in, like having to eat the edges of the cookie before the chocolate drop in the center can be gobbled. On this cookie, however, I can't always see where the edges are. I paddled up-channel against the wild wind, threading close to the six-foot-high silt bank to take advantage of the weaker current. I bottom out, step out and drag the boat, step into a hole, filling my left boot with

*A*laskans are travelers. This is probably because we're so far removed from contiguous America that traveling to another state involves distances difficult for "outsiders" to grasp. It's about the same distance from Fairbanks to Dallas as to Glasgow, Guadalajara, or Panama; Hong Kong, no farther than Rio or Nairobi. A three-day, thousand-mile weekend is not outrageous. I do them as often as I can.

♦

—Stephen Binns, "Road Reflections," *Alaska Passages: Twenty Voices from Above the 54th Parallel*, edited by Susan Fox Rogers mud and water. *Fuck. Arms ache, dusk near, damn wind...*To lighten the boat, I take out three dry bags and the ammo can, and stash them on a high outcrop of beach grass for later retrieval. Drag the yak upstream some more. Arms on fire. There in a tiny clump of trees, I can just make out a Forest Service cabin, still several hundred yards away. *Wasn't on the chart.* I can't pull the weight of the fully loaded boat through this muck anymore. I haul one armload up to the cabin, dump it, sigh, curse and sling a flashlight around my neck. There's maybe fifteen minutes' more light and another hour of hauling, in my fatigue. Back to the boat for more gear, through waist-high grasses. Mud holes for roots.

Too dark now to see the boat or find the stashed bags; I have to search by following my own boot holes back through the marsh. Looks like these early fall tides give little slack time. Almost as fast as the sound sucks itself back, it comes flowing in again. My boot holes begin to fill with incoming tidewater. Whole damned marsh will be under within the hour. I find the boat, and at the thought of having to move it all that way I feel tears rising. Looking at the ground, tidewater seeping into the depressions around my boots, I command my left foot to take a step. It barely moves. Muscle ache anchors me in mud and dark. *How in hell am I going to find that gear I stashed, gotta get it, too dark...*

Light floods the swamp, a sweeping gleam as though cast by a thousand icebergs. I throw back my head and open my arms wide to embrace the light, as over the ridge tops rises the fullest, roundest, most brilliant of all moons; the moon that lit the balcony when Romeo wooed Juliet; the moon that shone under the feet of the astronauts who first walked there; the moon that glints over the flukes of feeding humpbacks.

An hour later, I lift the last cargo out of the yak: two cans of Foster's Lager, just the right amount to wash down three Advils. I sit on the porch of the Forest Service cabin, muddy stuff bags piled all around, crusty paddle pants and jacket drying over the rails. In all this baggage rides the essence of seals and whales who have accompanied me on open crossings, the smell of salt-spray crust on my face and hands and its taste on my tongue, the tales of old companions, the advice of mentors and the gleaming dream visions of violet ice. Waves lap at the rocks a few yards away, and I inhale the salt smell. Gulls weave their aerial night patterns. "Ki-ree, ki-ree," they call. I can't see them, but I know the smooth, gray heads of seals bob offshore and will be there at dawnlight, their huge, curious eyes translucent like the marbles we called puries when I was a kid. To the southeast twinkle the electric lights of Wrangell, where tomorrow I will attempt a solo traverse through the streets of a town filled with people.

Sheryl Clough lives in Washington, and Alaska whenever possible. She holds an M.F.A. from the University of Alaska, Fairbanks. She has worked as a river guide, naturalist, and teacher. Her writing appears in Arnazella, Bellowing Art, Women's Outdoor Journal, *and other publications. She has written a book-length poetry manuscript and is currently finishing a collection of nonfiction essays with an emphasis on kayak travel.*

★

I asked the sailors casually, "Why race around Admiralty Island?" It is something they do every summer solstice, launching themselves on a 210-mile circumnavigation around the huge island and back to Juneau. They sail night and day, pausing only for an overnight stop at Baranof Warm Springs. For a week they run away to sea, deserting families, job, identities. They call the race the Spirit of Adventure, and it's true it offers most elements of the best Alaskan contests: potential disaster, a test of skills undervalued by society, the chance to be pummeled by awful weather, a certain grandeur of vision, and relative pointlessness. It is prac-tically irresistible.

The sailors considered my question, and then, in the intimate manner of the mildly intoxicated, one of them leaned against me and said the race illustrates the three essential conflicts she learned about in high school literature. She ticked them off against her fingers: Man against man. Man against nature. Man against self.

Bullshit, said her fellow sailor, the one drinking Jack Daniels—*it's all about terror and ecstasy*. That seemed right. We all raised our glasses to ter-ror and ecstasy.

—Sherry Simpson, "Circumnavigation," *Alaska Passages: Twenty Voices from Above the 54th Parallel*, edited by Susan Fox Rogers

MARIANA GOSNELL

Amelia in Kansas

The great aviator is nearly remembered.

THERE HAD TO BE AN AIRPORT NAMED FOR AMELIA EARHART *somewhere* in the country, I knew. It turned out to be in Atchison, Kansas, the town on a crook of the Missouri River where Amelia's grandmother lived and where she herself was born and went to school up to the fifth grade. On my way to Kansas City to visit my cousins I stopped in at the airport, to have a quick look around. I made a smooth touchdown on the single runway and the first turnoff—a landing any woman could be proud of. There was an elevated area on one side of the field with an obelisk on top and three pines planted in a row, so I went up there before the office. The obelisk was gray stone with a bas-relief carving on one side and a bronze plaque near the top. The carving was done in the convention of ancient Egypt, more or less: a woman, apparently nude, was kneeling with her torso facing front but her legs and head turned sideways. She was holding out to either side what looked like the stumps of arms: tapered wings. Clouds were billowing behind them on both sides. The clouds on her right were labeled Atlantic, those on her left Pacific. It was the Pacific side she was looking at.

The plaque noted that Amelia Earhart was "the first woman to fly the Atlantic (1932)," "the first woman to fly the Pacific (1935)," and "the first woman to receive the distinguished flying cross." Also, that she was "lost on Pacific flight July 1937." Before all these firsts (and last), however, in even bigger letters and at the top of the plaque, was, "Amelia Earhart...a courageous Zontian." Zontian? It had a definite sci-fi ring to it (first woman to have a close encounter?). Later I found out that a Zontian was a member of Zontia, an organization of "executive women in business," and Earhart had qualified because, as a pilot, she was "her own boss and exercised decision-making in her profession."

Inside the office were several large framed photographs on one wall, of Earhart sitting in the doorway of her Lockheed Electra, Earhart standing in front of the prop of her Electra, Earhart sitting by a fireplace, writing. Other than the photos and the obelisk, there didn't seem to be anything at the airport that had anything to do with her. I asked the FBO if that were so and he said he'd *thought* about holding a fly-in using her name as a draw but hadn't gotten around to it. When I phoned my cousins in Kansas City to let them know when I'd be landing, I mentioned where I was calling from. My cousin Joyce said her mother used to live in Atchison and had gone to kindergarten with Amelia. When she asked her mother what she remembered about her famous class-mate, "We had an ugly teacher with a mole" was all her mother would say.

For many years Mariana Gosnell reported on medicine and science for Newsweek magazine. She took a leave from her job for a three-month adventure, flying solo across America in her single-engine tailwheel airplane. She is the author of Zero 3 Bravo: Solo Across America in a Small Plane, *from which this piece was excerpted. She now lives in New York City.*

★

Airports are among the only sites in public life where emotions are hugely sanctioned. We see people weep, shout, kiss in airports; we see them at the furthest edges of excitement and exhaustion. Airports are privileged spaces where we can see the primal states—fear, recognition, hope—writ large. But there are some of us, perhaps, sitting at the departure gate, boarding passes in hand, watching the destinations ticking over, who feel neither the pain of separation nor the exultation of wonder; who alight with the same emotions with which we embarked; who go down to the baggage carousel and watch our lives circling, circling, circling, waiting to be claimed.

—Pico Iyer, "The Soul of an Intercontinental Wanderer," *Harper's*

MARILYN McCABE

✦ ✶ ✦

Fish for Thanksgiving

Thank goodness for a rotting carcass.

MAPS SHOW OREGON'S COAST AS A RAGGED EDGE. THE PRO-
nounced knobs of the coastline are often called "heads," although
they look like noses to me, or perhaps chins. We were headed to
Tillamook Head that night and the town of Oceanside perched
on its edge. It was Thanksgiving Day eve.

We were "Just Saying No" to Thanksgiving that year, my sister
and I. Her husband had recently left her and he had the kids for
the holidays. It would be the first Thanksgiving in more than fifteen years that she was not spreading the lace tablecloth over the
table they inherited from his grandmother, wasn't cooking up her
special cranberries, and filling the house with the flannelly smell of
Brussels sprouts. I was escaping from the obligatory dinner with
the east coast side of the family. Every year I trail after my mother
into my brother's pristine home where everything is either peach
or teal. We ask polite, but subtly puzzled questions about each
other's lives, then turn with relief to the familiar topic of local
politics and the latest traffic accident.

My sister and the dog picked me up at Portland's airport after
my long and turbulent ride from New York, and we headed
straight for the coast. Lyle Lovett was on the stereo and we talked

in fits and starts, as is often the case when you haven't seen an old friend for a while. She drove and I peered into the blackness on the edges of the headlights. The windshield wipers grumbled.

Route 6 from Portland winds west through Tillamook County, over the pine-dense hills into the rich farmland where Tillamook cheese is made. It crosses and recrosses the tumbling Wilson River. In the tempests of the winter of 1996, much of Route 6 and its bridges were washed out. Authorities weren't sure how long it would take to re-open the road. But that night, although wet and windy, the roads were clear.

We checked in at the Motel on the Hill in Oceanside and found our room, where rain streamed against the sliding glass door that faced the pounding sea down below. Tattered pieces of coast stand just off shore there, as if to better play in the waves. Crumbling cliffs meet the ocean, losing face with every storm.

When Captain Robert Gray first encountered the Oregon coast in his exploration of the Pacific in the late 1780s, he maneuvered carefully onto shore not far from Oceanside, in Tillamook Bay. As if the rocky coast weren't hostile enough, natives killed Gray's cabin boy. It's a rugged place.

The morning dawned grayly with rain still heavy. Although we were used to, even expecting, wet and gray weather at the beach in November, the rain was a little too hard for us. Finally hunger sent us out into Thanksgiving Day. We drove through the shiny deserted street of Oceanside. Bits of cloud were caught on the hill's trees, the sky was so low.

Oceanside is just beginning to be touched by creeping development. On its fringes a fancy hotel has erupted. Some lofty houses have been built on the cliffs above the town, gazing across the old wind- and time-worn buildings to the sea, as if the town weren't even there. There is still only one bar, one restaurant, and one place to get a quick cup of coffee. On the outskirts stand some tiny gas station and grocery store combinations, and down the road a few diners—fried fish, clam chowder, bad oil paintings of fishing boats and flowers.

Farther down the road at the next cluster of buildings—hardly a town, Netarts—we saw the dim glow of an open diner. The few natives in the diner turned and looked at us. We shuffled our feet uncomfortably and rain from our jackets dripped on the floor. I thought of the cabin boy. Finally one woman nodded and got us menus.

"We're closing in about twenty minutes," she said. "We opened for the fishermen, but we're closing for the rest of the day. Having a big dinner for the people in the area who are regulars and who have no place to go for the holiday."

Holiday comes from the words "holy day." But for those of us who have families we may wish we didn't or for those with no family at all, these days can be unholy indeed. And holy is etymologically linked to the word wholly, meaning entirely, altogether—or all together. The barrage of advertisement about holidays makes the absence of our "all together" wholly uncomfortable.

These people of Netarts had created their own family. I wondered whether they might recognize us for the orphans we felt like and take us in. But the woman just took our money and wished us a happy Thanksgiving.

My sister and I, a community of two, ran to the car. A community of three, I was reminded as I climbed in and was blanketed by the smell of kibble and wet dog. We stopped at a store and bought a Thanksgiving dinner of cheese popcorn, peppermint patties, and bottled water, and drove out to Cape Lookout.

Cape Lookout protects Netarts Bay on the south side as the coast continues on its wild way beyond. North of Oceanside, the tip of Cape Meares points north as Tillamook Bay dips inland. Cape Meares is a solitary slip, bounded by ocean and bay. We both find it disturbing and tend not to go there. You feel very alone on that slip of beach, as alone as the tide-washed trunks of broken trees that have washed up there, beached and bleached. Cape Lookout, in contrast, accepts the slap of the sea into its ample curve, and the lighthouse stands bravely facing the onslaught, making us feel in good company.

We didn't expect to share the beach with anyone except seagulls, but two cars were parked in the parking lot. In spite of the inclement weather, two intrepid people were spreading a picnic out on a sheltered table overlooking the frothing ocean. That's what I love about Oregonians. They just seem to become oblivious of the weather. We sat in the parking lot for a while and ate large handfuls of popcorn, watching the seagulls pace around our car on their skinny legs with knobby knees and feet like bats' wings. Then we filled our pockets with peppermint patties and set out.

The weather suited our mood. We spent a long time just standing watching the waves. And, of course, we walked. Our tradition is to walk the beach for hours, searching the sand for shells, colored rocks, interesting dead things washed up with the tide.

We go to Cape Lookout because of the baby sand dollars. Sometimes they are scattered across the beach as if the gods' pockets had holes. Sometimes they are nowhere to be found. We also go for the rocks that stand in a huge jumble at the end of the beach where they seem to have tumbled over the cliff. We can scramble over them, except at high tide, looking for starfish. Flumes shoot up with the waves in the gaps between rocks, soaking our shoes and slapping our faces.

The sea crashed in a constant snarl, and we often had to skitter to one side as waves came up especially high and tried to grab our ankles. A few black scoters flew low and fast over the breakers.

She saw it first, tangled in seaweed, the large head with gaping mouth. A sea bass, lower jaw jutting forward in useless pugnacity. It was quite dead and was washed clean, leaving only the skeleton draped with seaweed.

We poked at it, turning it over on the sand. We were entranced somehow. Eventually we picked the whole head up. Dead and disembodied it may have been, but it had such a funny expression on its face. My sister and I looked at each other, and started giggling.

I pulled my hood out as far as it could go and held the fish head in front of my face so it would replace me. I stared into its cavity, thinking fish thoughts of gray and cold darkness, of wet and scales and the garbage of oceans. The photograph my sister took shows a figure that might be death, but dressed not in a hooded black robe but blue Gore-tex. No sickle, but a red backpack. My sister took the head and held it up next to her face and imitated its expression exactly. I took a photograph of their likeness, and claimed that it called into question her lineage.

The dog bounded around us barking at our hilarity. Our mouths were tinged with the white of popcorn cheese, our pockets filled with crumpled peppermint patty wrappers. We were laughing in the wild wind, sand swirling into our mouths. We were scoured—this family of three and a dead fish, all together, on this deserted Oregon beach, where laughter was thanksgiving.

Marilyn McCabe is a freelance writer and editor living in Middle Grove, New York, far from any ocean, but comfortably close to the mountains. Her work has been published in several local and regional journals.

★

To go from anywhere to anywhere in Seattle it was necessary to cross at least one bridge. As a newcomer, I found them maddeningly hard to find, and the simplest journeys, like crossing from Queen Anne Hill to Capitol Hill, or from Magnolia to Ballard, used to defeat me, as I went under bridges that I should have gone over or came to an angry halt at yet another impassable waterfront. There were lift bridges, floating bridges, pedestrian bridges, bridges of Gothic wrought iron and of pale postmodern concrete. There were, I read, 161 bridges in Seattle, and I could well believe it. It occurred to me that any city so obsessively dedicated to bridge building as this must suffer from a fundamental anxiety about making connections.

—Jonathan Raban, "America's Most Private City," *Travel Holiday*

DOUGLAS PRESTON

* * *

Bewildered on Horseback

In the Arizona desert, a man's best friend
is his horse—until she runs away.

THE TRAIL BEGAN TO THIN OUT. THE PLEASANT GRAVEL STREAM-
bed turned into a deep arroyo jammed with rocks and boulders
slick with algae. At each crossing the horses scrabbled and slipped
among the boulders, trying to maintain a stable purchase. Soon
they were lathered up and blowing hard, the whites of their eyes
rolling in fear, and it became increasingly difficult to persuade
them to cross. Eusebio became eerily silent, no longer cursing,
hollering, or whipping his horses.

We stopped for lunch in a narrow meadow between Booger
Canyon and Hell Hole Canyon, two massive ravines that spilled
into Aravaipa Canyon.

We saw something we hadn't seen in 150 miles of wilderness
travel: hikers. A couple came jaunting by, dressed in colorful
Gore-tex clothing and carrying collapsible aluminum hiking
sticks. They looked so bright and clean and new that we, in
contrast, suddenly saw ourselves as we must have appeared to
them: three unspeakably foul (and no doubt criminally dangerous)
men. They eyed us with undisguised fear and hurried past on the
upwind side.

Past Hell Hole Canyon the going got much worse. We found

ourselves in a very dangerous situation. The horses began to panic for real. At one three-foot embankment, crowded with boulders, Robin, in a spasm of fear, leapt into the air. She landed in the stream with a roar of water and splashed about with the two-hundred-pound pack on her back. My heart nearly stopped and I was certain she had broken a leg, but she scrambled up with nothing worse than a few scrapes.

I insisted we stop on the far bank to look for an alternate route on the maps. Unfortunately, there was really no way out, unless we rode back 75 miles.

"Eusebio," I asked, "are we going to kill a horse in here?"

He shrugged.

I asked again without getting an answer.

Finally I became irritated. "*Goddammit, I want an answer. Are we going to kill a horse in here?*"

Eusebio stared at the ground. "Maybe," he said slowly, "and maybe not. I'm not saying *nothing*. You kill a horse in here, it ain't gonna be my fault."

When the Spaniards learned that Hawikuh —just a few houses "all crumpled together"—was the first of the seven glorious cities of Cíbola they were, to put it mildly, irate. They had nothing but curses for Fray Marcos—he was sent back to Mexico in disgrace—and, of course, Coronado was livid. He fired off a message to the viceroy about the mendacious friar: "I can assure you that he has not told the truth in a single thing he has said, for everything is the opposite of what he related except the names of the cities and the large houses. The Seven Cities of Cíbola are seven little villages." Actually the friar was wrong about the number— there were only six.

◆

—Bill Lawrence, *Wilderness: North America as the Early Explorers Saw It*

"What a load of bullshit," Walter said with disgust and got back on his horse. We continued on.

The afternoon sun had wheeled around and was now glowing off the eastern walls of the canyon. The canyon had become so narrow and twisting that we lost track of how much farther we had to go. The trail kept disappearing and reappearing. It wasn't a trail at all, just a place where hikers had worn down the vegetation. In several places the brush was so thick that the packed horses became wedged in it, unable to move.

At one point the canyon narrowed to less than fifteen feet wide, with sheer walls on either side. An uprooted cottonwood, with a trunk three feet in diameter, was jammed in the gap, with just enough room for a packed horse to squeeze through. Just beyond, Walter and I heard a tremendous ripping noise followed by a torrent of curses. Eusebio's packhorse had caught a pannier on the jagged rock wall of the canyon and the canvas had torn nearly in half. Stuff was spilling out into the creek and the pack was listing to one side.

Walter, always resourceful, improvised a hitch that temporarily held the pannier together until it could be repaired. With the canyon walls flaming blood-red in the evening sun, we came upon a small meadow with a little flat spot for our bedrolls. We would have to camp.

We unpacked the animals, smeared gall salve on their bloody legs, and staked them out in the rich grass. Eusebio sat down to sew the pannier back together, muttering angrily to himself in Spanish.

Walter hauled a fishnet out of the bottom of a pannier.

"We're gonna have ourselves some trout!" he said.

We found a likely pool, and as we peered into it we could see the flickering of silver. Walter cackled and smacked his palms together. We each took an end of the net and waded into the pool, lunged and scooped, and hauled the net out.

It was empty.

"Dammit," Walter said, "you're letting 'em get out from under."

I was annoyed. "It's not my fault. I saw the fish going right between your legs."

We thrashed through the pool a second time, roiling the bottom. Again the dripping net was empty.

"Damn, Doug, I *saw* 'em get right out from under your end."

"If you spent more time holding your own end down we'd have some fish by now," I said.

We tried driving them upstream into shallow water.

"Hold your end down!" Walter shouted.

We argued a while longer and then I lost my footing and fell head-first into the pool.

When I surfaced Walter was stomping around, laughing. "I didn't want to mention it, but you needed that bath!"

"Shut up," I said.

We hauled in the net. Somehow, in the confusion, we'd managed to catch two fish, barely larger than minnows, which wiggled in the folds of the net. We untangled them. Two big, ugly, rubbery mouths were gasping for air.

"Son-of-a-bitch!" Walter roared out. "These ain't trout! These are suckers!"

We straggled back to camp, dripping wet and laughing.

"Where's dinner?" Eusebio asked.

"Right there," Walter said, kicking a pannier. "Rice and beans."

"*Que chinga'os,*" he said with infinite disgust, and went back to his sewing....

We broke camp early. It was May 2nd, and we had to reach the mining town of Winkelman on the 3rd to meet Wicks, the cowboy who was to give us fresh horses and take Eusebio home. The canyon walls gradually opened up and the creek flowed into a land of arid, stony hills, dotted with giant saguaro cacti.

At the very foot of the canyon, on a bench of land above the river, we spied a magnificent horse ranch. The most prominent landmark was a costly and beautiful horse barn, with room for dozens of stalls. Next to that were corrals, hot walkers, exercise rings, and a swimming pool for horses. On the near side were more barns, a large main house with a swimming pool (for humans), and several guest houses. The ranch was surrounded by fields with miles of white pipe fencing.

As we got closer, the place began to look strange. A barn door hung on one hinge, swaying drunkenly in the breeze. The dirt road we picked up was full of weeds. Blue sky shone through the shattered window frames of the main house. The pool was half full of tumbleweeds. An old chair, its stuffing ripped out, stood outside in a patch of dead grass. The head of a doll, cracked by the sun, looked out of a broken window.

It was one more ranch gone bankrupt.

We followed the road back toward the San Pedro River. We started passing ugly modern houses. There were clusters of signs along the road. House for Sale. Aravaipa Subdivision. Choice Lots. Century 21 Realty. And everywhere: NO TRESPASSING, KEEP OUT. I realized with a start that these were the first No Trespassing signs we had seen in some 175 miles of travel.

We had come down on the Tucson side of the mountains, leaving rural Arizona behind. These were the vacation homes of city folk. The road turned to asphalt and the heat became ferocious. Cars whizzed by, big American cars packed with plump women and men wearing brand-new cowboy hats. We had entered as ugly a landscape as I believe I have ever seen.

Twelve miles of riding brought us to a small group of prefabricated metal buildings and a sign announcing them as Central Arizona College. As we were watering our horses, the ground suddenly shuddered beneath our feet, and a moment later I heard an unearthly roar rolling across the desert. I looked up. A gigantic cloud of mouse-colored dust was rising up in slow motion from some hills to the west. It continued to expand like a grotesque balloon, until it blotted out the sun itself. Some infernal mining operation was in progress.

We crossed a highway and rejoined the San Pedro. We camped in a patch of sand at a bend in the river, not far from the supposed location of old Fort Grant. Nothing was left of the fort, and its precise site has been forgotten.

The soldiers at old Fort Grant also despised this landscape, and the fort had finally been moved because of its "unhealthy location."

"Beauty of situation or construction it had none," an officer posted at the old fort wrote. "Its site was the supposed junction of the sand bed of the Aravaipa with the sand bed of the San Pedro which complacently figured on maps of that time as a creek and river respectively. They were generally as dry as a lime-burner's hat. It was a hot-bed of fever and ague."

We pitched camp in the dusk. I got a fire going and started dinner. While I worked, I could hear Walter in the brush, talking to his three horses while they grazed. (After several weeks we had found ourselves conversing with our horses as if they were human.)

Then I heard Walter's voice raised: "Whoa, Ped."

And a little louder: "I said whoa."

Uh-oh, I thought.

Then: "Ped! *Whoa*! Bobby! Whoa, you son-of-a-bitch, *whoa*! Hey! Robin! Goddammit, *whoa*!"

I began to feel sick. Faintly, from the brush, I could hear one last despairing cry:

"*Motherfuckers!*"

Walter's hysterical voice disappeared into the darkness.

Eusebio stood up and spat. "Shit," he said, "he just lost his horses."

Walter returned an hour later. All three of his horses were gone. In a moment of trust, he had let two graze free; they had taken off, and in the excitement he had dropped the lead rope of the third horse, who also escaped.

It was now pitch-black, a moonless night. We would have to wait until morning.

We had a short, depressing dinner. Eusebio took a grim enjoyment in the disaster. "You watch," he said, "them horses, they shag ass. Them sum-bitches *gone*, man. Ain't nothing gonna stop them now. You ain't *never* gonna find them sum-bitches." He smacked his palms together and spread his arms dramatically, his beady, darting eyes flaming in the firelight. "They *gone!*"

He kept up a steady stream of dreadful predictions, involving horses run over and people killed on the highway, horses lost in brush for months, horses traveling 40, 50 miles in a single night. As he talked, Walter sank deeper into a depression.

I finally pointed out to Eusebio that, as Bobby was one of the lost horses, and as Bobby was our payment for getting Eusebio back to East Pecos, and as Wicks would probably not accept a promissory note on a horse lost somewhere in the Arizona desert, *ergo*, Eusebio would not be going anywhere until we found Bobby.

There was a momentary silence while Eusebio processed this information, his brows knitting together until his entire face was a mass of puzzled wrinkles. Then his eyes popped open and he slapped his hand on his thigh.

"*Aiee*! Sum-bitches! We'll get out there, catch'em first thing to-morrow! There'll be a fence'll *stop* them sum-bitches, you'll see!"

I will not go into the painful details of our search for the lost horses. We could not track them; the brush was too thick and the ground, which hadn't been rained on in six weeks, was criss-crossed with horse tracks.

Our first step was to determine the area they were lost in. We located and rode the boundary fences and figured it at about 17,000 acres, or approximately 27 square miles—virtually all of it dense salt cedar, willow, and cottonwood brush.

I would submit that you cannot understand despair until you have looked for lost horses in 27 square miles of impassable brush, lousy with invisible rattlesnakes, under a white-hot sky in 107-degree heat with no wind and high humidity. (We learned later it was the hottest day southern Arizona had experienced at that time of year in 44 years.)

We saw, during that long day, something of the way the West had changed since Coronado's day. This was mining country, and there is something about working in an underground hole that breaks the human spirit. I'll never forget coming across the mining town of Dudleyville, emerging from the brush like some Boschean vision of hell: houses of unpainted cinderblock; trailers shedding strips of aluminum; dogs behind chain-link fences, racing back and forth in a frenzy of blood-lust hatred, slobbering and digging to get out; No Trespassing signs with a full-frontal picture of a six-shooter.

Later I rode alongside the highway, through heaps of trash, broken bottles of Night Train, used diapers, beer cans, oil-soaked dirt, and cacti draped with torn plastic and toilet paper. The only breeze was the backwash from passing trucks. Nowhere could I escape the distant clank and grind and roar of men and machines in the surrounding hills, extracting minerals from the earth.

Wicks, the cowboy with our fresh horses, arrived at 2 p.m. I met him on the highway. When he opened the truck door a dozen Coors Light cans tumbled to the ground. He had been refreshing himself since five o'clock that morning.

We rendezvoused back at our camp. Wicks staggered about, mightily annoyed that we had allowed his payment to take hoof. He asked us a lot of questions, none of which we answered satisfactorily, and after some thoughts he emitted a stream of tobacco juice and the following assessment:

"What a bunch of greenhorn assholes."

He then proceeded to give us some of the best advice we had during the entire trip. Among his instructions were (a) the minute you reach camp, stake out or hobble the horses—never let a horse be loose, even for a moment; (b) train them to come back to camp in the morning by whistling and giving them some grain; (c) just when you think you can trust them, don't; (d) watch them particularly carefully when they are fed and rested, as that's when they'll start causing trouble; and (e) identify the lead horse and watch him closely, as he's the one who will initiate the trouble.

To horse people this advice might seem a little elementary, but to us it was a revelation.

Wicks was a short cowboy with a mustache and an Arizona drawl. He carried a coffee can in his left hand, into which he regularly deposited, with a ringing sound, a stream of tobacco juice. When riding, he wore Adidas, a Lacoste shirt, and a trucker's hat. He was a good enough cowboy that he didn't even have to look like one.

Wicks had once been a champion calf roper. His greatest moment, he told me, was getting thrown off a horse in Madison Square Garden in New York City, for which he received a standing ovation. "I roped fifty head a cows every night for ten years to git there," Wicks said, "and then this son-of-a-bitch horse threw me comin' right out of the gate."

He was a very good roper, almost a world champion. I didn't ask him why he'd quit; the pile of Coors cans explained everything. He now trained horses for the movies, teaching them how to fall down when "shot," how to rear on command, and other tricks.

We finally found the horses at nine o'clock that evening. They were grazing alongside the highway, not even inside the twenty-seven-square-mile wilderness which we had been combing for the past fourteen hours. Somehow, they'd found a hole in the fence or jumped a cattle guard.

I thought it worthy of taking notice of a singular method the traders make use of to reduce the wild young horses to their hard duty. When any one persists in refusing to receive his load, if threats, the discipline of the whip and other common abuse prove insufficient, after being haltered, a pack-horseman catches the tip end of one of his ears betwixt his teeth and pinches it, when instantly the furious strong creature, trembling, stands perfectly still until he is loaded.

♦

—William Bartram,
Travels and Other Writings

The next morning I met my two horses, Banjo and Popeye. They were both large, powerful quarter horses, with sorrel coloring. Popeye had a white blaze on his forehead and Banjo a snip of white on his nose.

Wicks was a little worried about my ability to handle Popeye. He gave me detailed instructions on what to do if Popeye ran away with me or started bucking. "If somethin' starts to happen, you either git off right away or stay on for the ride—you cain't change your mind halfway through a wreck. If he stampedes with you, reach around and pull the son-of-a-bitch's head sideways with one rein so he cain't see where he's goin'. But don't do it to fast or he'll fall. If that don't work, steer him straight into a bush; that'll stop him."

I was a little perturbed at the advice.

"Now look here," Wicks cautioned, "if he acts up, you gotta punish him."

And how does one punish a 1,200-pound horse?

"The way you do that is to ride him around in a tight circle while kicking the shit out of him. They hate that. Or get off him and kick him hard in the ribs. But kick him with the side of your foot, not the toe."

"I guess you have to be careful not to break his ribs," I offered.

"Hell no!" he said. "You don't want to break your *toe*." He roared with laughter and turned to Walter. "I had a friend did that once, broke his toe kicking a horse. What a dumbshit."

It came time to depart. We shook hands all around while Eusebio sat silently in the truck.

Wicks got in and leaned out the window with a big grin.

"Now that Banjo, he's a lively son-of-a-bitch. As soon as I drive away, he's gonna buck that pack into the river and take off and you're gonna have another lost horse."

We all laughed at the joke. While they lurched off Walter and I sat in a patch of dust under a cottonwood, eating peanuts.

"I'm glad we got rid of that Mexican," Walter said. "That bastard was *diseased*."

"At least he'll make a good character in my book," I said.

"Yeah, and when he reads what you write about him he'll come and burn down your house."

"What makes you so sure he can read?" I asked.

We laughed, feeling enormously elated. The real adventure was now beginning.

"I'll tell you something," Walter said. "*This* is more like it, God *damn*. We're on our own now." He whooped and danced by the side of the river, shedding dust.

Then we formally shook hands.

I mounted Popeye and lightly touched his flanks with my heels, to get him started. The horse acted like he'd just received a load of buckshot in the ass. He sprang forward and went blasting through the brush at a dead run. I held on for dear life and followed Wick's advice for arresting a runaway horse. When I finally got him under control I saw what had spooked him. Banjo was in the middle of the river, leaping and twisting and kicking, trying to shuck his pack. Our gear was popping off every which way. Then, with the pack half undone, he galloped like hell up the river and disappeared.

We watched in stunned silence. I can hardly describe what my feelings were at this moment. We had lost another horse.

Douglas Preston, a frequent contributor to Smithsonian *magazine and former columnist for* Natural History, *is the author of the acclaimed book* Dinosaurs in the Attic. *This story was excerpted from his book,* Cities of Gold: A Journey Across the American Southwest in Pursuit of Coronado.

*

As I continue to run down the dirt road alongside the wagons where the Pony riders once raced I can't help but think about what happens to the human body as a man ages. When I was the age of the Pony riders, I felt nothing could hurt me. Muscle and bone were stronger than steel. The Pony riders must've felt the same way to take the risks they took. But now, with my youth gone, as I see old David, fragile and weathered driving his mules I know I too, will one day become that vulnerable, as surely as all the Pony riders are now dead and turned to dust. These thoughts don't depress me. They make me realize once again just how short and precious life is. At least in this heightened moment I don't even mind that my lungs begin to burn from running. I feel lucky to be in the race against time.

—Jerry Ellis, *Bareback! One Man's Journey Along the Pony Express Trail*

MIKE McINTYRE

A Night's Accommodation

What it takes to stay dry all night.

WILMINGTON IS THE BIGGEST CITY I'VE HAD TO SPEND THE NIGHT in since Billings, Montana. I can't count on the kindness of strangers. No shelters are listed in the Yellow Pages, so I get the address of the YMCA. Maybe they'll let me sleep there.

The Y is 27 blocks away. I start hoofing it. Naturally, it begins to rain. My umbrella snags on branches as I walk in the dark. I make it 23 blocks, then the sidewalk runs out. The shoulder of the busy boulevard is flooded. I walk back downtown.

I find the police station inside a brick building near the riverfront. The officer at the desk gives me directions to the Salvation Army. But when I get there, every bunk is taken. The receptionist calls Wilmington's other shelter. They are full, too. She tells me the police will let me sit in the station.

"I'm back," I tell the officer when I return. "The shelters are full. All right if I sit in here until daylight?"

The room glares with fluorescent lights and the chairs are wooden. But at least it's safe and dry.

"I can't let you stay here," the cop says. "It's against policy."

"Oh, shoot, the lady at the Salvation Army said you let people sit in here."

"It's up to the sergeant on duty. The sergeant's policy tonight is no."

I gaze over the cop's shoulder at the sergeant, a stern-looking black woman hunched over paperwork inside a glass office. From the way she grips her pencil, I know her policy is ironclad.

I ask the officer if there is an open public building in town where I can stay out of the rain.

The cop leans over the counter and whispers, so his sergeant can't hear. He says there is a closet in the lobby of this building. I can stay there.

It sounds like a crazy idea, and I wonder if the cop is kidding, but I thank him and go looking for tonight's lodgings.

I find the closet next to the automatic door that opens to the street. It stands across the lobby from the restrooms. It's about the width of a coffin, but not as long. The space is made smaller by the presence of a single sofa cushion, a two-by-four board, and a music stand.

After I remove my pack, there is barely enough room to curl up on the floor. I take off my shoes and socks and lay on top of my wet sleeping bag. My hip is bruised from sleeping on the cement slab last night in the park. I wish I hadn't thrown away my pad.

The closet door won't click shut. It's warped and keeps popping open. Light from the lobby filters through the crack. I toss and turn, trying to find a comfortable position. My feet press against the door, and my head rests on the base of the music stand.

I finally doze off.

I don't know how long I've been asleep when I hear the automatic door swing open. I listen for the footsteps to turn toward the police station, but they come my way. Still groggy, I bolt upright. The closet door is open an inch. A human shadow dances on the closet wall. It gets bigger. I place my feet against the door and try to lock my knees, but I'm too late. Whoever is on the other side barges in.

I spring up, reeling with panic. The intruder flicks a cigarette lighter. There is suddenly an angry black man in my face, attacking me with eighty-six-proof breath.

"*What the fuck are you doing in here???!!!*" he shouts.

I stumble back into the music stand.

"Who are you?" I say. "Who are you?"

All of us at various moments are the man on the bus gazing out and murmuring, "Isn't that a sight."

◆

—John Daniel, *The Trail Home*

He steps back out of the closet without a word. He's unshaven, and the cuffs of his baggy pants are frayed from dragging on the street. He stumbles across the lobby and drops in the doorway of the men's room. He lays his head on the greasy athletic bag he carries with him.

I shut the closet door and stand in the dark. I try to wedge the two-by-four against the door but it won't hold. I place the cushion between my feet and the door, as if that's going to keep anybody out. I sit up on my sleeping bag. I worry about what's happening on the other side of the door. I don't make a sound. I'm afraid to even shift. I don't want to remind the guy I'm in here. When I hear him snoring, I lay back down.

The automatic door rumbles open a while later. Someone leans on the closet door.

"Hey!" I shout, trying to sound scary.

"Oh, excuse me," says the man on the other side.

I hear him sit down next to the other man. He spreads out some newspaper and lies down. The man mutters something I can't hear, waking the guy with the lighter.

"There's a white guy in there," the man with the lighter says.

The new man is talkative, but he's hard to understand. I pick up snippets, wondering if any of it pertains to me.

"Night of the living dead…Lies in disguise…Revelations, chapter nine…Lies in disguise…"

The man rambles on, growing loud and belligerent. If he keeps it up, the cops will hear him and come kick us out in the rain.

Sure enough, the doors from the police station open at around one in the morning. I hear the authoritative click of heels start across the linoleum floor.

"You can't sleep here!" a woman barks.

It must be the sergeant.

"Let me see the chief," the new guy grumbles.

"I'm in charge here tonight. You gotta sleep somewhere else. People come in here and see you, they get scared. Not everyone who comes here is a criminal. There are some people who come here for legitimate reasons."

"Can't I just sit here, to avoid the elements?"

"How did you avoid the elements last night?"

"I slept in a friend's car at his apartment building."

"Well, I suggest you do the same tonight."

"He ain't there."

"My heart goes out to you, but you can't stay here."

A new voice enters the conversation.

"We get treated better by white people!" shouts the man with the lighter.

"Who is that talking behind that corner?" the sergeant snaps.

I hear the man with the lighter roll into the sergeant's view. He starts in about injustice, but the woman cuts him off.

"Who keeps the bathroom open for you? You get on out of here. I don't want to see you here again. You come back here when there's white folks working."

The two men gather their things and leave.

"You think this is funny," the talkative one says to the sergeant on his way out the door.

"No, I don't. I think it's sad. All the black people who died fighting for civil rights, and you ending up like this…"

"Civil rights! Whatta you done for civil rights? I marched in Mississippi for civil rights! You ain't done nothin' for civil rights! Don't go talkin' to me 'bout civil rights!…"

The argument carries on out into the street. I listen through the closet wall. My fellow vagrants don't rat me out. When the sergeant walks back into the police station, I try to get some sleep.

It's not long before the two homeless men return. They try to keep quiet, but their voices echo like they were camping in the Taj Mahal. The automatic door keeps swinging open as more bums stagger in. A few try the closet door. "Hey!" I shout over and over.

Finally the commotion is too great. The sergeant marches back into the lobby. This time she has help. The officers escort everybody out of the building. The night is again quiet. I breathe easy. Then somebody pushes on my door.

"Who is that in there?" the sergeant growls.

"Me."

"Who's 'me'?"

"Mike McIntyre."

"Come on out of there!"

I walk out of the closet rubbing my eyes. The sergeant glares at me. The officer who told me to crash in the closet stands behind her.

"How long you been in there?" the sergeant says.

"Since about ten," I say.

"What are you doing coming in and sleeping in the building without telling anyone you're here? You could be cited."

I don't tell her how I found the closet.

"Damn, he knows the building better than I do," the cop says with convincing amazement.

I drag my sleeping bag and pack out of the closet. I put on some dry socks and step back into my wet boots.

"Where are you from?" the sergeant says.

"California."

"California! And you end up in *Wilmington*?"

"Yep, it's the end of the line."

"California," she says, shaking her head.

It seems like a good time to laugh. And we do.

Stuck in a job he no longer found fulfilling, journalist Mike McIntyre felt his life was passing him by. So one day he hit the road to trek from one end of the country to the other with little more than the clothes on his back and without a single penny in his pocket. He wrote about his journey in The Kindness of Strangers: Penniless Across America, *from which this story was excerpted.*

I found an open boxcar and joined the half a dozen bums in it. When we reached Roseburg we all got out and down into a swampy place by the river. It was pitch dark and raining heavily, and we agreed to scatter and collect some wood to make a big fire. They scattered all right, and left me creeping along the dangerously swollen river among the cottonwoods, gathering water-soaked limbs and bark.

Finally with some damp newspaper that I carried around my waist under a sweater and some dry cedar that I'd come upon, I started a fire. As the flames rose and I scrounged around for more dry fuel, a particularly heavy downpour put out the fire. Crawling around, I couldn't even find where I'd made it, so I gave up and felt my way directly away from the sound of the river until I finally found the town, which was all locked up. After much wandering through the empty streets, I came upon the courthouse and, going nearer to find a place protected from the weather, I heard talking. It was the bums I had ridden with, who were all in the jail, warm and cozy. "Hunt up the night watchman," one of them said. "He'll let you in here."

—Clyde Rice, *A Heaven in the Eye*

SALLIE TISDALE

Where is Idaho?

*It definitely means more
than potatoes.*

BOISE IS LIKE THE LAND; PEOPLE WHO CAME HERE HAD BIG HOPES, and big plans. In the varied lands surrounding Boise, you can move in a few short miles through the broad wheat plains, past isolated houses huddled behind cottonwood windbreaks, past barns and giant silver silos, seed companies, and tractors with columns of dust rising from under their big wheels like smoke. North of Boise are dry, steep canyons that break open into tree-covered hills, shallow quick streams that spread into marshes before they squeeze down other canyons. Meadows, hills, wheat, dust, trees, meadows: one seems to lead inevitably to another. I drive along the winding, steep, two-lane highways too fast, past the FROST HEAVES signs, my van leaning precariously in the curves, up and down until I reach another lumbering RV, another slow trailer too wide to pass.

People say mean things about Boise, and Idaho. (The poet Linda McAndrew calls it Idahohum.) One of my favorite postcards shows two men driving in a car with two shaggy dogs in the back seat. The caption is "Idaho Double-Date." People have always said mean things about Idaho, crawling over the hot, dusty southern basin and leaning ever forward, to the farther West. "In the raw new land of South Idaho it was shove and scrape, and if you had bad luck or lost your strength you were done for." So wrote Nancy Stringfellow, who is now 80, of her childhood in Twin Falls, Idaho, "where the wind blows down like the hounds of hell."

Idaho was late settled, late to be a territory, a state, still an orphan of the West. In 1858, a travel writer, apparently serious, wrote, "Idaho is no chimera of the brain—*no terra incognita, no ignuus fatuus*—but an established fact." (Much later, after an extended visit to Idaho Territory, the same writer added: "Should we ever encounter an enemy, and his punishment be left to our decision, the sentence will be: 'Go, ride a fat, lazy, hard-trotting horse to Boise, and be forgiven.'")

Teddy Roosevelt liked to hunt in the varied wilderness of Idaho. He was that kind of man who is eminently logical to himself, and almost incomprehensible to me: the hunter who loves the virgin wilderness and the kill at once, who in fact connects the two. If Mr. Roosevelt had been my passenger one night near Fossil, Oregon, when I drove past two perfect fawns standing like statues in the road, he would have wanted me to stop and collect them. Roosevelt once had a piece of great good luck on a hunting trip in the northern mountains in 1888. He was able to catch a water-shrew, "a rare little beast," he wrote in his memoir of the trip. "I instantly pounced and slew it; for I knew a friend in the Smithsonian at Washington who would have coveted it greatly." He skinned the animal and laid the treasure aside, while the night darkened and his Indian guide—"He was a good Indian, as Indians go," wrote Roosevelt—prepared the meal. In the process, the guide accidentally threw the skin on the fire and that was the end of the rare little shrew.

Because it is stuck between the open land of Washington and Oregon and the Continental Divide of the Rockies, Idaho gets left out. Is it Rocky Mountain country? Perhaps. Is it the Northwest? Perhaps. Is it anything, but Idaho?

The Northwest would be another kingdom—isolated, anarchic, raising itself up like a wolf child in the wilderness. The West's anarchy is another terra incognita; unfound, unexplored. It has a dual nature, murky, a vague combination of conservative and radical, pride and backwoods shame that would be more interesting if it were more examined. The Pacific Northwest is provincial and progressive in the same breath, conformist, regressive, excessively tolerant and intolerant by turns. It walks the conservative line and then elects a Democrat. We have a history of escape.

Not long ago, petitions for a new state circulated from Sandpoint, Idaho, through Spokane in eastern Washington and Coeur d'Alene in northern Idaho. The call was for a movement to form Columbia, the 51st state—the Wilderness State—out of eastern Washington, western Montana, and part of Idaho. Columbia's state animal would be, of course, the grizzly bear.

Secession isn't usually thought of as a tradition, but it is here—at least, attempts at seceding variously from the states and the Union itself have gone on since the first settlers came. It is Frederick Jackson Turner's fear come to life: the West breeds independence, and the Far West a kind of defiance.

In 1852, there was a bill to form a state of Shasta from what is now northern California and southern Oregon, out of anger at high taxes and poor mail service; the bill died in committee. In 1853, there was a call for the same area to form the state of

> *I*daho presents the greatest challenge to easy classification. While most Oregon and Washington residents consciously locate themselves within the Pacific Northwest, those of Idaho cannot agree. Some Idahoans perceive their state as oriented toward Oregon, Washington, and the Pacific rim; other consider it part of an intermountain West that includes Montana and Utah. It has often been said that Idaho is the only American state with three capitals: Boise, Salt Lake City, and Spokane.
>
> ◆
>
> —Carlos A. Schwantes,
> *The Pacific Northwest:*
> *An Interpretive History*

Klamath; in 1854 and 1855, for the area to form the state of Jackson. In 1854, a group of men determined to prevent southern Oregon from joining the antislavery Union made a secession attempt; later, northern California was added to Oregon for the same purpose and a constitutional convention was called in 1857. In 1861, a secret society for secession, the Knights of the Golden Circle, was formed, and all through the 1860s there was talk of forming the Pacific Republic of Western States. The first mention of the state of Jefferson was in the 1890s. In 1908, eastern Washington and northern Idaho tried to form the state of Lincoln. Again in 1909 came an attempt to create the state of Siskiyou from the same northern California and southern Oregon area; and again in 1935 and 1940. In both 1915 and 1978, there were attempts to form a second California, called Alta California, from the sparsely populated, geographically defiant northern section.

In 1941, the Yreka Chamber of Commerce passed a resolution calling for a 49th state to be formed from parts of northern California and southern Oregon from roughly the 40th to the 44th parallel. A Proclamation of Independence was announced on November 27, 1941, declaring that regular and repeated secessions from the Union would occur every Thursday "until further notice." Cars were stopped on the main road through, Highway 99, and drivers were given informational pamphlets. A governor was elected, a flag was sewn, and rallies were held, complete with all-girl Drum and Bugle Corps. The momentum was high and mounting; it took the Japanese at Pearl Harbor to divert attention.

In places like Boise you can stop for a cup of coffee almost anywhere, even in a gun shop. I crossed the wide, empty Boise Streets, the short buildings so far apart that whole chunks of sun seemed to fall between them, to a gun shop for breakfast, remembering the sporting-goods store on the main street of my hometown. The four high walls are covered with taxidermy, examples of size and prowess cut off at the neck: a moose, a buck with rack as wide as a park bench, a snarling, frozen bear. The center of the store is a U-shaped soda fountain, and around it, any time of the day, sit men—young and old, wearing cowboy hats and baseball caps, eating pastrami and tuna fish. If I can't find my father at the Elks Club, or the fire hall, or standing behind the counter at the hardware store, I know he'll be at Dan's Sporting Goods.

My companion at Moon's Café in Boise was a handsome, diffident man named Rick Ardinger, a Pittsburgh boy who dreamed of coming west. Rick found Pocatello, in eastern Idaho, then tried Albuquerque, and in 1977 moved back to Idaho City, a small town outside Boise where he feels permanently, and happily, settled. He has red hair, a bushy red beard, wire-rim glasses. Rick is a letterpress printer and, with his wife Rosemary, owner of Limberlost Press, one of the breed of small presses in the Northwest turning out handcrafted editions of poetry, journals, pioneer diaries. The evening before, Rick and Rosemary had hosted the poet Robert Creeley for a reading. It is Rick who gave me a copy of Nancy Stringfellow's memoir, a small paperbound book he had set by hand, each copy bound singly, by hand. Nancy brought the love of serious reading to Boise in the form of a store called The Book Shop. She and her husband built a house that, her daughter Rosalie Sorrels writes, "looks like a bower and everywhere you put your foot a cloud of fragrance envelops you. The whole place seems to have grown from the ground."

We sat at a tiny table in the back, eating good, cheap food, and watched a succession of taciturn men examine shotguns and pistols. Hunting season was soon to start, and I could see boxes of ammunition pushed across the counter; a heavy-bellied man in a baseball cap sighted along a rifle toward the picture window at the far end of the narrow shop. We talked about the West's confusion,

A sked at the Boise, Idaho, visitor's bureau: "If you go to a restaurant in Idaho and you don't want any kind of potato with your meal, will they ask you to leave?"

♦

—John Flinn, "We Have Some Questions, and Answers, Too," *San Francisco Examiner* its adolescent ruminations on itself. "What is true for the West, is all most true in Idaho," Rick said, dipping into scrambled eggs. I could hear the murmur of men nearby, sipping good hot coffee, taking time. Idaho is isolated, Rick continued, running north and south the long way, split like a shingle by the Bitterroot Mountains. It is unclaimed, not quite set apart, but apart: Idaho is an orphan.

Idaho has a disproportion of millionaires; its conservatism and relative isolation seem to cushion the wealthy person seeking privacy and a big backyard. In 1980, Idaho had more millionaires per capita than any other state.

J.R. Simplot is one of the country's richest men, owner of one of the largest privately owned corporations in the world. His company employs ninety-five hundred people. Simplot sells McDonald's more than half its french fries. He is a symbol of Boise, and Idaho, not necessarily loved. When I was last in Boise, I stayed in a turn-of-the-century hotel in the center of downtown. Out my window I could see the western sky, a distant rivercourse, and a tall building right across the street, with big glass windows and a concrete sign as big as a small car: SIMPLOT.

Simplot is 82 now; he's lived in Idaho since he was a child. Simplot is a big, slow, sturdy man with a big, bald, freckled head. His voice has the drawl of a backcountry man, blunt and unpoetic. We met in his thirteenth-floor office, the windowed walls open to the short, squat city below. The valley beyond was spacious and light, dry, spreckled with trees following the winding course of the Boise River, up to the base of the soft, khaki-colored hills rising into the sun.

"I never wanted to live anywhere else—I know a good place when I find out. It's been good to me. And God, I've seen it come a long way. I started out with horses and farming, you know, and I know what you can get done with a couple or three teams of horses. I was a young fellow, didn't go to school, and I got to trading pigs and horses—I was a pretty good horse trader. Hogs got awful cheap, they got so cheap nobody wanted them. So my

Dad and I built this hog pen and I bought six, seven hundred head of hogs, bought them for a dollar apiece, big ones, little ones. People just went out of the hog business, that's all. Anyway, I fed those hogs and in the spring I got a hot hog market. I sold those hogs and I got about seven hundred dollars, and I bought a hundred and twenty acres and went farming, and I was on my way.

"Then I started growing potatoes. They've really been good to me. The old boy I rented my farm from, he was alcoholic. And one day he and I bought this electric potato sorter, fifty-fifty. I beefed it up quite a bit and started sorting potatoes, my own and then I started sorting the neighbors', and I had a hell of a crew. It was the first electric sorter in the county. Well, he got drunk one day and he said, 'Jack, I think it's time to put it up.' Well, anyway, we got in a little argument, and I said, 'Hell, there's only one way to solve this thing, let's flip to see who owns this sorter.' So he pulled a dollar out of his pocket and threw it up in the air and I called it. And that put me in the potato business."

Boise looks prosperous and lucky and clean from Mr. Simplot's window; it has that charm of plenty, like the dark fields of potatoes on the outskirts: winding rows dug in the soft dirt and filled with thousands of ovaline russets and yellow finns and whites shiny in the afternoon sun. Simplot sat behind an enormous desk made from a single polished burl, rocked back and forth, laid his heavy, thick hands on the tabletop: "I got so big in the potato business I quit farming. In the thirties I built me some thirty warehouses, clear into Oregon. By 1940 I was probably the biggest shipper in Idaho. I got into dehydration, and that turned out to be the key to the whole thing, because I happened to have the only dryer when the war come on. They got a colonel out here and he said, 'You're going to go to work for Uncle Sam. You're gonna dry potatoes for him.' And I did, and I got in the potato-drying business. And that led into the fertilizer business, and that led into the lumber business. Then, of course, we found out we could freeze french-fried potatoes, and that's just gotten bigger by the day.

"There was opportunities back then. What really made me was the fertilizer business, and then I got into the mining business. We came from nothing! Nobody used fertilizer when I started. I convinced myself by doing it. I got people to put phosphate on their hay, and that's the way we built the business. Well, honey, I've got some good mines. It's new money—you dig it out of the ground and sell it, it's all new money. And the farming business is the same way.

"I never went back to school. That's my whole thing. When we hire people we screen them, and we want the tops. If you walked in here today and said you only had gotten through the eighth grade, why, I don't think any of my people would even talk to you."

The company takes the leftover parts of the potato and mixes it with grain to feed cattle. Simplot also uses potato leavings to make ethanol, and the waste water from potato processing for irrigation. The cattle manure goes into methane production, and the company makes its own fertilizer from phosphate from its own mines. The potato muck left over from the ethanol is used to make food for tilapia fish, which are primarily turned into fillets for frozen dinners; the waste water from the tilapia tanks is run in to feed hyacinths, which pull the nitrogen out of the water and freshen it, to be fed back into the fish tanks. The hyacinths are fed to the cattle; the leavings from the fish-processing plant are mixed with potato sludge and fed back to the fish. Now Simplot is moving into robotic fast-food cookers and computer chips.

"Did you ever go down to California? It's all plugged up and costs are awesome. And we got water. We're going to be providing all the power for the Southwest. I know, I'm in it. We've got the coal! We've got the water! You've just got to bring the coal to the water. We're growing, we're growing, this whole country is growing. And we're letting in a million or so people every year. Now, I know we've got a lot of Mexicans working for us, and I don't know if we could get along without them or not. But you start letting them in by the millions and pretty soon we're going to be in the same boat as they are."

His company is slowly moving into Honduras, Turkey, Poland, Germany: he wants to teach the potato-eating Poles how to grow

potatoes the Simplot way; he calls it the New Frontier. He wants
to build coal-fired power plants along the Snake River: "The future's not ours to see, but I see democracy is making the most
progress in the world. It's going to change everything. Look at
the military budget—it's awesome. Get rid of that and start putting
it into our society. I can see what we can do with this system.
We can build a utopia. We've got everything. I tell you, I think
we're just getting started." The Simplot Company has a mandatory
retirement age of 65, without negotiation. Except for the boss.
J.R. is still president and won't consider stepping down: "If I'd
been working for the other guy, I'd have had to quit a long time
ago! But I'm not. I'm working for me." He has been a horse-rider,
skier, scuba diver all these years, and finally a bad hip has slowed
him down: "I haven't had a sick day in my life; in all these years I
haven't even had a pain! Nothing! It's hard to believe—but I can
buy a part for this hip and get it fixed, and I'm gonna, next month."

We stood by the windows above the town, suspended in silence.
Solid stone and brick buildings together on the floor of the valley,
near the water, out of the winds, lit by sunshine; already the glass
was beginning to reflect the fading light in tiny glints and squares.
On a small coffee table surrounded by armchairs was a large, polished piece of jasper pulled from one of Simplot's mines; it was
the size of a football.

"I like to see things grow. You've gotta have progress; that's
what's built America. The marketplace is the best mousetrap." He
points to the east, swings his meaty hands in an arc along the soft
brown hills walling in the valley: "I bought all this land here.
We've got lots of land, I'm a land-buyer and I just keep buying
ranches. I've got the most beautiful cattle ranches you've ever
seen, and I don't mean just one or two of them. They don't make
a lot of money, but someday. Do you see that place up there?
Someday my grandkids or my great-grandkids are gonna think
that old sonuvabitch was pretty smart."

He lives on 60 acres of unnaturally green grass on the undulant
khaki hills east of Boise; the 30-by-55-foot American flag flying
above his house used to flap and crackle so loudly in the night

winds that his neighbors complained it kept them awake nights. He raised the flagpole to 150 feet, and now the flag snaps so high and bright the sound flies down the valley and is gone.

Suddenly he turns to me: "Well, how about you? You got a family?"

"Married, with three kids."

"No kidding?" He seems pleased. "Well, I'm proud of you, honey. That's America for you."

Sallie Tisdale is the author of Sorcerer's Apprentice, Harvest Moon, Lot's Wife, *and* Stepping Westward: The Long Search for Home in the Pacific Northwest. *The winner of numerous literary awards, she has had essays in* The New Yorker, Harper's, Esquire, *and other magazines. She lives in Oregon.*

＊

Men are free when they belong to a living, organic, believing community, active in fulfilling some unfilled, perhaps unrealized purpose. Not when they are escaping to some wild west. The most unfree souls go west, and shout of freedom. Men are freest when they are most unconscious of freedom. The shout is a rattling of chains, always was.

—D.H. Lawrence, *Studies in Classic American Literature*

✦ ✦ ✦

Colorado Solo

Here comes a serious rapid.

NEXT DAY I CAME TO RED CREEK RAPID.

It was the tenth rapid shown in my river guide.

River guides are softcover books, printed on waterproof or water-resistant paper, that map a river's every twist and turn. They show mileages from some specific point, and just enough contours on both banks to help you identify your position. Photographs and quotes in the margins may add historical information. And there may be supplementary sections on geology, paleontology, anthropology. But the core is the ongoing map of the river. As you float down you keep turning pages, and the map-river flows on.

As a backpacker, I had long loathed trail guides. Loathed them strong and sour, from the pit of my gut. They tend to lead you by the nose, impose tunnel vision, predigest what should be fresh discoveries. To constrain, that is, the freedoms you are walking to find. But backpacking is not river-running. I guess I'd glimpsed differences between them—of nature, not merit—back in the planning stages, because I let experts coerce me into buying guides for the whitewater canyons. And now, after only one day's use, I was already halfway a believer.

My river guide could not limit a nonexistent choice of routes, and the information it gave was so sketchy and narrowly confined that it rarely threatened to damage discovery. It also did more than maps to help me select good campsites. Above all, though, it warned of imminent rapids.

Red Creek Rapid was, as I say, the tenth my guide had shown since the dam. The first nine had been little more than riffles: mildly good practice; just enough to whet my appetite—and cue latent fears.

The white slashes indicating Red Creek Rapid covered only a slightly longer stretch of river than had most of the others. There was no specific warning notation. But a margin photograph showed a wooden boat jammed beam-on against a rock, tilted almost vertical and half-filled with water. A more or less

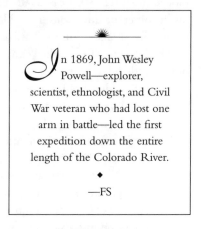

In 1869, John Wesley Powell—explorer, scientist, ethnologist, and Civil War veteran who had lost one arm in battle—led the first expedition down the entire length of the Colorado River.

♦

—FS

naked man perched on the gunwales was apparently struggling to free it. A caption read: *Current pins Todd-Page boat in Red Creek Rapid, 1926.* Powell's journal does not mention Red Creek; but I knew he'd lined or portaged many that he doesn't specify.

Two miles below my nightcamp, I floated down toward a bend. Beyond it I should be able to see Red Creek Rapid, and I tried to recall details of a conversation with Bill Russell, maintenance crew chief at the dam.

I'd not really expected any serious rapids before the Gates of Lodore, but to be on the safe side I'd asked Russell about them, and he'd said, "The only serious one is Red Creek. But it's given a lot of people trouble."

"How should I run it?"

Russell had offered what sounded like good, informed advice. But now I fumbled. The best I could come up with was that he'd said either "It looks as if you should go left, but you go right" or "It looks as if you should go right, but you go left." And that was hardly helpful.

I floated around the bend.

From above, the prospect looked uninviting. The main channel frothed white, close to the right bank. But the rapid was divided longitudinally into two distinct halves, and over on the left things looked more relaxed. I eased left. The wind, which had been gusting in different directions, now blew upriver and held us in the safety zone. I landed on the left bank, walked down, scouting.

The left run at first looked easy enough: rather shallow; no great power; little white water. But as I walked down beside it I saw that a maze of hidden boulders, barely submerged, posed a confused succession of problems that would come so fast, one after the other without break, that they'd leave no time for maneuvering.

From where I stood, the far run wasn't easy to assess. It cascaded white and wild, but there just might be a viable route, left of the main frothings. Halfway down, a boiling white turmoil looked like a "hole"—a pulsing water cavity downstream of a boulder, capable of flipping a boat or raft, even of holding it helpless. But this "hole" might be just a wave. I couldn't be sure. If I could maneuver the raft past its left edge, though, there should be time to pivot into ferrying position and avoid—either left or right—a boulder that thrust up from the foot of the run like a small haystack and looked remarkably like the one that had pinned the Todd-Page boat in 1926. Achieving the right line would largely depend on hitting the right point of entry.

I stood for a long time, there on the left bank, weighing pros and cons.

Red Creek would be by far the most challenging rapid I'd attempted alone. I'd made more difficult and dangerous runs during my thirteen-day initiation on the Idaho Salmon, two years before, but there'd always been experts ready to rescue me if things went sour. And now there wasn't much doubt about being alone. The day fishermen had all pulled ashore at a designated ramp. Since leaving nightcamp I'd seen no one.

I reassessed options. With a lightened load, I should be able to line the raft down the boulder-maze left run. Or I could portage. Portaging would be a sweat, but safe.

There was more to it than safety, though.

The far run was the challenge, because it scared me. If I let fear prevail here, this first time, I'd probably never overcome it. On the other hand, a successful run would give my confidence a vital boost.

In the end, there really wasn't much choice.

Much later I discovered that on October 9, 1937, at 2:30 in the afternoon—about an hour later in the day than I reached Red Creek Rapid—Buzz Holmstrom, also traveling alone, came to the same place. He, too, grappled with indecision. In his journal he called the rapid "a dirty son of a gun to put it mild," and hinted at thoughts much like mine.

Buzz Holmstrom and I shared more than just traveling alone. He was a mediocre swimmer, too. The year before, he'd run the Idaho Salmon. And there were things about his approach to river and journey, most of which I came to understand only slowly, that plucked empathetic chords in me.

But huge differences divided us. Buzz traveled not in a raft but in a 15-foot boat he'd built from a downed log of well-cured cedar he found near his hometown of Coquille, Oregon, where he worked as a filling-station attendant. It was a well-designed craft, stoutly constructed; but no wooden boat is as forgiving of fast-water errors as a good inflatable raft. And although Buzz had more river experience than I, he lacked the huge advantage of expertise honed and handed down by the river-running pioneers. Pioneers who, in my case, included him.

On the other hand, Buzz, at twenty-eight, had forty years less wear and tear on him. And he had, like Powell and with the same relief and elation, already run serious rapids now buried beneath Flaming Gorge Reservoir. Also like Powell, though, he'd launched at Green River, Wyoming, and so had had less time than I to forge confidence in boat or abilities.

One major difference between our situations at Red Creek

Rapid is difficult to evaluate. It's one that always intrudes when you try to compare journeys made before and after the big dams were built. The day I reached Red Creek Rapid, the river was flowing at a little over 1100 cubic feet per second—slightly less than the flow when I left Frontenelle Dam. Buzz's description of the rapid suggests that much more water was pouring through— yet the way he reports running the minor rapids I'd run the day before suggests the opposite. Remember, though, that some rapids are easier in low flows, some at high. And rapids change over the years. Remember these uncertainties when you read what Buzz wrote in his journal:

I might have tried to run it if close to home and everything favorable, but here there is too much to lose by a smashing, so I portaged the boat over a beaver dam down a little side channel, then ran down to the foot light… I hated to break down and portage, as I have not done so before, but what I am trying to do is to see how far I can get rather than how many I can run.

Now, more than fifty years later, as soon as I'd made up my mind, I battened the raft down.

Loose articles went into the big dry boxes, cameras and binoculars into their padded watertight box, lashed at my side. I told myself it was worth doing the job properly not because I really thought I might flip or even get bounced seriously around— though it paid to be careful—but because it was valuable practice for what I'd absolutely have to do beyond the Gates of Lodore— now less than forty miles ahead—and then, intermittently, for almost a thousand miles, until I moved out of Grand Canyon.

Everything ready at last. I cast off and rowed out across the smooth, swift water, keeping well above the place it slid over and down into the rapid.

The wind was still gusting, still changeable. But I managed without real difficulty to position myself at the head of the main run, not far from the right bank. There, by pulling gently on the oars, I held us stationary, bow leading.

The view downstream was less clear than I'd expected. Partly because of the drop-off. Partly because the obstacles and clear runs I'd carefully catalogued from the bank were now more or less lined up and difficult to distinguish one from the other. And partly, I think, because my heart was pounding.

A long, hanging interlude of uncertainty. Then I let us drift down toward the most likely-looking entry point. Before committing myself, I'd take a closer look.

At that moment the wind swung around and gusted hard, directly down-river. I felt it nudge the raft toward the brink. Felt the current grip us. Tried to pull back. Failed. Saw that the best course—by now probably the only one open—was to trust my preliminary choice of entry point. I pushed hard with both oars, downriver, the way you must if you're to establish enough momentum to carry you over big waves.

Almost at once we were racing through a boiling white cauldron. Slight pressure on the oars—their blades kept just below the surface—held the raft straight and true. Then the hole was there—a huge, white, glistening mound-then-pit. It throbbed, pulsated. We careered past, closer than intended; sort of ran through its left edge. I held my breath. But all that happened was a minor bump. And before I'd really asked myself, let alone decided, whether the hole had been hole or mere wave, we were beyond its pulsating grasp, without check and dead on course, hurtling on down toward the haystack boulder. The boulder's black shape was clear now, and I counter-pressured the oars so that we'd swing, stern right, into half-beam ferrying mode. The raft responded. I gave one or two quick strokes—and saw that we'd clear the boulder, right, with something to spare. I pivoted back bow-first. As we slid past the boulder, left gunwale three or four feet clear of its black, granular flank, I lifted my left oar from the water and slanted it back, out of the boulder's way. Then I had the oar back in place and the river's power had slackened and nothing loomed ahead except a few scattered boulders.

We moved clear of the last boulders. I took a deep breath. Now the oars seemed to keep the raft straight almost without my help.

Down beside my feet, something silvery caught my eye. A small can of chicken meat. I smiled. I'd opened it while scouting along the left bank, and before pulling out above the rapid had put the open, half-eaten can on the rubber-surfaced foot-thwart. It was still there, in more or less the same place. My little raft, in its first real whitewater test, had sat down like a sports car. But Red Creek Rapid had done much more than erase lingering doubts about the raft's stability. I'd run my first unchaperoned rapid. With luck, I no longer had to fear fear itself.

Colin Fletcher was born in Wales and educated in England. In 1956, he moved to California. Soon afterward he spent a summer walking from Mexico to Oregon across California's deserts and mountains. Later he became the first man known to have walked the length of Grand Canyon National Park within the Canyon's rim. Each of these feats generated a book: The Thousand-Mile Summer *and* The Man Who Walked Through Time. *He continues to explore—and to write books:* The Complete Walker *(revised twice),* The Winds of Mara, The Man from the Cave, *and* River: One Man's Journey Down the Colorado, Source to Sea *from which this story was excerpted.*

★

The large number of single, mobile men who came west presented the greatest challenge to western community formation. Nineteenth-century writings on the American West reflect a pervasive fear that such unattached men would never permanently settle. Failing to form community ties of their own, they seemed to present a constant danger to those communities that did establish themselves in the West. "Left by themselves, men degenerate rapidly and become rough, harsh, slovenly— almost brutish," Reverend William Goode wrote after visiting the Colorado mines.

—Richard White, *It's Your Misfortune and None of My Own: A New History of the American West*

FRED SETTERBERG

✦ ✦ ✦

Underneath Willa Cather's Nebraska

Nebraska isn't flat.

SCOTTS BLUFF TOWERS EIGHT HUNDRED FEET ABOVE THE NORTH Platte Valley floor, providing a firm, flat table upon which to view the country. Atop the headland's steep summit, Ann and I gasped for breath, massaged our quadriceps, and clapped our arms around each other's waists to stand at the cliff's edge and silently admire what I had feared as far as we both could see.

Throughout the spring, Ann and I had been debating the wisdom of planning a trip back to Nebraska in July. Ann wanted to visit her hometown during the hottest, dullest, flattest month of the year. Atop the bluff, everything we now saw, or didn't see, confused rather than confirmed my misgivings. Nebraska was certainly a flat, empty place. But there was nothing dull about the scenery.

"Nebraska can surprise you," Ann had warned back in California. "Most people don't appreciate the place. Sometimes I don't appreciate it."

Like many foolish partisans of either coast, I had long presumed that Nebraska was an unsuitable site for an agreeable visit. I envisioned a big, stolid hay bale of a place, composed largely of perfect right angles, with one ragged edge flagging the corn belt. I thought of Nebraska as the epitome of those crafty states whose

349

indeterminate location in the center of an unmarked map con-
founds the majority of our nation's young geography students.

Nebraska, the misperceived and misplaced.

In the midst of our argument, Ann shimmered off to the
bookshelf. She returned with a well-thumbed paperback edition
of *My Ántonia*, Willa Cather's novel about the immigrant
Scandinavians, Germans, French, and Bohemians who settled
southeastern Nebraska's farm country in the late nineteenth century. Over the years, Willa Cather has provided Ann with per-
suasive evidence that her home state has been largely maligned
and misunderstood by the rest of us. She told me to read the book.
And that's how we now found ourselves wiping the sweat from
our faces atop Scotts Bluff while admiring the infamous emptiness.

Nebraska is best perceived from this height. On top of the bluff,
everything below seems even flatter, more severe, endless. This
view mirrors the terrible sameness that assailed the first settlers
moving west. For every drugstore clerk and cobbler's wife departing from St. Joseph, Missouri, with an overfilled twelve-foot
Conestoga wagon and some appreciation for life's constant struggle, the western Nebraska plains—deemed, no less, the Great
American Desert—must have looked like the bottom of the world.

Historians of the westward migration maintain that the plains
drove some people crazy; it was so boring. Scotts Bluff was a
blessed change, rising up in swift relief to the infernal flatness.
Not as exciting as the feared but infrequent war parties of
Cheyenne and Sioux, but dramatic enough; and as welcome a
diversion as might be found along the trail until Denver.

But the far end of Nebraska, though impressive in its vacancy,
is still the rocky West, not the blazing middle of the nation; it
isn't Willa Cather territory. And it was the middle of the state that
had weighted Ann's argument in favor of spending several weeks
there. So when we climbed down from the bluff, we stepped into
our borrowed car and pointed ourselves toward the heartland.

Scores of miles blurred into hundreds. We caught roadside
glimpses of Lewellen, Gothenburg, and the North Platte River. By
the time we hit the middle of the state, where Nebraskan farmland

fits squarely into the shoulders of Iowa and Kansas, leaving behind the West to form that troika of ordinariness known as Middle America, Ann said that she felt in her bones once again the Nebraska could be the perfect place in which to grow up. And she told me the following story.

One summer afternoon, when she was a little girl visiting her grandparents in Beaver City, Nebraska (population 780), Ann slipped up to the attic to prowl around for hidden treasures. While she hadn't been expressly forbidden to explore the attic alone, she had been warned often enough about touching things that didn't belong to her. Nothing inside the attic belonged to her, but she furtively probed and peeked and quietly ransacked every closet, trunk, and cupboard until she had to conclude that the dark attic smelled provocatively of the mysterious past (it was damp and musky, like a decaying cardboard box) but it truly held no treasures.

Then in a corner, she stumbled upon a great wrangle of plastic sheeting wound around a bundle of white lace. When she peeled back the plastic, its hardened layers crackled noisily and then cracked open like sun-

> *A*t the end of the day we always knew how many miles we had driven. It was of only academic interest to us; we never had any reservations or any particular time we had to be anywhere. Still, we took some pride in covering ground. When I got old enough to travel with friends, we concentrated on making time as if we were trying to beat a rival expedition to the Pole. The summer I got out of high school, I drove with two friends to the Minnesota lake country for a canoe trip, and even on the way home we waited until red lights to change drivers so as not to waste any time—although I can't think of much we were doing with our time in Kansas City that summer beyond going down to LeRoy's Tavern to talk dirty.
>
> ◆
>
> —Calvin Trillin, *Travels with Alice*

split furrows in the summer garden. Ann heard footsteps on the stairs; spinning around on the heels of her bare feet, she suddenly faced grandmother. "That's my wedding dress," her grandmother declared, arms folded across her chest. But she wasn't angry. In a moment, they were huddled together, unraveling the dress from its plastic layers. The woman hugged the wedding gown up against her chest, her exaggerated hips budding from either side, and then she pinned it against Ann's shoulders and beamed.

Ann said that for years, she fancied her grandmother must have been thinking about passing the dress down to her someday for her own wedding; she'd never seen her looking so dreamy. But by the time Ann grew old enough to wear the dress, it proved an impossible fit. At eighteen, Ann stood six feet tall, while her grandmother's head bobbed barely up to her shoulders. Nobody ever wore the dress again.

Now when Ann thinks back on that summer afternoon when they unwound the delicate lace and let it flutter to the floor, she realizes that her grandmother probably had not been daydreaming at all about some child's future wedding; she'd been reliving her own. Much of Nebraska, Ann insisted, was like the dress resurrected in the dim attic light: some dream of passion stored away for decades, only now and then privately revived.

As we drove south through the barbed whiskers of wheat and corn, I began to grasp what she meant. It was certainly possible to write off the countryside as an interminable plain. ("The only thing very noticeable about Nebraska," admonished Willa Cather's worried narrator in the opening pages of *My Ántonia*, "was that it was still, all day, Nebraska.") But by the time we'd reached the middle of the state, the dead sea of flat, sprawling land had lapped up upon itself in foamy waves of bristling alfalfa and sugar beets to form one of the most gorgeous landscapes I'd ever seen.

Now perhaps it's just the contrariness of human imagination, but all this land sewn together in ample, undulating strips inevitably suggests its opposite to the scanning eye. In the language of the Omaha Indians, Nebraska means "flat water." And today people still talk persistently about the land in terms better suited to oceans, lakes, and rivers—probably because there isn't much real water around. Except for the Platte River, Nebraska is a dry place, renowned among the early pioneers for its nonexistent streams and ponds coruscating across the plains in maddening mirage. But once the plains break midstate, the shaggy grain fields wag and ripple in the breezes like an ocean about to rise up from its calm, and it's here that you make a discovery that's as startling as the first geographer's revelation about the roundness of the Earth: Nebraska isn't all flat. In fact, much of the hilly grassland streaming through the state's side roads and detours bucks and rolls so insistently as to almost make you seasick. Cather wrote that "the grass was the country, as the water is the sea. The red of the grass made all the great prairie the colour of wine-stains, or of certain seaweeds when they are first washed up. And there was so much motion in it; the whole country seemed, somehow, to be running."

> *I*t went on raining. It was still raining when I drove back to the motel, where the forecourt was awash and the kitchen carpet blackly sodden. I sat up listening to it; attuned now to what I ought to hear. When rain falls in these parts, in what used to be known as the Great American Desert, it falls with the weight of an astounding gift. It falls like money.
>
> ◆
>
> —Jonathan Raban, *Bad Land: An American Romance*

As we drove further into Nebraska and I scanned Ann's old copy of *My Ántonia*, I came to see how the book didn't merely reflect the landscape; it revealed the state's deepest secrets, penetrating the veil of shy Nebraska's most intimate nature with almost embarrassing sensuality. It was as though Cather had stormed in from the fields to cast back some small farmer's flour-sack bedroom curtains and there the author found Nebraska sprawled out upon the satin pillows, stripped of her flattening, plain-print frock; and naked underneath, she was ripe, fervent, and bodaciously curvy.

Nebraska, state of the steamy sensualists.

On the outskirts of Red Cloud, Nebraska, Willa Cather's hometown, we pulled to the side of the road and strolled for an hour through the Willa Cather Memorial Prairie, 610 acres containing hundreds of varieties of grass, now preserved by the Nature Conservancy. The sun held high at about three o'clock; the temperature had hit 108 degrees. Ann told me it was the kind of day she used to call "close" as a kid, when the air stands as thick as water. The waist-high grasses whipped our bare arms and legs, and as we moved slowly through the fields we both felt as though we were swimming.

In Nebraska, people talk constantly about the weather. Nebraskans chew over the temperature, humidity, daily wind-chill factor, barometer readings, cloud formations, rainstorm divinations, flashflood warnings, and tornado preparations with an abiding, quiet fascination that borders on mania because the weather in Nebraska can no more be ignored than a time bomb ticking at the breakfast table.

> *A*gain, in the coldest midwinter weather, not a breath of wind may stir; and then the still, merciless, terrible cold that broods over the earth like the shadow of silent death seems even more dreadful in its gloomy rigor than is the lawless madness of the storms.
>
> ◆
>
> —Theodore Roosevelt, *Ranch Life and the Hunting-Trail*

The mistake is to think that obsessive concern for rain, snow, wind, and sun is somehow indicative of an unimaginative or desperate people. The Nebraskan character, founded upon the unglamorous virtues of common sense, reticence, compression, and reserve, adds up to one of the great national models of grace under pressure. A more appropriate reaction to the state's climatic highs and lows—and more critically, to the enormous risks compounded by the weather for tens of thousands of people who still make their living in agriculture—would be a condition of gibbering hysteria.

Nebraskans are gamblers, always have been.

The romance of pioneering one of the nation's richest strips of farmland stands at the heart of Willa Cather's Nebraska novels. But the inherent drama of the immigrant farmers' lives was far from obvious to the young writer at the beginning of her career.

"Life began for me," Cather confessed, "when I ceased to admire and began to remember." Sarah Orne Jewett, the great Maine miniaturist and Cather's early mentor, urged the younger writer along with the oldest advice in the world: write about what you know. Write about Nebraska. Yet it wasn't until the middle of Cather's life—she was thirty-eight years old when her first novel was published—that she most fruitfully remembered the struggle of the immigrant farmers and the extraordinary beauty of the landscape upon which they suffered and triumphed.

Eventually Cather would write in numerous guises about her Nebraskan hometown of Red Cloud and its inhabitants. In *My Ántonia*, she called Red Cloud Blackhawk; in *O Pioneers!*, the town is Hanover; in *A Lost Lady*, Sweet Water; it's Frankfort in *One of Ours*; Haverford in *Lucy Gayheart*; and though *The Song of the Lark* is set in Moonstone, Colorado, the small town is, nevertheless, once again Red Cloud, the familiar setting still "anchored on a windy Nebraska tableland" and "trying not to be blown away."

The Cather family first moved to Red Cloud in 1884. Young Willa wanted to leave immediately, missing the forests surrounding her family's old Virginia farm. (More rueful than amused, she would later call Nebraska "distinctly *déclassé* as a literary background.") But over time, Willa found that the landscape of her new home whipped up in her an adolescent passion to which she could surrender with all the heat and single-mindedness of first love.

By the 1920s, Cather's vision of the fertile, rough land upon which the new country was founded had made her one of the nation's most respected writers. F. Scott Fitzgerald wrote to her, announcing himself to be "one of your greatest admirers—an admirer particularly of *My Ántonia*." When Sinclair Lewis won the Nobel Prize in 1931, he protested that the award should rather have gone to Cather, and he compared her favorably to other famous Nebraskans. "Willa Cather is greater than General Pershing," insisted Lewis, "she is incomparably greater than William Jennings Bryan. She is Nebraska's foremost citizen because through her stories she has made the outside world know Nebraska as no one else has done."

Red Cloud, Nebraska, population 1,300, stands upon the drifting plains, about thirty miles from Kansas, in the middle of nowhere. At the tail end of the last century, eight passenger trains traveling between Kansas City and Denver passed daily through Red Cloud, which was then several times its present size. In its own peculiar way, the town seemed to rest at the center of things, the locus of the thriving zigzag still twisting and bending the country into shape.

Today nobody would accidentally find himself in Red Cloud. The old railway station serves as a museum; the passenger line stopped decades ago. Yet each year, as many as six thousand visitors drabble into Red Cloud for the exclusive purpose, as the town librarian offhandedly told Ann and me, "to go Cathering."

On our first day in town, Ann and I visited the Cather family home on Third and Cedar Streets. The house where Willa Cather lived as a teenager is the centerpiece of Red Cloud's 190 historical sites that now make up the official "Willa Cather Thematic District." Since Cather's acute memory threatened Red Cloud readers with an unusually high degree of verisimilitude, the debut of each book had once been the source of considerable local anxiety. The wastrels, villains, heroes, and fools that peopled her novels could be readily identified as they paced down the small town's streets. "I am the husband of *My Ántonia*," proclaimed the character's real-life model when asked to sign in for admittance to a hospital not far from Red Cloud.

When we walked into the Willa Cather Historical Center on cobble-stoned North Webster Street, the wisdom of Cather's leaving home was emphatically reiterated, oddly enough, by the museum curator.

"People sometimes wonder why anyone would build a museum to honor one person," the curator admitted, shrugging his shoulders in a lugubrious fashion that hinted that perhaps he wondered too. For several minutes, the museum curator and Ann talked about Nebraskans' suspicion of the outstanding person. Nebraskans, they agreed, have never much cared for show-offs. In Willa Cather's case, even her boostering of the state could be interpreted as showing-off. With so much ordinary work each day binding together farm life and small town society, any dalliance with extraordinary labors, such as literature, had to seem remote, impractical, presumptuous.

After answering some questions about the Cather exhibits, the writer, her books, and Red Cloud, the museum curator confessed to us that he had been transferred by officialdom to Catherland, curtailing a far more satisfying twelve-year stint at the historical site in Lincoln that honored John Neihardt, the state's poet laureate back in the 1920s and, more famously, the author of *Black Elk Speaks*. Although two years had passed since the curator's new posting, he was obviously still uncomfortable with his public role in Catherland. In this sense, he was perhaps the ideal Nebraskan civil servant, reticent of the limelight. Only when the conversation veered back toward Black Elk and John Neihardt, with whom the curator had spent a more insulated and happy past, did he brilliantly wake up, his face flushed and full of life. Black Elk was a Nebraskan treasure whose value the curator could estimate. About Cather, he could only ponder and glumly say, "It seems like the land overshadowed her characters."

Of course, he'd skipped over the point, or rather the soul, of Cather. Bereft of the land, Cather's characters were unimaginable; she needed Nebraska as Balzac depended upon Paris, as Dickens required London.

Later that afternoon, Ann and I strolled to the edge of Red Cloud to watch the sun slip into a swaying, knee-high field of alfalfa, and I better understood why Cather had valued Nebraska so highly from the distance of Greenwich Village. It's not just that sunset over a glistering field of grain can be lovely. In this part of Nebraska, where there seems to be nothing *but* waves of grain rolling back into an unreachable horizon, the landscape feels everlasting, abundant, and, somehow, intensely moral.

At the edge of this alfalfa field, I thought I grasped for the first time why people twenty years ago in the Midwest—there, particularly—threw up their hands in disgust and confusion over the young people who collected most noticeably on either coast to decry America's corruption in Vietnam. Upon Nebraska's sublime, resplendent, and harmonious landscape (words that nobody would use, but everybody feels) such talk about American malevolence, our nation's original sins blistering into a field of evil, had to sound fundamentally screwball. The most obvious argument against the young radicals was the land itself: *just look at it!* No other country had repaid its people so generously for the cultivation of its raw potential. America was too abundant to be malignant, too much the beautiful woman above suspicion.

We like to pretend we're an innocent people. And even now, it seems as though small-town America largely perceives the country's present decline as pertaining exclusively to the jungle of cities. But out here in Nebraska, in the midst of the most generous and yielding landscape, the fierce sun shines through this illusion like blood on parchment.

Back in California, it's always easy to get Ann talking about her fellow-Nebraskan Charlie Starkweather.

A few days later I drove across America from Dallas to Boston with the top down, hopped up on Dexedrine, my mind flying. I rode between the wheat fields and cow pastures, past the shotgunned road signs, across a country that was at war with itself, a country that was stewing in its own bitter juices. I despised America. I hated its meanness. It wasn't my country anymore. It had resurrected Richard Nixon from his own angry exile and made him President—Nixon, the hit man of the bourgeoisie—and as I drove across the vast belly of Nixon's America I felt defeated and afraid.

◆

—Lawrence Wright, *In the New World: Growing Up with America from the Sixties to the Eighties*

In 1957, Charlie Starkweather, seventeen years old, left his home in Lincoln, Nebraska, to ramble around the state for two months with his fifteen-year-old girl friend, gunning down nine people for no reason at all. When Starkweather was finally captured, Ann's father was serving as a district judge, and he'd actually caught a glimpse of the murderer in jail. For that reason at least, Starkweather is lodged in her memory.

One evening, shortly after Ann and I had first met, we were invited to a dinner party with three other couples whom neither of us really knew. At some point, Ann became heatedly, though mistakenly, convinced that the gabby architect sitting across from her was talking about Nebraska's most infamous criminal, rather than the fact that the skiing that winter in Colorado had been compromised by rude weather that he characterized as inhospitably chilly—and stark.

"He wasn't in Colorado," Ann told the architect, speaking above the dull hum of polite table talk. "Just Nebraska. They caught him in Wyoming."

"Pardon me?" asked the architect.

"Starkweather. Martin Sheen played him in the movie *Badlands*, did you ever see it? Sissy Spacek was the girlfriend. They killed nine people."

"Who's that?" asked our hostess.

"Martin Sheen," answered somebody else at the far rim of the table, hoping to squirm into the conversation. "He just killed somebody."

"That was Brando's son."

"He killed nine people. With Sissy Specek's help."

"Martin Sheen, the actor?"

"No, Charlie Starkweather. He was a garbageman in Lincoln, Nebraska."

"Is this a movie? I haven't seen it."

"Where was Martin Sheen a garbageman?"

"This lady said Lincoln, Nebraska, of all places. I'm sorry, I didn't get your name."

"Ann," she said, "but it was Charlie Starkweather who shot all those people."

"Martin Sheen's sons were in a movie about two garbagemen, but I didn't see it either."

"No, Starkweather. Charlie Starkweather. He's from Nebraska."

"You don't ski, do you?"

"Martin Sheen killed Charlie Starkweather?"

"All I said was that there was rather stark weather out in Vail this winter."

"No, the other way around. Some guy named Starkweather killed Martin Sheen."

"Oh, my God! When?"

"Why?"

"It's just a movie."

"No, it's the weather."

"No," exclaimed Ann righteously, "this really happened. It happened in Nebraska, where I grew up. I can't believe you people don't know about Charlie Starkweather. I wasn't even born in California and I can quote you chapter and verse about people like Jim Jones and Charles Manson."

The table quieted down because she was really quite upset, and besides, nobody actually knew us. Nebraska, the ignominiously ignored. But folks can't keep quiet for long.

"Is Martin Sheen making a movie about Charles Manson?" asked the architect.

"This lady from Nebraska said it's called *Chapter and Verse.*"

Over the salad, Ann whispered in my ear: "I'm really tired, can we go home now?"

When Bruce Springsteen released *Nebraska* (his somber acoustic album with the black-and-white cover photo, whose title song concludes with Charlie Starkweather's soul being hurled into the "great void" via the state penitentiary's electric chair), the singer explained that he'd fallen under the influence of Flannery O'Connor's short stories. But Springsteen could have read Willa Cather to the same effect.

Cather never amended her memories of Nebraska to fashion a sentimental Middle America. In her fiction, the edenic days of childhood on the farm are penetrated by the slippery entrance of vipers. Dispirited, incompetent farmers shoot themselves in the unforgiving winter. In the fall, crops can fail and families starve. (A mean, hungry Charlie Starkweather might have prowled around Red Cloud, Blackhawk, Hanover.) The story in *My Ántonia* about the pair of Russian bachelor farmers who throw the bride and bridegroom from their wedding party's sleigh to a pack of ravenous wolves is as barbarous and more believable than any horror tale conceived in the cities for today's jaded movie audiences.

That's the difficulty with remembering the places from which we've sprung: from the distance of years, we squint so hard as to make our upbringing all one thing or the other. It's all bounteous heartland or it's all stark, ominous plains. Cather looked in both directions; that's part of her greatness. She never indulged herself in the national amnesia that strikes our country with such terrible ferocity and frequency. Her fictional Nebraska is a booming, contradictory place—a portrait of the bustling human comedy underscored by the emptiness of the prairies. Cather once remarked that she had taken the small themes of rural life that hid in the grass and then woven them into the landscape's larger story, including its uncelebrated harm, mischief, and buffoonery. Like Dvořák's New World Symphony, inspired in part by several weeks the Czech composer had spent in Nebraska during the 1880s, Cather's memory wells up grandly enough to contain both her state's isolation and its solitude, the arbitrariness of sudden death as well as the land's insistent rebirth. Everything good and bad grew there.

Nebraska seems to be one of those places that you leave in order to love. Nebraska, the adored and abandoned.

From Red Cloud, it's less than a half-day's drive to Beaver City, where Ann's grandparents had lived for decades. They were both dead now, but Ann wanted to see the town once again. Beaver City consists of seven square blocks, and its population is about half the size of Red Cloud—another puddle of a town evaporating under the Nebraska sun. We arrived around dusk, following into town a trail of rolling hills lined with patches of sunflowers and hollyhocks. In the distance, cottonwoods sparkled along the horizon's rim, and cicadas hummed like rattlesnakes in the trees. When the lightning bugs swarmed, the darkening road was suddenly illuminated by what looked like an air force of floating light bulbs.

We found Ann's grandparents' house and walked right up to the front door.

On the porch, behind the screen door, the old woman who lived there greeted us warmly and urged us inside. She was a newcomer to Beaver City, having arrived less than twenty years earlier; she hadn't known Ann's grandparents. We wandered through the house's crooked hallways, inspecting each room. Finally Ann mounted the ladder to the attic, where she and her grandmother years before had unwrapped the wedding dress from its sun-cracked wrapper of plastic. To fit under the attic's drooping eaves, she had to fold herself in half at the waist.

"I'd think about selling the house," the old woman told us, "if I could ever find a buyer." In the living room darkened with heavy muslin curtains, we sat chatting and sipping tea. "But these days, people only seem to move out of Beaver City." And then more confidentially: "The house must be worth at least eleven thousand dollars."

After a half-hour or so, Ann graciously thanked the old woman for taking two strangers into her home. We stood at the front door shaking hands and exchanging addresses.

As we strolled past the front yard's summer garden, Ann said, "It's not what I remember."

"Isn't it the right house?"

"Yes, well, I suppose it is—as much as that's possible after all these years. But I remember something else, something different. I can't say what."

We wandered down to the town square and sprawled upon the lawn for an hour to watch the fireflies. I bought an apple and a bottle of beer from the market across the street for dinner. When I returned, Ann suddenly scrambled to her feet and pointed to a large sign hanging above a storefront at the edge of the square. The sign read: Beaver City Locker. She grabbed my hand and pulled me down the block.

The Beaver City Locker is the town's cold storage for slaughtered livestock. Ann explained that her grandfather had taken her to the meat locker as a child to pick up portions of some cow or pig chopped up and stored in the freezer throughout the year to be parcelled out for Sunday dinners. Almost every family in town had their own locker drawer in the freezer compartment and their own set of keys.

We stepped inside to watch two young men and a young woman hack and saw ribbed slabs of splayed carcasses. The entire enterprise consisted of one small carving station equipped with several stainless-steel butcher blocks and a huge refrigerator banking the deep-freeze.

"We don't get a lot of people asking to visit the meat," admitted the young man who seemed to be in charge. He swiped his cleaver into a loin of veal. "But sure," he told Ann, "go right in."

The heavy locker door swung open. Inside the refrigerated vault, we found a whole scalded pig and marbled strips of beef dangling upon their sharpened metal hooks. The locker felt unbearably chilly. It stank of blood, flesh, and refrigerated air. Ann turned to me, grinned innocently, and said, "It's funny what you can't forget." She drew a huge breath, stretching her arms up towards the butchered pig's snout as though she were a spreading cottonwood reaching for the sun on the most fragrant summer's day, and she refilled her lungs with memory.

Fred Setterberg is the editor of Travelers' Tales America *and the author of* The Roads Taken: Travels Through America's Literary Landscape, *from which this story was excerpted.*

✳

On long and arduous expeditions men are apt to become irritable and ill-natured, and oftentimes fancy they have more labor imposed upon them than their comrades, and that the person who directs the march is partial toward his favorites, etc. That man who exercises the greatest forbearance under such circumstances, who is cheerful, slow to take up quarrels, and endeavors to reconcile difficulties among his companions,

is deserving of all praise, and will, without doubt, contribute largely to
the success and comfort of an expedition.

—Randolph B. Marcy, *The Prairie Traveler: The Classic
Handbook for America's Pioneers*

✦ ✦ ✦

Adventures in Dreamland

Along the Alien Highway, visitors may
come from far, far away.

WE SAT IN CHUCK CLARK'S NAVY BLUE JEEP CHEROKEE WAITING for full night to settle upon the Nevada desert. Chuck was in a jolly mood, because we intended, in Chuck's words, to harass the guys with guns.

Chuck and I were parked near the black mailbox. The black mailbox appeared black only because it was dark outside. During the day, the black mailbox is white. It used to be black, but then rancher Steve Medlin got a new one, which is white. But everyone still calls it the black mailbox. A white, black mailbox is an apt metaphor for how things work out here.

To anyone with a serious interest in the nexus between UFOs, extraterrestrials and government conspiracies, the black mailbox is an icon. Here in the Tikaboo Valley, it's a shrine.

"It's like the monolith in *2001*; they worship the damn thing," said Chuck, his anticipatory cheer marred only slightly by his annoyance at the airy-fairy, ETs-as-beneficent-beings crowd who gather here most nights.

To the casual motorist on this stretch of Highway 375 in Lincoln County, the black mailbox is the only human-made object in sight; the surveillance tower on 9,468-foot-high Bald

365

Mountain, the area's highest peak, appears as little more than a speck even during the day. The rest is relentlessly barren desert save for scattered low scrub and Joshua trees.

To those in the know, the black mailbox signifies that some twenty miles away, just beyond the mountains to the west, lies a military base so top secret that the federal government denies it exists, yet so legendary its mythology grows exponentially.

The legendary military base that doesn't exist is called Area 51, although that is probably not its official name. Only government officials, on a need-to-know basis, know its official name. It is also commonly called Groom Lake for the dry lake bed upon which the base sits. More colorful names, at once sinister and ironic, include the Box, the Ranch, Dreamland, and the Dark Side of the Moon.

The nonexistent military base contains the world's longest paved runway, almost six miles long. By all accounts except the official one, America test flies its most advanced military aircraft from this runway. The U2 spy plane first burned rubber there in the 1950s, followed by the SR-71 Blackbird spy plane, the F-117 Stealth fighter, and now the latest aerial phantom, a supposed spy plane called Aurora.

As great as these revelations may be, students of space-alien activity believe Area 51 conceals an even greater secret than spy planes and Stealth fighters. They believe the alien spacecraft that purportedly crashed near Roswell, New Mexico, in 1947—a seminal event in UFO lore—is being held underground at Papoose Lake, one dry lake bed south from Groom Lake. What's more, they say, its alien crew is there, too. Some also believe the military has resurrected the damaged spacecraft and is test flying it within sight of the black mailbox. Some claim to have seen it.

These strange reports emanating from the Nevada desert had intrigued me for years. Fool that I am, I needed to see for myself if they were true.

Now in full darkness, Chuck fired up the Jeep Cherokee and we slowly rolled through the cool night air down the dirt road toward The Boundary, as everyone here calls the Area 51 borderline.

"It would be a real bummer if I took them prisoner," said Chuck with a self-satisfied chuckle, referring to the guys with guns, otherwise known as the Area 51 security guards.

"I've captured them before," he boasted. "I've cornered them, run them out to where they couldn't go any farther, and they just sat out there and stewed. Outside the boundary, they'll go off road to avoid you."

Inside the boundary, it's an entirely different matter, however. Step one foot over the line and they quickly put a gun to your head, flop you face down on the ground, and snap on the cuffs. Resist, and they shoot you.

Chuck chuckled whenever he talked about the guys with guns and how he harasses them—"It's great sport!"—although he also guffawed, yucked and occasionally snorted. Chuck enjoys his work.

Chuck's work is to monitor Area 51 activity; he's one of a handful of such self-appointed, citizen investigators. Chuck is a former computer consultant and a custom, salt-water-rod maker, a divorced man with an even tan that bespeaks his time logged in the outdoors despite an otherwise sedentary image suggested by a full-body, middle-aged paunchiness. When not harassing security guards or attending to other Area 51 duties, Chuck writes an astronomy textbook he hopes will penetrate the popular

> The people and the land are inseparable, but at first I did not understand. I used to think there were exact boundaries that constituted "the homeland," because I grew up in an age of invisible lines designating ownership. In the old days there had been no boundaries between the people and the land; there had been mutual respect for the land that others were actively using.
>
> ◆
>
> —Leslie Marmon Silko, *Yellow Woman and a Beauty of the Spirit*

book market (he's also written a self-published Area 51 guidebook). In 1994 he moved to the nearest town, Rachel, from

Lompoc, California, from where he monitored missiles launched from Vandenberg Air Force Base.

As we drove close to the boundary, Chuck said, "Let's see if they're on that ridge ahead of us; it's one of their favorite hiding spots."

We swung off the road and ascended the low ridge. At the top, the Cherokee's headlights caught a momentary reflection.

"There they are! There they are! We've got'em!" Chuck exclaimed gleefully.

"Watch this." Chuck guffawed as he parked and pulled out a million-and-a-half-candlepower spotlight (fourteen bucks at Wal-Mart; helluva deal). With the flip of a switch and a clean, sharp yuck, Chuck ripped back the blanket of night concealing the security guards' own Jeep Cherokee. The bone-white Jeep looked horribly vulnerable in the bright light, exposed on the ridge like some weird, naked, metallic baby. We could see two indistinct figures inside.

Thanks to Chuck's previous shenanigans at the boundary, the guards were prepared with their own heavy artillery.

"OK, OK, there's his floodlight," said Chuck. "We're going to go at it. Here they come, two of 'em…"

We took a double-barrel shot—a million candlepower each light—right between the eyes.

"ALL RIGHHHT!" cried Chuck, and we laughed uproariously—I can't tell you why; pure, childish mischievousness, I suppose.

Chuck and the security guards shined spotlights at each other for the next several minutes. It was a useless exercise for all concerned as far as I could tell, although Chuck insisted he was doing them a favor: "It's pretty boring sitting out here eight, ten hours a shift watching the cactus grow." Chuck chuckled. A jackrabbit, no doubt bewildered by the sudden onset of day, scampered through the light beams and disappeared in the blackness.

"Security knows exactly who they're dealing with," Chuck announced. "They usually carry one spotlight but they started carrying two ever since I started doing this to them. We'll sit here and play this game until they get tired, and then they'll back off."

Chuck turned his spotlight away from the Jeep and toward a nearby ridge, to show me a surveillance camera.

"Does it have night capability?" I asked.

"It did, until I hit it with the spotlight. That turns it off." Chuck snorted; that was a good one.

Meanwhile, another white Jeep Cherokee from inside Area 51 had driven along Groom Lake Road, which lay just below us, and parked within a few dozen yards of the boundary.

Chuck hit it with the spotlight and then drove down the ridge and onto the dirt road, stopping several yards outside the boundary, just to get in their faces—a favorite Chuck Clark phrase. He urged me to get out and take photographs of the boundary warning signs. Caught up in the taunting, I blithely obliged. No fence marked the boundary, but big signs on a metal pole warned that beyond was a restricted area. The fine print on the bottom got my attention: "Use of deadly force authorized."

I stayed close to the Jeep—my two-and-a-half-ton security blanket—because I pictured myself stubbing my toe on a rock in the dark, vaulting head first over the boundary line, and falling into the hands of some really pissed-off security guards, who are reputed to be retired Navy SEALS.

Having accomplished what we came for, though I wasn't sure exactly what we came for, we called it a night and drove back up Groom Lake Road. We turned left at the last Joshua tree—that's how they give directions around here—and onto the dirt road to the black mailbox. Soon we were back on asphalt and headed for Rachel.

"If you want to see what's going on, you have to be out here at night when they're doing it," said Chuck, explaining our nocturnal foray. "These airplanes are stealth, painted black, and fly at night. And the UFO stuff...I don't know anyone who's seen it during the day; they see it at night. I've seen four fairly good incidences myself."

Chuck's first sighting took place in autumn of '94, shortly after he moved to Rachel. Driving north on Highway 375 near Groom Lake Road, Chuck and a companion saw an orange light appear suddenly in mid-air, move slightly upwards, make a quick sharp V-turn, zip back to near its starting point, and just as suddenly disappear.

"I don't know how big it was, how fast it was going, or how far away it was, I just know it defied the laws of physics," said Chuck. "The whole thing took about seven seconds."

The majority of Americas believe in UFOs, according to public opinion polls, as spacecraft carrying space aliens. Chuck, however, ventured an alternative theory: "The most likely scenario is that these things are from a parallel reality. They are indigenous to Earth, but they are from a world, a dimension, that is beyond our perception."

I peered out the window and searched for fissures in the space-time continuum, but saw only the road in our headlights and the stars overhead. I felt at once relieved and disappointed.

It occurred to me, however, that perhaps Chuck and I live in parallel realities.

Suddenly, several white lights appeared in the distance. They hovered just above the desert floor and grew ever larger as we approached. I grew ever more anxious and regretted my condescension toward Chuck. Perhaps there is some merit to this fourth dimension stuff, I thought. Perhaps that's them!

> The United States is not a nation in the sense that that England or France is. It is a society, a political system, which is still in a somewhat experimental state. Hence our panics of various kinds.
>
> ◆
>
> —Edmund Wilson, *A Piece of My Mind: Reflections at Sixty*

I was rattled, I admit. I started to panic. I broke out in a cold sweat. I was about to shout out a warning...

Then I realized: they're the lights of Rachel.

I regained my composure just as we pulled into the parking lot of the Little A'Le'Inn (that's right, pronounced like "alien"). The Little A'Le'Inn was composed of a squat, boxy, pre-fab building that housed the inn's bar and restaurant along with a cluster of mobile homes that comprised its ten rooms.

Rachel, population 100, was in fact more mobile-home encampment than town. It is the only town, however, located along the nearly one hundred miles of Highway 375, which parallels the eastern edge of Nellis Air Force Base. (It's not clear whether Area 51 is part of Nellis, which is two-and-a-half times the size of Connecticut, or exactly which government agency has jurisdiction; the feds have ably covered their paper trail.)

Except for the Quick-Pik gas station and mini-store located at the far end of town, the Little A'Le'Inn is Rachel's only public accommodation. This fact makes the Little A'Le'Inn command central for the UFO-curious who stop by Rachel on their way to and from the black mailbox.

A handful of cars and pickup trucks were parked in front; a decent-size crowd for a Saturday night. The inn's hand-painted sign in front included a drawing of an alien head in what has become the cultural consensus of what space aliens look like, based on Roswell reports: an absurdly over-sized, bald cranium (aliens are a lot smarter than we are) tapering to a sharp chin, and enormous, vacant, almond-shaped eyes. The sign read, "Earthlings Welcome."

Inside, the Earthlings were having a grand time. Locals and visitors in equal measures finished their dinners at Formica-top tables or enjoyed after-dinner drinks, mainly Bud in a bottle, at a long bar. Two men shot pool while a young man and a middle-aged woman plunked quarters into slot machines. The din of conversation, clacking pool balls, ringing slot machines and Country-Western jukebox music bounced off the brightly lit room's hard surfaces.

The museum, as proprietors Joe and Pat Travis call it, mainly consisted of low bookshelves lining one wall, while the souvenir shop—nook—consisted of another set of shelves located in a far corner. Both mostly contained UFO-Area 51 paraphernalia: logo-laden t-shirts and coffee mugs, books on UFOs, and photographs of Area 51 taken from a mountain ridge that the feds finally placed off limits when too many people climbed it to see the base. A drawing of a space alien was captioned: "Trust no one."

"This UFO thing has worked out real well for us," Joe Travis had told me that afternoon. State officials had recently dubbed Highway 375 the "Extraterrestrial Highway" in a shameless ploy to hype tourism to this remote part of Nevada.

Joe appreciated the state's helping hand, which was surprising, given Joe's distrust of big government. A wildly bearded, choleric figure redolent of modern militia, Joe habitually inveighs against the New World Order, his orations backed by a chorus of bumper stickers adorning the cooler behind the bar.

"Don't steal. The government hates competition," read one, succinctly expressing Joe's sentiments. The best barbs, however, were reserved for Bill and Hillary Clinton; "S/he didn't inhale but S/he swallows" had a certain malevolent charm all its own.

Chuck and I settled in at Joe's library of political thought. A waitress, Mary Marrier, came over and with friendly enthusiasm asked, "Did you see anything?"

"Not really," said Chuck. "We just drove out to the boundary and played spotlight wars with security."

Mary had recently moved to Rachel to be near the action. She looked like an aged Vegas showgirl except for her tiny, doll-like stature. She wore a pink, terry-cloth jumpsuit and ultra-thick makeup, which included sparkles on her cheeks. Her auburn hair was teased into a stiff, cotton-candy confection. She had a high, sing-song voice and sweet, ingenuous personality. In the afternoon she had hovered over me like a hummingbird as I spoke with Joe and Chuck. She was anxious to talk, but Chuck had brushed aside her few incipient attempts.

When everyone else finally left for the night and she had me to herself, Mary would talk till two a.m. She would tell me about how the aliens implanted a bead in her nose when she was eleven years old, how in 1981 she and a Las Vegas radio talk-show host brought the first group of people to the black mail-box, how she knew aliens who live here on Earth disguised as humans, and how for years she dreamed of building a city for children and then how someone else finally built it and called it the Mall of America.

But before Mary could tell me her life story uninterrupted, Chuck bid me good night and I fell into a conversation with my trailer mates, Don and Dan.

Don and Dan were fiftyish, identical twins from Illinois on a month-long swing through the Southwest to look at Indian petroglyphs. They inhabited slender frames of about five-nine, and they had willowy limbs and remarkably long, delicate fingers. Their balding heads tapered to gaunt cheeks and sharp chins, and they had large, pellucid, blue eyes. They chain-smoked the same off-brand of cigarettes.

Don and Dan told me their interest in petroglyphs stemmed from an interest in ancient history.

"Many of human civilization's 'firsts' come from Sumer, the first known civilization," Don began. "The Sumerians were a highly developed people. They accurately described the solar system thousands of years before the invention of the telescope. Now, wherever did they get that information?

"Well, they got it from the gods, as they were later called. The Sumerians originally called them *Anunnaki*, which means, 'Those who from Heaven to Earth came.' The Bible speaks of them in Genesis as *nephilim*, which is sometimes mistranslated from the original Hebrew as 'giant.' But some Hebrew scholars now agree 'nephilim' means the same as 'Anunnaki:' 'Those who from Heaven to Earth came.'"

"Are you suggesting the Anunnaki were extraterrestrials?" I asked, incredulous. "That's a bold statement."

"Well, when you read all the information, you can't suggest otherwise," Don replied. "It has to be because of the petroglyph. Not entirely, but that's part of it."

"What petroglyph?"

"The cross. It's a very common sight throughout the world. The cross was the symbol for a tenth planet, which the Sumerians called Nibiru. The tenth planet has a highly elliptical orbit, so it crosses over the paths of the other planets. It travels in our vicinity only once every thirty-six hundred years, which is why no one has seen it in modern times. The Sumerian texts say the Anunnaki came from the tenth planet and that the Anunnaki taught the Sumerians everything they knew."

"So why did they come here?" I posed the question as a challenge, although I should have known Don would have a ready answer.

"Because they were suffering an ecological disaster; their atmosphere was deteriorating. They needed to put gold in their atmosphere to block out X-rays and gamma rays."

"There's gold dust in the space shuttle's windows to protect the astronauts," Dan interjected.

"They dug for gold in mines in Africa but the work was too hard," Don continued, "so they crossbred ape-men with themselves and produced the first humans—that was the missing link. This is all explained in *The Twelfth Planet* by Zecharia Stichin."

Mary nodded her head; she knew the book. Why was this no surprise?

"The original Hebrew in Genesis refers to Adam as 'the Adam,' and Adam is derived from adamah, which means earth, so Adam literally means, 'the Earthling,'" Don revealed. "What's more, the Hebrew word for God is *Elohim*, which is plural, and in Genesis God speaks in the plural: 'Let us make man in our own image.' The Elohim are the same as the Anunnaki."

"Jesus said, 'My kingdom is not of this world,'" Dan offered.

Don went on to explain how Jerusalem had figured into Anunnaki plans for a space station, but I couldn't follow, for I had become distracted by an astounding sight.

Don and Dan stood facing me side by side, and on the far wall directly between their heads hung a drawing of the head of a creature with a huge, bald cranium tapering to a sharp chin, and enormous, almond-shaped eyes. It was one of the several drawings of extraterrestrials in the Little A'Le'Inn's gallery of ETs.

The resemblance was uncanny; shocking, really. The mere possibility staggered me.

The twins had become triplets!

The sight of those three heads mesmerized me. I felt lightheaded, disoriented, delirious, as though I were about to lose my balance. Or my mind. Or both.

It didn't help that Don constantly gesticulated, waving his long, slender fingers in my face. I recalled the mega-long finger with which ET phoned home.

Don stressed a point about the missing link, but I couldn't concentrate on what he was saying. My mind reeled from my own linkage theory.

At last, they finished their discourse and departed for bed— Don and Dan; the picture stayed. Mary then started in on me about nose beads and other matters. Finally, at the end of a very long day, I ventured into the chilly black night for the trailer I shared with Don and Dan; a tiny vestibule separated us. I locked the door and wedged a chair underneath the doorknob like they do in the movies. The room smelled musty; the trailer creaked and moaned under pressure from the constant wind.

The next morning I awoke, seemingly intact. The chair was still pushed against the door, but that was no guarantee. I gently pinched my nose, and then carefully inserted my index finger way up each nostril—I had to know.

No bead.

Thank you, sweet Jesus! Whoever you are, and from wherever you came.

Writer Marshall Krantz has traveled extensively on Earth. His writing has appeared in many places including the San Francisco Chronicle *and* Travelers' Tales Spain.

✳

Eastgate was for years the most-talked-of stopping place for tenderfoot travelers, for here the buckaroos (*vaqueros*) put on Wild West exhibitions that visitors believed genuine. One of the favorite stunts was a fictitious shooting. After the victim was "murdered" and carried out of sight, presumably for burial, the "killer" was seized, not for murder but for cattle rustling—for it was intended to impress on greenhorns that the slaying of a man was a trifling offense compared with cattle-stealing. While the visitors gazed in horror, the killer-rustler would be strung up by a rope that seemed to be around his neck but was actually around his body under his arms. As the man dangled, the avengers pretended to

riddle the body with bullets. Many a traveler left Eastgate, yarn-spin-
ners gleefully relate, convinced that he had seen an actual murder and
lynching.

—Bernard A. Weisberger, *The WPA Guide to America*

TRACEY SELTZER

* * *

The New York Dog
Show Hotel

New York is the capital of ambition—
for all species.

FIRST, I'D LIKE TO MAKE IT clear that I love my kids. Having said
that, I'll confess that the longer I'm a mother, the more I like hotel
rooms. Hotel rooms represent the exact opposite of a mother's life.
A hotel room is quiet; a hotel room only has about four things in
it (each there for your personal enjoyment); and you're supposed
to let somebody else clean the bathroom. I've never understood
why meditation experts ask you to conjure up a deep forest or a
blooming meadow; I can lower my blood pressure simply by
mentally positioning myself inside a brightly lit, freshly scrubbed
hotel room that has a crisply wrapped mini-soap waiting like a
little present by the sparkling bathtub and a courtesy note on the
bedside table asking me, "How Are We Doing?"

This affinity for hotel rooms is the best explanation I can come
up with for why I spent a lot of money I didn't have to attend the
Westminster Kennel Club Dog Show in New York City one
February. I certainly didn't make the trip because I knew anything
about purebred-dog competitions (which I learned are collectively
called "the Fancy" by many insiders). I've never owned a purebred dog, and I'd never been to a dog show until four months
before I travelled 2,000 miles to Westminster. Back then, I'd started

going to a few shows near my hometown of Fort Collins, Colorado, basically as something to do with my kids on weekends. But I'd even stopped doing that after the time my two-year-old son offered a sandwich to a Bullmastiff heading into a show ring.

Judging from the handler's reaction, Bullmastiffs must get marked down for peanut butter breath.

Now, here I was, in the back seat of a rented town car on my way into Manhattan from Newark International Airport. In the back seat with me was Ch. Jordean All Kiddin' Aside, the best Brittany show dog of all time. ("Of all time" is a phrase you hear a lot at dog shows, where setting records is the name of the game for serious competitors.) His "call name" is Ollie. Ollie's owners, Dennis and Andrea Jordan of Arvada, Colorado, whom I'd only met a few weeks earlier at the Flatirons Kennel Club show in Longmont, were letting me tag along with them to Westminster. They were in the front seat. Dennis was attempting to make small talk with the driver, who'd emigrated from Russia fifteen months ago and was still struggling with English. When Dennis told him we were in town for the dog show at Madison Square Garden, the driver did his best to connect with this friendly American. "I have Poodle," he said, "from Moscow. Ten hours."

None of us knew where to take the conversation from there, so the rest of the ride was pretty quiet. Eventually the driver pulled up outside the Hotel Pennsylvania on 7th Avenue and 33rd Street,

> *N*ew York is a city with virtually no habitable public space—only private spaces expensively maintained within the general disaster. While popular journalism focuses on the possible collapse of Los Angeles and San Francisco into chasms opened by earthquakes, here on the East Coast, on its oblong of solid granite, the country's greatest city is sinking into the chasm of itself.
>
> ◆
>
> —John Updike, *Odd Jobs: Essays and Criticism*

just across from Madison Square Garden. As we got out, I couldn't help noticing a large sculpture just west of the hotel's front doors. It depicted three people, two women and a man, sitting on a bench. The man, buck naked, was in an earnest love-clutch with one of the women, also naked. All three looked uncomfortable sitting out there like that in early February, and I was glad to gather my luggage and swish through the revolving door, shivering as I entered the hotel.

The Westminster Kennel Club Dog Show is the second oldest continuous sporting event in the United States; only the Kentucky Derby is older. Besides its age (over 120 years old), Westminster is the Fancy's premier dog show for two other reasons. First, each of its 2,500 contestants is a "Ch.," or champion (meaning it's earned fifteen show points), and second, the show takes place in "the nation's most celebrated blood pit," as sportswriter Red Smith once facetiously called Madison Square Garden. This means it gets a lot of publicity. The Madison Square Garden cable network telecasts the show live in the New York metropolitan area, and the USA cable network takes it live everywhere else in the country. The year I was there, the USA network was even featuring a Westminster special report by June Lockhart, star of the *Lassie* TV show from 1958 to 1964. And spot interviews with celebrities at the dog show were being handled by Andrea McCardle, a former Broadway "Annie."

As I passed under the huge chandelier to join the check-in line at the back of the long lobby, I could tell that the Hotel Pennsylvania played as big a role in Westminster proceedings as did "the Garden," as everybody was calling the concrete, drum-shaped building across the street. Although Westminster didn't start until the following Monday, the lobby on this Thursday afternoon was crammed with "doggers" settling in for a pre-show weekend of specialty competitions, awards dinners, judges' luncheons, and trade-show exhibitions—in short, the annual convention of the Fancy. (Andrea had told me that, during Westminster last year, the lobby had served an unexpected purpose: 800 people and whole packs of showdogs had streamed down here from the guest rooms while the fire department checked out an alarm call, which had turned out to be nothing.) The Penn Bar, which opened onto the lobby, was decorated with a Carlsberg Beer banner that said "Dog Show Entertainment Center," and signs near the escalators gave directions to weekend events on the mezzanine. These included hospitality rooms hosted by dog food companies and a pug show on the dance floor.

When I'd booked my room two months earlier, the reservations clerk had told me that the Hotel Pennsylvania, like its annual Westminster guests, held some impressive records: it was one of the largest hotels in New York, with 1,705 rooms, and its phone listing (perhaps the city's oldest continuous one) had been immortalized in the Glenn Miller song, "Pennsylvania Six Five Thousand." "Really?" I asked in delight. Oh yes, said the clerk, back in the Big Band days, Glenn Miller and his orchestra had played legendary dates in the Café Rouge on the hotel's top floor. *New York, New York.* I'd hung up the phone utterly thrilled, although stung by the price-tag (it was going to be my most expensive hotel stay ever, even with the special deal the hotel was giving us dog-show people). Remembering a travel-safety tip I'd heard on *Oprah* (and thinking about the fire scare last year), I called back. Could I have a room close to the ground? Absolutely, said the clerk.

"You're in Room 1440. Take the elevators, they're right over there; 1440 is half-way down the center hallway. Okay? Enjoy your stay. May I help you?" The check-in clerk had already turned her attention to the next person in the long line of doggers and dog travel-crates snaking across the lobby. Although I could hear Oprah's voice nagging me that it was going to be pretty exciting jumping from the 14th floor during the hotel fire, I decided to keep my assigned spot when I looked again at the check-in line. The doggers wore one of two expressions: exhaustion, or ultra-alertness, as if preparing for battle. One woman stood behind a cart loaded with six sky kennels, stacked double; from each poked the button nose and Bambi eyes of a Bichon Frise. The line inched forward, and she bent low and shoved the cart ahead. The Bambi eyes shrank back, then ventured into the light again, with question-mark looks. Suddenly, I was tired, too, and just wanted to get up to my room, even if it was *awfully* up. I rode the elevator with a group that included an airline pilot not happy that hundreds of dogs were checking in. "I'm gonna pink-list this place," he grumbled to his co-pilot as they moved over to make room for two Rottweilers.

When I stepped out onto the 14th floor and the elevator doors closed behind me, I felt like Vic Morrow's character in *Twilight Zone: The Movie* when he walks out of a crowded bar in the 1980s to find himself inexplicably on a deserted street in Berlin in the 1930s. The 14th floor was so different from what I'd anticipated for two months—so different even than the bustling lobby—that all I could do was blink. Hallways covered in tired carpeting led out in three directions. The halls were silent, so silent I had a hard time believing there was anybody else staying on this floor. As I started down the center hallway, I would have welcomed a friendly dog bark, but the only sound I could hear was of water dripping in a utility closet.

To the employees of the hotel, the lizards were familiar oddities. They were elderly individuals who liked to stop by around four o'clock in the afternoon, when the daily violin and piano music started up in the Palm Court, and just sit serenely in the Fifth Avenue lobby and soak in the solace. "Jules and Paul" were the attraction—Jules on the piano and Paul on the violin. The lizards never took a table in the restaurant. They didn't eat or drink anything. They didn't spend a cent. Some of them jabbed cigar butts into the hotel's gleaming ashtrays or dragged mud over the sparkling carpeting. What did they care?

♦

—Sonny Kleinfield, *The Hotel: A Week in the Life of The Plaza*

Room 1440 had a dead TV, a broken lamp, an ancient carpet with burn marks in it, and a shallow, five-hanger-capacity closet.

Between the scary bed and the water-stained drapes was the room's focal point: a big brown chair that seemed to exude the dusty despair of some phantom Garment District salesman. There he was, clutching a greasy glass full of warm Scotch as he ruminated on some botched deal and thought about blowing his brains out. Not wanting to disturb him, I placed my suitcase near the door and tiptoed out, fleeing back to the lobby and the 1990s, where I was to rendezvous with the Jordans and head over to the Garden.

When I'd met the Jordans at the Flatirons show the previous fall, immediately I'd felt like a loose electron sucked into their victory-charged orbit. At the time, I was wobbling in that strange Who-Am-I land that some women can stumble into after they've moved from working professionally to baby-raising. It hadn't been an effortless transition for me, and for a couple of years, I was having difficulty planning anything past dinner and the next diaper change. The Jordans had made different life choices. At approximately age 30, they were happily childless and living with a houseful of Brittanies. Although that wasn't for me, I did admire their laser-like focus on their goals for Ollie's "campaign" (as a show-dog's competition appearances are called). With Andrea attending to Ollie's grooming and also charting his campaign course, Dennis (a veterinarian and seasoned show-dog handler) was leading Ollie to Best-in-Show victory at events in which Brittanies had never even placed before. The source of Ollie's drive was dog-simple: he was in love with Dennis, and lived to please him. So close was their connection that Ollie could read—and compensate for—Dennis's adrenaline level in the show ring: the more nervous Dennis got, the calmer and more spectacular Ollie became. This year, the Jordans were hoping to set Westminster records that no Brittany had ever gotten close enough to sniff at: Best of Breed for the third straight year, and a placement in the Sporting Group (the next step up after a Breed win). Just a few days after meeting the Jordans at Flatirons, I called to ask if I could come to New York to watch them go for it.

During the pre-Westminster weekend, the lobby of the Hotel

Pennsylvania turned into Dogger Central. While the dogs rested upstairs (Ollie spent some of his leisure time eating rawhide snacks and watching TV), the doggers packed into the Penn Bar to smoke, drink, and schmooze. As I got to know a few of them, I learned that this socializing, for some, served a dual purpose. One woman told me she'd had an especially successful drink in the Penn Bar with a show judge who sometimes judged Sporting Group (the group in which her dogs competed). She'd invited the judge for a drink, just to be friendly and just in case, in the course of conversation, he revealed something about which dogs he liked to "put up" (award victory to), and which he didn't. Sure enough, the judge had told her that it was hard for him to put up Chesapeake Bay Retrievers ("Chessies") with a coat color called "dead-grass." When he was growing up, he said, his father—a Chessie breeder—used to drown dead-grass puppies at birth, believing they'd never grow a coat pretty enough to win in the show ring.

Friday afternoon, I got invited to the Hills Science Diet Awards dinner at the Hilton that night. I went up to my room and rifled through my tiny closet again and again, trying to find something right for a Night Out in the Big Apple. But it was hopeless; it was either the

I fly back from any homogeneous country, from a place where every person I see is blond, or black, or belongs to only one religion, and then disembark at JFK. I revel in the cadence of many accents, catch a ride to the city with a Nigerian-American or Russian-American cab driver. Eat Thai food at a Greek restaurant next to a table of Chinese-American conventioneers from Alabama. Get directions from an Iranian-American cop and drink a cup of Turkish coffee served by a Navajo student at Fordham who's majoring in Japanese literature. Argue with everybody about everything. I'm home.

♦

—Michael Dorris,
Paper Trail: Essays

black cotton pants and brown cotton blouse, or nothing. The only other female who showed up at the Hills event in something other than a spangly cocktail dress was Mary Tyler Moore, stunning in a black tuxedo and silver bow-tie. I'm not sure why she'd agreed to attend this dog-food dinner, but her brief address was more than a little courageous. She gently corrected the man who'd introduced her. "The Collie that Mr. Frei mentioned I have is a Collie in his dreams," she said, flashing her brilliant smile. "He's a foundling—a poundling, I call him. Without any disrespect to the purebred dogs we love, go to the pound and get a dog. Rescue a dog," she entreated this ballroom full of show-dog breeders and owners. For her trouble, she received a smattering of polite applause and some derogatory comments at our table about the fact that she was wearing pants.

The crowd clapped wildly a few moments later, though, when Robert burst through the back door and raced to the front of the room as the band played "Hey, Look Me Over." Robert, or Ch. Salilyn's Condor, the best English Springer Spaniel of all time, was there to receive the award as top dog of the year. He'd won that distinction on the basis of "most dogs defeated"; that is, he'd beat more dogs in competition than any other dog campaigning that year. In fact, he'd defeated 115,651, which made him the best dog defeater of all time. Not only that: Unless he came down with rabies before Tuesday, Robert, everyone was saying, was going to win Westminster. Partly this was due to his innate skills at dog defeating, and partly it was due to the fact that he was the carefully rendered product of a now-elderly breeder who'd been active in the Fancy for 50 years and had never won Westminster. Had never won Westminster despite the fact that she was widely thought of as the person most responsible for breeding the leg speckles out of the coats of English Springer Spaniels. In short, she was due.

Because I was pretty certain I had "Mug Me: I'm from Colorado" stamped in big letters on my forehead, for the rest of the weekend I stuck pretty close to the hotel. Once, I talked to housekeeping director Natalie Moss, a pleasant, round-faced woman with a flouncy taffeta choker around her neck and a heavy set of keys on a long chain down the front of her blazer. Natalie didn't seem to mind that, for a week every February, Westminster transformed her hotel into the biggest dog kennel of all time. "We just do a little more airing out and shampooing after they leave," she said. As a downtown hotel catering to weekday business people, the Hotel Pennsylvania was glad to be sold out this weekend. Natalie had even put a letter in doggers' rooms wishing them good luck at the show and encouraging them to please use the "doggie pads" and "doggie towels" she'd provided. She herself owned two Shih Tzus named Little Bit and Dr. Watson. Dr. Watson was Little Bit's son and had been born by Cesarean section—a tense moment for Natalie. Was she going to the Westminster show? No, she said, she was too busy here at the hotel, "but I'll tape it on cable."

The more I snooped around, the more I became aware that the hotel was also "taping it." With the exception of the rather ornate lobby, it turned out that duct tape was a prominent design feature in the Hotel Pennsylvania. From the two dark, apparently closed restaurants in the grim basement (or "lower lobby," as the staff called it) to the frayed public rooms on the mezzanine, parts of the place seemed riotously ripped up, even violated. In my worn-out guest room at night, I'd try to imagine the Hotel Pennsylvania in her heyday, a lithe young party girl table-hopping in the Café Rouge on the top floor, her beautiful head thrown back, laughing, as some midnight Romeo grabs her none too gently and heads for the dance floor when Glenn Miller breaks into "Chattanooga Choo-Choo." Maybe she ended up in a room like this on a night like that. Maybe she ended up in rooms like this for years, until nobody invited her anymore. Now, much later, her only trick was denial, smearing on the pancake make-up in the morning, duct-taping it all together for one more day. It reminded me of the story doggers told of a once-spectacular Bouvier des Flandres with the grandiose call name of Iron Eyes, whose owners, trying to set every record they could with him, extended his campaign so embarrassingly long that people started calling him Tired Eyes.

By the time Westminster opened on Monday, the hotel was looking decidedly weary. The lobby, which had hopped with activity all weekend, was deserted, with the doggers now focused on competing, not partying. As a symbol of their mass exodus to the Garden, the hotel's revolving-door entrance was broken and boarded up; foot traffic was being shunted to the glass doors to the right and left. The temperature in the lobby was bitter-cold, and there was a certain hung-over feeling. A few stragglers were complaining about the hotel's sudden request that dog-show guests use the service elevators. I asked the elevator security guard about this. With practiced joviality, he shrugged and said, "We've had some incidents. A few dogs got a little upset, so a few people got a little upset. So now, only dogs in crates can go up these elevators. Dogs on leashes have to use the service elevators." Continuing to smile, he added, "Those are usually faster, anyway. They'll shootya right up to y'room."

Over at the Garden, the benching area was hopping. It resembled what it must be like to be backstage at the Miss America Pageant, if the pageant's backstage hallways were lined with vendor booths hawking better-breeding software and meat-flavored doughnuts, and if the contestants having their hair blow-dried were dogs. Anyone who paid the Westminster show fee could visit this "backstage," and hundreds of people passed freely from the show rings to the benching area to see the dogs up close. Seventy-five Best of Breed competitions would be held today. Tomorrow—the second and final day of the show—70 other Breed competitions would be held. That night, as millions watched on television, the 145 Breed winners would be narrowed down to seven Group winners, and these seven would then vie for Best in Show.

Brittanies didn't compete today, so I had no agenda. I wandered around, listening to conversations at ring-side. ("I like this dog's mother. Oh God, is she beautiful?" "They've reduced the benching spaces this year. To try to get a Bedlington into eighteen inches is about impossible." "C'mon Huskies! C'mon Huskies! I want *Huskies* to win!" "I wish he was still here. I'd breed to him.") This crowd—which included more than a few fur coats and expensive coifs—was different from any I'd seen at a dog show. A lot of dog shows are held in what one full-time handler described to me as "the crummiest places in the crummiest little towns—the crummiest fairgrounds or somebody's crummy barn." They didn't tend to attract celebrities. This show was different. As I lingered at the Chinese Shar-Pei ring, a nervous teenaged voice addressed somebody right behind me. "Excuse me, would you mind if I took your picture? For my sister?" the voice asked. "It would mean a lot to her." "No, guh-head," said a young woman, in New Yorkese. I really wanted to, but I just couldn't turn around, even if I *was* from an agricultural state. I eavesdropped like crazy on the New York woman's conversation, though. But instead of providing clues to her identity, she was telling her male companion that she'd heard that Shar-Pei, known for their abundantly folding skin that makes them look like they're wearing way-too-big pajamas, have trouble with something called wrinkle rot.

That afternoon, reading the *Daily News* in the Willie Loman chair in my hotel room, my eyes fell on a good-sized ad in the classifieds listed under "Join the Pet Set." An organization called the North Shore Animal League in Port Washington, Long Island, was giving away free pets. "MANY VALUABLE PUREBREEDS!" it yelled. "Poodle, Collie, Shepherd, Pug, Pointer, Dalmatian, Boxer, Westie, Scotty, Samoyed, Malamute, Lab, Husky, Irish Setter, Airedale, Beagle…." The ad said that if you hurried in to adopt, as a bonus they'd give you some free valentine candy worth $2.95.

Somehow I didn't feel like going back to the Garden just then. Instead, I got in the elevator and pushed "18." The top floor…Glenn Miller and the Café Rouge…satin and champagne. On Christmas Eve, 1939, hours after the band had broken a 14-year attendance record at the Savoy Ballroom in Harlem, the gleeful members of Glenn Miller's orchestra—who'd risen from obscurity to become America's favorite dance band almost overnight—had surprised Miller with a brand new Buick Roadmaster. They'd presented it to him here in the lobby of the Hotel Pennsylvania, probably right near the poster I'd walked past this afternoon giving the hours for tonight's karaoke singing in the bar. As I rode the elevator all the way up, I was hoping for some hint of the romance that must have pervaded the hotel back when Glenn Miller started off an evening here with "Moonlight Serenade."

The elevator opened onto a hallway covered in threadbare, sporadically duct-taped carpeting that led to the entrance of what was once the Café Rouge (now called the Penn Top Ballroom).

The wall paint in the hallways was chipping, and wires hung from one of the broken ceiling panels. The ballroom itself was almost empty of furniture; a few chairs were stacked haphazardly by the windows, and two long utility tables held a couple of over-flowing ashtrays and several piles of winter coats. The coats be-longed to dog-show judges attending a meeting in the nearby Sky Top Room. Next to the tables, in a travel crate on the dance floor, stood a nervous-looking Whippet.

"Ask not what the sport can do for you, ask what you can do for the sport," the speaker at the judge's luncheon was saying in the Sky Top Room as I passed by to investigate the other end of the floor. A large amount of space was taken up by a vacant suite of offices that looked like the most recent occupants had raced to make the last helicopter out of Saigon. The floors were littered with wadded office paper, two chairs and a desk were thrown on their sides, and a control panel had been ripped away with such force that wires stuck straight out from the wall, like witches' fingers.

That night, around 10:30, I was just dozing off when I became aware of another life-form on my hotel floor. Heavy boots were stomping around by the elevators. A man's voice, amplified by an electronic megaphone, crackled, "Attention. There is no fire. I repeat. This has been a false alarm. The elevators will be turned on again as soon as the fire department arrives." When my heart finally stopped jack-hammering, I could hear the wail of sirens many, many stories below.

Tuesday morning, the Jordans were in a semi-composed state of extreme agitation. The previous night, Ollie had started limping, and when Dennis had examined his paw, Ollie had cried. "He never does that," said Dennis. Because Dennis had found pus in the paw, he'd given Ollie antibiotics, and this morning, he'd gaited Ollie up and down the hallway to watch his movement. In the show ring, a lame dog would be disqualified.

Under heavy skies, we walked to the Garden, past New York's main post office on 8th Avenue with its famous frieze paraphrasing Herodotus: "Neither snow, nor rain, nor heat, nor gloom of night, stays these couriers from the swift completion of their appointed rounds." Two hours later, in typical fashion, Dennis and Ollie took Best of Breed. Nobody was even close.

In my estimation, Ollie's most taxing assignment at Westminster was doing the TV promotional spot with Gilbert Gottfried. Gilbert Gottfried's celebrity status stemmed from the fact that he hosted the show *Up All Night* on the USA cable network and had served as the voice of Iago, the malevolent parrot in Disney's movie *Aladdin*. If Ollie could read other people's emotions like he could read Dennis's, his circuits must have been smoked by Gilbert Gottfried. Gottfried's professional trademark is a metallically screechy voice. Ollie was placed in his lap for the promo, and when the crew turned on their lights and camera, Gottfried would break into a huge, cheesy grin and recite a raspy spiel that began, each time, "I'm Gilbert Gottfried. No, *I* am. Not him, *me*. *I'm* Gilbert Gottfried...." Between takes, Gottfried's smile would vanish, and he'd sit staring without expression at nothing. Ollie was uneasy in Gottfried's lap. He watched Dennis hard, as Dennis knelt on the floor just off-camera with a bit of liver bait in his hand. In the middle of one take, a dog-show official suddenly burst onto the public-address system to ask a certain handler to "check your Foxhound on the bench. It appears in distress. Please check your Foxhound." When the TV crew finally got the take they wanted, Gottfried handed Ollie to Dennis as if he were turning over a bag of groceries to the help. He and his crew moved off into the sea of people flowing through the benching area, in the general direction, as it happened, of an NBC-TV crew taping a segment featuring *Today Show* weatherman Al Roker and a pug. It registered with Dennis that Gilbert Gottfried had barely acknowledged him or Ollie, but that was OK, it was worth it, he said, "for the publicity."

As the time for the Group competitions (and the nationwide telecast) drew near, Dennis headed for the public bathrooms to change into his competition tux. The excitement and tension increased steadily as the clock ticked away and groomers gave their dogs a final "once over." Passing by Robert on his prep table, I asked his groomer what it was she was putting on his eyes. "Eyeliner," she said irritably, without looking up. Nearby, another groomer ripped two matches from a matchbook and inserted them (unlit, of course) up the anus of her dog, who, knowing his cue, defecated on the spot.

As Dennis and Ollie left the ramp and headed into the TV lights in the arena, Dennis was focusing on the need to pace Ollie's performance through the judicious use of Ollie's "buttons." "Buttons" are little distractions—bits of liver bait, or a ball, or a small bird wing—that handlers keep in their pockets and use to heighten their dog's alertness when the judge's eye is on them. Last year, in the Westminster Sporting Group competition, Dennis hadn't kept Ollie's attention riveted on him and the buttons, and Ollie had happened to glance up at the huge video screen on the Garden's imposing scoreboard. There Ollie had discovered, as Dennis phrased it, "the biggest Brittany he'd ever seen" suspended near the ceiling. There was no way Dennis could tell Ollie that he was watching himself on television. Emotionally, Ollie was a dog defeated, and they were out of the running for a placement in Group.

This year, Dennis and Ollie were masterful. The Sporting Group judge was an extremely tall, commanding woman with so many years of judging experience and so much physical authority that all week Dennis and Andrea had been referring to her simply as "God." She watched Ollie move out as the first of the 25 Sporting Group competitors. The conditions favored Ollie: unlike the cramped competition rings used for the 145 breed competitions, Group competitions at Westminster were held one after the other, so each competition was able to use all of the arena floor space. This allowed handlers to let their dogs out on a very long lead, so a good mover like Ollie could really "pour it on" and "ask for the win" (as doggers say) through sheer, spirited movement. When Sporting Group was over, Ollie had placed an impressive, Brittany-record-setting fourth. First place went to Robert, who minutes later went on to take Best in Show.

I hung around the photography area while Ollie had his winner's picture taken with Dennis and God. Andrea stood nearby, beaming and holding a grooming brush. I congratulated them, and we said our good-byes: I'd be staying in the east for a few days to visit my sister, and the Jordans were returning to Colorado before that. But their business tonight wasn't quite finished. As soon as the pictures were taken and the press interviews were given, they would be rushing back to their hotel room, where Ollie had a breeding date with a bitch from Canada.

Since my stay there, the Hotel Pennsylvania has been sold and spruced up. The game plan of the new owners seems to be to convert a lot of square footage to office space. The two bars in the lobby are gone, as is the escalator, and the mezzanine—site of the pug show four years ago—has been rented out to various small business concerns. All of this would seem to make the hotel considerably less dogger-friendly, and at least a couple of hotel employees hint at their own hesitations about the change. (When asked whether he thought the remodeling was for the better, one of the lobby staff said, "I couldn't say, Miss…but they've closed all the ballrooms.") On the 18th floor, both the Sky Top Room and the Penn Top Ballroom (the old Café Rouge) are chained shut for renovation, and the powder room down the hall from them is closed, too.

As I checked out of the hotel the morning after the Westminster show and made my way past the sculpture of the naked lovers (their toes now resting in a slushy pool of yellow dog water), I was thinking about how the old radiator in that powder room reminded me of a dog. I'd noticed the radiator right away when I'd entered the empty room, because it was really chugging away, rattling and pinging and giving everything it had to the assignment of warming the place. Directly above the radiator was a big window. It was wide open. A freezing breeze was zinging snowflakes into the room as easy as paper airplanes. But the radiator didn't care. Unaware of the absurdity of its situation, it just leaned into the task at hand.

That's just like a dog, I thought, as I turned the corner and walked north to meet my sister at the New York Public Library. A dog has a radiator's faith when it comes to humans. Whether they're campaigning in dog shows or waiting at the North Shore Animal League for somebody to take them away with a free box of valentine candy, dogs spend their time trying to figure out what we want, and they're tail-waggingly happy when they can provide it. They don't ask for annual cost-of-living raises or for two weeks off in the summer. They just aim to please. Walking up 8th Avenue, I saw an old black dog in a red sweater staring through the glass door of a corner deli. She stood there motionless, intent, but rattling inside with a radiator's faith that somebody would be out in just a minute to take her home.

Tracey Seltzer lives in Fort Collins, Colorado. Her work has appeared in the Christian Science Monitor, Wigwag, *and other publications. She often writes about the uncommon link between people and dogs.*

*

Their love of animals. Pet stores with several floors: on the first floor the canaries and on the top floor the big monkeys. Several years ago on Fifth Avenue a man was arrested for driving a truck with a giraffe in it. He explained that his giraffe lacked fresh air in the suburbs where he kept it, and that this was his solution.

—Albert Camus, *American Journals*

EDDY L. HARRIS

★ ★ ★

Over the Mason–Dixon Line

Watch out for the cops.

ACROSS THE DIVIDE, ACROSS THE MASON-DIXON AND BACK BACK backward in time. Deeper into the South, deeper into the labyrinth, following the line that connects, searching for the Minotaur, the monster to blame for the way things are and have been, looking for someone to hate, wanting something ominous to happen. Deeper I slide into the South whose past owns my nights, owns the darkness of my imaginings, and lurks in the shadows of my dreams, lurks in my memory like the hideous monster of a childhood nightmare. Deeper into the past that the South clings to in a deathlike grip.

Confederate battle flags flutter along my route. They hang from front porches. They dangle in pickup truck rear windows. They are pasted on car bumpers, decorate caps and jackets and shop windows. They color the covers of books. They are a constant reminder.

The South.

I drive the motorcycle with near abandon. By now I, who had never ridden before, am comfortable on the machine after already so many thousands of miles, and so many more to come, comfortable with the bike's speed and with its power, comfortable with its size and with its heft. I have learned by doing, learned to ride by climbing on and holding on, have seen the beauty in this beast and have learned to love the animal. Now I live constantly with it. I have become one with it and through it have become one with the road. I can feel every rut and every ridge. I anticipate every turn....

Corn fields surround me. Bean fields and tobacco. Clapboard houses line my route. Dirt farmers and their families look up to watch me speed by. Like flies languid in the dense autumn heat, they sit slow-moving on rickety front porches, the women in soiled gingham, the men in torn undershirts, their bellies swollen from too many beers and from diets designed with little more in mind than to quiet the long night's hunger. They are poor and they are very tired, even the young ones among them, the babies and the little children in shoes too big that have been handed down from some older relative or bought from a neighbor's yard sale. There is surrender in the soft smiles of them all, and something akin to resignation. Poor like soil that has played out, tired like overworked mules, fatigue in their faces, they gather in groups and sit on the steps. They watch the cars pass like a parade.

An old man in a rocker sits alone in the shade of a tree. Slowly he waves, but too late. I have passed him before I realize the gesture of his hand is a wave. Too late to throw up a hand in return, I tap two toots on the horn and send them back to him. I speed on as if in a hurry, as if something down this road is waiting for me.

But no one waits for me, only Bowling Green and lunch.

Why Bowling Green?

Why, then, the cop?

Why turn left when the road right seems just as fair? Why the motorcycle, this make and this color?

Why anything?

Five years ago, I canoed down the Mississippi. I saw an Indian canoe as the only suitable vessel for such a journey on such a mythic American river—something about getting closer to the water and to the spirit of the river, something about the canoe's connection to American history and to others who had gone before me. I see now that I did not choose the canoe, any more than I chose to walk across the Sahara, or to squeeze with eight others into the back of a car built for six and travel Africa, or to steam up the Congo River on an ancient barge held together by magic and spit. No, I did not choose these things. The canoe, the steamer, the camel, and now this motorcycle, I realize all of a sudden, they chose me. And none of it could have happened any other way.

I did not choose Bowling Green. Nor did I choose the South. Bowling Green, the South, the cop down the road: they—or the weaver—chose me....

Specters of the past loom in the clouds. The South is as the South was—and always will be, though nothing is forever. The past and the present coexist here as nowhere on earth, side by side, as though the one cannot live without the other, the way evil sustains good, the same too as white and black in the South are inextricably linked. You can hardly think of the South without thinking of blacks, could not have one without the other. And how can you think of blacks and their predicament without considering their links to the South?

> $\mathcal{G}$oing south always seems to me rather desolate and fatal and uneasy. This is no exception. Going north is a safe dull feeling.
>
> ◆
>
> —F. Scott Fitzgerald, letter to Ernest Hemingway written on a train heading south, June 5, 1937

The distant past is as fresh in the South as yesterday. History is a living thing still played out, forever battled, the future at stake, the past winning at least as often as the present. The effects of history and the effects of the battle are evident in the many angry eyes, the suspicious glares, the friendly smiles, in a man's hands and in his thoughts.

It is a very hot day. The wind blows slowly. Dust spirals in the fields. Heat swirls all around. The wispy clouds that had been hanging on the horizon are now thunderheads roiling together and threatening an autumn electrical storm. They billow in the sky's high breeze. I run inexorably on, toward those clouds as if toward the future. They slide overhead and all around, suggesting shapes that my imagination can play with, but not playful ones, no swans, no elephants upside-down, no faces of dead presidents.

In the clouds before me I see hooded men dressed like angels in flowing white robes. They are burning the symbol of their Christianity, and at the same time incinerating Christianity itself.

And in the clouds behind me, as real as any hallucination, lurks the fat-bellied figure of Bull Connor, surrounded in the clouds by policemen and dogs.

How can it be real? How could it ever have been real?

May 1963. Birmingham, Alabama. A hot day in a very hot week. The streets are crowded with young blacks protesting against racism, against not being able to sit at a lunch counter or swim in a public pool, demonstrating with no weapon, defenseless hands, nonviolence.

And then comes Bull Connor. The man whose given name, Eugene, is so genteel, but whose nickname speaks of the fury and violence that pervades the South.

Bull Connor is a fleshy man with a soft puffy face, large ears, and a glass eye. His belly hangs over the top of his belt. He looks like a hick gas station attendant, a good old boy at the Coon Hunters' Club. But he is the Commissioner of Public Safety, in effect the sheriff of Birmingham. He controls the police. He controls the police dogs. The fire department belongs to him as well. It is on his orders that these weapons, the police, the dogs, and the hoses, are loosed on the black crowd.

Most of them are high school and college students. Most of them do not resist.

The dogs attack and bite them. The water from the hoses slams into them with force enough to take the bark off trees.

Day after day they are repulsed back to the black sections of town. They are beaten and bloodied. Others are arrested, more than two thousand in a five-day stretch. And for the time being Connor's edict holds: "We ain't going to segregate (he means integrate) no niggers and whites together in this town." He doesn't want blacks and whites eating at the same lunch counters, or using the same toilet, or doing anything else together either.

Whatever was this man named Bull thinking, that he and his dogs could hold back the swelling tide of the past surging into the future's momentum suddenly upon him? Did he not care how history would remember him? Or did he think what he was doing would be too small for history to remember? Did he think his name would go down in the book of heroes? Or do men not think of such things? Did he think he was doing what was good, what was morally right? Or was he not thinking at all, just reacting the way his daddy would have reacted, the way his daddy would have wanted Bull to react?

Bull Connor's face still hangs in the clouds.

It is a dream. It is a very hot day. I need a break, but I speed on as if in a hurry, as if time will save me. I am afraid to stop. I worry that fear and anger will overcome me. (I am afraid too of this almost unthinkable other thing taking shape in the clouds, an impossibility that shall for now remain nameless.)

And so I hurry, trying to outrun the fear and the anger. But I cannot escape them. Time puts no distance between me and my nightmares. They travel with me. The South is my nightmare. Time, it seems, has healed no wounds. The old sores open. The past is indeed as fresh as yesterday, my own past awakening in me just by my being in the South.

The sun is high overhead. I have on a black leather jacket and it's hot. Even at eighty miles an hour, the wind rushing by me is not enough to cool me. I stop the bike when I come to Hartford, Kentucky, stop to stretch my legs, to cool off, to clear my head.

There is a sameness to American small towns. As you approach the town, the houses get closer and closer together. Sidewalks appear. Trees lining the road at the outskirts give way to utility poles. Buildings crop up. Cars are parked roadside. Suddenly you are in the center of town.

So too with Hartford. One minute you are on the outskirts,

the next minute you're in it. Only the houses closer together to warn you.

I pull to the curb and stop at the corner. I shut off the engine, get off the bike, and have a look around.

The buildings are low, none over two stories high, old and made of brick. A few shops, a courthouse across the street, a tiny library halfway down the next block. Right here on the corner where I stand is a bank. I can see my reflection in its big glass windows. Standing here with my helmet on, my black jacket shining in the sun, gathering heat, I look like a road warrior hell-bent on finding trouble. Beyond my reflection I can see the bankers and their customers regarding me with small town curiosity, the recognition and suspicion of strangers. When they see me watching them watching me, they look nervously away.

I peel off jacket and gloves and finally the helmet. I drop everything right on the ground. I stretch and flex. There is a phone booth on the other side of the street. I walk over toward it.

And of course here comes the cop, down the steps of the courthouse and right toward me.

He is the spitting image of Bull Connor to me. But then all cops are Bull Connor to me.

I prepare myself for trouble.

I have not been very lucky with the police. Every encounter with a cop on duty has been disaster, and I long ago lost my every-kid's desire to be one of them, long ago lost my respect for them as a profession. Not a single encounter has been friendly.

> *You show me a black man who isn't an extremist and I'll shows you one who needs a psychiatrist.*
>
> ◆
>
> —Malcolm X

As a seventeen-year-old kid, just beginning my wandering ways, traveling the country by bus, I sprinted across a busy street in downtown Houston. A motorcycle cop spotted the crime, hurried behind me, screeched to a sudden stop.

"Boy!" he shouted at me. (I was young, yes, but why do they always have to call you "boy"?)

"Boy," he said. "You better have some ID."

I handed over my driver's license.

"You ain't up north, boy," he said. "And down here we take jaywalking serious." He kept calling me "boy" and my heart was beginning to pound. I didn't know why.

"Now there's two ways for a boy like you to end up," he said. "In jail. Or in the morgue." He waited. "Now what's it going to be?"

"Pardon me?"

"Pardon me, *sir*," he corrected, but I didn't oblige. Looking back on it now, I suppose he wanted me to lower my eyes, bow my head, and apologize. I looked him in the eye instead and frowned seriously. I wondered what jail would be like. He stared back.

Eventually he let me go.

"You be careful, boy," he said finally. "And from now on cross the street like you're supposed to—at the light." I had forgotten about the entire incident until now, repressed it, the psychologists would say.

Five years later, another situation that I did not so easily forget. The Los Angeles police were not so easygoing.

Once more I was traveling by bus, in the station and trying to buy a ticket to San Francisco. Twelve people stood in line ahead of me and my bus's departure had just been announced over the PA. In a panic I asked each person in front of me if I could skip ahead. But even with their permission the ticket agent refused to sell me a ticket.

"Why not?"

"Because you jumped in line," he said. But no, that couldn't have been it.

"I asked first. You saw me. And everybody agreed."

I turned to them all for confirmation. They still agreed.

"Doesn't matter," he said. "Now get back at the end of the line or I'll call security."

"Go ahead and call security, you jerk. I'm not moving until I get my ticket."

Security came, but what could they do? I still wouldn't budge. But then the police were called. One tough cop kept fiddling, as tough cops like to do, with the pistol in his holster. I thought it might be a good idea to get back in line, but not before I told them all, cops included, what jerks they were.

The line moved quickly—of course. Without the panic and without the fuss I would have had my ticket by now, been on the bus and gone. And that made the entire incident all the more frustrating.

The cops stayed right beside me. They gloated now about how easy it could have all been if I had just stayed in line in the first place.

"That didn't take long," one cop said. "Now did it?"

But I was still angry.

"You see?" he said. "We're not such jerks, are we? We're just doing our jobs."

I saw red.

"Calling it your job doesn't make it right," I said. "But no, you're not a jerk. You're very little more than a pea-brained penis-head."

Now he was the one who saw red. Before I could finish insulting his mother, he grabbed me by the wrist and yanked my arm hard behind my back. He twisted my wrist until the skin burned. I struggled. Together the two cops slammed me to the floor and while one of them held my head against the filthy tile, the other cop handcuffed me. Then they dragged me off and threw me into a little holding room with a couple of drunken vagrants trying to sleep off their DTs. The room reeked of vomit and urine, the odor of stale alcohol and sweat. The two cops pushed me in and bounced me off the walls a couple of times. They punched me and one of them kicked me hard in the stomach. He had been trying to kick me lower, but I sidestepped and he missed.

They didn't book me. They merely harassed me, held me there just long enough that I missed my bus.

I brooded about this incident for a long time then, but put it behind me. Never funny to begin with, it is now even less amusing, almost absurd, slightly sad, and, when I think of the return-ing black soldier who had his eyes gouged out at the bus station in 1945, infuriating.

Like my father's old stories, over time my own remembrances take on new shapes, gain in significance, alter my outlook. What's most important, they connect me to my father in ways I had never considered. They connect me to so many others.

As I was driving in New Jersey the police pulled me over one evening, searched me, searched my car. My offense? I had changed lanes without signaling.

"With all the maniacs out here driving a hundred miles an hour, since when," I wanted to know, "do you pull people over and search their cars for changing lanes without signaling?"

In Delaware, another cop, another search, another lie.

"Come," I said, "why'd you really pull me over?"

I was smiling. I wanted a good laugh and would have gone along with this joke if only they had guts enough to tell the truth. But what could they say?

"You were speeding. We clocked you doing seventy-five."

I had just gone through a toll booth. It couldn't have been more than five seconds from a dead stop.

"Does this look like a race car to you?" I said. "It doesn't to me."

They looked through the car and told me to open the trunk.

"Have you guys got probable cause?" I asked.

They looked up then, paid me more serious attention.

"Are you a lawyer?"

Now it was my turn to lie.

"You got it," I said. "I sure am."

They left me alone.

The police and I just don't get along....

Being black is still the crime. And every cop, black or white, is Bull Connor to me. Every cop is a southerner at heart.

And now here in Hartford was another one. A southern one.

He had a slight paunch that hung over his belt, but otherwise was lean. He wore a clean white shirt, sweat stains at the armpits, collar buttoned to the last button but one. Clipped to his belt was his pistol. I waited for him to touch it, was sure he would before long.

Hartford is the county seat. The courthouse sits up on a grassy hill. At the base of the hill is a retaining wall. On the very corner is the phone booth. That's where I was when the cop, a deputy sheriff, came to me.

I was thumbing through the little phone book hanging from a small chain. You hardly ever find directories hanging in phone booths anymore. People rip pages out of them. People steal them.

I was trying to find a phone number for the Coon Hunters' Club. It wasn't listed. When I dialed directory assistance, they didn't have a number for them either. So I stepped out of the booth and leaned against the wall. The cop was waiting for me.

"How y'all doing?" he said.

"Okay." Suspicious. Cagey. "How about you?"

"About as well as can be expected," he said. And then he touched the gun. He tugged at the waist of his pants and adjusted the way the gun hung on his belt.

His accent was soft, hardly southern at all, almost midwestern but slower and with a slight twang.

"Sure is hot," he said. He pointed with his chin across the street. "Is that your bike over by the bank?"

"Yeah."

"Sure is a pretty thing," he said. "How's she run?"

"Smooth," I said.

"And fast, I bet."

"Fast enough," I said. "Speed limits, you know."

"Yeah, right." I don't think he believed me.

"You're loaded down," he said, never taking his eyes off the bike. "Going far?"

"Just to Bowling Green right now. After that I'm just going."

"Living every man's dream," he said. "Ooo-wee! That's just about heaven."

He started to walk away, around the corner and to his car parked there, but he came back.

"Hey, you ain't lost, are you?" he asked. "You looking for something you can't find in that phone book?"

"Well, yeah. I'm trying to find a number for the Coon Hunters' Club I passed a while back."

"You passed it on this road? How far back?

"Not too long ago," I said. "Back between here and Owensboro."

He scratched his head and shook it. "Naw, sir," he said. "I don't remember ever seeing no Coon Hunters' Club on this road."

"But I just saw it."

"Naw. Not in this county. If it was here I'd know about it. I know where just about everything is in these parts. That must have been back in Daviess County. And you won't find that number in this phone book. This here is Ohio County."

He gave one more long glance toward the bike, shook his head and smiled.

"You be careful on that thing," he said. "I'm not going to tell you to have fun. That's not something I even have to worry about, is it?"

He walked away, still adjusting the gun on his belt and pulling at his collar. I heard him muttering to himself. "Man oh man," he was saying. I couldn't tell if he was talking about the heat or talking about the bike.

I took a long look at the bike myself. It certainly was a beautiful machine, big and blue and sleek and all loaded down, two black saddle bags, one on each side, a canvas duffel strapped to the luggage rack on the rear, and a fishing rod attached. I admired my choice. The first bike I ever owned. The first I ever rode. BMW K75s. A sport bike that looked like a racer but built for long-distance touring. It had six miles on the odometer when I picked it up, twenty-two at the end of the first afternoon I owned it. The dealer and I went to Forest Park on it and he taught me how to ride it. Twenty minutes it took and he told me I was on my own. By the end of the next week, I had put six hundred miles on it. The bike was ready for its first routine service, and I was ready to hit the road. I wondered how the odometer would read by the time I got home again.

I crossed back over and suited up, slowly for all the world to see and envy, jacket, gauntlets, helmet. I looked like a road warrior, I *felt* like a road warrior. As slowly as possible I climbed on. A light squeeze on the clutch handle and the kickstand retracted by itself. I stuck the key in the ignition and started the engine. An instant of slight pressure on the little green button was all it took. She fired right up. I said to myself: Ah! Those Germans! as I always did when I had climbed on and was about to take off. When I applied the brakes, the red light on the instrument panel went off, telling me the rear brake light was working. Ah! Those Germans.

I checked for traffic. I put the bike in gear. In half a moment I was gone. I forget all about Bull Connor and the hateful past, forgot I was in the South. And for the moment I was back to my old self, a tall man with a beard, now with a hot-looking motorcycle. I was king of the world again. Being black hardly mattered.

Eddy L. Harris graduated from Stanford University and studied in London. His first book was the critically acclaimed Mississippi Solo, *which was followed by* Native Stranger, Still Life in Harlem, *and* South of Haunted Dreams: A Ride Through Slavery's Old Back Yard, *from which this story was excerpted.*

★

I myself think that people in general have no notion what widely different nations will develop themselves in America in some fifty years, if the Union breaks up. Climate and mixture of race will then be enabled fully to tell, and I cannot help thinking that the more diversity of nation there is on the American continent the more chance there is of one nation developing itself with grandeur and richness.

—Matthew Arnold, letter to his sister, 1861

PART FOUR

IN THE SHADOWS

LUIS ALBERTO URREA

⋆ ⋆ ⋆

Borderland Blues

*Crossing the line means
hardship and danger.*

EARLY EVENING, AS DAYLIGHT TURNED VIOLET–GRAY AND THE SEA horizon torched copper, I stood at the end of E Street in Chula Vista. Chula Vista (the Precious View) is one of the little scraps of town between San Diego and Tijuana—a buffer zone consisting of National City, Nestor, Imperial Beach, Chula Vista, and San Isidro, the whole region oddly flattened by the pressure of the twins above and below it.

Cutting through it all is the massive flow of Interstate 5 in the west and 805 in the east. There are many ways across the line for "wetbacks" (an odd name for people who don't have to swim across the Rio Grande to get here—maybe they're wet only with blood). Those who don't get out of Tijuana through Colonia Libertad or by being smuggled by car often get trapped by 5's concrete river. It flows dead west along the Mexican border, then veers north and heads all the way up the West Coast. The Border Patrol has come to count on the freeway to siphon the wetbacks along the coast, in a thin strip easily patrolled by helicopter. They get trapped in the saltbogs, the brackish swamps, the Navy yards and slag heaps that run from the border to San Diego. Often at night they try to run across the lanes of traffic, and they are run down.

I was in front of Anthony's Fish Grotto restaurant, poking around for no obvious reason. A helicopter cut in a bit closer on its fly-by, checking to see what this gringo-looking fool with a notebook was doing down here. I can imagine one of the agents saying, Some sort of reporter. Looking to get shot, I guess. I wonder if they thought of me as a drive-by poet.

E Street dead-ends at the edge of Anthony's parking lot. Across the street from the restaurant is a weed-choked lot with the foundation of a house in it. Beyond the dead end is a farm, and this property spills into the Deep South swamps of San Diego Bay. Near here, a colony of sea turtles has immigrated into the hot-water ponds off the electric company's big turbines. Apparently the steaming effluent mimics the tropical tides of the Caribbean. Sea World officials, zookeepers, and animal control officers regularly stop them and check them for papers; the bright-hued plastic tags punched into their fins pass for turtle green cards. The Mark of the Aquatic Beast.

Another road runs at right angles to E, and the two form a dusty T. The arm of this T that runs north, toward San Diego, ends abruptly at the edge of a briny area of tide marshes and bogs. It is barricaded. Parallel to this road is a set of rusted train tracks. It was here, along this road, that I found myself among the remnants of what seemed a lost race, the spoor of courage and desperation.

I walked north along the closed road, veering around a barricade that kept cars from the area. Grass had worked its way through the blacktop, cracking and lifting triangular pieces of it. There was a ditch on the left, and every few yards there were clumps of tired pine trees. I could see the abandoned rail line through the trees. There were peeling PRIVATE PROPERTY signs posted all along the edge of the farm. A crumpled pair of blue jeans in the road. The silence. A cottontail broke from cover in the crumbling foundation and ran in panicked jags. The river-hiss of 5 to my right underlined the quiet. A blue-and-yellow CAT baseball cap was dangling from a twig.

It was so lonely out there. Not restive, not solitary; *lonely.* I began to feel sad, then furtive. I was convinced somebody was watching me. I imagined a rifle scope trained on my back. I wanted to hide.

It was like a smell. I looked around for its source and suddenly got a hunch. I cautiously stepped down one of the little banks into the ditch between the road and the tracks. I crawled under a pine.

They'd been there.

There were cardboard sleeping mats, small white roses of crumpled paper, flat liquor bottles, dry scat. All along the ditch there were hidey-holes burrowed out among the roots and pine needles, dens scraped out between a flood of cars and a dead railway.

I moved into the hole. There was dust all over the cardboard mats. It had clearly been a while since anyone hid here. Had the people been arrested? Had this spot been compromised, discovered by *la migra,* and rendered permanently unsafe? Perhaps they made it north. Maybe locals found them and made sport of them. (The Ku Klux Klan had been patrolling the region, "assisting" the U.S. government in the roundup of unwanted humans.)

A broken bottle of Mexican beer. Magazine pages smashed into petrified stools. I could feel the pulse of these men, lying here, hiding night after night. Who, I wondered, who? I might have known them. I might have fed them the week before they came here.

One stained mattress. A shattered TV set on the tracks. There was nothing left here. Not a voice. I felt watched by shadows as I climbed out, hurried away from the traces of sorrow downwind of the city.

Luis Alberto Urrea is the author of two books about life on the border, Across the Wire *and* By the Lake of Sleeping Children, *from which this story was excerpted.*

✳

This so-called war zone, where illegal immigration is at its most brazen and where enforcement is concentrated, runs from the Pacific Ocean through brushland and city streets to the first desert mountains, a distance of only fourteen miles. The official crossing point, the port of entry, is a dryland gate in an urban sprawl. It is in fact two gates—one Mexican and one American—big, boastful structures spanning a north-south freeway.

Together they tally fifty million crossings a year and claim to be the busiest border point in the world. Southbound traffic slows but rarely stops. Northbound traffic backs up for miles and crawls through a multi-lane marketplace that has grown up around it. Day after day in the fumes, boys wash windows, girls sell gum, and Indian mothers beg for charity. From the comfort of your car, you can buy what you need: genuine peasant clothes, cartoon dolls, Maria and Jesus, a giant beer mug, a plastic dog or cactus, an etched mirror, a pelican on a piling, and even death itself— a grinning skeleton in an infantry helmet riding wide open on a dirt bike. The waiting can last hours. At the end a green light says come, one car at a time, and a gatekeeper says stop, now prove your right to proceed.

—William Langewiesche, *Cutting for Sign*

★ ★ ★

The Train to Hell

On a downhill run to nowhere.

THE TRAIN IS AN HOUR LATE. I BOARD, FIND MY SLEEPING COM-
partment. The attendant says, "Oh boy, bad news. The dining car
won't open until nine p.m." When nine o'clock comes I am rav-
enously hungry. I sit across from a fat young man who exudes a
miasmic stink. I cannot eat, take a buttered roll and return to my
compartment. The people in the swaying coaches already seem
exhausted, sprawl in their seats with babies, blankets printed with
words bunched over them, their bruised eyes closed, mouths gaping and choked. The car sways, the wheels roar.

At midnight, lying in the bed with the shade up, I see we are
entering Toledo. And fall asleep before we arrive.

An hour after dawn I am awake. The train is motionless. I feel
it has been motionless for some time. There is breathy hissing. I
dress in my stale clothes. The sky is cloudy, there is a view of graffiti on concrete. The sleeping car attendant comes with coffee
and juice.

"Oh boy," he says, "oh boy, I have bad news. We are still in
Toledo, we have been here all night. There is a problem."

"What?" The coffee is lukewarm, with a grassy taste as though
from an infusion of hay.

411

"A boat is stuck under the railroad bridge at the Maumee River."

Up and down the train the passengers buzz. The sleeping car passengers laugh at first. The coach passengers, who have known for hours, are sullen, cramped in their seats with the hard armrests.

As the hours crawl by there is no information. Rumours seethe: the train will go back to Chicago; the train will be rerouted to the north; the passengers will all be sent on by bus or plane; the boat under the bridge cannot be freed; powerful tugs are coming down from Detroit to pull it out.

Free coffee and doughnuts for all. People are getting off the train and wandering into the station to telephone, to explain to bosses and spouses that although they should have been in Boston by now they are still—ha-ha—in Toledo, home of the Detroit Tigers' minor-league team, the Toledo Mud Hens. The train has no cellular phone. In the station only two telephones are working. There are long lines. No food in the station either, only vending machines displaying "empty" signs. The ticket agents know nothing. Yes, this has happened before, last November another boat was stuck under the same bridge.

I get back on the train. I pass through the club car. The attendant is piling bags of peanuts on the counter; on a napkin he writes the word "FREE." The peanuts are intended as solace. I take some. In my cubbyhole I take up my book and read. The peanuts are stale.

All at once the train begins to move, cautiously but steadily. Inside the station the passengers waiting to use the telephones see the train leaving and they run out onto the platform. But it is no use. The train is on its way and they are left behind.

The train crosses the bridge. There is no boat in sight, no tugs, only splintered pilings and the rough brown current of the Maumee. We gather speed. The train is twelve hours late. I have missed my connection to Montreal. Everyone has missed everything. We pass a vast cemetery at the edge of a cornfield.

Things are seriously awry. The train has lost its slot in the great flow of rail traffic. The sleeping car attendant has dark circles under his eyes, answers the querulous complaints of passengers by saying,

"I don't know, they don't tell us anything." The train chief, the conductor walk briskly through the cars, trying not to look at the bitter passengers. When their sleeves are seized, they grimace, say they are awaiting instruction, all will be made right. "That's as much as I know, ma'am." Then they are gone. Later, an insistent passenger demanding the train chief is told that he is sleeping, the poor fellow has been up all night.

In Cleveland we pass boats shrink-wrapped in royal-blue plastic near a cliff of scrap metal. The sleeping car attendant's eyes are bloodshot. He limps on swollen feet. At noon he brings his passengers each a bag of barbecue-flavoured potato chips and a cup of coffee. The train has run out of food. He brings each of us three mint chocolates of the sort hotels put on a guest's pillow.

We are the fly in the ointment, the drunk uncle at the wedding party. The train moves slowly past a desolate station. All the windows are broken—there is no pane intact in 504 lights. A fine, wind-streaked snow begins. This is a nerved-up, strained time of waiting for nothing but the cessation of waiting.

Sighing and groaning, the train halts in a wasteland, once a marsh and now a combination swamp-and-appliance-disposal depot. Toppled stoves and yellowed refrigerators lie in ice-rimmed water, in the sedges and cattails. A male mallard duck hovers and drops down through a maze of wires. A few minutes later he flies up with a female, into the wind.

A passenger is carrying on in the corridor, insisting he be let out to make a phone call. Perhaps there is a telephone booth in the marsh.

"Sir, the train will not wait. If we start you will be left."

I can tell when the train is going to start—there is a straining sensation, though without movement. I feel this strain now. The passenger jumps out. At once the train jerks forward and the marsh dissolves to an abandoned, ramshackle station. The passenger, halfway between the train and the station, looks back—his bag is on the train. It is snowing heavily and almost dark. Everyone is hungry. There is not even coffee now. The train glides through more wetlands. Snaking through the boggy ground beneath the high-tension wires are dirt bike trails crooked as dropped ropes. The handlebars of a motorcycle project from a scummed pool; is there a rider under the water? In the dusk we pass junkyard after junkyard, one of them filled with nothing but the cut-off tops of bulldozers and back-hoes and graders. The word "CUT" is spray-painted on the doors. More ducks, like bowling pins with wings.

Outside Rochester the train stops again. The attendant, lurching and grey-faced, comes with more bad news; of the two eastbound tracks ahead, one is flooded. On the other a freight train has derailed and run over its own drawbar and behind it seven other freights have right of precedence over us. There will be a minimum wait of four-and-a-half hours to get the derailed freight off the tracks, and then the track repairs…The train is on a downhill run to nowhere. The crew lost their chance at the on-time bonus last night.

There is no reason for getting this train to its destination aside from passenger anxiety and pleading—and that counts for nothing. It is money reward that runs the train and now the reward has shifted from the on-time bonus to the sweeter lure of massive overtime. In every car plastic sacks of trash block the corridors.

The car attendant is strung out and crazy. He is at the end of his rope. There is no food, no coffee, the chocolate mints are gone.

> *T*he subway car is full but not crowded. Crowded is when you aren't actively worried about being attacked because there isn't enough room for someone to wield a knife or snatch your bag. Full is when there are so many people in the car that were someone to stab you or grab your purse you wouldn't be able to get out of the way or give pursuit. We take the last two seats, near the door, the subway equivalent of the suicide seat; that's where the muggers get you as they're leaving the train.
>
> ◆
>
> —Dyan Sheldon,
> *Dream Catching: A Wander
> Round the Americas*

"Cheer up," says a second attendant, who has appeared from nowhere, "it can't last forever."

"It seems like it already has," the first says in a sullen, dropping voice. He coughs. "I'm going to change my clothes." I hear him go into the empty roomette across the corridor.

After a few minutes I take my aspirin bottle from my purse and open it. The lid cracks up noisily, the pills rattle. From the corridor the second attendant shouts in a rough voice, "John! What are you taking!"

"What?"

"What are you taking? I heard the pills rattle, goddamn you. You better not be taking anything!"

"What are you talking about?"

"You push me, I'll break that damn door down."

The voices have a delirious, feverish quality. There is a long silence.

"Don't go to sleep, John," says the voice of the second attendant close to the door, "you'll be up all night... John, what saved his ass was that flood. The general inspector coming on here like gangbusters. They couldn't get hold of him—he used the flood for an excuse. I tell you, John, this is unbelievable, unbelievable." There is a long silence.

*E*tymologically a traveler is one who suffers travail, a word deriving in its turn from Latin *Tripalium*, a torture instrument consisting of three stakes designed to rack the body.

◆

—Paul Fussell, *Abroad: British Literary Traveling Between the Wars*

"John, you want a beer? You got the white one, right? I'll tell you what I got now. John, you got a pen on you?"

"Yeah."

"It black?"

"We were out of Cleveland at 12:33."

"5:26. What time we pull up? 5:26?"

"Yeah." There is a long silence. "Hey. Open up!" The door

opens and the second attendant goes inside. Their conspiratorial voices are clearly audible.

"O.K., Johnny. How many tennis racquets you got? I might borrow one from Tubby. You got balls? Want to play on Monday? I'll tell you something, John." The second attendant's voice drops. "Twelve hours overtime, that's like two days' pay! Two days' pay! Hey, Johnny. Did you call up Carmen when you were here?"

"No. I was thinking about her."

"Hey, the hormones getting to you."

"You see now, you tell me if he's thinking clearly? Where are you, Scotty?"

"Oh, I'm right across from Van Damme."

It is dark outside. Huge green letters appear. THE SPAGHETTI WAREHOUSE. I am starving. I have a headache and a ringing buzz in my ears like cicadas. The train slows, slows, and stops before a deserted station, a brick colossus in the dirty snow, the waiting room lit by a dim high bulb. Luggage trucks on the platform in random positions. The door across the corridor opens and the attendants come out, walk away. After a long time the first attendant, John, brings word to his few remaining passengers. He is startled to see me. "Oh. I thought you got off the train back there."

"No."

"Well, the conductor is holding up the train for some food."

"Better luck if he would hold up a restaurant. There isn't any food on the train." A feeble joke.

An hour passes. Two cars pull into the station parking lot. A few train crew people are on the platform, go into the dirty waiting room, come out again. A taxi cab arrives and they run to it. The driver opens the trunk. The train people pull out large cartons. The train chief, he who escaped the inspector's discovery of his illegal nap, strips small bills from a large wad of money and pays the taxi driver.

"Arunh!" A man grunts with the weight of the boxes. Money is in the hands of the vehicle drivers. More taxis, more boxes arrive, cartons of soft drinks, and someone brings up a baggage wagon. A voice issues from a loudspeaker.

"All train attendants. They're relaying the chicken to your cars. Please be ready."

John, enveloped in the perfume of salty, greasy Kentucky Fried Chicken, brings me a striped box. A dozen more taxi cabs pull up, disgorge other men. The vehicle drivers hang around on the platform staring at the train as though at a road accident. More taxis.

"They're changing the train crew," says John, yawning.

"You can finally get some sleep."

"No. The car attendants don't ever get relieved. We're on for the trip, even if it takes a million years."

Outside on the platform the train chief is staggering, perhaps with weariness, his stumbling figure backlit by the bulb in the open baggage-cart storage shed. In the corridor I hear the voice of the second attendant again.

"John, Johnny, we have to take care of each other. Right or wrong!"

I go to the club car. It is like a tableau from hell, crammed with flushed drunks, thick smoke, and the stink of dirty travellers. People are shouting, snoring, kissing, scratching, arguing, dealing cards, bending down, coughing, drinking, rotating their glasses to make the ice swirl up the sides, tapping ash into striped boxes of bones and wadded napkins, throwing down torn magazines, picking up torn magazines, stumbling toward the toilet, standing in line at the toilet, vomiting inside the toilet. I buy a small bottle of warm white wine, think a moment, and buy another.

Back in the claustrophobic cubbyhole a terrible knowledge comes. Somehow, in Chicago, I have boarded the Train from Hell on its endless circling route, clanking and lurching through dirty days and nights until the universe runs down, and then on into the void. The passengers who debark along the route drop straight into the fiery pit. Here at least is greasy chicken and warm wine.

"Hey, hey Johnny, you see this? Saudis behead five?"

Mumble.

"Aw, give me a break!"

Mumble.

"We got time. They got this other crew waiting at Amsterdam. Imagine bringing this thing in?" His mocking voice drops to a whisper. "Amtrak is the bessssst..."

In Syracuse the train holds up for more than an hour in a labour dispute. The question is, is it legally necessary to put on a new crew? There is an enormous wrangle on the platform while the passengers grow old. A woman in a white leather coat gets off the train, approaches the chief, and screams in his face that he and his fucking train are utterly, utterly fucked up. She gets back on. And so the second night grinds away, the train jerking forward, running for fifteen or twenty miles, then stopping in snowy junkyards, at way stations where crew members are replaced, where union representatives shake their fists, again and again.

"That's two complete changes of the train crew since yesterday morning," says John in dawn light. His face is ghastly, great black circles under his eyes, gaunt and stubbled, numb mouth.

On this second morning, as the sky lightens in the east, the train enters rural countryside in upstate New York. The landscape is grey and dense. The trees are plastered with clots and rinds of snow. There is a man coming down a steep path toward the railroad track, frowsy, half-asleep. He is carrying a white enamel pail, an old-fashioned object from the days before indoor plumbing— the thundermug, the slop bucket.

The chief tells me I can make my Montreal connection at the next stop. I carry my bag to the platform of the sleeping car. The train pulls in. I press money into John's hand. I cannot believe I am free of this train. In the station I present my ticket at the window.

"Montreal? There's no Montreal connection here. You should have got off at the last station. No, there's nothing going anywhere until tomorrow. You better get back on that train. At least it's going east. *Hurry!*"

I run for the hated train, the heavy bag pounding against my leg. John sees me coming, extends his hand for my bag. The train pulls out.

"What happened? What happened?" His distress is real.

"You can't get there from here."

The train lumbers on for hours, hopelessly compromised, filled with exhausted, reeking humans entering a curious state of mind—irrational, manic. Nothing that has once defined the journey counts any longer—tickets, arrival times, connections, accommodations, business meetings, family reunions, all are meaningless. The passengers' only hope is some compromise that will not leave them homeless in Yellowknife or hitchhiking north from Miami. A kind of euphoria sets in as the conductor shuffles along asking people where they want to go. Not that he cares. Passengers begin to choose strange new destinations that have nothing to do with their former lives.

"Let me off in New York, haven't been there for years."

"I was going to Schenectady, but I think I'll take Boston now."

My connection to Montreal is dead. Dead in an unmarked grave.

"White River Junction?" I murmur. It is only thirty miles from where I live.

"Yes," says the conductor, "get off at Springfield, there'll be a taxi to take you to White River Junction. There's other ones going."

Six of us disembark at Springfield. There is no taxi but we are off the train. The cold air smells wonderful. After long discussion with the ticket clerks—how clean and fresh they look, how energetic, filled with careless confidence in contrast to the demoralized, wretched passengers—a vehicle arrives, a small sedan driven by a 300-pound woman. We squeeze into the rump-sprung seats. Four of us sit in back. I am between a homeopathic physician who recites know-all accounts of Chinese herbal cures and a pair of teen sweethearts who kiss and fondle. In the front, next to the huge driver, is a businessman who says he has now conquered his fear of flying and a frail grandmother who seems unconscious.

This last hour-and-a-half is the worst of the entire trip: crushed against strangers, head swimming, in a car speeding over an icy road while the radio plays country and western and machine-gun advertisements to "get hooked on phonics," this final leg is nearly unbearable. It is an eternity until I am in White River Junction eating burned eggs at the Polka Dot Diner and waiting for a friend to pick me up. I think it is over.

But the journey does not end, cannot end. A year later I am still on that train, you are with me, and there is no getting off. The train is a metaphor, bearing us through the junkyards and despoiled landscapes at the end of the century, past mean houses and the casually dead, through broken trees, deserted stations and transmission towers, a train staffed by the exhausted, the sly, the conniving, the uncaring.

E. Annie Proulx won the Pulitzer Prize in 1993 for her novel, The Shipping News. *She lives in Vermont, travels a great deal, and may be recognized by her yellow pencils, feedstore cap, and heavy suitcase full of books. Her most recent novel is* Accordian Crimes.

★

The range of service and consequently, the experience of riding across country on an Amtrak train can run from the sublime to the ridiculous. The country is divided into regions with some of the better service found along the West Coast, and on the East Coast running west to east, rather than north to south. Who can understand what kind of system could produce the stunning insolence of Stalinesque-era waiters who will take a reading break at an otherwise empty table with an overloaded dining car crammed with anxious and impatient diners? Who has not gazed into the eyes of service personnel who react with all the swiftness of a bored postal clerk at noon, and wondered what kind of union could tolerate such behavior? If Amtrak perishes it will not be for lack of equipment or funds; it will be because the public cannot find romance on trains serviced by improperly trained personnel. Other than this simple complaint, one can have a lovely time on the new sleepers which can house two or four individuals depending on the size paid for. And really, despite the poor service rendered by some, the truly dedicated and enthusiastic individuals who love the railroad can make any segment of the journey a joy.

—Sean O'Reilly, "The New Amtrak"

Boston Escalator

At a certain height, New England gets chilly.

I AM IN THE HEART OF THE CITY, BENEATH THE COLD MOIST EARTH of the Boston Common, where the glare of the Park Street subway station slides icily along concrete and tile. I am watching an old man.

The old man sits alone on a bench, cradling a battered paper bag. The bag has a curious shape. Is it a bottle? I wonder. It seems too large. The bag top has been twisted along an expanse of neck. The bottom is bulbous. The old man peers inside. He smiles a secret smile. Then, he twists the bag closed.

People clip past, moving briskly toward some private future. The old man is invisible to them. He exists on some slower, dreamier plane. He peers into the bag again and squirms with anticipatory delight. As if to restrain himself, he fusses with the folding of a tattered overcoat. Finally, he cannot resist. He reaches into the bag and unveils its contents. It is a child's ukelele, with faded pink and blue paint.

The old man smiles shyly. He rests the ukelele against his cheek and gently plucks one string. Twang. The sound echoes once and is lost. After a moment, the old man tenderly slides the ukelele back into its bag. He stands and shuffles away.

★

Often a person interacts with a place and time in a manner that fails "to take." Occasionally, the result is a combustive moment when history is made—when revolutions and inventions and abominations are born. More frequently, the result is a drying and darkening, like a grafted bough that cannot thrive and fails to die, not a raging despair but a mild confusion upon waking. A "Where am I?" that lingers through the day. In time, it may create a timidity, or an anxiety, or a quiet sweet lunacy. In Boston, for two years, I lived at such a juncture.

Call it a youthful identity crisis. It was not a time of great trauma. I suffered no grave psychic or social wounds. But if it is true that when translated by the Chinese "crisis" becomes the words "danger" plus "opportunity," then it indeed was a crisis. For, eventually, its unsettling passage would lead me toward a greater fortune.

I moved to Boston in August. I was very young and had in my possession: a brand-new tenure-track contract to teach graduate studies at a large university and a doctorate that was two weeks old. I had asked for—no, I had *negotiated*—a salary that was twice the sum of the graduate stipend I had been receiving. My latest issue of the *American Psychologist* had informed me that in the United States of America there were four women of Asian descent who were counseling psychologists. I was prepared to swell their august ranks.

The apartment that I leased hovered on the cusp of grandness. Two blocks east was the crest of Beacon Hill. There baronial mansions stood shoulder to shoulder in fraternal confidence—the clearly favored sons of an ungenerous god—looking down across the Capitol, Common, and finally back to England.

My apartment building nestled among a line of nineteenth-century tenements and boarding houses. The gas-lit cobblestone alley was in a perpetual din. The tenements were being converted into luxury housing; a hotel for elderly vagrant men was being renovated. Massive pieces of construction equipment sprawled across the street, sandblasting the facades of buildings never built to be graceful until they could face the street with a stolid scrubbed prettiness.

The interiors of these buildings were being gutted. If you looked behind the scoured veneer, through the open windows, you could see huge chomping machines devouring walls and ceilings. It was like looking into the startled eyes of a decent housewife going mad.

Amidst the commotion, the elderly vagrant men wandered in mild confusion. They peered up at the buildings, with the nibbling fear of old men who no longer recognize their neighbors, and urinated on the polished stoops.

Like the neighborhood, my neighbors and I sought entry to a more gracious state of being. We awaited glorious, imminent metamorphoses. We lived in tiny, kitchenless, walk-up apart-

> $\mathcal{S}$uch was the condition of the Charles Street ghosts, it seemed to me—shades of a past that had once been so thick and warm and happy; they moved, dimly, through a turbid medium in which the signs of their old life looked soiled and sordid.
>
> ◆
>
> —Henry James, *Collected Travel Writings: Great Britain and America*

ments with multiple dead-bolt locks on our doors, with neither views nor light from our windows. Yet we were undaunted. We had hardwood floors and marble fireplaces. We had a foothold on Beacon Hill.

Larry and Tricia, my upstairs neighbors, were newlyweds. They were twenty-five years old. Larry was an insurance agent and Tricia was a substitute teacher. Both had grown up in an Irish working-class section of Boston; both were the first in their families to have attended college. They were proud to live so near to America's oldest, wealthiest families. Someday, they told me, they hoped to buy one of the luxury apartments that were emerging along the street.

The first year I lived in Boston, I frequently would wake to the sound of Larry singing in the shower. Tricia would be laughing and calling to him. Often I would hear them playing a game of make-believe. Larry was a puppy. Tricia was a kitten. "Woof, Woof," he would skid across the floor. "Meow," she would purr. Each evening, the young husband would rush home to his bride: whistling his way up four flights of stairs, jingling his keys, bearing his bicycle before him like a tribute.

One winter night, I woke to hear Tricia sobbing. "I know that I'm changing. I know you're not happy, but what can I do?" Larry keened. "I'm making it; I'm moving up. I'm happy. I'm happy. I'm a happy, happy man."

They separated in April. On the narrow stairwell, I met the man who leased their former apartment. He was a thirty-four-year-old lawyer, in the midst of a divorce. He told me that he loved his new apartment: the marble fireplace, the fact that he could walk to work. "And do you know what?" he confided. "After my divorce settles, I think that I will buy one of the luxury condominiums coming up along the street."

During the 1950s, I was born in the United States of America. This event placed me among the ranks of a powerful cohort group—the postwar generation. Through the simple act of being born, in a country where majority rules, we were destined to wield inordinate influence on our society. We have grown, like infant emperors, watching our social environment continually re-create itself to mirror our changing whims.

I was ambivalent about my new career, about my possibilities. Psychology and university teaching are "helping" professions requiring long years of training. They exert a simultaneous pull toward altruism and egotism, toward self-sacrifice and self-enhancement. Serve humanity and live well, I joked to myself. But it was an uneasy humor.

"I hate to sound like I'm manufacturing angst in the face of bounty," says Ann, "but what's more valuable to us—our life as it has been or as it could be?"

We are drinking tea on a Sunday afternoon in Ann and Danny's attic apartment. The apartment is furnished in homey comfort with hand-me-down furniture. Everything seemed to carry a family story: a desk given by Danny's father, crocheted cushions from a great-grand-auntie, a shell-rimmed anniversary mirror made by a sister. Two plump cats doze at our feet.

"Real estate, stock portfolios, tax shelters," she lists in gloom, "lately, that's all I hear."

Ann is completing her doctorate in counseling. Danny is completing his medical internship. This year, they have earned approximately thirty thousand dollars. It is the first time in their five-year marriage that they jointly have earned over ten thousand dollars, and it seems a staggering sum. Yet they suddenly have realized its puniness when compared to the amounts they potentially could earn. The knowledge is unsettling.

"When we were in college, choosing our careers, I never thought that one day we would be preoccupied with nurturing our money, that we'd become gluttons for ownership," says Ann with a shiver.

"You two will never be gluttons for ownership," I chuckle.

On a postal clerk's salary, Danny's parents raised eleven children. Ann's father supported a family of seven by working in a chemical plant. Backed by their families' values, encouraged by the

> *M*oving away is the American way. "We are a nation of leavers," Ellen Goodman said. The country was founded and built by people moving away, from repression or lack of opportunity in the Old World, from repression and lack of opportunity in Connecticut or Massachusetts or Oklahoma. Tocqueville was surprised to discover that the settlers at the frontier of 1831, Michigan and Ohio, were not from Europe but from Connecticut. They were moving away, seeking more opportunity, a chance, a new beginning.
>
> ◆
>
> —Richard Reeves, *American Journey: Traveling with Tocqueville in Search of Democracy in America*

idealism of the era, Danny and Ann dreamed of a life devoted to family and public service. He wants to work in medical research. She wants to be a counselor for nontraditional students. "You know," she explains, "older adults, single mothers, ethnic minorities: the people who usually don't get a chance to go to college."

Now, however, Ann is working at a Seven Sisters college. Danny is interning with the sons of doctors. Their colleagues have referred them to tax accountants, stock brokers, real estate agents; and Ann and Danny are beginning to feel defensive about the simpleness of their dreams.

"I get the feeling that *real* professionals want the most visible, most prestigious jobs; that *committed* parents place earning money as their highest priority," says Ann. "We want to be realistic and responsible, but will we end up as people we no longer recognize or like?"

In her kitchen, Ann sits deep in thought. Her husband reads in the next room; her cats sleep by her feet. Her future shimmers before her. Suddenly she laughs.

"A prominent woman professional, whose first child is fifteen months old, invited me to lunch," she recalls. "Danny and I are planning to start our family. Woman to woman, professional to professional, she wanted to help. 'Motherhood can be emotionally turbulent, in ways you never expected,' this woman confided. I waited to hear—oh, I don't know—maybe about the aching helplessness you feel the first time your baby suffers from a cold." Ann pauses and starts to giggle.

"So what did she say?"

"She told me about the frustrations of trying to locate designer-labeled infantwear."

When I read Margaret Mead's autobiography, I was astounded by how matter-of-factly she stated that sometimes she did not like a culture. It seemed to lack ritual, or celebration, or tenderness. Sometimes there was nothing really wrong with the culture. It simply did not provide the fodder necessary to satisfy her personal or professional aims. When I lived in Boston, I assumed that a good social scientist should be able to create a sustaining day-to-day existence through the sheer power of discernment. There must be something here to satisfy you, I told myself. If only you would observe keenly enough; if you would just *perceive* with all your might.

In practically all my memories of Boston, it is winter. My spirit hovered outside my body, observing from a dispassionate distance. Psychologists call this disassociation. It is considered a defense mechanism—a way to keep life in abeyance. It was a phenomenon that I welcomed.

Boston is not a lighthearted city, like Paris or New Orleans. It is not a mystical place, like Kyoto or Lhasa, where ancient spirits brush past you in the morning markets. It does not trumpet with the brash confidence of New York or Hong Kong. Bostonians refer to Boston as the Hub. It is an abbreviation for the Hub of the Universe.

"I'd attribute Boston's *je ne sais quois* to the weather and to the Puritans," laughs Ann. "Those Puritans were a strange and enduring bunch."

We are on a ferry bound for Provincetown, the tip of Cape Cod. We hope to see some whales on our voyage. We are in a playful mood.

"Recall the self-absorption in their industriousness, the weird vanity of their austerity. Imagine, if you can, the sheer terrifying gall of a people who could be so certain of the correctness of wearing black that they could despise the Pilgrims for wearing gray."

Ann recently has become steeped in Puritan lore. She has left the Seven Sisters college and is working in the heart of witch trial territory, providing mental health services on Boston's north shore.

At Ann's community agency, there is a legend. In the mid-1970s—when the agency first opened—a consultant was hired to deliver a training workshop. The consultant was a young African American woman. She wore her hair unstraightened in what was called an Afro. Now, at that time, community mental health cen-

ters were distrusted by the American public. After all, the centers
dealt with crazy people and endorsed going into schools and
telling *children* about sexual assault and drug usage. Additionally,
African Americans were never seen in villages like Beverly, Prides
Crossing, or Salem. They did not live there. They did not work
there. They did not vacation there. African Americans were people seen on television. So when the consultant was seen entering
the community mental health center, why it was only natural that
a telephone call would be placed to the village police. "The community mental health center is harboring a fugitive. Angela
Davis has been sighted entering the premises." Legend has it that
the word spread quickly. A village vigilante group was formed and
dispatched. In the basement of the mental health center, the consultant was drawing a diagram on the chalkboard when the bull-
horned message rang out. "The building has been surrounded. We
advise you to surrender peacefully."

Ann laughs as she tells the story. "Sometimes it's hard to tell
a legend from a tall tale," she says. Then suddenly, she is serious.
"But one thing you quickly learn in the Boston area is never to go
outside your ethnic territory, never to do the unexpected."

Perhaps it is a lesson learned from unexpected hurricanes rav-
aging the shoreline. Perhaps it is a legacy from the Puritan's self-
righteous fury, but in Boston the unexpected creates immediate
suspicion, causes sure surveillance, and often ends in sadness.

*Lydia Minatoya is a counselor on the faculty of a community college in
Seattle. She received a supporting grant from the Seattle Arts Commission
and the PEN/Jerard Award honoring an emerging American woman writer
of nonfiction for* Talking to High Monks in the Snow, *from which this
story was taken. She is married and has two young children.*

★

Usually a number of people were already sitting there or standing around.
Gradually more and more would come until most of the space along the
whole wall was occupied. I always found this an interesting occasion;
every type of sitting or reclining pose was sketchable, and I also overheard
animated discussions from one group or another from time to time.

Though I could hardly follow any of their topics, it interested me, for it reminded me both of the Sunday free lectures and discussions in Hyde Park, London, and of similar gatherings on Boston Common week-end afternoons. Don McPherson told me that this wall had been dubbed the "War Street." But he also remarked that this "War Street" has long been condemned as disfiguring the city and would soon be overshadowed by some new structures. Freedom of speech is one of the symbols of democracy. If the free discussion with "soap-box-orators" disappeared from Hyde Park, Boston Common and San Francisco's Civic Center, where else should I find such a genuine symbol of democracy?

—Chiang Yee, *The Silent Traveller in San Francisco*

LARS EIGHNER

* * *

Hitchhiking
with Lizbeth

Thumbing across country
can be beastly.

FRIDAY MORNING WAS OVERCAST WITH HIGH CLOUDS. THE GRASS was very dewy and, in patches, frosty. Because I was bigger and stronger I eventually dislodged Lizbeth from the bedroll. As we were up at first light, I believe I had packed and we were down at the road before sunrise. Very many semitrailers passed us. I tipped my cap or waved at most of them and a few of them sounded their horns. So far as I know, no trucker has ever done me any good in my travels, but I had heard it was a good idea to be friendly toward the truckers, so I was. Lizbeth curled up on the gear and shivered. I hate it when she shivers.

Quite soon, although at the time it seemed not so soon, we got another ride. I did not notice him until he had passed us and stopped and honked his horn.

The old pickup was very battered, mostly lime green, with a Florida license plate taped in the rear window of the cab. It sat on the shoulder under the crossover some two or three hundred yards beyond us. As fast as I could move with all the gear was hardly more than a brisk walk, even with Lizbeth towing me as hard she was able. The truck did not pull away as sometimes happens in these situations. The cab was nearly full of gear and delicately balanced arrangements for brewing coffee with power from the cigarette lighter. The bed of the pickup was loaded with exactly what all I never discovered, but Lizbeth would have to ride there.

Lizbeth is a fool. Off her leash she cannot be trusted not to dart out into traffic. In the last couple of days she had ridden more than she had in her whole life before and she had never been in the back of a pickup alone. I tied her leash to the hub of a loose spare tire in the bed of the pickup.

It was far from clear that she could not hang herself by jumping overboard or be lost over the side by slipping her collar. There was not room for me to ride with her. I worried about her constantly for she rode standing on various objects and precariously balanced. The worst was when we would overtake a livestock truck. She clearly appreciated only the very slight relative motion of the vehicles and gave every appearance of being willing to dash herself against the slats of the livestock trucks, just as she might jump against a stationary fence.

The driver's story was that he had been a couple of years in Florida with a girlfriend, but the relationship had gone sour. So he was returning to Tucson, his hometown, and a previous girlfriend.

To Tucson seemed quite a ways and I was very much encouraged. I had pored over the map without absorbing many facts of geography. I thought, for example, that the continental divide was somewhere in California, rather near the San Gabriel Mountains. I was not entirely sure how far I would have got when I reached Tucson, but from the mile markers I could see this ride would put at least five hundred miles of Texas behind me.

We stopped fairly soon at a rest stop. I scraped a razor over my face, washed my neck and forearms, and since I had a ride already, changed into my most ragged jeans. The driver wanted to be sure that Lizbeth was walked. She seldom wants walking more than twice a day. But I welcomed the chance to lash her to the tire again, this time with much less slack. Nonetheless, she managed to get up and about and to keep my heart in my throat for the rest of the ride.

The last of the grass and the trees petered out a little past

Junction, Texas, and then for many miles there was nothing except what is called cedar in Austin but elsewhere is known as juniper scrub. This is a long and desolate stretch, but what is more, the few wretched settlements that exist are several miles from the highway and no cafés, gas stations, or even tourist trips are visible from the road. I was set to work brewing coffee. The driver was well into his second day on the road without stopping and had no intention of resting until he reached Tucson. Again I was offered a part of a roach from the ashtray, but once it was clear I had no interest in marijuana, I was given the job of rolling joints for the driver from a stash in a Bull Durham bag. We did not talk much. The driver was determined to coax something out of the radio. For the most part we got static and whenever he did pick up something he overpowered his speakers so the result to me was little different from static.

I was suitably impressed by the mountains as we got to them. I had seldom seen mountains and never such as these, young and rising from a treeless landscape.

It was another hot day and we were climbing. The temperature gauge in the old pickup read hot, but the driver insisted it was stuck. We pulled into Las Cruces to get gas and the radiator blew.

The cap is supposed to blow first, just as a safety valve on a boiler blows before the boiler reaches the bursting point. But this cap had not. Yet as the steam dissipated and things cooled off, it appeared the radiator had only split a seam. A welder was found who would draw a bead down the seam for seven dollars.

This exhausted our folding cash and I was set to the task of sorting through the driver's change pot. There was enough for a couple of packs of cigarettes and, perhaps, gasoline to get to Tucson. I had about three quarters besides of my own, which I did not mention. We would press on.

As we pulled out of the service station in Las Cruces, Lizbeth finally managed to hang herself, but inadequately. She was attempting to get from the back of the pickup to the cab window. I made a bed for her in the hub of the spare tire and then lashed her to it again with as little slack as I thought possible. Night was falling and I knew it would be cold. I hoped she would nest in the tire. Of course she did not. I was set back to square one in worrying about her. I became accustomed to the shadow of her head in the lights of the vehicles that overtook us, only to be alarmed again by the absence of the shadow when she finally fell asleep.

The sun set as we passed Vail, Arizona. We were climbing again. The driver explained that Tucson was in a box canyon and if we reached the top of this climb we could coast into town. This was far from an idle observation, for fuel was precariously low. Eventually the truck did make it to the top and it was all downhill from there.

The driver let us off about 9:00 p.m. at a truck stop south of town. I have since learned that this was a famous truck stop and elegantly appointed as these things go, but I had no chance of learning that firsthand. Immediately Lizbeth sat on a prickly pear and thus struck the keynote of our tenure in Tucson.

The shoulder of the frontage road was under construction for as far ahead as I could see. That would pose a problem in getting away from the truck stop.

I know now what I should have done. I should have found a dark spot and gone to sleep. Our situation did not appear to me to be good, but it was far from desperate and unlikely to deteriorate overnight. "Things will look brighter in the morning" was the sort of adage I always sneered at. Now I was to learn it was valuable advice and in Tucson it was a dear lesson. A long ride is such a piece of luck that one is tempted to try to press on before fortune shows its other face. I suppose that was why I hoped to get farther that night. But instead, Lizbeth and I were fallen upon by thieves.

A young Latin man distracted me with some discussion that I never understood. I was holding Lizbeth and we were not more than twenty feet from our gear. When I turned to the gear, it was gone, and when I turned again, so was the young man.

His confederates must have had a car, for there was no other way they could have made such a pile of gear disappear in so short a time. Naturally, I had laid my heavy coat on the bundle.

I find it hard to believe that anyone would have thought I had anything of much value. My clothes, besides being worn, would not fit many other people, and this should have been obvious to look at me. The little radio was of no appreciable value. Besides my papers, most of the bulk of what was taken was the remainder of Lizbeth's food and the bedding, which was warm enough, but could not have been sold. Other than a few dollars in postage, nothing could have been readily converted to cash. I was left with what I was wearing, a football practice jersey and my most ragged pair of jeans, and Lizbeth.

My mistake, besides not getting us out of harm's way after dark, was in not lashing Lizbeth to the gear the minute I set it down. While Lizbeth is harmless, most people would require some time to discover the fact and in the meanwhile she would make noise.

Tired and disheartened, I sat by a telephone pole, and in spite of the cold I must have dozed sitting up.

When I awoke I discovered a further disaster. Lizbeth had curled up at the base of the telephone pole, and cold as it was, she had heated the tar on the pole until it flowed all over her back.

> I have met with but one or two persons in the course of my life who understood the art of Walking, that is, of taking walks—who had a genius, so to speak, for *sauntering*: which word is beautifully derived "from idle people who roved about the country, in the Middle Ages, and asked charity, under pretense of going *á la Sainte Terre*," to the Holy Land, till the children exclaimed, "There goes a *Sainte-Terrer*," a Saunterer, a Holy-Lander. They who never go to the Holy Land in their walks, as they pretend, are indeed mere idlers and vagabonds; but they who do go there are saunterers in the good sense, such as I mean.
>
> ◆
>
> —Henry David Thoreau,
> *Walden*

Clearly no one would want this mess in his vehicle. When the sun rose I saw it was even worse than it had first appeared.

My own stamps and envelopes had gone with our gear. But just before I left Austin, Billy gave me a whole book of stamps with a face value of $4.40, which I had put in my wallet. By chance the wallet was in my jeans and not in the pocket of the coat that had been stolen.

Billy had told me his phone credit card number and I used it to call a bookstore that was listed in the copied pages of a gay travelers' guide that Billy had given me with the stamps. I supposed the bookstore was a gay one, and in my experience these little stores, which are not to be confused with adult bookstores, take a proprietary interest in their authors. The clerk I spoke to, however, seemed less than gracious and only grudgingly agreed to give me cash for the stamps. My object was to buy some rubbing alcohol to clean the tar off Lizbeth's back.

The immediate problem was to get to the bookstore.

South Tucson consists of huts and shacks and sand dunes, with here and there the occasional obvious federal housing project. It is unremittingly barren and ugly. There are few improvements of any kind. Street signs are restricted to the housing projects where they identify various *stravs*. Using the dictionaries of several languages, I have been unable to discover what a *strav* is, and have concluded that it is a compromise between *street* and *avenue*.

South Tucson simply has no sidewalks. I thought at first this was merely in keeping with the general wretchedness of the place, but eventually it seemed to me that the public policy in Tucson is to impede pedestrians as much as possible. In particular, I could find no way to walk to the main part of town in the north except in the traffic lanes of narrow highway ramps.

I could not believe this at first, and Lizbeth and I spent several hours wandering on the south bank of the dry gash that divides Tucson as I looked for a walkway. More than anywhere we have been, adults like teenagers shouted threats as well as insults at us in Tucson, and did so whether I was trying to hitchhike or was merely walking. More than one man found it necessary to brandish a firearm at us although we were afoot and presented no conceivable threat to those cruising past us at upward of fifty miles per hour. This atmosphere did not make the walk across the high ramp in the traffic lane any less exciting.

The usual medium in Tucson for vulgar displays of wealth appeared to be the conspicuous and wasteful consumption of water. As we walked north things got greener and more affluent. The ritziest neighborhoods were positively swamp-like. Lizbeth could drink from the runoff of the sprinkler systems that ran throughout the heat of the day. Still, there were no continuous sidewalks.

Perhaps the bookstore was no more than seven miles north of the gorge, but it was late in the afternoon when Lizbeth and I got there. The bookstore was not of the sort I expected. It was not after all a little gay bookstore, but was a very large general-interest bookstore with a gay-interest section.

The clerk took the book of stamps and said he would have to check with the owner, although I mentioned having phoned earlier. I suppose they counted the stamps

As in Phoenix, water availability in Tucson has been inextricably linked to growth. The concern has been that the lack of an existing supply or delays in obtaining it can interrupt future patterns of growth. It became important, then, for the Tucson water industry to demonstrate that it had little fear of water shortage and that water was available without any limits imposed on its use. Thus, there could be found artificial lakes (more lakes per capita than any other state); rapid increases in water hookups to new urban subdivisions; low water rates, which further decreased with higher levels of consumption and thus acted as a disincentive for conservation; and an increasing and relatively high per capita water use that peaked at slightly over two hundred gallons per day in the early 1970s.

◆

—Robert Gottlieb,
A Life of Its Own: The Politics and Power of Water

each and every one, for it was some time before he returned to give me $4.40. I noticed that a couple of magazines that contained my stories were on display behind the counter, over the clerk's head.

I took the money to a nearby drugstore to get some rubbing alcohol.

If I had then had a better grasp of the geography I might have saved us considerable trouble and heartbreak. The bookstore was not so very far to the east of the interstate. But as we had crossed the gorge, the interstate appeared to veer off sharply to the west. I thought the nearest point of the highway was in the south, and to the south we returned.

We were quite in darkness by the time we crossed the gorge again. Lizbeth could no longer walk.

We were far enough west now that convenience stores no longer had faucets and hoses on the outside. I went into a convenience store and bought a gallon of water. I returned to Lizbeth and carried her a few feet from the road, behind a sand dune.

I would never have thought a stout middle-aged man could outwalk a healthy young dog. I have since learned I cannot expect much more than five miles a day out of Lizbeth on a consistent basis, and then only when conditions are favorable. In Tucson conditions are not favorable. Without sidewalks or grass, she had walked on cinders, sand, and rocks. The trip to the bookstore had worn the pads off her paws.

Lars Eighner has been described as the "Thoreau of Dumpsters," and as a "Latter Day Candide." He and Lizbeth were living under a shower curtain in a stand of bamboo in a public park when he began his book, Travels with Lizbeth: Three Years on the Road and on the Streets, *from which this story was excerpted. He is also the author of the novel,* Pawn to Queen Four.

※

It is well known that our roads are dangerous. And here I admit I had senseless qualms. It is some years since I have been alone, nameless, friendless, without any of the safety one gets from family, friends, and accomplices. There is no reality in the danger. It's just a very lonely, helpless feeling at first—a kind of desolate feeling. For this reason I took one companion on my journey—an old French gentleman poodle known as Charley. Actually his name is Charles le Chien. He was born in Bercy on the outskirts of Paris and trained in France, and while he knows a little poodle-English, he responds quickly only to commands in French. Otherwise he has to translate, and that slows him down. He is a very big poodle, of a color called *bleu*, and he is blue when he is clean. Charley is a born diplomat. He prefers negotiation to fighting, and properly so since he is very bad at fighting. Only once in his ten years has he been in trouble—when he met a dog who refused to negotiate. Charley lost a piece of his right ear that time. But he is a good watch dog—has a roar like a lion, designed to conceal from night-wandering strangers the fact that he couldn't bite his way out of a *cornet du papier*. He is a good friend and traveling companion, and would rather travel about than anything he can imagine.

—John Steinbeck, *Travels with Charley: In Search of America*

TERESA JORDAN

✦ ✦ ✦

Playing God on the Lawns of the Lord

In Oklahoma, the bison once again roam.

THERE ARE A THOUSAND OF US AND THREE HUNDRED OF THEM. We are *Homo sapiens* and they are *Bison bison bison*. We have come to this spot in the Flint Hills of northern Oklahoma to watch them released onto five thousand acres of native tallgrass prairie. The prairie and the bison evolved together over thousands of years. They have been separated for well over a century. They are coming together now, some order is being restored, and we are in a celebratory mood.

Each of us feels honored to be here. This is an invitational event, open to members of the Osage Tribe, which owns the vast oil reserves under this ground but not the ground itself; to members and friends of The Nature Conservancy, which now owns the ground; to General Norman H. Schwarzkopf, Retired, of the U.S. Army, who has just a few hours before, at dawn, received his Osage name of Tzizho Kihekah, or Eagle Chief; and to a swarm of schoolchildren, who sit restlessly on the grass waiting for the bison to appear.

No one denies that we are part of a spectacle. CBS is here. NBC is here. CNN is here. *The New York Times* is here. They have the best seats in the house, on the elevated platform near the gate through which the bison will run. Excitement fills the air, something akin to what one feels at a homecoming game, and we all have our cameras in our hands. Now we see the bison in the distance, a bounding line of darkness above the tallgrass, heading the wrong way at a dead run.

The cowboys do not ride horseback, but in pickups and on four-wheel all-terrain vehicles. They turn the bison toward the gate; the animals turn back the other way. The cowboys turn the bison again; once more, they refuse. The cowboys try a third time, and this time the great shaggy beasts come through the gate on the run, three hundred head, a diversified herd, ranging from calves born only a few months earlier, in the spring, to massive bulls a dozen years old that weigh nearly a ton.

We have grown quiet, as we've been instructed to do in order not to startle the animals, and our silence turns quickly to awe. So it's true, what we have read in books and seen in movies. The sound of bison on the run really does travel over a long distance. This is a quintessential American sound, something we must carry in our genes, bred into Native Americans by thousands of years hunting and eating and living side by side with the beasts; bred into Euro-Americans as a haunting legacy of what our ances-

> The elk and, more surprisingly, the bison, ranged east in the woodlands to Pennsylvania and New York, and possibly to western New England, and their range extended south through the Atlantic States at least as far as Georgia; probably both species once strayed to the coastal savannas, but had commenced their retreat at the time of the first white settlements. East of the Appalachians, the last bison was killed in 1801, at Buffalo Cross Roads, near Lewisburg, Pennsylvania, and a cow and her calf killed at Valley Head, West Virginia, in 1825, were the last east of the Mississippi.
>
> ◆
>
> —Peter Matthiessen,
> *Wildlife in America*

tors annihilated in a few short years only slightly more than a century ago. This is the sound of history and valor and triumph and squalor and sorrow, and it really does sound like thunder. But thunder would be borne by the air. We would feel it in our chests, our diaphragms. This sound comes up from the ground, through the soles of our feet. The sensation increases as the bison near, and they move like a dark roiling sea, swift and high bounding, closely packed. The damp overcast of the sky brings out the full spectrum of gold in their shaggy roughs and darkens the burnt sienna of their atavistic forms. They pass and we are no longer members of a crowd of spectators. Each one of us is alone, watching as if from great distance something primal and real. And most of us are weeping.

Teresa Jordan is the author of Riding the White Horse Home *and* Cow-girls: Women of the American West *and writes frequently about the West and rural culture. Her fiction, nonfiction, and poetry have appeared in* Ms., Lears, *and* The Washington Post.

*

When the course of history has been told
Let these truths here carved be known:
Conscience dictates civilizations live
And duty ours to place before the world,
A chronicle which will long endure.
For like all things under us and beyond
Inevitably we must pass into oblivion.

This land of refuge to the stranger
Was ours for countless eons before:
Civilizations majestic and mighty.
Our gifts were many which we shared
And gratitude for them was known.
But later given my oppressed ones
Were murder, rape and sanguine war.

Looking from whence invaders came.
Greedy usurpers of our heritage.

For us the past is in our hearts,
The future never to be fulfilled.
To you I give this granite epic
For your descendants to always know
"My lands are where my dead lie buried."

—Dedication Plaque at Crazy Horse
National Monument

PHILIP CAPUTO

Alone

*A man seeks respite from
the moral wasteland.*

FINDING CONNECTIONS BETWEEN APPARENTLY DISCONNECTED
facts or events is a sign of genius or of madness. Isaac Newton
linked the rise and fall of tides to the gravitational attractions
between the Earth and the moon. At the loony end of the scale
is the right-wing militiaman who weaves the federal government,
the United Nations, and the helicopter he heard fly over his
house into a conspiracy to land saboteurs in preparation for a U.N.
takeover of the country. I'm no Isaac Newton; therefore I wonder, as I sip whiskey beside a campfire deep within New Mexico's
Aldo Leopold Wilderness, if I'm a little gone. For several days,
something has been causing my brain to see conjunctions between
things that any normal person would say have nothing to do with
one another. Maybe it's too much solitude: For three weeks before this solo backpacking trip, I was living alone on a remote
Arizona ranch, which is when the symptoms first appeared.

One night when a violent storm knocked out the power, I was
crumpling newspapers to get a fire going in my adobe cabin. Two
horrific crime stories on the front page of the *Arizona Republic* got
my attention, and I found myself reading them by candlelight and
then clipping them instead of consigning them to the fireplace. As

443

I continued, a few other stories about subjects seemingly unrelated to the homicides also caught my eye. I read them and cut them out, too, and then, without quite knowing why, joined them to the crime stories with a paper clip.

Now, leaning against a log close to the campfire, I'm pondering what relationship the stories could possibly bear to one another. Whatever it is, I sense that it also has something to do with why I am here, alone in one of the vastest and possibly one of the last authentic wildernesses left in the contiguous United States.

The region is called the Gila, a term of convenience that applies to the 5,200-square-mile Gila National Forest in southwestern New Mexico, as well as to the three wildernesses that form its primitive core—the Gila, the Aldo Leopold, and the Blue Range. Logging, mining, livestock grazing, roads, and motor vehicles are prohibited in the wilderness areas, whose combined territory could easily accommodate Rhode Island. Within them are mountain ranges nearly two miles high—the Mogollon and the Diablo, the Mimbres and the Black. Ancient forests of ponderosa pines, Douglas firs, and Englemann spruces bristle up the slopes while agave and prickly pear cling to the canyon bottoms. Rare Gila trout hold in the pools of the streams and rivers, waiting for what food the swift currents bring them; elk graze in high alpine meadows, desert bighorn sheep stand poised on steep ledges, black bears prowl remote gorges. All in all, it's territory that at least resembles the America that stretched from sea to sea before the "stern impassioned stress" of Pilgrim feet began to beat a path that appears to have led our civilization to the shopping mall.

It is early spring and, because of the freakish weather stirred up by El Niño, still cold—nighttime temperatures of 10 degrees at the higher elevations. The Gila is most heavily visited in summer and early fall, though it draws only a fraction of the mobs that descend on Yellowstone and Yosemite. Now, with the weather nippy and unpredictable, it is virtually unpopulated, solitude all but guaranteed.

Before I'd hiked in, I told John Kramer, the chief wilderness ranger (I'd love to have a title like that), that I wanted to minimize or, if possible, eliminate any chance of running into my fellow bipeds for the next five days. He suggested a route in the Aldo Leopold, which is named for the great conservationist who wrote *A Sand County Almanac.* The Gila Wilderness, twice the size of the Aldo Leopold and bordering it on the west, attracts more people because it contains prehistoric Indian cliff dwellings and its gateway is reachable by a paved road. The Aldo Leopold has no tourist attractions, and New Mexico State Highway 61—a narrow, rutted, washboarded stretch of dirt—is the only way to get to it by car.

Shortly before noon, I started up Route 61. It was posted with two signs that read "CAUTION ROAD AHEAD RESTRICTED 4 WHEEL DRIVE AND HIGH AXLE VEHICLE. NO FOOD LODGING OR GASOLINE NEXT 120 MILES." The road turned out to be less formidable than advertised, but the side track to the trailhead for the Continental Divide Trail was a real axle breaker if taken at speeds faster than five miles per hour. I tucked my dust-cloaked, mud-splashed Pathfinder behind the ruins of a corral, shouldered my pack, and hiked off. In the distance, scraping a heaven scrubbed clean of clouds, was my destination: the 10,100-foot crest of the Black Range, mantled in snow and the dark spruces and firs that, I surmised, give the range its name.

On this night, my first in the boondocks, I am somewhat pleased with myself. I have hauled a 60-pound backpack through some 5 miles of wilderness, all of it uphill: a gradual ascent for the most part, but in a few spots fairly steep, the path a treachery of shale and rubble. I have pitched my tent, gathered firewood, strung my food bag high in a tree to avoid presenting bears with an occasion to sin, cooked my dinner of freeze-dried beef stew, and managed to get a good fire going in a woods still wet from the storm that passed through a couple of days ago.

But I haven't come all this way to prove what a manly fellow I am. Been there done that, bought that t-shirt ten times over as a marine platoon commander in Vietnam, then as a war correspondent in the Ethiopian desert and in Afghanistan Hindu Kush. I don't regard the great outdoors as a fitness center or an arena for athletic contest. Having hunted, fished, backpacked, and run rivers everywhere from Alaska's Brook's Range to Florida's Everglades, I've learned that merely getting from point A to point B in wild country provides sufficient challenge for anyone.

I have come all this way to take a kind of American walkabout. My reasons are contained in a remark Theodore Roosevelt Jr. made to one of his brothers, expressing his loathing for the sort of holiday we would call a "family vacation." "When I go," he said, "I go hard and I go alone." That should be every backpacker's motto.

I am going hard because I think it's important to test yourself. I am going alone because I wish to follow my own agenda, not a guide's and because I don't want to deal with the needs, wishes, and complaints of a companion. I am seeking more than escape from the toe-jam of contemporary American society. I seek what wilderness engenders in me—the feeling and state of mind that I am supposed to have in church but seldom, if ever, do: joy. Fulfillment. Happiness. "To be dissolved into something complete and great," as Willa Cather wrote. The natural world is whole and sufficient unto itself, it doesn't need us or want us. It is stunningly indifferent, and yet, to immerse yourself in its completeness, if you can manage that surrender, is to grasp happiness.

Unfortunately, those ugly newspaper stories keep intruding. They hobble my pursuit, reminding me that if I am in a vast and beautiful cathedral, it is one surrounded by a much larger aesthetic and moral slum.

> This, then, is not the tale of a great hunter or of a great warrior, or of a great traveler, although I have made much meat in my time and fought for my people both as boy and man, and have gone far and seen strange lands and men. So also have many others done, and better than I.
>
> ◆
>
> —John G. Neihardt, *Black Elk Speaks: Being the Life Story of a Holy Man of the Oglala Sioux*

On February 24, 1998, in Phoenix, the *Arizona Republic* reported, a 31-year-old unemployed laborer, John Sansing, high on crack with his wife, Kara, telephoned the Living Springs Assembly of God Church, asking for help in feeding his family. The church sent Elizabeth Calabrese, a 41-year-old mother of two, to deliver a box of groceries. According to the *Republic*, this is what happened next. When the good Samaritan appeared at Sansing's door, he pulled her into the living room, threw her to the floor, beat her over the head with a club, and then, with his wife's assistance tied her to a chair. The couple did this in full view of their four children ages 9 through 12, who couldn't understand why their parents were hurting the lady who'd brought them food. Their father explained it was for the money and showed them the cash he'd netted from Mrs. Calabrese's purse: $1.25.

Sansing then blindfolded and gagged her, dragged her into the master bedroom, and raped her while Kara watched. When he was through he got a kitchen knife and stabbed Mrs. Calabrese to death. It had been quite a day for John and Kara; they left the body in the bedroom, went into the living room, and promptly fell asleep.

On March 22, 1998, the *Arizona Republic* reported mixed reactions to the news that Maricopa County, which encompasses Phoenix and its suburbs, was the fastest-growing county in the nation. It even outpaced Clark County, Nevada, where Las Vegas has been spreading like a gigantic oil spot. Between 1990 and 1997, according to the U.S. Census Bureau, Maricopa County welcomed an astonishing 574,097 newcomers. Developers and cheerleaders of laissez-faire growth were elated. "I think it's very exciting," gushed Jan Brewer, the chairwoman of the county board of supervisors. But some residents thought their desert paradise was repeating the mistakes of postwar Los Angeles, subjecting them to urban sprawl, overcrowded schools, polluted air, traffic jams, and more crime.

About the same time that the Census Bureau report was issued, this headline appeared in the *Republic*: "MOM TORCHES KIDS." Kelly Blake, a 34-year-old unwed mother of three, telling her children that they were going to play a game, lured them into a shed beside their Phoenix house. Once they were all inside, their mother poured gasoline on the children and set them on fire, then exited the shed. The two boys—John Fausto, 14, and Ramon Fausto, 12—managed to escape. While John was trying to extinguish the flames that engulfed his brother, Blake doused herself in gasoline and set herself ablaze. Firefighters who arrived on the scene saved her life and John's, but 9-year-old Vanessa Fausto burned to death, while Ramon died of his burns the next day.

Meanwhile, back on the growth front, Tucson's *Arizona Daily Star* reported in its March 29 edition that as of 1996 there were 247 golf courses in the state, 129 in the Phoenix area (average annual rainfall 8 inches) and another 35 in Tucson (average annual rainfall 12 inches). The metastasizing of greens and fairways is devastating the Sonoran Desert's ecology and draining the state's aquifers. It takes 185 million gallons of water per year—as much as is used by about 3,600 people living in single-family houses—to keep the average 18-hole course looking lush. Conservationists were gearing up to battle developers and politicians eager to draw more tourists and retirees to the state by building still more links, the *Star* said. But one statistic cited suggested that the conservationists have about as much chance of halting the advance as the Polish cavalry had of stopping German panzers in 1939. Golf in Arizona brings in approximately $1 *billion* a year.

And, finally, this item, reported in the *Arizona Daily Star*. Scattered across a ridge in northwestern Albuquerque—New Mexico's capital and another Sunbelt city busting its seams—are some 15,000 petroglyphs that ancestors of today's Pueblo Indians carved into boulders spewed from five now-extinct volcanoes. The figures of horned serpents, masked men, flute players, birds, spirals, and stars are revered by Zunis, Hopis, Sandias, and Cochitis, who believe that the volcanoes link living people to the spirit world and the afterlife.

A six-lane commuter highway abruptly stops at the foot of the ridge, which was designated a national monument in 1990. Beyond it, out in the pristine Chihuahuan Desert, subdivisions for

60,000 people are going to be built early next century, and the developers and their political allies want to extend the highway through the monument to connect the new communities with the rest of the city. They defend this plan by saying that the extension would slice off only a sliver of the petoglyphs: a little more than 8 acres out of a total of 7,244. To the highway's Indian opponents that is like saying that a proposed widening of Fifth Avenue in New York City will lop off only the front of St. Patrick's Cathedral.

"In Albuquerque, major roads stop at golf courses," a Cochiti Indian leader, William Weahkee, told a reporter. "Are those sacred sites to you guys?" He must have known the answer. A proposed alternative to the route had already been dropped, after residents realized it would amputate a few holes from a golf course in the suburb of Paradise Hills.

> *To go into solitude, a man needs to retire as much from his chamber as from society. I am not solitary whilst I read and write, though nobody is with me. But if a man would be alone, let him look at the stars.'*
>
> ◆
>
> —Ralph Waldo Emerson, "Nature"

So now I am a long way from the places where little white Spaldings soar over the bones of Anasazi shamans, farther still from neighborhoods where sociopaths prompted by drug-jangled neurons rape and murder churchwomen. But I am still no closer than I was days ago to connecting the dots between golf and homicide and Indian petroglyphs.

I stoke the fire, flick on my penlight, and begin rereading *A Sand County Almanac*, both because I like it and because it seems a good way to express my gratitude. June 3, 1999, will mark the seventy-fifth anniversary of the creation of the Gila's wilderness areas. If God was their father and Nature their mother, Aldo Leopold was their midwife; he was working for the U.S. Forest Service in the early half of this century, and thanks to his impassioned advocacy, the wild heart of the Gila National Forest was spared from the ax, the chain saw, and the bulldozer.

The opening of his book, published almost 50 years ago, has always struck me for its clarity: "There are some who can live without wild things, and some who cannot. These essays are the delights and dilemmas of one who cannot...Like winds and sunsets, wild things were taken for granted until progress began to do away with them. Now we face the question whether a still higher standard of living is worth its cost in things natural, wild, and free. For us of the minority, the opportunity to see geese is more important than television, and the chance to find a pasqueflower is a right as inalienable as free speech."

The only thing wrong with backpacking solo is that you have to do everything yourself; the chores involved in pitching and striking camp take twice as long. But the brain-cleansing effects of solitude make it worth the effort. It is past ten-thirty before I am on the trail the next morning. The going is pretty easy, but the 60 pounds on my back make my progress less than mercurial: a little less than two miles an hour. Because of the weather, I'm carrying more warm clothes than I'd originally planned, and because Kramer told me the springs up ahead have run dry, I've tanked up on water—a two-quart saddle canteen and two one-quart water bottles.

After an hour, I take a short break, faintly hearing in memory's ear a drill sergeant barking, *Take five, troopers. Lamp is lit. Smoke 'em if you got 'em.* Don't got 'em. Quit 'em, though I have brought five cigars: one for each night. I am looking westward, out across Rocky Canyon, at a landscape of such breadth and beauty that it seems to stretch the ligaments of my soul. The tiered foothills and mountains go from dark green to blue to purple at the horizon, where the Mogollons rise and their highest summit, Mogollon Baldy, is so slabbed with snow that it might be in the Canadian Rockies. In the middle distance, a pair of hawks orbit over a side canyon. They ride the thermal until something is revealed to their keen eyes, and they glide down and away, in a line so perfect it's as if they are sliding down an inclined cable. In 30 seconds they disappear over a ridge that looks to be a mile from where they'd been circling. It would take me half an hour to cover that mile on the ground. Backpacking in rough country revalues the currency of distance, the mile cheapened by the car and rendered almost worthless by the jet plane once more costs something, and so means something.

I set off again. I do not intend to wander aimlessly on this walkabout. My plan is to reach Reeds Peak (now some 6 miles away and another 2,500 feet up), follow the Black Range crest southward, past Mimbres Lake to McKnight Mountain, and then descend to the South Fork of the Mimbres River, tracing that to the main stem of the Mimbres, which will eventually lead me back to the trailhead. Thirty-five to forty miles altogether. Kramer warned me that I might not make it, however: there is deep snow on the crest, and the drifts could be waist-high on the north faces of the slopes below it.

And they almost are, as I discover around noon, when I reach 8,500 feet. I am following fresh elk tracks, in the hopes of photographing the animal, but for the moment my attention is focused on the impressions its hooves have made in the drifts. I try to walk where the prints are only a few inches deep and to avoid those places where the elk's legs have drilled what look like post holes. As the day warms, the frozen crust thaws fast, and several times I plunge to my thighs. It takes an hour to get around the north face of this particular hill and I'm chilled from the thighs down, drenched in sweat from the waist up. I've also worked up a raging thirst and empty one water bottle and half the other. The map says that Aspen Spring is about a mile and a half farther on. Maybe with all the precipitation, it has water in it.

The hike there is easy and exhilarating at first, but the trail then wraps around the north face of another slope and I am again hobbled by snow. Aspen Spring is dry; I am, too, and I drain my second water bottle. It is now two in the afternoon, and I will have to find a decent campsite in an hour or so. At about 9,000 feet, I encounter more deep drifts. Reeds Peak and the western face of the Black Range loom ahead. A brisk wind has risen from the south and the sound it makes as it moves through the pines is sometimes like a waterfall, sometimes like the rush of an approaching train. Scanning the crest with my binoculars, I can see only snow, cascading down the slopes. It looks very cold and forbidding up there and I remember that just last week Kramer and his rangers rescued seven young adventurers who had been trapped in the Gila by a sudden storm. They had run out of food and two were in advanced stages of hypothermia and had to be taken out on packhorses. "That's our best case scenario in search-and-rescue work, a large group of fit young men," Kramer told me, leaving unsaid what was a worst-case scenario: a middle-aged man on his own. I decide to leave my trek along the crest for the future—maybe the fall, when the aspens turn gold.

I camp for two nights in as flat and sheltered a spot as I can find on a ridge overlooking the named and unnamed canyons that lace their way downward into the Mimbres River valley. I gather pine needles, pine cones, and dry grass, cut shavings from a dead stick of gamble's oak, then make a tepee of twigs over the tinder and strike a match. Advocates of minimal impact camping frown on fire making. I carry a backpacker's stove, but mostly for emergencies or for use in places where ground fires are prohibited. I think it's important to know how to make a cooking fire out of what's around rather than relying on a gas bottle. And a backpacker's stove can't keep you warm or provide cheer in the darkness.

At around 8:30 p.m. on my second night at the site while I am thinking about absolutely nothing and savoring my nightly whiskey ration, I hear the most bizarre noise I have ever heard in the wilderness. It is coming from the east near where the land falls steeply into a small canyon: a piercing screech with a pulse as regular as a metronome. With my flashlight, I walk toward it, and it never varies in tone, pitch, or rhythm. Could it be some high-tech signaling device used by lost hikers? "Is someone there?" I call out. "Somebody in trouble out there?" The noise stops. "Hello? Anyone there?" Silence. Ten or twenty seconds later, it starts again. Now I can hear that it's coming from up in a tree somewhere. A bird? I cannot think of a bird capable of making such an absolutely unearthly cry. Some sort of tracking collar?

But tracking collars don't emit sound. A weather balloon that's fallen to earth and is sending a distress signal? But weather balloons are pretty big in the bright moonlight. I would see one if it had fallen this close. How about space aliens? After all, this is New Mexico, land of Roswell. Once more I shout, once more it falls silent. All right to borrow a line from the horror flicks—it's alive! I'm sure of that now. It also flies, because in a few seconds the sound starts coming from the south and from high above. Shrill, insistent, not frightening so much as irritating. At one point, I yell "Shut the hell up!" And it does, but soon resumes and doesn't stop. After a while, I get used to it, so used to it that I actually crawl into my tent and fall asleep to that SCREEP-SCREEP-SCREEP.

In the morning, while I'm melting snow for my morning coffee, I scour the woods, looking for bird droppings. I scan the branches but can't find a clue about the night's strange visitor. Two days later, the biologist for the Gila Wilderness will clear it up for me. I will learn that I had an encounter with a famous endangered species. The screech was the alarm cry of the female spotted owl, and I was what she was alarmed about.

If climbing through the snow to the crest would be too much adventure, backtracking to my truck would be too little. I break out my topo map, orient it, and see that the anonymous canyon below me strikes southeastward and joins another, which in turn tumbles down to meet the Mimbres River. On paper, a trek of about two and a half miles, but figure a good three and a half to four on the ground. And a fairly rugged walk for the first two, judging from the crowded contour lines.

Even in a wilderness following blazed trails dilutes the adventure. The idea of going off-trail, into unnamed canyons, appeals to me. Also, there is sure to be fresh running water in the bottoms—my coffee and breakfast were seasoned with dirt, bark, and bits of leaves embedded in the snow I'd melted. Silencing the memory of the Robert Service poem that Aldo Leopold quotes in his book—"Where nameless men by nameless rivers wander and in strange valleys die strange deaths alone"—I hoist my pack and start on down.

Soon, I hear the rush of water. A clear swift stream, no more than a foot across, descends in a series of rocky steps. I fill my water bottles, drop in some iodine tablets, and while I'm waiting for them to take effect I shoot an azimuth down the length of canyon to make sure I've read the map right. Yes, 120 degrees magnetic. There is a lot of satisfaction in navigating cross country with map and compass. I prefer that to turning everything over to a GPS. For one thing, you never know when the little box of microcircuits will go on the fritz, for another, not knowing where you are right down to the yard creates a certain pleasurable *frisson*.

The canyon is almost a slot canyon, with nearly sheer walls of sedimentary rock—sandstone, mudstone, conglomerate, ash tuff fused by volcanic eruptions and the collapse of calderas 30 million years ago. I am walking on ground perhaps trod by dinosaurs. I haven't seen any humans for three full days, but I've seen signs of them. Down in No-Name Canyon, however, I don't see a single boot print. The only trail is one blazed by elk and bears. The going is tricky, for the canyon falls in rocky ladders, creating tiny cataracts. There are windfalls and deadfalls everywhere, but I can see where the elk and bears have gone around these obstacles. I follow their lead—what the hell, they live here. Several times, I have to do some nontechnical rock-climbing to find a way around narrow gorges. I am very careful. The surtax for a lack of caution or a lapse in attention could be a broken ankle or leg, and I know Ranger Kramer and his rescue team would have a devil of a time finding me here.

An hour and a half later, I reach the junction of No-Name Canyon No. 1 with No-Name No. 2, which is twice as wide. I come across a recent bear dig, 10 feet long by 4 wide by nearly 2 deep. To be on the safe side, I call out "Bear, hey, bear," and make a lot of noise as I walk along. Grizzlies are gone from the Gila, the last one was shot in the 1920s by Ben Lilly, the famous mountain man and hunter. But I am not complacent about black bears; it's a matter of record, I've been told, that they have killed more people than the infamous *Ursus horribilis.*.

Another two hours brings me to the Mimbres, which curves

southwestward, glittering like a brightly jeweled cord. I make good time for the next three miles. Compared to the side canyons, the river valley is a park. White and violet wildflowers are beginning to bloom in the meadows. Far above rise cliffs fissured by eons of rain, sculpted by millenniums of wind into towers and minarets and spires.

Farther downstream, I have to make eight river crossings within a mile—and that slows me down. Tired, I decide to pitch camp in a trail-tramper's Eden: a knoll above the river, with soft, flat ground and plenty of standing and fallen deadwood. I perform the usual chores, wolf down dinner and take up *A Sand County Almanac* while there is light enough to read. The line "Now we face the question whether a still higher standard of living is worth its cost in things natural, wild, and free" leaps out from the page and discloses the common thread in the stories I clipped from the newspapers.

It is growth. The one thing our society does hold sacred is growth. Not intellectual or spiritual growth but economic growth, and not stable, sustainable economic growth but let-'er-rip, boomtown, pave-it-don't-save-it growth. Our grail is an ever higher standard of living that must be sought and grasped at almost any cost: polluted air, a soaring crime rate, a degraded quality of life. But there is this difference between today and Aldo Leopold's day: then, getting and spending was a big part of what we Americans were all about; now, it seems to be *all* that we are about. Our national religion is a kind of evangelical consumerism. We even consume things that aren't really things—we swallow the salt water of information by the gallon while our throats are parched for the springs of wisdom; we consume violence in computer games and on tabloid TV while we gorge on a home-delivered pizza.

Of course, we pay a price for a consumer culture such as ours, a culture that demands its instant gratifications. It isn't paid only in the coinage of rivers drained dry to irrigate golf courses or of sacred petroglyphs bulldozed to make travel more convenient for commuters. Our bodies pay a price: study after study has shown that Americans are more obese now than at any time in history; we are the fattest people on Earth. We pay in lowered quality of our moral lives. Heinous crimes like John Sansing's and Kelly Blake's are not anomalies but signs of our spiritual emptiness, signs that what we have built over the past half-century is not civilization. It may be development, but it's not civilization. It seems that the more we despoil the land and divorce ourselves from the rhythms, cycles, and beauty of the natural world, the less civilized we become.

Well, I am still no Isaac Newton, so am I crazy for making these connections? Hope not. In the past, this country needed a frontier as an outlet for people seeking to build new and better lives for themselves. I wonder, here beside the Mimbres River, if we need more wild places like this one as sanctuaries in which we can restore and renovate our inner lives. I think we would all benefit if more of us spent more time watching geese instead of television; if more of us devoted more time to absorbing the information wild creatures leave instead of filling our brains with the data-babble on the Internet. Woods and rivers can teach us lessons about patience and humility, about the interconnectedness of all living things, about discerning what is important and lasting and what is trivial and transient. Thoreau said that in wilderness lies the salvation of mankind. John Muir, in one of his essays on the California Sierras, wrote that each alpine wildflower was "a mirror reflecting the Creator." Maybe you don't believe in a Creator, so put it like this: through that window we can see the grandeur in all creation, from atoms to galaxies; we can catch at least a transforming glimpse of something bigger than ourselves, something ineffable to remind us that consumption isn't the point of being human.

I have spent four nights in the Gila. Tomorrow, I will hike the remaining four miles to the trailhead, get in my truck, and return to what is commonly called the real world. But I'm not so sure it is.

Philip Caputo, a 1973 Pulitzer Prize winner, is the author of seven books, including A Rumor of War *and, most recently,* Exiles. *He is at work on a new novel.*

＊

This past Tuesday evening my 16-year-old nephew and two friends went out for pizza. They ate at Peter Piper's next to Arrowhead Mall. The store closed and as they made their way through the parking lot, masked gunmen accosted them.

The gunmen apparently mistook them for employees with access to the restaurant. My nephew was promptly shot in the back. Then the boys, with guns pointed at their heads, were forced to lie prone, hands behind their heads, as the robbers demanded something the boys could not give them.

The bullet traveled through my nephew's body and lodged in his neck. Presently, he is in the ICU ward of John C. Lincoln Hospital. Extracting the bullet required an incision that runs 180 degrees around the base of his neck. He cannot speak because there is a breathing tube bisecting his voice box. A boy who I highly doubt has ever tasted beer is now being given large doses of morphine at regular intervals.

The perpetrators are still on the loose. A mere razor's edge of variance in a bullet's random course through a boy's body is all that separates these non-humans from child murderers. They were willing to prey on the innocent in the most innocuous place I can imagine. They were prepared. This was planned. Is this not a community danger worthy of note? Could a well-told story not possibly aid in their capture?

Apparently not, according to the media. I watched Fox 10 at 6 p.m. The lead story was about a cat. A cat. None of the other newscasts mentioned it at 6, but they all found time for the cat. I'm sure the same held true for the later broadcasts, but I cannot be certain—forgive me, I was too disgusted to watch. No story in *The Republic*, either, but you certainly didn't miss the cat (and the obligatory photograph).

Now I've heard that America West Airlines is offering a large cash reward for the cat perpetrators. I guess we should just accept that teenagers being shot at the mall is just a normal part of suburban Phoenix life, nothing very newsworthy about that. But cat torturers, now that's where we draw the line. Let's get those guys!

This is shameful.

—Richard Senatro, Letter to the Editor, *Arizona Republic*

∗ ∗ ∗

Surviving the City
of Angels

If you hear any noise it's just
me and the boys...

MY MORNING BEGAN IN A TIME ZONE IN ANOTHER PLACE. FIVE p.m., L.A. time, I found myself a lone passenger on a bus heading north, cutting through left-over desert littered with metallic trash jutting out of the sand like some recently-forgotten, half-buried treasure. The sun shone on those barren scrap-fields, and they sparkled like a stage of fallen stars.

So much luminous waste can make you start seeing things. I could have sworn that dinosaurs (real live versions of those in the La Brea tar pits) were advancing in a state of frozen motion. I blinked. Turned out it was only the sun setting on cranes at rest.

"Where you from?" asked the bus driver, a guy in his late fifties with a belly which boasted years of taking in the beer. He hadn't spoken before so it took me a moment to come out of myself and respond to him.

"Paris," I finally said, my voice dropping low so he wouldn't get the idea of striking up a conversation with me just because he was bored. Hell, I was tired. What else, after a twelve-, thirteen-hour trip?

"What's it like in Paris? Guess it's a real culture shock going there, huh? Guess there's a lot of parley-vous français and wine-drinking going on in that city. I hear they drink a hell of a lot over there. Don't take baths either from what I've been told. Must be one funky place!"

Going to Paris had never produced a shock to my system. Not even the first time. Villages connected by tunnels serviced by reliable trains (when they aren't on strike). Paris, like many of its inhabitants, is thoroughly modern, utterly sophisticated, and hopelessly provincial. What's so shocking about that?

I told the driver that all his guesses were better than any of mine, chuckling so he wouldn't take offense. After all, I was back in America where a chortle or a smile might mean everything. But knowing I couldn't keep up pretenses, I stuck a pair of lightweight headphones in my ears, and plugged into a Walkman playing Gilberto Gil, from which audio-vantage point I viewed my entry into L.A. as though it were no more than a film of my own making. The bus, meanwhile, moved on, stopping frequently (picking up passengers, letting them off), which broke its momentum the instant it seemed to gain some.

I tried to visualize the end of the road; imagine the moment when I would get off, greet the friend at whose home I would be staying. Settle in for the night. But every time the bus covered some small, obscure distance, a length of road seemed to open up to one of two possibilities: either the trip would go on forever, or I'd never get where I was going alive.

Around 6:15 I found myself a lone passenger again. But only for a moment. The bus stopped. Five boys got on wearing colors which signified they belonged, if only to each other. Not one of them paid.

It occurred to me that the driver might comment on their little oversight, *le genre*: "Back in my day when people got on the bus, they paid their fare. Fare was fair. Know what I mean? Nowadays folks don't believe in nothing but a free ride. People just be assuming that without paying a price they can get somewhere. Now ain't that a hell-of-a-way to look at life!"

But the driver's tongue must have sat thick and stiff in his mouth. He didn't say a word as four of the free-riders swaggered to the rear of the bus, as if by silent command. Silence (I was listening carefully) also commanded that I belonged to the leader, a eighteen-year-old baby with droopy pants and rotten teeth overlaid in gold, who stood looking down at me like a whip-snapping young overseer.

The boy flashed a smile that glimmered like those metal scrap-fields that had deluded me into seeing things that are not. But this was no time to abandon myself to a space in my head where dinosaurs danced with figments of my imagination.

I stared up at this man-child, to whom life had promised so little. Glowing like luminous waste, violence lay low in his eyes, hiding behind the gold-decked smile. I wanted to smile back but my face got stuck, so I averted my eyes.

"Look at him!" I told myself, "and remember where you are for Christ's sake!" You're not in Paris where flirting doesn't necessarily lead to fucking; where titillation is not a prelude to mutilation; where a man might follow you up the subway stairs (walking a careful distance behind you to get a good look up your dress), invite you for coffee when you've both reached the air, then tell you on the way to a café that he's a cameraman and you're like light to his eyes. This is not Paris where, if a man or two do decide to take you on, you can tell them to make their move as long as they are fully aware that one, two, or all three of you are going to end up dead in a struggle over your body. "This is L.A.," I screamed silently to give myself a good, hard mental pinch. "You could get shot in the face for looking at that boy the wrong way!

"So look at him the right way," I whispered inaudibly, "or close your eyes and pray, if you remember how."

So many women have met their deaths kneeling. I looked that boy in the eyes. I looked beyond his eyes. Recognized him. I reached out to touch his hand, knowing, explicitly, that that gesture might save my life. Besides, with his arm extended, an open palm approaching my lap, the boy's hand was already mine for the taking.

I grasped it firmly. And when I did, the boy's fingers wrapped around my knuckles like a steel coil. Locked in his grip, I heard laughter in the back of the bus, bottles crashing to the floor. I no longer felt the bus moving. The bus driver had turned zombie on me. I was on my own, and had played one empty hand. Now the boy would play his.

"What's your name?"

I heard a slurred voice sing out: *I wanna know your name!* A chorus swooned in the background, gurgling and laughter fizzled in my ears. I wanted my hand back. But I waited. I've waited before. I waited for Christmas when I was little. I waited small eternities for RTD buses (L.A.'s rapid transit bus system) once upon a time when I lived in this tropical, edge-city sprawl. I've waited hours to be picked up from airports by family who'd forgotten I had come to town. I've waited for phone calls from lovers, for their on-line names to light up my screen.

I waited for my hand. While I did so I told the boy my name. Three times I repeated it because, like most Americans, he couldn't get it in one go.

"Janine."

"Janey."

"No. Janine"

"Jeannie."

"Ja. Say Ja." He said Ja. "Neene. Like mean. That's what my little brother called me when he was a baby."

He said Neene, then put the two syllables togther. Smiling, he began to rub his stomach with the satisfaction of a man who's just wolfed down a feast. I wasn't complaining. With both hands on his belly, I had my hand back! I shoved it between my legs, though on hindsight, that wasn't the safest place to keep it.

"My name's Capone," the boy told me.

I swallowed hard to stop myself asking this child if that was the name his mother had given him at birth or some label he'd branded himself with in a violent rite of passage. I made sure the only thing he saw me do was shake my head gently in acknowledgment of what he said, the name falling quietly from my lips.

"Janine, where you stay at? I stay over by the Coliseum."

"I live in Paris."

I will never understand the boy's reaction to this piece of information. He left me, walking tall to the back of the bus, his pants riding the tail-end of his narrow butt. I should have kept my head still, which might have signaled that I considered our encounter a thing of a not so distant past. But when someone whets your curiosity it's hard to close anything, even when fear is fuming in your stomach.

My head turned, and I watched as the boy told his friends, "She stay in Paris." He said it with pride. They sat silent for a moment, as if awe-struck, then watched respectfully as Capone made his way back to me like the Lone Ranger staking out a claim.

There his hand was again, this time reaching for my face. I grabbed it, like I might take hold of a baby's foot, before it could connect with my skin.

"You got some pretty eyes. Anybody ever tell you that?"

He started grinning and teasing me.

"Come on now, they tell you that all the time, don't they?"

I laughed and told him the truth: "Not all the time."

After a moment of silence (he was thinking, rubbing his chin) he asked: "You wanna go with me?"

Now when boys and men tag after you on busy sidewalks speaking nonsense to you and every other female between the ages of 8 and 50, ridiculous things like, *Baby can I come?*, you usually laugh, shake your head (as if in pity) and continue on your way. Or you might ask them in play, "I don't know, can you?" But this boy wasn't playing. His proposition was about as serious as the heart attack I could have had that very moment.

What in the world, I wondered, did this boy see in my face that would have him believe that I would even consider accompanying him and four other drunken boys to some place unknown to me, near the Coliseum? It should have been a joke. He wasn't laughing. Surely this was one of those moments I had to stop and consider who I might be from the world's point of view.

The boy stood there looking down at me, patient. He didn't seem to mind my silent deliberation. He even dropped my hand, as if to say, "Here, take as much of yourself as you need while you make up your mind."

My mind wasn't the problem. You've got to be careful how you say 'no' to a man, even one you think you know. How many times had I had to learn that lesson?

I decided that I couldn't. I couldn't tell Capone no.

"I'm thirty-three years old," I told Capone, thinking that might dissuade him. Tell a 40-year-old man you're thirty-three and the fantasy he fancied will evaporate like a late morning dream. But it turns out there's all the difference in the world between a man who needs to suck the youth from a young woman to bolster his own flagging mast and a man-child who's still strong enough to suck and be sucked all on his own juice. Capone all but laughed in my face.

"Thirty-three! Baby, that ain't nothing but a number to me!"

Good thing I have a sense of humor. Our moment of mutual joy bought me some time. A few moments later I served him another line, a true one for what it's worth.

"I can't go with you Capone. I'm going to have an operation the day after tomorrow. That's why I've returned to L.A."

I don't know what I expected Capone's reaction to be. For all I knew he had banged a few bodies deathside in his time. Why should the state of my health mean anything to him?

The grin dropped out of Capone's face. His eyes lost a layer of glaze, making him actually appear sober for a second or so. He extended his arm, reaching neither for my lap nor my face. Touching me lightly on the shoulder he said, as though speaking to a distant cousin (which I may well be) "You take care of yourself, you hear?" A twinge of something southern softened his voice. Probably came from Texas, as a little boy; his family in search of a better life.

"Thanks," I said.

I stared into the boy's face for the last time. Some doors don't shut on their own. You have to help them along, gently. I had to recognize him once more, let him know I did indeed catch sight of *him* behind Capone's golden grin. I sought to speak to the ghost-writer before the boy named Capone changed his mind.

"Thank you."

Capone made his way to the rear, his strut deliberately slow, lazy, and crooked. (Odd how a person can gain strength from pretending to be a cripple.) I knew he had to be grinning. Capone had resumed his role. Man has a tendency to survive.

About fifteen minutes later I got off the bus, still *kicking it*, as Capone might have said. Heading down an isolated sidewalk, which ran alongside an abandoned tract, I felt that bus in my back, standing there, the doors probably wide open, like the gates to heaven. Only when I heard the bus pull away did I feel my legs come back to me, as I stumbled around in that lamp-lit dusk breathing breathing breathing that gorgeous, polluted, L.A. air.

And while echoes of drunken laughter and clanging bottles rang in my ears I couldn't help but wonder: Here, in this City of Angels, how many invisible souls remain locked inside the bodies of boys with names like "Capone" merely as a means of staying alive?

Janine Jones grew up a military brat. so there is no place she really calls home, except where she happens to be living. She received a Ph.D. in philosophy from UCLA; lived, on and off, for ten years in France; and traveled throughout Europe. She is now living in Brooklyn, New York, where she makes a virtual living working for a global company located in Emeryville, California.

★

Strange thoughts, in the dead of night: America is a virus, invading my soul, destroying my Britishness, my faith in humanity, my quiet calm and natural reserve.

—Alexander Stuart, *Life on Mars*

PART FIVE

THE LAST WORD

JONATHAN RABAN

Always Arriving

By sea, he approaches the
land of the possible.

THE CITY WAS HIDING BEHIND THE LOW HILLS OF BROOKLYN AND
the thick weather—a distant glow of ruddy smoke, like a forest fire
in another county. It took an age to reach the Verrazano Bridge
and enter the Narrows, from where New York was suddenly on
top of us. Manhattan was a dozen glittering sticks of light, through
which livid storm clouds were rolling, lit from below, sooty orange
in color, as they swirled past the middle and upper stories of the
buildings. The choppy sea in the harbor was like a lake of troubled
mercury, and the water glared so fiercely that it was almost impossible to find the tiny red and green sparks of the buoys marking the
deepwater channel. Then one's eye adjusted and the city's famous
icons began to emerge from the general dazzle of things. *There* was
Brooklyn Bridge, a sweeping curve of white lights to the north;
there, on her rock, was Liberty, weirdly floodlit in leprechaun
green. Manhattan's freakish height and narrowness, rising in front
of the low dark industrial sprawl of the Jersey shore, defied gravity, proportion, nature. It was brazen in its disdain for the ordinary
limits of human enterprise. I watched the storm and the city bat-
tling it out, high in the sky. For a few moments, the sailing clouds
exposed a large, low moon. It was drifting over the boroughs like

a huge corroded gilt medallion. Given the air of high melodrama in the surrounding landscape, I would have been only mildly surprised to see the moon come crashing out of heaven and set the whole of Queens on fire.

If the moon had crashed, the event would not have much interested the crew of the *Conveyor*, who were otherwise engaged, getting ropes out to tugs and talking into radios. With his back firmly turned on the brilliant scene to starboard, Captain Jackson was saying, "You see, you have to keep an eye on the set of the tide in the Kill Van Kull; it's very narrow there, and there are some nasty shallow patches…"

I tried to think about the set of the tide in the Kill Van Kull, but it was no match against the scowling splendor of the illuminated city in the storm, the racing clouds, the hideous light in which Liberty was bathed, the exaggerated sense of occasion that this moment must always have inspired. The immigrants, crowding against each other's backs, shoving and straining, must have felt that all the reports and letters home had understated the awful truth about New York. The real thing was even taller and more intimidating than the tallest story. So you looked out, numbed by the gigantism of the city, asking the immigrant's single overriding question: is there really a place *there*, for *me*?

With tugs attached to the bows and stern, the *Conveyor* rounded the corner of Staten Island and nosed her way slowly into the tricky canal of the Kill Van Kull. The darkness was turning to gray now, and Manhattan began to dissolve into the clouds astern of us, as if it had just been one of those vividly awful things you see on a disturbed night. We docked, in the dead light of dawn, at a container terminal that looked like nowhere at all.

After breakfast, the ship's New York agent volunteered to drive me to Newark Airport, from where I could catch a bus to the city, and we drove through a landscape that only a guard dog could have looked at with any pleasure or anticipation. There were several miles of wire mesh, concrete, sheds, containers, dumps. The place, if it could properly be called a place, was a storage and service area for New York. Everything the city didn't want, or didn't want yet, or was just about to run out of, landed up here, where it lay about in mounds and piles and crates and tins. It was a glutton's backyard, on an epic scale. As evidence of Manhattan's insatiable appetites, it was impressive. Here came the fleets of ships, trucks and cargo planes that were needed to keep the city fed and entertained. To these heaps of packaged consumables, the *Conveyor* was now adding its minuscule contribution.

The airport was quiet, the bus stop deserted. I waited with my bags, feeling marooned and short of sleep. I missed the easy community of the ship and the imminence of New York felt oppressive.

"Hey! You want the bus? I sell the ticket—" The man was light on his feet, his walk close to a dance step. He looked as if he was wearing a fatter man's clothes, and his black pant-legs flapped thinly round his knees. I suspected that he was working some kind of minor scam, but the ticket looked official.

"Where you from?"

I explained my eccentric way of getting from London to Newark Airport, and he shook my hand up and down, beaming ferociously.

"I am…Sam Zokar." He said it importantly, as if it ought to ring a bell. It didn't. "From Liberia."

He'd been in America for three months. He was staying in Newark. He was alive with the springy hopefulness of the greenhorn. "This," he said, waving his wad of bus tickets, "is, for me, just *tempo*-rary."

He laid his plans out for me. Everyone was going places today, so Sam Zokar was going to get into the travel business. There were a few things to sort out, but pretty soon he was going to have his own agency, right here in Newark.

"Start small, right? But then you got to *expand*. Move out to Manhattan…maybe a chain…"

In seconds, Zokar Travel grew from a single room over a derelict grocery in downtown Newark to a corporate giant with branches scattered over the subcontinent.

"Don't have no business card right yet, but if you have a piece of paper on you…?" He wrote out his name in careful block capitals, with a Newark phone number. "Just ask for Sam. They'll know. Soon, I get Telex. Next time you need a plane flight, call that number—maybe then I'm in business already."

When the bus arrived, he loaded my bags into the hold, and as it was about to move off he stuck his head through the door and shouted, "Hey, John! Give me that call, right? You never know!"

I watched him dancing back into the shelter of the airport terminal. He was on air, fired up with the sense of his own boundlessness. Like the other immigrants whose ghostly company I'd been keeping, he had discovered the world's capital of *maybe* and *you never know*.

Jonathan Raban also contributed "The Minnesota State Fair" in Part Two. This story was excerpted from his book, Hunting Mister Heartbreak: A Discovery of America.

WHAT YOU NEED TO KNOW

*W*HEN TO GO/WEATHER

The climate of the United States is as diverse as the country itself, and as a result, we do not subscribe to the idea that there is one fixed tourist season. Thus, your destination determines the time of visit. For example, if you want to observe the breathtaking fall foliage of the Berkshires in the northeast USA, you want to arrive during the months of September and October. If you love rain and can't get enough of it, then you should visit San Francisco and Seattle in winter. But if you prefer snow and ice and skiing, then you may want to check out the slopes in Vermont or Colorado.

If your desire is simply to wander around as much of America as possible, then the best time is summertime when weather does not close down airports or highways (although rain, thunderstorms, and hurricanes may cause some delay). But summer time also is when Americans go on vacation and highways, hotels/motels, airports, parks, museums, and other tourist attractions are crowded and the prices tend to be higher.

*V*ISAS

Citizens of most European countries, Australia, and New Zealand require only a valid passport to enter the USA for 90 days. They must also have enough money to support themselves during their stay.

Citizens of other nations must check with the local American embassy or consulate about obtaining a visa. Besides a valid passport, minimum requirements often are a round-trip air ticket, enough money to make the visit possible, or a letter and various official documents (e.g. a bank statement) if the visit is being funded by a friend or a relative in the U.S.

A Note of Caution: Before the fall of the Evil Empire, Communists, leftists, or their sympathizers were also denied entry into the land of the free and the brave. Some notables who could not visit the Statue of Liberty in person included the British author Graham Greene, the Nobel Laureate Gabriel García Márquez, and the Canadian writer Farley Mowatt (see below for more about Canadians).

As for Canadians, often they do not even need a passport when visiting their southern neighbors. A photo i.d. will do fine, thank you. But like all other "alien" visitors, Canadians too may not work legally in the U.S., a rather surprising piece of legislation when we realize (with a shock!) that some of the most well-known Americans are actually Canadians! (Such as Peter Jennings and Dan Akroyd.)

You may be denied a visa or entry into the United States if you declare yourself to be HIV-positive, have AIDS or TB—and if you are poor.

𝒞USTOMS AND ARRIVAL

If you are over 21, you are allowed to bring 1-liter bottle of alcohol; if you are over 17, you can bring 200 cigarettes and 100 cigars (but not Cuban), and $100 worth of gifts.

Declare at Customs if you plan to bring in or take out more than $10,000.

The customs officers will also want to know if you are bringing in any fruits, vegetables, seeds, cooked meat, or exotic plants and animals. All these are forbidden and you must notify the Customs people. If you try to smuggle any of these items (as a special surprise gift to your American friend or cousin who is sponsoring you), you will be fined and perhaps even jailed. So get rid of that smelly durian, the moldy cheese, baby python, or special herb before the full weight of the United States Department of Justice bears down upon you.

Getting into the City

Visitors can enter the country at major metropolitan centers through-out the land. Some of the busiest and most important places of arrival are New York City, Chicago, and Los Angeles.

The **New York** metropolitan area is served by three international air-ports, John F. Kennedy (JFK), La Guardia, and Newark International which is actually located in Newark, New Jersey.

From both JFK and La Guardia airports, you can get into mid-town Manhattan by bus or a combination of bus-and-subway. The latter combination costs under two dollars but travel time is longer (over an hour) because of bus-and-subway connections.

Both airports are serviced by the Carey Bus Service and costs $13 from JFK and $10 from La Guardia into mid-Manhattan where you are dropped off at the Port Authority Bus Terminal or Grand Central Station. The bus service runs from 6 a.m. to midnight and takes be-tween 45 minutes to an hour.

From Newark International Airport, it's a 40-minute ride to Manhattan on Olympia Trails buses. It costs $10 and buses stop at the Grand Central Station, World Trade Center, and Penn Station. A cheaper alternative (under $4.00) is the New Jersey Transit buses which will drop you at the Port Authority Terminal.

You can also hire cars, mini-vans, and metered taxis from each of these airports. Taxi fares range approximately from $25–35 (insist on the meter being on, just as if you were in Delhi or Bangkok). Mini-vans and cars will cost around $15–20, depending upon the airport and your destination in New York City.

O'Hare International Airport in **Chicago** is seventeen miles from the city center and your choices are bus, train, or taxi. The Blue Line Rapid Train is the cheapest at $1.50 and runs twenty-four hours. The train station is under Terminal 4; it's a 40 minute ride into the city. The Continental Air Transport stops at most first-class hotels. One-way fare is $15.50 and operates from 6 a.m. to 11:30 p.m. Taxis cost between $25–30, or you can share a ride at $15 per person. Because of the traffic, the ride between the airport and downtown Chicago can sometimes take almost two hours; normally it should take one hour.

The Los Angeles International Airport, better known simply as LAX, is fifteen miles southwest of downtown **Los Angeles**. The cheap but long way to get there is to take the free 24-hour shuttle bus to the Los Angeles Transit Center where you transfer to a local bus to your destination. Various door-to-door minibuses will cost you $20 and upwards, depending upon where you get off—is it Hollywood ($30, plus tip, naturally) or Disneyland (as much as $90!). Metered taxis start around $25 (Santa Monica) and upwards; for example, $30 to Beverly Hills. Depending upon traffic, it will take at least a half hour to get downtown.

No matter at which international airport you arrive in America, rest assured that if you ask (for information), you will receive. Often you will receive more information than you can handle. Maps, brochures, and other paper products will be given to you for free.

America also is a land where laws are normally observed. So do not think of bargaining when a minibus driver says it will cost you $25 to get to your hotel. And if you feel you are being cheated, there are legitimate avenues of complaint. Or decline the services offered and try another bus service or a taxi. Remember, you are now in the land of choices, of freedom, of many, many individual rights and very few responsibilities or obligations.

If you are arriving overland, either at the Canadian or Mexican border, the customs procedures may be fairly short and painless—or long and tortuous, making you wish you had never heard of these United States of America.

A word of warning: Keep your bags by your side all the time. Do not leave them unattended. If airport thieves don't run off with them, the security people will. Every unattended bag is considered a potential bomb!

*H*EALTH

When Americans go abroad, one of their biggest concerns is, "Can you drink the water?" You may find asking yourself the same question, especially in a hip, urban setting where you may notice many people, young and old, drinking from large and small plastic bottles. And these people will tell you, fiercely to put the fear of God in you, that "No! You cannot drink the tap water in this country anymore!" Ignore these people. These are the same kind of people who will also inform you that you will drop dead before 40, or worse, become ugly, fat, and stupid if you don't jog or join an expensive health club where you pay to sweat. Now simply turn the tap water and drink long and deep to quench your thirst. Do not be surprised the next morning if you still feel healthy and energetic.

Unless you come from a country, or stopped over in one, where dreaded diseases such as cholera, malaria, yellow or dengue fever are a fact of daily life, you do not need inoculations to enter America.

Availability of certain drugs are also restricted. What you have been able to get at your neighborhood pharmacy in your country may require a doctor's prescription. So if you take medications, (e.g., for blood pressure or cholesterol), you must find an American doctor who can prescribe them for you. Or bring extra enough to last during your stay.

To avoid or battle major and minor health hazards, we have listed below **Some Helpful Tips:**

- See a doctor and dentist prior to departure for general health checkups.
- If necessary, record all current immunizations on your yellow International Health Certificate and carry it with you.
- If you wear prescription glasses, bring an extra pair.
- Rehydrate, rehydrate, rehydrate.
- It's a good idea to take a medical kit which includes: aspirin or aceta-minophen, antihistamine, antibiotics, Lomotil or Imodium for diar-

rhea, rehydration mixture, antiseptic such as iodine or Betadine, Calamine lotion, bandages, bandaids, tweezers, scissors, thermometer, cold and flu tablets, insect repellent, sunscreen, chapstick, water purification tablets, and possibly even sterile syringes with needles, dressings, and gloves.

- Also consider taking a travel kit of basic homeopathic remedies and a homeopathic first aid book. Such remedies can provide rapid relief from common travel ailments including gastrointestinal problems, fevers, and many acute conditions.

Notes on Personal Safety

- Anyone who is familiar with American media receives the impression that Americans are not too far removed from the days of the Wild West when guys with guns took care of business, both private and public. While American media, like media everywhere, exaggerate and distort, there is a core of truth in these reports. Compared to many countries and cultures, America, especially urban America, does appear to be constantly plagued by violence of all sorts (and as an antidote, a bumper sticker you may see on cars: "Practice Acts of Random Kindness and Senseless Beauty").

- To avoid being a victim, use your common sense as you would when traveling anywhere else. Don't be poring over maps and guidebooks at street corners; avoid wandering, especially alone, in dimly-lit streets or dark alleys; even if that's where the "real" bars and clubs are; don't leave valuables in your hotel room; don't go off jogging or walking very early in the morning until you have familiarized yourself with the neighborhood.

- Finally, mugging is a very familiar word among Americans. It means someone pointed a gun, a knife, or some other lethal object and demanded your money and valuables. It can happen anywhere, anytime. Do not think that because you are in a "nice" neighborhood or an exclusive shopping area it will not happen. People can follow you to your expensive hotel room, confront you in a city park or even when you are in your car (known as carjacking). Do not argue or resist. Do what you are told and hope that you will be able to report it to the police later.

♦ In case of emergency, medical or otherwise, and if a phone is nearby, dial 911 immediately or ask someone to do so.

Travel Insurance and Assistance

Unlike Britain, Canada, and some European nations, there is no national health service in America. Consequently, health care is very expensive. We recommend that you buy an insurance policy to cover any health problems that might occur during your trip. Several companies in the U.S. and Europe provide emergency medical assistance for travelers worldwide, including 24-hour help lines. Travel agents and tour companies can recommend policies that can work for you.

 IME ————————————————————————

The USA is wide rather than narrow, and spans four time zones plus one more for Alaska and Hawaii. The four time zones are Eastern, Central, Mountain, and Pacific. There is a three-hour difference between Eastern and Pacific time zones. Thus, when it is noon in New York (Eastern time), it is 9 a.m. in San Francisco (Pacific time), 8 a.m. in Alaska, and 7 a.m. in Hawaii, which is five hours behind the Eastern time zone.

Greenwich Mean Time (GMT) is five hours ahead of **Eastern** time zone. Thus, when it is noon in New York, it is:

9 a.m. in San Francisco
5 p.m. in London
6 p.m. in Paris
1 a.m. the following day in Hong Kong
2 a.m. the following day in Tokyo
3 a.m. the following day in Sydney

 USINESS HOURS ————————————————————

Operating hours vary from place to place but generally speaking, government and private offices, stores, post office and banks open

Monday–Friday from 9 a.m. to 5 p.m. Some private companies may open as early as at 8 or 8:30 a.m. and close at 6 p.m. Many banks and post office are open Saturdays from 9 a.m. to noon. While Saturday and Sunday are the official days of rest, many stores, especially large department stores, stay open throughout the weekend and late into the evening, since many Americans shop not to fulfill a need but to satiate various wants and desires. An urgent American expression you will certainly encounter is "Shop till you drop."

𝓜ONEY

By now, even a reclusive monk in a Himalayan cave has been made aware of the America dollar. It requires 100 cents to make 1 dollar. Coins come in six denominations:

1 cent (copper, known as a "penny")
5 cents (a silver "nickel")
10 cents (a silver "dime")
25 cents (a silver "quarter")
50 cents (a silver "half dollar")
and that seldom-seen "Susan B. Anthony" dollar coin.

Paper money comes in denominations of 1, 5, 10, 20, 50, and 100. You may occasionally come across a two dollar bill too. Paper money is also know as a "buck"; thus, a can of coke in a store could cost you a "buck," meaning one dollar, and a pair of blue jeans 25 "bucks."

It is very easy to travel in America with very little cash on you because you can use credit cards and travelers' checks for most of your needs—from paying hotel bills to renting cars to shopping. Automatic Teller Machines (ATMs) are scattered throughout cities and towns (in airports, banks, and grocery stores) to enable you to get cash using your credit or bank cards. (Remember to note or memorize your PIN number.)

Travelers' checks are accepted almost everywhere—banks, hotels, restaurants, stores, etc., and are a safer method of carrying your money.

*E*LECTRICITY

Power runs on 110–120 volts AC, 60 cycles. If you come from a country that uses 220–250 volts AC, 50 cycles, bring your own adapter with two flat vertical plugs because converters that change from 220 to 110 are difficult to find here.

*M*EDIA: NEWSPAPERS, RADIO, TELEVISION

America is awash in information, and many Americans erroneously equate information with truth, if not also wisdom. There are probably more newspapers, magazines, and television stations in the USA than any other nation. Besides internationally-recognized media outlets (*The New York Times, Newsweek,* CNN, etc.), Americans crank out newsletters, pamphlets, and broadsheets devoted to any and every interest a human being might have, no matter how quirky or questionable. Drop into a bookstore and look at the magazine racks. The arrival of multimedia and mushrooming of web sites has only added to this information overload. If you find yourself in a tiny settlement in the middle of nowhere, you can bet your bottom dollar that it has a local newspaper, and it will want to interview you, a foreigner from a faraway land. Don't be shy. Go for your fifteen minutes of fame!

*T*OUCHING BASE: PHONE, FAX, POSTAGE, EMAIL

Communication is simple, easy, very reliable and not very expensive. You can use the post office to mail letters or parcels to anywhere in the world. Americans heap tons of abuse upon their postal system simply because a letter arrived in seven days instead of four. If you want your package or letter to arrive faster, you can contact private companies such as Federal Express, UPS, or DHL that promise delivery within the USA in 24 hours. Worldwide delivery takes a little longer.

Local telephone calls made from a public phone booth cost a minimum of 25 cents. If you are calling beyond your immediate area, you dial "1", the three digit area code, and then seven digit numbers. Dial 411 for the local operator.

𝒯HE NEXT STEP

Many businesses such as hotels, car rentals, airline offices, government departments, travel agencies, etc. have toll-free numbers, so you can call them for free. These numbers usually begin with 800 or 888. Call 1-800-555-1212 to get the toll-free number of the company you want to contact.

If your credit card cannot be used to make phone calls, buy a phone card. These can be purchased at airports, post offices, many supermarkets, and other convenience outlets. To make international calls, dial 011 first, followed by your country and city codes, and then your home number. To contact the international operator, dial 00. You can make international calls from most public phones.

And don't forget fax and e-mail. Many photocopying stores have fax and even e-mail facilities, not to mention the many cybercafes that have opened in hip, cool cities such as San Francisco.

Courtesy Alert! Do not call your far-away home when you are staying with American friends (or relatives). You may never hear from or see them again after they get their phone bill! Always ask your host's permission before using the phone.

CULTURAL CONSIDERATIONS

𝓛OCAL CUSTOMS: DOS AND DON'TS ───────────

America is well-known for its equality, liberty, fraternity. Everyone is very friendly and informal. Children often call their parents by their first names and at work, subordinates do not normally use "Mister" when addressing their supervisors. To those visitors who come from a more rigid and stratified society, such casualness can be confusing, leading to egregious blunders. Conversely, many worldly, sophisticated Americans appear mortified because they feel America is not "civilized," with a capital "C." However, we know of—and have experienced—terribly embarrassing incidents from

mistakes which only an innocent foreigner would have made. Listed below are some tips which will help you avoid making the foreigner's faux pas:

- Americans shake hands when introduced for the first time. "Hi" and "hello" are the informal greetings. Some greet old friends and family members with a hug and a kiss, especially when saying good-bye. If your guests feel they have made a deep "connection" with you the first time around, you too will be embraced and perhaps pecked on the cheek.

- Public displays of affection between the sexes are very common, unlike perhaps where you have come from. In many cities, especially San Francisco, homosexuality is an accepted way of life. You may therefore see men being affectionate with men and women with women. If you disapprove of homosexuals (also known as gays) because of your religious or cultural beliefs, please keep it to yourself. You might even find yourself a guest in a gay person's home—and might become shocked to realize that your host is a normal human being like any other and that you are actually enjoying his hospitality. Many couples also live together without being married—and may never marry. But you must realize their bond is probably as strong as the bond of marriage. So don't think one of them is available for a "date."

- America is a notoriously "open" society, and to most foreigners Americans often appear exceptionally and "instantly" friendly. But sometimes such openness can lead to serious misunderstanding, especially between men and women. A casual invitation to have drinks and/or dinner does not mean that your American host also wants to become "intimate" with you afterwards. So be careful not to read too much into a friendly invitation. Just prepare yourself to "go with the flow," as Americans are fond of saying.

- Perhaps more than any nation in the world, the relationship between men and women in America is becoming more equal, and therefore more complex. Each demands and expects a lot from the other, especially when it comes to sharing household and family responsibilities. Your opinions and attitudes will be openly challenged if you still hold the old-fashioned notion that women should still remain uneducated, barefoot, pregnant, and in the kitchen. Thus, do not expect to be served, especially by women. If you are a dinner guest, ask if you can help—and do not flinch in shock if you are asked to set the table or help clear the dishes after dinner. If you are a long-term guest (a visiting scholar, an exchange student), you might even be asked to wash the dirty dishes, do the laundry and other household chores.

- Try not to burp and slurp when eating. Whereas in some cultures a long-drawn belch indicates that the guest enjoyed the meal enormously, in America you stifle it, or cover your mouth as the belch surfaces despite your best effort.

- Americans love compliments. Let them know if you like their homes, clothes, cars. A simple statement such as "Nice jacket, you look cool!" will make your host smile for the rest of the day and night.

- Despite indications to the contrary, the majority of Americans are very polite. They say "thank you" and "excuse me" and "please" and such all the time. These simple words are much appreciated. Utter them like a mantra. Much merit will be gained right here on earth.

- Americans usually go "Dutch" when they are out with friends for food and drinks. You are expected to pay your share even though you have been invited by someone else. When the check arrives, do not stare at the ceiling and pick your teeth, but reach for your wallet.

- In stark contrast to their openness, Americans are actually very private when it comes to their "personal space." What this means is that you can't just barge into their room (which will be probably closed anyway) without first knocking.

- Do not pry into personal affairs, such as their salary or even marital status.

- A word about pets. Many Americans love and cherish their dogs, cats, birds, and even more exotic animals such as a snake or a rat. Many foreigners have observed that Americans appear to love their pets more than even their own family members. A slight exaggeration, perhaps, but do understand that Americans are very close to their pets and do not appreciate flippant remarks about them. In this situation, observe the rule that if you have nothing nice to say, don't.

- Americans are punctual and expect you to be the same, especially if it is a business appointment. While you may get away with arriving at 2:15 for a 2 p.m. appointment, you will find yourself alone if you arrive at 3 p.m. So remember, *be on time.*
- If you realize you've made a mistake or offended someone inadvertently just say, "I'm sorry."
- Those who smoke cigarettes, cigars, or pipes are in big trouble. All internal flights within the United States ban smoking. There are very few places left where you can smoke in peace, and that is mostly outside on the sidewalk or some smoky bar in an obscure town. Even in private homes, you may be asked to smoke outside. The reason most Americans jog, join a gym, or become a vegetarian is they want to be healthy. So smoking is out.
- Curb your habit of spitting indiscriminately.

EVENTS & HOLIDAYS

Since America is a relatively new nation, there aren't as many festivals, especially the religious kind, one encounters in older cultures and nations. This has usually been made up for by having music festivals, art and craft fairs, Hog- or Husband-Calling competitions. But assertive multiculturism and diversity are loosening the grim workaholism of Puritan America. As a result, holidays and festivals in America are increasingly reflecting—and celebrating—the multi-ethnic heritage of immigrant America. Nowadays, most Americans are equally eager to let it all hang out during the excess of a Latin-and-Caribbean-influenced Carnaval as well as reflect quietly upon race relations in contemporary America while observing Martin Luther King, Jr. Day. Another indication that Americans want more play and less work is their habit of shuffling holiday dates around so that they can have a three-day weekend instead of the standard Saturday and Sunday. Many holidays are officially observed on Mondays to accommodate this desire, a sure sign of the decline and eventual fall of the treasured American Work Ethic.

Some Important Events and Holidays celebrated in America are:

January

January 1 is **New Year's Day**. One of those rare days in America when **almost** everything shuts down. Most are recovering from a hangover of the night before, celebrating New Year's Eve. Some have been partying since Christmas Eve (see December), and everyone knows after New Year's Day is over, it's back to the grind of work, and the prospect of becoming a year older. The human spirit is somber, the streets and bars cold and deserted, as inviting as a tomb.

January 8 is the day to put on your "blue suede shoes" and howl like a "hound dog." Music lovers, you will want to be at Graceland in Memphis to celebrate the birthday of the one and only **Elvis Presley** (who may show up unannounced).

January 19 is **Martin Luther King Jr.'s Birthday.** An important day to reflect upon the actions of the pre-eminent civil rights leader of African Americans. On the third Monday in January, Martin Luther King's electrifying speech "I have a dream…" is recited on the steps of the Lincoln Memorial in Washington, D.C.

In Atlanta, a whole week is devoted to commemorate Martin Luther King's life. Speeches, music, parades, seminars. Be There!

February

February 14 is **Valentines Day.** Originally observed in honor of a 3rd century martyr. Modern times celebration of this day includes sending cards (known as valentines), chocolates, and/or flowers to sweethearts, spouses, schoolmates.

February 16 is **President's Day.** A national holiday when government offices and banks are closed. This day was originally meant to honor George Washington, America's first president and now also honors Abraham Lincoln, the 16th president. The day is celebrated with colonial costume dinners and balls in Alexandria, Virginia. Revolutionary battles are re-enacted with period costumes and blank bullets. Parades occur in some cities to rouse the patriotic spirit. Department stores will have huge "President's Day Sales."

Mardi Gras in New Orleans. Also known as fat Tuesday or Shrove Tuesday, the last day before Lent. The date varies depending on when Lent occurs each year. Like Rio, New Orleans has a week-long Carnaval around the Mardi Gras period. While most events taking place indoors, such as the balls, may be by invitation only, sold out, or horribly expensive, the street festivities and parades are free, and that's where the real action is anyway—on the streets. If colorful costumes that reveal rather than clothe bodies and drinking and dancing offend you, get thee to a nunnery.

Perhaps your taste is more Oriental. Head west to San Francisco and celebrate the **Chinese New Year Festival and Parade.** This is probably America's largest Chinese celebration. This festival occurs annually between February and April, based on the Chinese lunar calendar. Besides the usual food and street fair, do not miss the parade in the evening with dragons and lion dancing. Bring warm clothes and a raincoat, just in case.

March

March 17 is **St. Patrick's Day**. A day when many people drink **green beer** for the first and probably only time in their lives. Parades are staged in cities such as New York, Boston, and other heavily Irish-populated areas. The best place to be is any Irish bar. You will cry, you will laugh, you will sing, you will embrace total strangers—and you will drink green beer. Old-fashioned restaurants will serve the evening's special—corn beef with boiled potatoes and cabbage—at a discount price.

Several weeks in late March/early April are also set aside for **Spring Break** for college students. The beach towns of Florida such as Fort Lauderdale or Miami Beach are especially notorious for this event which highlights wet t-shirt and bikini contests, informal beer guzzling competitions, and the usual naughty events that take place when young men and women gather without chaperones.

April

Easter occurs on the first Sunday after the date of the first full moon that occurs on or after March 21. This is a Christian holiday celebrating the resurrection of Jesus. Religious ceremonies vary from community to community. The President of the United States invites 3–6 year-old children onto the White House lawn to hunt for Easter eggs. Easter parades are held in some towns and cities such as New York on Easter morning.

A week after Easter, head for **Hawaii** where the **Merrie Monarch Hula Festival** takes place in Hilo—three nights of ancient and modern Hawaiian dance competition.

May

May 5th is **Cinco de Mayo.** The day when cities with large Hispanic populations such as Los Angeles, Miami, San Antonio, and San Francisco recall the Mexican victory over the French in 1862. There are parades in colorful costumes, dancing, music, food and other expressions of Hispanic pride.

This fair often coincides with **Memorial Day.** This holiday occurs on the l**ast Monday in May** and is celebrated over the preceding weekend. This time is spent honoring the dead servicemen of all wars. Special ceremonies in Washington, D.C. and national cemeteries, as well as parades throughout the country.

June

The legendary **Chicago Blues Festival** takes place on the **second weekend of June**, followed by the **Gospel Festival** the next weekend. Both events take place at **Petrillo Music Shell** in **Grant Park, Chicago.**

July

Independence Day, July 4th, the day the United States exuberantly celebrates its freedom from British colonial bondage, with

parades in almost every village, town, and city. Free concerts, exhibits and special events everywhere. Fireworks in the evening! The place to be is **Philadelphia,** where the independence was proclaimed in 1776 and the "Declaration of Independence" is read as part of the festivities.

August

Music lovers gather at **Fort Adams State Park** in **Newport, Rhode Island,** usually held the first weekend in August, to hear some of the best jazz and folk musicians during the **Newport Jazz and Folk Festival** (also know as The Ben & Jerry's Folk Festival-Newport). Stick around for the following weekend to enjoy more of the same great music at the JVC Jazz Festival-Newport.

September

The **first Monday in September** is **Labor Day.** Summer vacation is over. Parents are grateful that school is open again. It is also the day to honor the workers of America and their labor which has made the American Way of Life the envy of the rest of the world.

Meanwhile, the state of **Hawaii** celebrates its own culture and tradition by holding **Aloha Festivals**. Time to do the hula.

October

In certain politically correct cities such as **Berkeley, California,** the **second Monday in October** is declared as **Indigenous Peoples Day** whereas the rest of America is honoring **Christopher Columbus**, an Italian who "discovered" America. Thus on **Columbus Day** certain people will be reminding others that this was the beginning and end of "Indians" or "Native Americans." Others will be doing the usual activities of a three-day weekend: going away somewhere quiet to fish, hike, or visit friends and possibly have the last barbecue before snow, ice, rain, cold and wind will force life indoors.

October 31 is **Halloween** or All Hallow's Eve. A celebration that includes masquerade and merry-making. Children dress up in costume and go door-to-door in their neighborhoods trick-or-treating (asking for sugared treats).

November

America has sent its sons and daughters to fight in wars all over the world, both for just and unjust causes. **November 11** is know as **Veterans Day** to honor these brave men and women who gave their lives when the nation called upon them to do their duty. It is a somber sight to observe young and old war veterans, especially those in wheelchairs, marching down avenues and boulevards.

Perhaps the least commercial holiday in America is **Thanksgiving Day,** celebrated on the fourth Thursday of the month. It commemorates the event when the first immigrants broke bread with the Native Americans, who helped them survive in the alien New World. Family and friends gather together and consume roast turkey with stuffings and cranberries, squash, mashed potatoes, and other delicacies that their Puritan forefathers shared with their hosts, the Native Americans. In certain quarters, especially in the radical San Francisco Bay Area, Native Americans gather with their supporters at dawn on **Alcatraz Island** in **San Francisco Bay** to protest and grieve over the injustice done to their ancestors by the white people.

Thanksgiving Day also kicks off the official holiday season. You are constantly reminded that only 30 days remain for Christmas shopping. To bring home this message loud and clear, Macy's department store sponsors **Macy's Thanksgiving Day Parade** in **New York City.** A parade dominated by huge balloons depicting beloved American cartoon characters such as **Snoopy, the Pink Panther, Betty Boop**, etc.

From now until after January 1st, America slows down. People get into the holiday mood. Workers arrive late and take off early not just on Fridays but also throughout the working weekday.

December

December 25 is **Christmas Day.** Open those presents. Tears of joy and disappointment (if the expected present was not given). Brood or smile as you warm yourself by the living room fire. Everything, and we mean everything, is closed (or ought to be!)

December 31 is **New Year's Eve.** The Last Hurrah! Eat, Drink, and Be Merry—for tomorrow begins another new year!

IMPORTANT CONTACTS

OREIGN EMBASSIES

All embassies are located in Washington, D.C. Several countries also have consulates in major cities such as New York and Los Angeles.

Foreign Embassies in **Washington, D.C.** and their phone numbers (If you are outside the city code, first dial "1" followed by 202, and then the remaining numbers):

- Australia   202-797-3000
- Canada   202-682-1740
- China   202-328-2500
- France   202-944-6200
- Germany   202-298-4000
- India   202-939-7000
- Ireland   202-462-3939
- Israel   202-364-5500
- Italy   202-328-5500
- Japan   202-238-6900
- New Zealand   202-328-6900
- South Africa   202-232-4400
- UK   202-462-1340

⌃HE NEXT STEP

⌃OURIST OFFICES ─────────────────────────────────

There is no national tourist information office. However, every state has an information bureau as well as a website. Call 1-800-555-1212 to get the toll-free phone number of the state(s) you plan to visit. Besides the state tourism office, every city, town and even a village has an official visitor center that will hand out free information and maps and brochures. The Chamber of Commerce often offers free information to visitors.

ACTIVITIES

⌃WENTY FUN THINGS TO DO ──────────────────────

+ The automobile defines America, and every American driver has one, if not more, favorite drive, usually along an ocean beach, the open desert or a winding mountain road. We urge you to join the Jeep Jamboree on the 26-mile Rubicon Trail over the California High Sierras near Lake Tahoe. You need a reliable four-wheeler and must be confident of your ability to navigate your machine over boulders, across streams, and up and down steep inclines and slopes. In other words, visualize trekking in a vehicle. You ride at about one mile per hour, the perfect speed to appreciate the gorgeous mountain-and-forest scenery. But don't take your eyes off the "road" too long.

+ Perhaps you prefer motorcycles to cars? Well, if you are a dedicated "hog" rider, then your heaven is in Sturgis, South Dakota, where for one week in mid-August thousands of bikers gather to participate at the annual Sturgis Rally & Races. Sacred and profane come together. According to one newspaper report, it can be "Mecca or Mardi Gras, Sodom and Gomorra." A woman commented that you not only can smell the testosterone, you can hear it.

+ If machines leave you cold and you prefer the beauty of Nature, then set aside a few summer nights and camp in the Gates of the Arctic National Park in Fairbanks, Alaska. You will be rewarded by the sight of the northern lights that make the sky dance.

♦ Maybe your bent is toward the supernatural? Then go South, young man. Georgetown in South Carolina has the reputation of being the most haunted county in the entire USA. Ghosts, spirits, and other beings have been sighted in as many as 100 homes, and quite a few of them are bed-and-breakfast inns!

♦ Beer lovers, make sure you are in Currigan Exhibition Hall in Denver on the first weekend in October for the annual Great American Beer Festival. You get to sample every sort of flavor, from blackberry to chili pepper to chocolate beer. This three-day event draws over 25,000 people and every brewery is present to try to win one of 37 medals.

♦ The Cold War may be over, the Evil Empire in ruins, but you remain a passionate anti-nuclear activist. To bolster your argument, tour the world's first nuclear-powered ship, the submarine Nautilus. Decommissioned in 1980, it is now a museum operated by the U.S. Navy. The "sub-museum" is in Groton, Connecticut, where it was built and launched in 1954. An indication that the Cold War may not be over: visitors are barred from the engine room, the ship's nuclear heart.

♦ On to a more pleasant and authentically American activity—shopping. In mid-August, bargain hunters converge on U.S. Highway 127 and cruise along the 450-mile route of the "World's Longest Yard Sale" that spans four Southern states: Alabama, Georgia, Tennessee, and Kentucky. Everything from used blue jeans to antique furniture is on sale.

♦ Everyone has told you that you must visit at least one of the great national parks, probably Yellowstone or Yosemite. Instead, why not visit Hot Springs National Park, the smallest national park, in Hot Springs, Arkansas. Only 5,549 acres, its thermal waters attracted visitors as diverse as Native Americans, Al Capone, and Bugsy Malone—and President Bill Clinton lived in Hot Springs between 1953 and 1964.

♦ A very quick way to visit four states at once is to arrive at Four Corners where New Mexico, Arizona, Utah and Colorado meet. A concrete slab, 20' x 20', marks the spot and it takes approximately 20

THE NEXT STEP

seconds to "tour" each state. On the other hand, if you'd rather be in the geographic center of continental USA, drive 2 miles northwest of Lebanon, Kentucky until you arrive at a stone monument.

* North Carolina's Outer Banks is a paradise for hang-gliders. The wind is consistent and gentle off the Atlantic coast and the sand dunes rise as high as 140 feet. The Wright Brothers experimented with flying in this area at the beginning of this century. High dunes to take off from, steady winds to stay afloat, soft sand to land. A perfect spot to get high.

* Haters of Hollywood and fans of generously endowed Dolly Parton must visit "Dollywood" in Pigeon Forge, Tennessee, 35 miles southeast of Knoxville. Covering 125 acres, this amusement park will enchant the adult and the child. A star attraction is a 60-foot waterfall, "the world's highest and fastest water ride"; you can observe local crafts people who are continuing the artistic traditions of the Great Smoky Mountains region. There is also a sanctuary for injured bald eagles. And on Paradise Road, a whole show is devoted to the life of Dolly Parton through her songs. Ms. Dolly Parton herself appears live four times a year.

* So you've been touring for a week, a month, even a year—and your visa has expired, but you've fallen in love with America and want to stay on. Well, grab an American and get married in Las Vegas. A "no-frills" ceremony costs $70, and this includes the marriage license. If you want something fancier in a wedding chapel with "Elvis" sere-nading you as you utter "I do" then the sky is the limit. Paul Newman and Joanne Woodward, Hollywood stars, got married in Vegas and still are together; alas, we cannot say the same for Bruce Willis and Demi Moore, also Vegas victims.

* Get educated as you shop. Mount Pleasant, a Charleston, South Carolina suburb, combines specialty-item shopping (sweetgrass baskets) with the complex history of African Americans. When slaves first arrived here, they brought with them from Africa the art of basket weaving. The baskets are made from local sweetgrass and palmetto strips. Along Highway 17, the main artery of Mount Pleasant, sweet-grass baskets of every shape and size woven by the local African American women are for sale. At nearby Boone Hall Plantation,

which contains original slave quarters, the annual sweetgrass festival is held in July.

• In the Black Hills of South Dakota, a project to sculpt the likeness of Lakota (or Sioux) Chief Crazy Horse has been going on since 1948. The sculptor, Korczak Ziolkowski, died in 1982; his widow continues the project, to be completed early in the 21st century. When completed, it will be 563 feet tall, 641 feet long, claiming the title of the world's largest sculpture. Should we be surprised though when we learn that the Native Americans do not approve of this project? When he was alive, the Chief did not allow himself to be sketched or photographed.

• James Dean, the young, dead but hip Hollywood star, was just the opposite of Chief Crazy Horse when it came to being photographed. He certainly would not object to his shrine, The James Dean Gallery, in the farming town of Fairmount, Indiana, his birthplace which is 70 miles north of Indianapolis. On September 30, a graveside service is held in Fairmount's Park Cemetery to mark the anniversary of his death at age 24 in a car accident in 1955.

• On the third week in July get yourself to Key West, Florida, especially if you have white hair and beard and craggy good looks so you can take part in the Hemingway look-alike contest at the Hemingway Day Festival. A love of liquor will make things go quicker. Pens, typewriters, laptops optional.

• For intellectual pursuits, the Strand in New York City considers itself to be the largest bookstore in the world. Two million books on 8 miles of shelves.

• Feeling lonely? Allow the kindness of strangers to comfort you. The Miracle Mile on Panama City Beach, Florida, is where the meat market is. Dive into the pool at Spinnaker and jostle with other semi-naked bodies; if you're proud of your body, compete in hot body contests. Also in this hedonistic 'hood, Club LaVela, which claims to be the largest club in the U.S., has multiple dance floors booming with all sorts of music. And the usual acts: wet t-shirt, bikini, and hard body contests. If you've got it, flaunt it!

• It's that millennium time again and the only place to be is at The

Burning Man Festival held every Labor Day Weekend (the first weekend of September) in the Black Rock Desert 100 miles north of
Reno, Nevada. A truly modern Dionysian celebration, this is an event
where anything and everything goes. Voyeurs are disdained, creativity
and participation are encouraged, if not enforced. Hundred bucks
entrance fee to groove to lots of New Agey, hippyish, love-thy-
neighbor nonsense.

♦ The third weekend in May, grab a live frog and register as a participant
in the world famous Calaveras County Fair and Jumping Frog Jubilee
in Angels Camp, California. Read Mark Twain's "The Celebrated
Jumping Frog of Calaveras County" to prepare for the competition.
Besides frogs, there will be livestock competition, rodeo, and lots of
country boys and gals in tight-fitting jeans, pointed cowboy boots,
and ten-gallon hats.

𝒩ATIONAL PARKS

One of the unexpected joys of traveling in America is the discovery
of large and diverse wilderness areas in every geographical region,
many of them only an hour or two by car. They are managed either
by the federal or the state government. There is an entrance fee, ranging between $5–20. For $50 you can buy the Golden Eagle Pass
which gives a specifically named driver and all the passengers in the
car one year's unlimited access to almost every national park and monument. There are 48 national parks in the USA stretching from Maine
to California, Alaska to Hawaii. When combined with protected
forests, seashores, monuments and other nature reserves, visitors reel
with the possibilities of activities they can indulge in. They can camp,
hike, raft on rivers, or just gaze upon the abundant beauty of nature
spread out before them; they can explore deserts, swamps, rainforests,
wildlife habitat.

Because of the vast range of possibilities, we suggest that you access the
official park service website: http://www.nps.gov/parklists/nm.html
and get updated information regarding opening hours, best time to
visit, entrance fee and visitor facilities. Or call the park service office

in Washington, D.C. at 202-208-4747. You can also call 202-205-0957 for a copy of *A Guide to Your National Forests*. It lists all national forest addresses and other information.

Listed below are some of the parks, forests and other natural recreation spots you will enjoy. Please call before you visit the park of your choice because each park has its own specific rules governing entry fee, pets, camping, automobile entry, dates and time when it opens or closes, etc. Once in the park, please obey all the rules, especially regarding feeding or disturbing wildlife, collecting any historical or natural objects (including gathering wood or picking wildflowers), off-trail use, hunting, snowmobiling, bicycling on park trails, and so on. These are fragile environments, and that is why they are being protected in the first place.

• The Appalachian National Scenic Trail is the Mother-of-all trails. A 2,158-mile (3,480.6 km) footpath, it traverses the ridge crests and the major valleys of the Appalachian Mountains that stretch across the states of Maine, New Hampshire, Vermont, Massachusetts, Connecticut, New York, New Jersey, Pennsylvania, Maryland, West Virginia, Virginia, Tennessee, North Carolina and Georgia. The Trail has more than 500 access points and is used primarily by weekend or short-term hikers. If you want the whole hog, it is recommended that you start from the South in early spring. It takes five to six months to hike the entire length, as you slog through 8 national forests and 60 state parks that make up the Appalachian Trail. The Trail has been hiked by the blind, persons on crutches, and other persons with disabilities. Do not ignore the abundant bird and wildlife on this trail.

• If your secret fetish is stones and rocks, visit Bryce Canyon National Park, named for one of a series of horseshoe-shaped amphitheaters carved from the eastern edge of the Paunsaugunt Plateau in southern Utah. Forces of nature have shaped colorful limestones, sandstones, and mudstones into thousands of spires, fins, pinnacles, and mazes that are knows as "hoodoos." Sitting at an elevation of 8,000 feet, the park and the surrounding area are also renowned for the air quality, and at night for unparalleled opportunities for star gazing. The park also has over

50 miles of hiking trails with a range of distances and elevation change. It is also especially inspiring to visit in winter, when tops of "hoodoos" rise above field of snow. Cross-country skiing and snow shoeing are popular activities during this season.

• Steven Spielberg probably got his idea for his movie *Jurassic Park* after visiting the Dinosaur National Monument, two-thirds of which is in Colorado and the rest in Utah. A "diamond in the desert," the park was created in 1915 after more than 1,600 deposits of Jurassic dinosaur bones were discovered in an ancient riverbed turned to stone. Make sure you visit the Dinosaur Quarry building where a layer of sandstone has been exposed to display fossilized dinosaur bones in its natural state.

• Creepy, crawly, reptilian creatures welcome you in the Everglades National Park in Homestead, Florida. The largest remaining subtropical wilderness in the continental United States, it has extensive fresh- and saltwater areas, open Everglades prairies, and mangrove forests. It is also the only place in the world where alligators and crocodiles exist side by side. Besides reptiles, the Everglades is also known for its diverse temperate and tropical birdlife. Boating and canoeing are popular activities, especially along the 99-mile canoe trail, known as the Wilderness Waterway. Park rangers also offer walking tours. The park is a World Heritage Site, an International Biosphere Reserve, and a Wetland of International Significance.

• Eloquent volumes have been written—and continue to be written—about the grandeur of the Grand Canyon, yet even the most accomplished writers have confessed that it remains "beyond the grasp of human imagination." So, with apologies to Nike, we'll simply say "Just Do It!" Meanwhile, some facts and highlights for you to ponder. It is located in northern Arizona and encompasses 277 miles of the Colorado River and surrounding uplands. It is almost one mile deep and between four and eighteen miles wide. The vistas offered from the rim of the Grand Canyon are unmatched and incomparable, attracting over five million visitors per year. This, unfortunately, means it is very crowded, especially during the peak season which runs from April through October; any three-day weekend and even winter holiday weekends are crowded. Visitors can hike or take mule trips along the various canyon trails. Bus or helicopter tours are also available. All hiking at Grand Canyon is strenuous, due to altitude (the South Rim is 7,000 feet above sea level) and extreme temperatures, up to 120° F in the inner canyon. To beat the heat, you can raft the white-water rapids of the Colorado River. Desert wildlife include rabbits, mountain lions, snakes, as well as eagles and vultures. There are traces of human life that go back as early as 2000 B.C. Special events at Grand Canyon include the Grand Canyon Chamber Music Festival each September, regularly scheduled theatrical productions in the summer, and art exhibits at Kolb Studio. The South Rim is open 24 hours a day, 365 days a year. The North Rim is closed from late October to mid-May.

• Hawaii Volcanoes National Park, 30 miles from Hilo on Hawaii's Big Island, is the perfect place to observe Nature in action! Two active volcanoes, Mauna Loa and Kilauea, are inside this 230,000-acre park; the dramatic landscape also includes desert, tundra, and rainforest. But it is the awesome sight of volcanic activity (past and present) that will impress you most. You can hike or drive to appreciate the scenery. For example, the Crater Rim Drive is an 11-mile loop road that encircles the summit caldera of Kilauea Volcano; it also passes through the Ka`u Desert and tropical rainforest. The Chain of Craters Road descends 3,700 feet in 20 miles and ends where a 1995 lava flow crosses the road where there may be opportunities for viewing active lava flows. Since the park is situated on two active volcanoes, there are many hidden hazards for those unfamiliar with volcanic environments. Stay on designated trails and do not enter closed areas. Also, volcanic fumes are hazardous to your health and can be life-threatening. Those with heart or breathing problems, infants, young children, and pregnant women should be especially careful and avoid areas where volcanic fumes are present.

• If you detest heat (of volcanoes), confess to possessing a "Monsoon" mood and like your environment all cool, damp, wet, and lushly green, you'd rather be in Olympic National Park, an area that occupies the central portion of the Olympic Peninsula which lies west of the Seattle/Tacoma metropolis and Puget Sound. The park's headquarters are located in Port Angeles, Washington. Also referred to as "three parks in one," it has three distinctly different ecosystems—rugged glacier-capped mountains, over 60 miles of wild Pacific coast, and magnificent stands of old-growth trees and rainforest. Approximately 95% of the park is designated wilderness. There are nearly 600 miles of trails and 168 miles of roads (69 of which are gravel) to provide vehicle access to various points around the park. All park roads are "spur roads" to provide vehicle access, no roads traverse the Olympic wilderness. The rain and the river waters combine to produce giant trees, mosses, lichens, ferns, and almost 300 species of plants. In the Queets River Rainforest stands the world's tallest Douglas fir tree, standing 220 feet. tall and 45 inches in circumference. The park boasts that eight kinds of plants and five kinds of animals found here live nowhere else in the world. Activities include fishing and hiking, especially the 36-mile Hoh River Trail in the Hoh Rainforest to the base of 8,000 ft. Mount Olympus. The rare Roosevelt elk and cougars are some of the wildlife you will see.

• The Petroglyph National Monument in Albuquerque, New Mexico, has more than 15,000 prehistoric and historic Native American and Hispanic petroglyphs (images carved in rock) that stretch 17 miles along Albuquerque's West Mesa escarpment. They provide a tantalizing glimpse into a 12,000 year-old story of human habitation in the Albuquerque area. The best time to visit is September and October. Hiking trails are quite primitive and vehicle access is limited. Please do not touch petroglyphs because you will damage them.

• To test the authenticity of the "call of the wild" in you, visit Denali National Park & Preserve, 125 miles south of Fairbanks, Alaska. In Denali's 6 million acre wilderness, there are very few trails or roads. There are, however, spectacular mountains and large glaciers. The sub-arctic ecosystem supports intimidating animals such as grizzly bears, wolves, caribou, and moose as well as less dangerous beasts such as Dall sheep, hare, and foxes. Over 160 bird species make their home in this park. It also has North America's highest mountain, the 20,320 foot. Mount McKinley, known as "Denali" (the Great One) to the local Athabascan natives. It is actually the highest mountain in the

world when you consider that it rises from 2000 feet at its base to over 20,000 feet at the peak. Mountaineering, therefore, is a siren call to many, but, alas, there is at least one fatality every climbing season. If upon arrival, the call of the wild in you suddenly becomes tamed when confronted by the vast uncharted wilderness, there are shuttle bases to take you around and even a 90-minute "Circle McKinley" airplane ride. Or you can raft down the Nenana River. The tourist season runs from May 1 to September 15, but if you want to get in touch with your inner machismo, arrive in winter when motor vehicles are banned and your options are skiing, snowshoes, or dog sleds. Write a romantic poem as you gaze at the glittering northern lights at night.

- Yellowstone National Park, like the Grand Canyon, suffers from being too famous. If there is one wilderness that an urban rat has heard of, it's most likely Yellowstone, thanks of course to that dependable geyser Old Faithful (there are more geysers and hot springs here than in the rest of the world combined). Yellowstone is the first and oldest national park in the world, established by an act of Congress on March 1, 1872. Although most of the park's 3,400 square miles (2.2 million acres) are within Wyoming, parts of it extend into Idaho and Montana. Given its popularity, it also comes as a shock to discover that 99 percent of the park remains undeveloped, making it a true wilderness. Besides its stunning natural scenery and the geological rumblings, gurglings, and eruptions, Yellowstone is especially noted for its wildlife. Moose, elk, bears, and the bison roam freely. In 1995, a pack of wolves were introduced in the park, despite opposition from local ranchers who feared loss of livestock. The usual activities are available: boating, hiking, camping, horseback riding. In winter, cross-country skiing and snowmobile riding are popular.

- Yosemite National Park became America's first state park in 1864. Compared to other protected areas, Yosemite Valley is quite small, about seven miles long and a mile wide. Small enough anyway for John Muir, the conservationist and founder of Sierra Club, to explore the entire area on foot. But within its narrow confines are some of the most impressive cliffs, valleys, meadows, waterfalls, and flora and fauna.

The park ranges from 2,000 feet above sea level to more than 13,000 feet. Among its most famous peaks are El Capitan, the largest piece of exposed granite in the world, and Half Dome. Some of the most spectacular waterfalls, such as the Bridalveil Falls, are only a short hike from the Yosemite Valley floor. The view of the Valley floor from the top of 3,200 foot Glacier Point, 32 miles away by road, is considered by many to be the most impressive of all. When you are not feeling "stoned" by the sheer cliffs that circle the valley, be aware of the black bears that no longer appear to fear humans and have known to brazenly walk into campsites and raid food. Coyotes and other denizens of the forests are more cunning and less visible. There are 196 miles of paved roads within the park and 840 miles of trails. Since it also has 8 miles of paved bike path, rent a bike and explore the relatively flat valley floor. To prevent congestion and overcrowding, there have been proposals to ban automobiles in Yosemite, especially during the very busy and crowded holiday weekends such as Memorial Day, Fourth of July, and Labor Day. But don't let a trifle like that stop you from visiting one of the most fabulous natural wonders of the world.

ADDITIONAL RESOURCES

*U*SA ONLINE

You can easily spend hours, days, weeks, months, and years surfing the internet and getting information from various web sites. Check out the ones below:

* **Destinations:EcoTravel:** Information on ecotravel in the United States.
  http://www.ecotravel.com/Destinations/countries/united_ states/:
* **FreeTime Guide, Inc.:** Index of states and their attractions as well as events and attractions in the USA.
  http://www.ftguide.com/:

+ **Great Outdoors Recreation Pages (G.O.R.P.):** Links to national parks, forests, monuments, preserves in 50 states.
  http://www.gorp.com/gorp/resource/US_National_Park/main.htm:
+ **LocalEyes: Local Web Guide, Find Web sites Near You:** Find Web pages in a particular area anywhere in the US.
  http://www1.localeyes.com/1US/:
+ **Lodging Finder of America:** Helps you find vacation accommodations & resorts in the USA. A national directory of condominium, home rental, and yacht charter companies.
  http://webworks.tislink.com/webworks/full.htm
+ **The National Atlas of the United States of America:** Maps and information from the USGS and its partners.
  http://www–atlas.usgs.gov/:
+ **National Parks and Conservation Association:** A private nonprofit citizen organization dedicated solely to protecting, preserving, and enhancing the U.S. National Park System.
  http://www.npca.org/home/npca/:
+ **The Rough Guide to Online Travel:** Expert advice on USA provided by The Rough Guide, a guide books series published in UK. Links by state and region.
  http://www.hotwired.com/rough/usa/:
+ **Travel Directory: Unique International Travel Resources:** Search for bed and breakfast lodgings and accommodations, vacation cottage rentals, wilderness adventure travel companies, chamber of commerce and city pages, and regional travel resources.
  http://www.triple1.com/usa/usa.htm:
+ **The USA CityLink Project:** Directory of links to information on cities across the United States. **http://usacitylink.com/:**

GIVING BACK

If you want to do volunteer work while in America, we suggest that you contact the appropriate organization after your arrival. While most charity, community, and social service agencies welcome volunteer help, they require a minimum training period as well as a certain amount of time commitment. Many will not accept you if you have only a week or ten days for volunteer work.

Almost every city and county in America has a "Volunteer Center" which is a clearinghouse for the community, matching volunteers with nonprofit organizations in its area. It is listed in the local phone book and welcomes inquiries.

In Europe, some travel and tour companies arrange trips in the USA where you visit and spend time among communities where your services will be appreciated.

A Reminder: You may be deported by the U.S. Immigration and Naturalization Services department if it determines that you are working illegally in the USA, especially if you receive any money for your work.

RECOMMENDED READING

Abbey, Edward. *Desert Solitaire: A Season in the Wilderness.* New York: Ballentine Books, 1968.

Ambrose, Stephen. *Undaunted Courage: Meriwether Lewis, Thomas Jefferson, and the Exploration of the West.* New York: Simon & Schuster, 1996.

Ambrose, Stephen E. *Eisenhower: Volume Two, The President.* New York: Simon & Schuster, 1984.

Baldwin, Neil. *Edison: Inventing the Century.* New York: Hyperion, 1995.

Barbato, Joseph and Lisa Weinerman [eds]. *Heart of the Land: Essays on the Last Great Places.* New York: Vintage Books, 1994.

Barry, Dave. *Dave Barry's Only Travel Guide You'll Ever Need.* New York: Ballentine Books, 1991.

Bartram, William. *William Bartram: Travels and Other Writings.* New York: The Library of America, 1996.

Baudrillard, Jean, translated by Chris Turner. *America.* London/New York: Verso, 1988.

Bellow, Saul. *It All Adds Up: From the Dim Past to the Uncertain Future.* New York: Viking Penguin, 1990.

Bergman, Charles. *Wild Echoes: Encounters with the Most Endangered Animals in North America.* New York: McGraw-Hill Publishing Company, 1990.

Boorstin, Daniel J. *The Americans: The Democratic Experience.* New York: Random House, 1973.

Bordewich. Fergus M. *Killing the White Man's Indian: Reinventing Native Americans at the End of the Twentieth Century.* New York: Doubleday, 1996.

Branch, Taylor. *Parting the Waters: America in the King Years 1954–63.* New York: Simon & Schuster, 1988.

Brandon, Ruth. *The Life and Many Deaths of Harry Houdini.* New York: Random House, 1993.

Brown, Dee. *Bury My Heart at Wounded Knee: An Indian History of the American West.* New York: Bantam Books, 1972.

Brown, Kenneth A. *Four Corners: History, Land, and People of the Desert Southwest.* New York: HarperCollins, 1995.

Browne, Waldo R. *Barnum's Own Story: The Autobiography of P. T. Barnum.* Magnolia, Massachusetts: Peter Smith Publisher Inc., 1972.

Bryson, Bill. *Made in America: An Informal History of the English Language in the United States.* New York: Avon Books, 1994.

Bryson, Bill. *The Lost Continent: Travels in Small-Town America.* New York: Harper & Row, 1989. London: Black Swan, 1997.

Bull, Debby. *Blue Jelly: Love Lost and the Lessons of Canning.* New York: Hyperion, 1997.

THE NEXT STEP

Buryn, Ed. *Vagabonding in the USA: A Guide for Independent Travelers and Foreign Visitors.* California: And/Or Press, 1980.

Carson, Rachel L. *The Sea Around Us.* New York: Oxford University Press, 1951.

Carter, Jimmy. *An Outdoor Journal: Adventures and Reflections.* Fayetteville, Arkansas: University of Arkansas Press, 1994.

Chapple, Steve. *Kayaking the Full Moon: A Journey Down the Yellowstone River to the Soul of Montana.* New York: HarperCollins, 1993.

Clarke, Thurston. *California Fault: Searching for the Spirit of a State Along the San Andreas.* New York: Ballantine Books, 1996.

Codrescu, Andrei. *Zombification: Stories from National Public Radio.* New York: St. Martin's Press, 1994.

Coster, Graham. *A Thousand Miles from Nowhere: Trucking Two Continents.* London: Penguin Books (UK) Ltd., 1995.

Covington, Dennis. *Salvation on Sand Mountain: Snake Handling and Redemption in Southern Appalachia.* Reading, Massachusetts: Addison-Wesley, 1995.

Cox, Harvey. *Fire From Heaven: The Rise of Pentecostal Spirituality and the Reshaping of Religion in the 21st Century.* Reading, Massachusetts: Addison-Wesley, 1995.

Daniel, John. *The Trail Home: Essays.* New York: Pantheon Books, 1992.

DeVoto, Bernard. *Across the Wide Missouri.* Boston: Houghton Mifflin, 1947.

Doig, Ivan. *Winter Brothers.* New York: Harcourt Brace Jovanovich, 1980.

Dorris, Michael. *Paper Trail: Essays.* New York: HarperCollins, 1994.

Egan, Timothy. *The Good Rain: Across Time and Terrain in the Pacific Northwest.* New York: Alfred A. Knopf, 1990.

Eighner, Lars. *Travels with Lizbeth: Three Years on the Road and on the Streets.* New York: St. Martin's Press, 1993.

Ellis, Jerry. *Bareback! One Man's Journey Along the Pony Express Trail.* New York: Delacorte Press, 1991.

Ellis, Jerry. *Walking the Trail: One Man's Journey Along the Cherokee Trail of Tears.* New York: Delacorte Press, 1991.

Ellmann, Richard. *The Artist as Critic: Critical Writings of Oscar Wilde.* New York: Random House, 1969.

Fadiman, Anne. *The Spirit Catches You and You Fall Down: A Hmong Child, Her Doctors, and the Collision of Two Cultures.* New York: Farrar Straus & Giroux, 1997.

Fitzgerald, Frances. *Cities on a Hill: A Journey Through Contemporary American Cultures.* New York: Simon & Schuster, 1986.

Fletcher, Colin. *River: One Man's Journey Down the Colorado, Source to Sea.* New York: Borzoi Books, 1997.

Fussell, Paul. *Abroad: British Literary Traveling Between the Wars.* New York: Oxford University Press, 1980.

Giovanni, Nikki. *Shimmy Shimmy Shimmy Like My Sister Kate: Looking at the Harlem Renaissance Through Poems.* New York: Henry Holt, 1996.

Gioia, Ted. *West Coast Jazz: Modern Jazz in California, 1945-1960.* New York: Oxford University Press, 1992.

Goodwin, Doris Kearns. *No Ordinary Time: FDR and Eleanor Roosevelt and the Homefront During World War II.* New York: Simon & Schuster, 1994.

Gosnell, Mariana. *Zero Three Bravo: Solo Across America in a Small Plane.* New York: Touchstone, 1993.

Gottlieb, Robert. *A Life of Its Own: The Politics and Power of Water.* Orlando: Harcourt Brace & Company, 1988.

Gruchow, Paul. *Grass Roots: The Universe of Home.* Minneapolis: Milkweed Editions, 1995.

Grumbach, Doris. *Coming Into the End Zone: A Memoir.* New York: W. W. Norton, 1991.

THE NEXT STEP

Hall. Edward T. *West of the Thirties: Discoveries Among the Navajo and Hopi.* New York: Doubleday, 1994.

Harris, Eddy L. *South of Haunted Dreams: A Ride Through Slavery's Old Back Yard.* New York: Simon & Schuster, 1993.

Harrison, Jim. *Just Before Dark: Collected Nonfiction.* Boston: Houghton Mifflin, 1992.

Hoagland, Edward. *The Edward Hoagland Reader.* New York: Random House, 1976.

Hoffman, Eva. *Lost in Translation: A Life in a New Language.* New York: E. P. Dutton, 1989.

Hongo, Garrett. *Volcano: A Memoir of Hawaii.* New York: Vintage Departures, 1995.

Horwitz, Tony. *Confederates in the Attic: Dispatches from the Unfinished Civil War.* New York: Pantheon Books, 1998.

Hubbell, Sue. *Far-Flung Hubbell: Essays from the American Road.* New York: Random House, 1995.

Hurston, Zora Neale. *Mules and Men.* New York: HarperCollins, 1963.

James, Henry. *Henry James: Collected Travel Writings—Great Britain and America.* New York: The Library of America, 1993.

Johnson, Haynes. *Divided We Fall: Gambling with History in the Nineties.* New York: W. W. Norton, 1995.

Johnson, Haynes. *Sleepwalking Through History: America in the Reagan Years.* New York: W. W. Norton, 1991.

Kazin, Alfred. *A Writer's America: Landscape in Literature.* New York: Alfred A. Knopf, 1988.

Kerouac, Jack. *On the Road.* New York: Signet, 1985.

Kleinfeld, Sonny. *The Hotel: A Week in the Life of the Plaza.* New York: Simon & Schuster, 1989.

Kuralt, Charles. *Charles Kuralt's America.* New York: Anchor Books Doubleday, 1995.

Lamb, David. *Stolen Season: A Journey Through America and Baseball's Minor Leagues.* New York: Random House, 1991.

Landau, Diana and Shelley Stump. *Living with Wildlife: How to Enjoy, Cope with, and Protect North America's Wild Creatures Around Your Home and Theirs.* San Francisco: Sierra Club Books, 1994.

Langewiesche, William. *Cutting for Sign.* New York: Pantheon Books, 1993.

Lawrence, Bill. *Wilderness: North America as the Early Explorers Saw It—From Norse Sagas to Lewis and Clark.* New York: Paragon House, 1991.

Lee, Li-Young. *The Winged Seed: A Remembrance.* New York: Simon & Schuster, 1995.

Legler, Gretchen. *All the Powerful Invisible Things: A Sportswoman's Notebook.* Seattle, Washington: Seal Press, 1995.

Levine, Lawrence. *High Brow/Low Brow: The Emergence of Cultural Hierarchy in America.* Cambridge, Massachusetts: Harvard University Press, 1988.

Louis-Philippe, King. *Diary of My Travels in America.* New York: Delacorte Press, 1977.

Marcy, Randolph B. *The Prairie Traveler: The Classic Handbook for America's Pioneers.* New York: Perigree Books.

Marling, Karal Ann. *As Seen on TV: The Visual Culture of Everyday Life in the 1950s.* Cambridge, Massachusetts: Harvard University Press, 1994.

Matthiessen, Peter. *Wildlife in America.* New York: Viking Penguin, 1987.

Mayle, Simon. *The Burial Brothers.* London: Hamish Hamilton, 1996.

McCullough, David. *Truman.* New York: Simon & Schuster, 1992.

McIntyre, Mike. *The Kindness of Strangers.* New York: Berkley Books, 1996.

McLean, Duncan. *Lone Star Swing: On the Trail of Bob Wills and His Texas Playboys.* London: Jonathan Cape, 1997; New York: W. W. Norton, 1997.

McPhee, John. *The John McPhee Reader.* New York: Farrar Straus & Giroux, 1976.

Merwin, W. S. *Houses and Travellers.* London: Atheneum, 1977.

Minatoya, Lydia. *Talking to High Monks in the Snow: An Asian American Odyssey.* New York: HarperCollins, 1992.

Mitchell, Joseph. *Up in the Old Hotel.* New York: Pantheon, 1992.

Morison, Samuel Eliot. *The European Discovery of America: The Southern Voyages A.D. 1492–1616.* New York: Oxford University Press, 1974.

Morris, Jan. *Pleasures of a Tangled Life.* New York: Random House, 1989.

Naipaul, V. S. *A Turn in the South.* New York: Alfred A. Knopf, 1989.

Neihardt, John G. *Black Elk Speaks: Being the Life Story of a Holy Man of the Ogala Sioux.* Lincoln, Nebraska: A Bison Book, 1961.

Nicolson, Adam. *On Foot: Guided Walks in England, France and the United States.* New York: Harmony Books, 1991.

Nickerson, Sheila. *Disappearance: A Map.* New York: Doubleday, 1996.

Niemann, Linda. *Boomer: Railroad Memoirs.* Berkeley, California: University of California Press, 1990.

Norris, Kathleen. *Dakota: A Spiritual Geography.* New York: Ticknor & Fields, 1993.

O'Connor, Joseph. S*weet Liberty: Travels in Irish America.* Boulder, Colorado: Roberts Rinehart Publishers, 1996.

Patterson, James T. *Grand Expectations: The United States, 1945–1974.* New York: Oxford University Press, 1996.

Pindell, Terry. *Making Tracks: An American Rail Odyssey.* New York: Grove/Atlantic, 1990.

Preston, Douglas. *Cities of Gold: A Journey Across the American Southwest in Pursuit of Coronado.* New York: Simon & Schuster, 1992.

Raban, Jonathan. *Hunting Mister Heartbreak: A Discovery of America.* New York: HarperCollins, 1991.

Raban, Jonathan. *Old Glory: A Voyage Down the Mississippi.* New York: Vintage Departures, 1981.

Rawls, Thomas H. *Small Places: In Search of a Vanishing America.* New York: Little Brown & Co., 1990.

Reeves, Richard. *American Journey: Traveling with Tocqueville in Search of Democracy in America.* New York: A Touchstone Book, 1982.

Reid, Robert Leonard. *Mountains of the Great Blue Dream.* New York: North Point Press, 1991.

Rice, Clyde. *A Heaven in the Eye.* Portland: Breitenbush, 1984, 1990.

Rockland, Michael Aaron. *Snowshoeing through Sewers: Adventures in New York City, New Jersey, and Philadelphia.* New Jersey: Rutgers University Press, 1994.

Rodriguez, Richard. *Hunger of Memory.* Boston: David Godine, 1982.

Rogers, Susan Fox. *Alaska Passages: 20 Voices from Above the 54th Parallel.* Seattle: Sasquatch Books, 1996.

Rogers, Susan Fox [ed.]. *Solo: On Her Own Adventure.* Seattle: Seal Press, 1996.

Russell, Sharman Apt. *When the Land Was Young: Reflections on American Archaeology.* Reading, Massachusetts: Addison-Wesley, 1996.

Schwantes, Carlos A. *The Pacific Northwest: An Interpretive History.* Lincoln, Nebraska: University of Nebraska Press, 1989.

Setterberg, Fred. *The Roads Taken: Travels Through America's Literary Landscapes.* Athens, Georgia: University of Georgia Press, 1993.

Sheldon, Dyan. *Dream Catching: A Wander Around the Americas.* London: Little, Brown & Company, 1995.

Shukman, Henry. *Savage Prilgrims: On the Road to Santa Fe.* London: HarperCollins Ltd., 1996.

Silko, Leslie Marmon. *Yellow Woman and a Beauty of the Spirit.* New York: Touchstone, 1996.

Sprague, Stuart Seely (ed.). *His Promised Land: The Autobiography of John P. Parker, Former Slave and Conductor on the Underground Railroad.* New York: W. W. Norton, 1996.

Stegner, Wallace. *Where the Bluebird Sings to the Lemonade Springs: Living and Writing in the West*. New York: Random House, 1992.

Steinbeck, John. *Travels with Charley: In Search of America*. New York: Viking Press, 1962.

Stuart, Alexander. *Life on Mars*. New York: Bantam, 1988.

Taylor, Michael Ray. *Cave Passages: Roaming the Underground Wilderness*. New York: Scribner, 1996.

Terkel, Studs. *Hard Times: An Oral History of the Great Depression*. New York: Pantheon, 1970.

Theroux, Peter. *Translating L.A.: A Tour of the Rainbow City*. New York: W.W. Norton, 1994.

Thoreau, Henry David. *Walden*. New York: Random House, 1950.

Trillin, Calvin. *Travels with Alice*. New York: Avon Books, 1989.

Turner, Frederick. *A Border of Blue: Along the Gulf of Mexico from the Keys to the Yucatán*. New York: Henry Holt, 1993.

Twain, Mark. *Life on the Mississippi*. New York: The New American Library of World Literature, Inc., 1961.

Twain, Mark. *Roughing It*. New York: The New American Library of World Literature, Inc., 1962.

Ugresic, Dubravka. *Have a Nice Day: From the Balkan War to the American Dream*. London: Jonathan Cape, Ltd., 1993.

Updike, John. *Odd Jobs: Essays and Criticiscm*. New York: Alfred A. Knopf, 1990.

Urrea, Luis Alberto. *By the Lake of Sleeping Children: The Secret Life of the Mexican Border*. New York: Anchor Books, 1996.

Utley, Robert M. *The Lance and the Shield: The Life and Times of Sitting Bull*. New York: Henry Holt, 1993.

Walton, Anthony. *Mississippi: An American Journey*. New York: Alfred A. Knopf, 1996.

Weisberger, Bernard A. *The WPA Guide to America: The Best of 1930s America as Seen by the Federal Writers' Project.* New York: Random House, 1985.

White, Richard. *It's Your Misfortune and None of My Own: A New History of the American West.* Norman: University of Oklahoma Press, 1991.

Wilson, Darryl Babe. *The Morning the Sun Went Down.* Berkeley: Heyday Books, 1998.

Wilson, E.O. *Naturalist.* Washington, D.C.: Island Press, 1994.

Wilson, Edmund. *A Piece of My Mind: Reflections at Sixty.* New York: Farrar, Straus Giroux, 1956.

Wolfe, Linnie Marsh Wolfe. *John of the Mountains: The Unpublished Journals of John Muir.* New York: Houghton Mifflin, 1966.

Wolfe, Tom. *The Purple Decades.* New York: Farrar Straus & Giroux, 1982.

Wright, Lawrence. *In the New World: Growing Up with America from the Sixties to the Eighties.* New York: Vintage Books, 1989.

Yardley, Jonathan. *States of Mind: A Personal Journey Through the Mid-Atlantic.* New York: Villard Books, 1993.

Yee, Chiang. *The Silent Traveller in San Francisco.* New York: W. W. Norton, 1964.

Young, Al. *Drowning in the Sea of Love: Musical Memoirs.* Hopewell: Ecco Press, 1995.

"THE NEXT STEP" WAS COMPILED BY RAJENDRA S. KHADKA AND THE STAFF AT TRAVELERS' TALES, INC.

Index

Index of Contributors

Acknowledgements

Heartfelt thanks and appreciation to James O'Reilly and Larry Habegger, dauntless examples of grace under pressure; the ever-enterprising and tenacious Raj Khadka; Susan Brady and Jennifer Leo for moving mountains of words; Leslie Martin and Sarah Ferrell who gave me the opportunity to see more of the country and write about it; Mike and Kim Caple for innumerable discussions paring East from West; Lonny Shavelson for our continuing conversation; and Ann Van Steenberg, my collaborator in almost everything important, who once again contributed far beyond the call of duty.

"Walking the Trail of Tears" by Jerry Ellis excerpted from *Walking the Trail: One Man's Journey Along the Cherokee Trail of Tears* by Jerry Ellis. Copyright © 1991 by Jerry Ellis. Used by permission of Delacorte Press, a division of Bantam Doubleday Dell Publishing Group, Inc. and Writer's House, Inc.

"Nashville Cats" by Duncan McLean excerpted from *Lone Star Swing: On the Trail of Bob Wills and His Texas Playboys* by Duncan McLean. Copyright © 1997 by Duncan McLean. Reprinted by permission of W. W. Norton & Company and Random House Ltd. (UK).

"Battle Acts" by Tony Horwitz excerpted from *Confederates in the Attic: Dispatches from the Unfinished Civil War* by Tony Horwitz. Copyright © 1998 by Tony Horwitz. Reprinted by permission of Pantheon Books, a division of Random House, Inc. and International Creative Management, Inc. Originally published in somewhat different form in *The New Yorker.*

"Desert Dreams" by Henry Shukman excerpted from *Savage Pilgrims: On the Road to Santa Fe* by Henry Shukman. Copyright © 1996 by Henry Shukman. Reprinted by permission of HarperCollins Publishers Ltd.

"Good People" by Charles Kuralt excerpted from *Charles Kuralt's America* by Charles Kuralt. Copyright © 1995 by Charles Kuralt. Reprinted by permission of Penguin Books USA Inc. and Bellon Enterprises Ltd.

"Going Places" by Jim Harrison excerpted from *Just Before Dark: Collected Nonfiction* by Jim Harrison. Reprinted by permission of the author. Copyright © 1991 by Jim Harrison.

"*Dose!*" by Darryl Babe Wilson excerpted from *The Morning the Sun Went Down* by Darryl Babe Wilson. Copyright © 1998 by Darryl Babe Wilson. Reprinted

"Washington, D.C. for Beginners" by James Fallows reprinted from the February 1995 issue of *The Atlantic Monthly*. Copyright ©1995 by James Fallows. Reprinted by permission of the author.

"The Minnesota State Fair" by Jonathan Raban excerpted from *Old Glory: A Voyage Down the Mississippi* by Jonathan Raban. Copyright © 1981 by Jonathan Raban. Reprinted by permission of the author.

"The Mountain of Love and Death" by Robert Leonard Reid excerpted from *Mountains of the Great Blue Dream* by Robert Leonard Reid. Copyright © 1991 by Robert Leonard Reid. Reprinted by permission of Farrar, Straus, Giroux and the author.

"The Walt 'You Will Have Fun' Disney World" by Dave Barry excerpted from *Dave Barry's Only Travel Guide You'll Ever Need* by Dave Barry. Copyright © 1991 by Dave Barry. Reprinted by permission of Ballantine Books, a division of Random House, Inc. and the author.

"Taken by Storm" by Dashka Slater reprinted from the May/June 1995 issue of *Sierra*. Copyright © 1995 by Dashka Slater. Reprinted by permission of the author.

"The Only Good Bear" by Cathy Petrick published with permission from the author. Copyright © 1999 by Cathy Petrick.

"Diamonds!" by Sean O'Reilly published with permission of the author. Copyright © 1999 by Sean O'Reilly.

"Enjoying the Louisiana Rodent" by Calvin Trillin originally appeared as "The Nutria Problem" in the February 1995 issue of *The Atlantic Monthly*. Copyright © 1995 by Calvin Trillin. This usage granted by permission.

"Philadelphia Stroll" by Michael Aaron Rockland excerpted from *Snowshoeing through Sewers: Adventures in New York City, New Jersey, and Philadelphia* by Michael Aaron Rockland. Copyright ©1994 by Michael Aaron Rockland. Reprinted by permission of Rutgers University Press.

"Texas Heartache" by Debby Bull excerpted from *Blue Jelly: Love Lost and the Lessons of Canning* by Debby Bull. Copyright © 1997 by Debby Bull. Reprinted by permission of Hyperion, a division of Disney Book Publishing, Inc.

"A Day in the Lake" by Michael Covino originally appeared as "The Holy Cow" in the March 1990 issue of *California Magazine*. Copyright © 1990 by Michael Covino. Reprinted by permission of the author.

"Trucking the Distance" by Graham Coster excerpted from *A Thousand Miles from Nowhere: Trucking Two Continents* by Graham Coster. Copyright © 1995 by Graham Coster. Reproduced by permission of Penguin Books Ltd. (UK) and Curtis Brown Ltd.

"Cincinnati Ho!" by Jon Carroll originally appeared as "My Visit to America" in the June 14, 1998 issue of the *San Francisco Chronicle*. Copyright © 1998 by the San Francisco Chronicle. Reprinted by permission of the San Francisco Chronicle.

"Icebergs in My Dreams" by Sheryl Clough excerpted from *Solo: On Her Own Adventure* edited by Susan Fox Rogers. Copyright © 1996 by Sheryl Clough. Reprinted by permission of Seal Press.

"Amelia in Kansas" by Mariana Gosnell excerpted from *Zero Three Bravo: Solo Across America in a Small Plane* by Mariana Gosnell. Copyright © 1993 by Mariana Gosnell. Reprinted by permission of Alfred A. Knopf, Inc. and the

"Alone" by Philip Caputo reprinted from the August 1998 issue of *Men's Journal*. Reprinted by permission of Men's Journal Company, L.P. All rights reserved. Copyright © 1996.

"Surviving the City of Angels" by Janine Jones published with permission from the author. Copyright ©1999 by Janine Jones.

"Always Arriving" by Jonathan Raban excerpted from *Hunting Mister Heartbreak: A Discovery of America* by Jonathan Raban. Copyright © 1991 by Jonathan Raban. Reprinted by permission of HarperCollins Publishers, Inc. and Gillon Aitken Associates Ltd.

Additional Credits (arranged alphabetically by title)

Selection from *Abroad: British Literary Traveling Between the Wars* by Paul Fussell copyright © 1980 by Paul Fussell. Used by permission of Oxford University Press, Inc.

Selection from *All the Powerful Invisible Things: A Sportswoman's Notebook* copyright © 1995 by Gretchen Legler. Reprinted by permission of Seal Press.

Selection from "America's Most Private City" by Jonathan Raban reprinted from the November 1991 issue of *Travel Holiday* . Copyright © 1991 by Jonathan Raban. Reprinted by permission of the author.

Selection from *American Journals* by Albert Camus (translation by Hugh Levick) copyright © 1987. Reprinted by permission of Editions Gallimard and Marlowe & Company.

Selection from *American Journey: Traveling with Tocqueville in Search of Democracy in America* by Richard Reeves copyright © 1982 by Richard Reeves. Reprinted by permission of Simon & Schuster, Inc. and Janklow & Nesbit.

Selection from *American Places: A Writer's Pilgrimage to 15 of this Country's Most Visited and Cherished Sites* by William Zinsser. Copyright © 1992 by William K. Zinsser. Reprinted by permission of the author.

Selection from *The Americans: The Democratic Experience* by Daniel J. Boorstin copyright © 1973 by Daniel J. Boorstin. Reprinted by permission of Random House, Inc.

Selection from *An Outdoor Journal: Adventures and Reflections* by Jimmy Carter copyright © 1996 by Jimmy Carter. Reprinted by permission of the University of Arkansas Press.

Selection from *The Artist as Critic: Critical Writings* of Oscar Wilde edited by Richard Ellmann. Copyright © 1968, 1969 by Richard Ellmann. Published by Random House, Inc.

Selection from *As Seen on TV: The Visual Culture of Everyday Life in the 1950s* by Karal Ann Marling reprinted by permission of Harvard University Press, Cambridge, Massachusetts. Copyright © 1994 by the President and Fellows of Harvard College.

Selection from *Bad Land: An American Romance* by Jonathan Raban copyright © 1996 by Jonathan Raban. Reprinted by permission of Pantheon Books, a division of Random House, Inc.

Selection from *Bareback! One Man's Journey Along the Pony Express Trail* by Jerry

Book Publishing Inc. and IMG Literary Agency.

Selection from "Encounters with the Serpent" by James O'Reilly excerpted from *Travelers' Tales Food: A Taste of the Road* edited by Richard Sterling. Reprinted by permission. Copyright © 1996 by Travelers' Tales, Inc.

Selection from *Four Corners: History, Land, and People of the Desert Southwest* by Kenneth A. Brown copyright © 1995 by Kenneth A. Brown. Reprinted by permission of HarperCollins Publishers, Inc. and John A. Ware Literary Agency.

Selection from "Ghost Wards: The Flight of Capital from History," by Mitchell Schwarzer reprinted from the Spring 1998 issue of *thresholds 16: speed, impact, change*. Copyright © 1998 by *thresholds*. Reprinted by permission of the author.

Selection from *The Good Rain: Across Time and Terrain in the Pacific Northwest* by Timothy Egan copyright © 1990 by Timothy Egan. Reprinted by permission of Alfred A. Knopf, Inc.

Selection from "The Grab Bag" by L. M. Boyd reprinted from the *San Francisco Chronicle*. Copyright © by the *San Francisco Chronicle*. Reprinted by permission.

Selection from *Grass Roots: The Universe of Home* by Paul Gruchow copyright © 1995 by Paul Gruchow. Reprinted by permission of Milkweed Editions.

Selection from "Greetings from Burning Man!" by Bruce Sterling reprinted from the November, 1996 issue of *Wired*. Copyright © 1996 by *Wired*. Reprinted by permission of the author.

Selection from *A Heaven in the Eye* by Clyde Rice copyright © 1984, 1990 by Clyde H. Rice, Sr. Reprinted by permission of Breitenbush Publications, Inc.

Selection from *Henry James: Collected Travel Writings—Great Britain and America* by Henry James. Reprinted by permission of Library of America.

Selection from *His Promised Land: The Autobiography of John P. Parker, Former Slave and Conductor on the Underground Railroad* by Stuart Seely Sprague, editor. Copyright © 1996 by The John P. Parker Historical Society. Reprinted by permission of W. W. Norton & Company, Inc. and The John P. Parker Historical Society.

Selection from *The Hotel: A Week in the Life of the Plaza* by Sonny Kleinfeld copyright © 1989 by Sonny Kleinfeld. Reprinted by permission of Simon & Schuster, Inc. and Philip Spitzer Literary Agency.

Selection from *Houses and Travellers* by W. S. Merwin copyright © 1977 by W. S. Merwin. Reprinted by permission of Georges Borchardt, Inc. for the author.

Selections from *The Hovering Hindu: An Education on Two Continents* by Rajendra S. Khadka published by permission of the author. Copyright © 1999 by Rajendra S. Khadka.

Selection from *In the New World: Growing Up with America from the Sixties to the Eighties* by Lawrence Wright copyright © 1987 by Lawrence Wright. Published by Vintage Books, a division of Random House, Inc.

Selection from *It All Adds Up: From the Dim Past to the Uncertain Future* by Saul Bellow copyright © 1990 by Saul Bellow. Used by permission of Viking Penguin, a division of Penguin Books USA, Inc.

Selection from "It All Ends on Labor Day" by Larry Habegger published with permission of the author. Copyright © 1999 by Larry Habegger.

Selection from *It's Your Misfortune and None of My Own: A New History of the American West* by Richard White copyright © 1991 by University of

Selection from *Mules and Men* by Zora Neale Hurston. Copyright © 1935 by Zora Neale Hurston, renewed 1963 by John C. Hurston and Joel Hurston. Reprinted by permission of HarperCollins Publishers, Inc.

Selection from "My Grizzly Story" by Rick Bass reprinted from the January-February 1996 issue of *Audubon*. Copyright © 1996 by Rick Bass. Reprinted by permission of the author.

Selection from "Navigational Information for Solo Flights in the Desert" by P.K. Price excerpted from *Solo: On Her Own Adventure* edited by Susan Fox Rogers. Reprinted by permission of Seal Press. Copyright © 1995 by Gretchen Legler.

Selection from "The New Amtrak" by Sean O'Reilly copyright © 1999 by Sean O'Reilly. Published with permission from the author.

Selection from *Odd Jobs: Essays and Criticism* by John Updike copyright © 1991 by John Updike. Published by Alfred A. Knopf, Inc.

Selection from *On the Road* by Jack Kerouac copyright © 1955, 1957 by Jack Kerouac, copyright renewed © 1985 by Stella and Jan Kerouac. Used by permission of The Viking Press, a division of Penguin Books USA, Inc

Selection from *The Pacific Northwest: An Interpretive History* by Carlos A. Schwantes copyright © 1989 by Carlos A. Schwantes. Reprinted by permission of University of Nebraska Press

Selection from *Paper Trail: Essays* by Michael Dorris copyright © 1994 by Michael Dorris. Reprinted by permission of HarperCollins Publishers, Inc.

Selection from *Parting the Waters: America in the King Years 1954-63* by Taylor Branch copyright © 1988 by Taylor Branch. Reprinted by permission of Simon and Schuster, Inc. and the author.

Selection from *A Piece of My Mind: Reflections at Sixty* by Edmund Wilson copyright © 1956 by Edmund Wilson. Reprinted by permission of Farrar, Straus, Giroux.

Selections from *Pleasures of a Tangled Life* by Jan Morris copyright © 1989 by Jan Morris. Reprinted by permission of Random House, Inc. and the author.

Selection from *The Prairie Traveler: The Classic Handbook for America's Pioneers* by Randolph B. Marcy copyright © by Randolph B. Marcy. Reprinted by permission of Berkeley Publishing Group.

Selection from "Road Reflections" by Stephen Binns excerpted from *Alaska Passages: 20 Voices from Above the 54th Parallel,* edited by Susan Fox Rogers. Copyright ©1996 by Susan Fox Rogers. Reprinted by permission of Sasquatch Books.

Selection by Sean O'Reilly excerpted from *The Road Within: True Stories of Transformation* edited by James O'Reilly, Sean O'Reilly and Larry Habegger. Reprinted by permission. Copyright © 1997 by Travelers' Tales, Inc.

Selection from *The Roads Taken: Travels through America's Literary Landscapes* by Fred Setterberg copyright © 1993 by Fred Setterberg. Reprinted by permission of the author.

Selection from *Roughing It* by Mark Twain, Afterforward copyright © 1962 by The New American Library of World Literature, Inc. Published by Signet Classics, a division of Penguin USA.

Selection from *Savage Pilgrims: On the Road to Santa Fe* by Henry Shukman copyright © 1996 by Henry Shukman. Reprinted by permission of HarperCollins Publishers Ltd.

Selection from *The WPA Guide to America: The Best of 1930s America as Seen by the Federal Writers' Project* by Bernard A. Weisberger copyright © 1985. Published by Random House, Inc.

Selection from *Walden* by Henry David Thoreau copyright © 1950 by Random House, Inc. Published by Random House, Inc.

Selection from "We Have Some Questions, and Answers, Too" by John Flinn reprinted from the September 8, 1996 issue of the *San Francisco Examiner.* Reprinted by permission of *the San Francisco Examiner.* Copyright © 1996 by the *San Francisco Examiner.*

Selection from *West of the Thirties: Discoveries Among the Navajo and Hopi* by Edward T. Hall copyright © 1994 by Edward T. Hall. Reprinted by permission of Doubleday, a division of Bantam Doubleday Dell Publishing Group, Inc.

Selection from *When the Land Was Young: Reflections on American Archaeology* by Sharman Russell Apt [excerpted from page 184] copyright © 1996 by Sharman Apt Russell. Reprinted by permission of Addison Wesley Publishing Company, Inc. and Felicia Eth Literary Representation.

Selection from *Where the Bluebird Sings to the Lemonade Springs: Living and Writing in the West* by Wallace Stegner. Copyright © 1992 by Wallace Stegner. Published by Random House, Inc.

Selection from *Wild Echoes: Encounters with the Most Endangered Animals in North America* by Charles Bergman copyright © 1990 by Charles Bergman. Reprinted by permission of McGraw-Hill Book Company.

Selection from *Wilderness: North America as the Early Explorers Saw It—From Norse Sagas to Lewis and Clark* by Bill Lawrence copyright © 1991 by Bill Lawrence. Reprinted by permission of the author.

Selection from *Wildlife in America* by Peter Matthiessen copyright © 1959, revised and renewed 1987 by Peter Matthiessen. Used by permission of Viking Penguin, a division of Penguin Books USA, Inc. and Donadio & Ashworth.

Selection from *William Bartram: Travels and Other Writings* by William Bartram, published by the Library of America (1996). Reprinted by permission of the publisher.

Selection from *A Writer's America: Landscape in Literature* by Alfred Kazin copyright © 1988 by Alfred Kazin. Reprinted by permission of Alfred A. Knopf, Inc.

Selection from *Yellow Woman and a Beauty of the Spirit* by Leslie Marmon Silko copyright © 1996 by Leslie Marmon Silko. Reprinted by permission of Simon and Schuster, Inc. and the author.

About the Editor

Fred Setterberg is the author of *The Roads Taken: Travels Through America's Literary Landscapes* which won the Associated Writing Program's award in creative nonfiction. The book's paperback edition is published by Interlink Books. He is also the co-author of several other nonfiction books, including *Toxic Nation: The Fight to Save Our Communities From Chemical Contamination,* written with Lonny Shavelson, and published by John Wiley and Sons.

Fred Setterberg's articles, essays, and stories have appeared in a wide range of publications, including *The New York Times, Mother Jones, The Nation, The Utne Reader, The Iowa Review, The Georgia Review,* and *The High Plains Literary Review.*

He is the recipient of numerous journalism awards and a creative writing fellowship from the National Endowment for the Arts.

TRAVELERS' TALES GUIDES

LOOK FOR THESE TITLES IN THE SERIES

$\mathscr{S}$PECIAL INTEREST

THE GIFT OF TRAVEL:
The Best of Travelers' Tales
Edited by Larry Habegger, James O'Reilly & Sean O'Reilly
ISBN 1-885211-25-2, 240 pages, $14.95

THERE'S NO TOILET PAPER ON
THE ROAD LESS TRAVELED:
The Best of Travel Humor and Misadventure
Edited by Doug Lansky
ISBN 1-885211-27-9, 207 pages, $12.95

A DOG'S WORLD:
True Stories of Man's Best Friend on the Road
Edited by Christine Hunsicker
ISBN 1-885211-23-6, 257 pages, $12.95

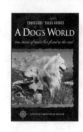

Check with your local bookstore for these titles
or call O'Reilly to order:
800-998-9938 (credit cards only—weekdays 6AM–5PM PST)
707-829-0515, or email: order@oreilly.com

𝒲OMEN'S TRAVEL

SAFETY AND SECURITY FOR WOMEN WHO TRAVEL
By Sheila Swan & Peter Laufer
ISBN 1-885211-29-5, 159 pages, $12.95

WOMEN IN THE WILD:
True Stories of Adventure and Connection
Edited by Lucy McCauley
ISBN 1-885211-21-X, 307 pages, $17.95

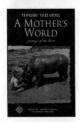

A MOTHER'S WORLD:
Journeys of the Heart
Edited by Marybeth Bond & Pamela Michael
ISBN 1-885211-26-0, 233 pages, $14.95

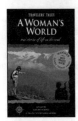

A WOMAN'S WORLD:
True Stories of Life on the Road
Edited by Marybeth Bond
Introduction by Dervla Murphy
ISBN 1-885211-06-6
475 pages, $17.95

Winner of the Lowell Thomas Award for Best Travel Book – Society of American Travel Writers

GUTSY WOMEN:
Travel Tips and Wisdom for the Road
By Marybeth Bond
ISBN 1-885211-15-5, 123 pages, $7.95

WOMEN'S TRAVEL

GUTSY MAMAS:
Travel Tips and Wisdom for Mothers on the Road
By Marybeth Bond
ISBN 1-885211-20-1, 139 pages, $7.95

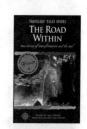

BODY & SOUL

THE ROAD WITHIN:
True Stories of Transformation and the Soul
Edited by Sean O'Reilly, James O'Reilly & Tim O'Reilly
ISBN 1-885211-19-8, 459 pages, $17.95

LOVE & ROMANCE:
True Stories of Passion on the Road
Edited by Judith Babcock Wylie
ISBN 1-885211-18-X, 319 pages, $17.95

FOOD:
A Taste of the Road
Edited by Richard Sterling
Introduction by Margo True
ISBN 1-885211-09-0
467 pages, $17.95

THE FEARLESS DINER:
Travel Tips and Wisdom for Eating around the World
By Richard Sterling
ISBN 1-885211-22-8, 139 pages, $7.95

COUNTRY GUIDES

JAPAN

Edited by Donald W. George
& Amy Greimann Carlson
ISBN 1-885211-04-X, 437 pages, $17.95

INDIA

Edited by James O'Reilly & Larry Habegger
ISBN 1-885211-01-5, 538 pages, $17.95

ITALY

Edited by Anne Calcagno
Introduction by Jan Morris
ISBN 1-885211-16-3, 463 pages, $17.95

FRANCE

Edited by James O'Reilly, Larry Habegger
& Sean O'Reilly
ISBN 1-885211-02-3, 517 pages, $17.95

MEXICO

Edited by James O'Reilly & Larry Habegger
ISBN 1-885211-00-7, 463 pages, $17.95

COUNTRY GUIDES

THAILAND
Edited by James O'Reilly
& Larry Habegger
ISBN 1-885211-05-8
483 pages, $17.95

SPAIN
Edited by Lucy McCauley
ISBN 1-885211-07-4, 495 pages, $17.95

NEPAL
Edited by Rajendra S. Khadka
ISBN 1-885211-14-7, 423 pages, $17.95

BRAZIL
Edited by Annette Haddad & Scott Doggett
Introduction by Alex Shoumatoff
ISBN 1-885211-11-2
452 pages, $17.95

$\mathscr{C}$ITY GUIDES

HONG KONG
Edited by James O'Reilly, Larry Habegger & Sean O'Reilly
ISBN 1-885211-03-1, 439 pages, $17.95

PARIS
Edited by James O'Reilly, Larry Habegger & Sean O'Reilly
ISBN 1-885211-10-4, 417 pages, $17.95

SAN FRANCISCO
Edited by James O'Reilly, Larry Habegger & Sean O'Reilly
ISBN 1-885211-08-2, 491 pages, $17.95

SUBMIT YOUR OWN TRAVEL TALE

Do you have a tale of your own that you would like to submit to Travelers' Tales? We highly recommend that you first read one or more of our books to get a feel for the kind of story we're looking for. For submission guidelines and a list of titles in the works, send a SASE to:

Travelers' Tales Submission Guidelines
P.O. Box 610160, Redwood City, CA 94061

or send email to ***ttguidelines@online.oreilly.com***
or visit our Web site at **www.oreilly.com/ttales**

You can send your story to the address above or via email to ***ttsubmit@oreilly.com***. On the outside of the envelope, ***please indicate what country/topic your story is about***. If your story is selected for one of our titles, we will contact you about rights and payment.

We hope to hear from you. In the meantime, enjoy the stories!